P9-DGE-336

Praise for

WHISTLING PAST DIXIE

"A prescription for Democratic presidential victory . . . Schaller's overall argument stands up pretty well."
—Nicholas Lemann, *The New Republic*

"*Whistling Past Dixie* makes a strong historical and numerical case that the Democrats can win presidential elections without depending on Southern votes and gratifying Southern mores."
—Michael Tomasky, *The New York Review of Books*

"Well-documented and thoughtful . . . if you read it before the midterms, you're likely to feel a rush of revelation as you realize how crucial battles in Ohio, Colorado and Nevada are. Schaller's suggestion that Democrats improve their national security credentials by focusing on homeland security is tightly argued. . . . Schaller also challenges liberal orthodoxy by proposing that Democrats embrace the language of Second Amendment rights to capture the votes of Midwestern and Western gun owners."
—John Dickerson, *The Washington Post Book World*

"Cutting-edge applied political science, with 21 statistical charts and the sort of state-by-state, even district-by-district, analysis that will delight political junkies."
—*Kirkus Reviews* (starred review)

"[A] focused, tactical account . . . the basic truth of the author's fight-fire-with-fire strategy is undeniable; a much needed shot of realpolitik in the arm of the modern Democratic Party."
—*Publishers Weekly*

"Timely . . . Schaller and his fellow advocates of a Rocky Mountain strategy are persuasive . . . there can be no denying that the demographic transformation has opened large parts of the West to political change."
—E.J. Dionne, *The American Prospect*

"Engrossing. . . . Angry and well-reported . . . gives ammunition to a party eager to regain power . . . bristles with charts and builds its point carefully."
—*Chicago Sun-Times*

"Mr. Schaller is on solid footing . . . [he] rightly advises Democrats to forget about the South."
—Brendan Conway, *The New York Sun*

"Schaller offers a comprehensive argument . . . painstakingly documents how the [South] votes differently than the rest of the country . . . ambitious."
—*Baltimore Sun*

"Schaller draws a complex and even daring blueprint . . . differs from others in the recent spate of political literature most notably because it takes a forward-looking approach to give Democrats a ray of hope for 2008 and beyond. Supported by enough electoral number crunching to satisfy political junkies, the author effectively dispels the pervading theory in national Democratic circles that the party needs to contend in the conservative South in order to win elections."
—John Frank, *The St. Petersburg Times*

"Highly accessible. . . . An absorbing look at politics and demographics."
—Vanessa Bush, *Booklist*

"He may be onto something, especially if Republicans continue to push themselves as the party of social conservatives and refuse to re-engage their limited-government constituents."
—David Weigel, *Reason*

ALSO BY THOMAS F. SCHALLER

Devolution and Black State Legislators
(with Tyson King-Meadows)

WHISTLING

THOMAS F. SCHALLER

PAST DIXIE

How Democrats Can Win Without the South

Simon & Schuster Paperbacks

New York   London   Toronto   Sydney

SIMON & SCHUSTER PAPERBACKS
A Division of Simon & Schuster
1230 Avenue of the Americas
New York, NY 10020

Copyright © 2006 by Thomas F. Schaller
Afterword copyright © 2008 by Thomas F. Schaller

All rights reserved, including the right to reproduce this book or portions thereof in any
form whatsoever. For information address Simon & Schuster Paperbacks Subsidiary Rights
Department, 1230 Avenue of the Americas, New York, NY 10020.

First Simon & Schuster trade paperback edition January 2008

SIMON & SCHUSTER PAPERBACKS and colophon are registered trademarks
of Simon & Schuster, Inc.

For information about special discounts for bulk purchases,
please contact Simon & Schuster Special Sales at
1-800-456-6798 or business@simonandschuster.com.

Book design by Ellen R. Sasahara

Manufactured in the United States of America

1   3   5   7   9   10   8   6   4   2

The Library of Congress has cataloged the hardcover edition as follows:

Schaller, Thomas F.
Whistling past Dixie : how Democrats can win without the South /
Thomas F. Schaller.
p.   cm.
Includes bibliographical references and index.
1. Democratic Party (U.S.)   2. Southern States—Politics and government—1951–   .
3. United States—Politics and government—2001–   .   I. Title.
JK2316 .S34   2006
324.2736—dc22   2006049312

ISBN-13: 978-0-7432-9015-9
ISBN-10:   0-7432-9015-1
ISBN-13: 978-0-7432-9016-6 (pbk)
ISBN-10:   0-7432-9016-X (pbk)

To Traci

Contents

WHISTLING PAST DIXIE

1

Partisan Graveyard

[A]nyone who believes Democrats can consistently win the
White House without puncturing the Republican dominance across the South is just whistling Dixie.

—*Los Angeles Times* columnist Ronald Brownstein

For Democrats, the South has become the Sahara of the
Electoral College. Give it up.

—*Slate* columnist Timothy Noah

THE DEMOCRATS are in disarray. National politicians are unsure what
to say about everything from gay marriage to late-term abortion, and
what to do about everything from tax rates to Iraq. The party is losing
a manufactured culture war and watching its labor union base lose a
very real manufacturing war. Rank-and-file Democrats from coast to
coast are increasingly frustrated with the party's lack of a coherent
message, and they are not alone: Fewer than half of all Americans agree
that Democrats "know what they stand for." In presidential elections
especially, the party somehow seems to self-destruct, picking bad candidates who run poor campaigns based on myopic advice from over-
paid consultants.

Desperate and fearful of being relegated to minority status for decades, some Democrats reflexively think back to the halcyon days of party dominance and conclude that the only solution is for the party to somehow restore its lost glory in the South—the most solidly Democratic region since the end of the Civil War, the backbone of the New Deal, and home to the party's three most recent presidents. To become a national majority party again, they insist, the Democrats must compete in Dixie. Strategists Steve Jarding and Dave "Mudcat" Saunders, both southern Democrats, articulate this view most forcefully in their 2006 book, *Foxes in the Henhouse*. "Democrats cannot afford to keep writing off the South," they write. "If you don't start getting a message there, if you don't start listening to people there, if you don't start spending time, energy and money there, you can say good-bye to any notion of realigning political power and instead say hello to the numbing reality that you are relegating yourself to the status of a permanent minority party."

The truth is that the geographic coalition the Democrats forged during the New Deal has come undone. The dramatic economic, social, and political changes of the past half century can be neither rewound nor ignored. The old "three-party" model of regional American partisanship—with northern and southern Democrats outvoting western Republicans—is now defunct, replaced by a new three-party model that pairs southern and western Republicans against urban-based Democrats of the Northeast, Midwest, and Pacific Coast states. Simply put, the South is no longer the "swing" region in American politics: It has swung to the Republicans.

That said, Democrats should forget about recapturing the South in the near term and begin building a national majority that ends, not begins, with restoring their lost southern glory. Most of the South is already beyond the Democrats' reach, and much of the rest continues to move steadily into the Republican column. White southerners used to be among the most economically liberal voters in America but are now among the most conservative. The South is America's most militaristic and least unionized region, and the powerful combination of race and religion create a socially conservative, electorally hostile environment for most statewide Democratic candidates and almost all Democratic presidential nominees.

Meanwhile, there are growing opportunities for Democrats to improve their electoral fortunes in other parts of the country, where demographic changes and political attitudes are more favorable to Democratic messages and messengers. Citizens in the Midwest have been decimated by globalization and are looking for economic salvation. In the Southwest where white and, most especially, Hispanic populations are booming, a strong platform on immigration reform and enforcement could divide the Republicans and put the region up for grabs. In parts of the Mountain West, Democrats can pair the lessons learned from Ross Perot's fiscal reform campaigns with an emphasis on land and water conservation to establish traction among disaffected libertarians and the millions of coastal transplants who either moved westward or bounced back eastward from California in search of open spaces and more affordable suburban lifestyles. If the Democrats can simultaneously expand and solidify their existing margins of control in the Northeast and Pacific Coast states—specifically by targeting moderate Republicans for defeat, just as moderate Democrats in the South have been systematically terminated by the GOP—the Democrats can build a national majority with no help from the South in presidential elections and little help from southern votes elsewhere down the ballot.

That's a pretty big checklist, no doubt. But these tasks are far more doable than trying to rewind history to re-create a pre–civil rights era Democratic South in post–civil rights America.

The South has long been America's regional political outlier. When the Republicans dominated national politics for seven decades between the Civil War and the New Deal, they did so with almost no support from the South. Thanks to the significant African-American population base in the South, the Democrats will never be so handicapped from the outset because there will always be a minimum degree of Democratic support and number of Democratic elected officials in the region. Building a non-southern majority, therefore, should be much easier for Democrats today than it was for the Republicans a century ago. Anyone who claims otherwise is willfully ignoring partisan history, not to mention contemporary demography.

As Democrats expand their non-southern support, the South will continue to assimilate into the national political culture from which it had mostly divorced itself until recent decades. Then and only then can Democrats begin to rebrand themselves in Dixie. In the interim, the Democrats' near-term goal should be to isolate the Republicans as a regional party that owns most of the South, but little else.

FLUNKING THE LITMUS TEST

The Republicans now dominate the South. Neither Al Gore nor John Kerry won a single southern state in their consecutive, failed presidential bids. The GOP controls solid majorities of southern governors and members of Congress, and a growing share of state legislative chambers and seats. In 2004, Republicans barely broke a sweat in claiming all five U.S. Senate seats vacated by retiring southern Democrats, and George W. Bush improved his vote share compared to 2000 in every southern state except North Carolina—the home of his opponent's running mate.

Why do Democrats struggle so mightily in the South? The reasons are many and include specific factors such as the historical absence of organized labor presence in the region, as well as more general factors like a political tradition of stubborn contraposition to northern political attitudes. The short answer, however, is that social and cultural issues tend to trump economic considerations for many voters in the South, where race and religion are woven through almost every aspect of the region's political culture. There are cultural conservatives outside the South and libertarian populists inside the region, of course. But southerners hold distinctly conservative values and have long prided themselves for their obstinacy, for resisting the social transformations unfolding elsewhere across America. What Thomas Frank laments has gone wrong in Kansas is even more wrong in the South, where cultural issues weigh heavily in the minds of voters in America's poorest region.

Against this backdrop of cultural conservatism, political candidates running in all but a few isolated pockets of the South essentially must pass a values "litmus test." Stuart Brunson, campaign manager for Tennessee's popular Democratic governor Phil Bredesen, explained how it works. "Voters go through a two-step process," says Brunson. "The first is a credentialing filter, which asks if a candidate shares their values. The second is on issues—education, health care, the economy." Howard Dean was roundly criticized during the 2004 Democratic primaries for openly referring to this phenomenon with his pithy, "god, guns, and gays" tagline. The blue-blooded Vermont governor and future Democratic National Committee chair did not need to speak in folksy aphorisms to prove he understood the underlying dynamics of modern southern politics.

Bickering Democrats are divided about how to attract, or at least pacify, culturally conservative voters. Some believe the party must moderate its positions on social issues. The truth is that moderation is unlikely to assuage, no less convert, wary southern conservatives. Besides, whatever small gains might come from abandoning support for reproductive choice or gay rights will likely be erased by the votes lost, both inside and outside the South, from projecting moral ambiguity. Frustrated Democrats tend to either avoid social issues altogether or, worse, make clumsy attempts at cultural contortionism. We are thus treated to campaign images of Al Gore wearing cowboy boots with his belt-clipped Blackberry, or a barn jacket–clad John Kerry buying a goose hunting license. These hollow, inauthentic gestures only accentuate and magnify the Democrats' cultural disconnect, forcing liberals to avert their eyes in horror, while conservatives look on from afar with a mixture of disdain and disbelief.

Others think Democrats can bridge the cultural gap by emphasizing the destructive impacts of Republican economic policies. But it's extraordinarily difficult for Democratic candidates to differentiate themselves sufficiently on economic policies to compensate for the built-in advantages Republicans enjoy on social issues, and post-NAFTA Democrats are having a hard time convincing many working-class voters that there is any meaningful differentiation at all. Besides, no matter how attractive their economic messages may be, Democrats must first pass through the "cultural credentialing" filter to get a full hearing from southerners on economic policy. The best Democrats can do is hope for fate to drop in their laps a huge electoral windfall, like an economic collapse of such magnitude that it eliminates the culture filter or a natural disaster like Hurricane Katrina that allows Democrats to play the incompetence card. This is neither a workable long-term strategy nor a noble way to run a political party.

In theory, the Democrats' economic messages ought to be embraced by working-class white and black southerners with equal gusto. Yet nowhere in America do people who come from similar economic stations vote so differently from one another. The self-comforting belief among Democrats that southerners vote against their interests is both condescending and false: White southerners are aware of their economic interests, but simply assign more weight to social issues than economic ones, and accordingly vote Republican; because they experience far less internal dissonance between the partisan implications of their cultural and economic preferences, African Americans in the South vote Democratic. Consequently, because white southerners far outnumber African Americans, neither hedging on cultural issues nor highlighting economic policy differences—or even both approaches in conjunction—can save the Democrats in the South. The only task more difficult than crafting a series of economic ideas capable of convincing white southern conservatives to ignore their social values is persuading them that the Democratic Party shares those values in the first place.

So why bother trying to leap the wide cultural chasm to reach them? Rather than superficial and mostly futile pandering to the nation's most conservative voters, Democrats should begin to build a non-southern majority by unapologetically tailoring policies and targeting messages to more receptive audiences outside the South. Bowing and scraping to salvage a few southern votes here and there only leads to the sort of ideological schizophrenia that does little to improve the Democrats' southern fortunes and, worse, muddies the party's image outside the South.

SISYPHEAN SOUTHERN SITUATION

The Democrats' situation is exacerbated by two glaring political liabilities in the South. The first is that racial polarization has created a virtual Republican monopoly of the southern white vote that prevents Democrats from winning statewide races. The second is that religion plays a more prominent role in the South than in any other region.

The central irony of southern politics is that the nation's most Republican region is home to half of all African Americans, the Democratic party's most loyal voters. Unfortunately, racial antagonisms exacerbate the Democrats' electoral problems in the South, creating a white countermobilization—a "blacklash," so to speak—that fuels Republican victories. In the 2000 and 2004 elections, many of George W. Bush's biggest wins came in southern states with the highest share of African Americans, and some Democratic congressional candidates are capturing as little as 30 percent of the white vote in the South. By contrast, the African-American vote in presidential elections and statewide contests is most successful for Democrats when it is part of multiethnic voting coalitions outside the South, as it is in states such as Illinois, Maryland, Michigan, New Jersey, New York, Ohio, and Pennsylvania. Republicans have established a virtual monopoly on the white southern vote—and *need* to, given the partisan head start Democrats enjoy by virtue of the size of the African-American populations in most southern states. Meanwhile, as we will see later, the Republicans have systematically diluted the power of African Americans by packing them into as few congressional and state legislative districts as possible. Unless the Democrats are prepared to abandon shamelessly their commitment to racial justice in order to win elections, these realities do not suggest a Democratic revival in the South any time soon.

Whereas secular electorates elsewhere are more likely to hold religion aside or even reject the interference of church into state matters, the party's second liability is that churchgoing faithful are very skeptical of Democratic candidates. The partisan effects of southern piety are astounding. No region boasts a greater share of evangelicals than the South. According to surveys conducted by the University of North Carolina, southerners are more likely than non-southerners to believe that God exists and answers prayers, in the biblical account of creation, and that people are sometimes possessed by the devil. A Pew Forum study conducted prior to the 2004 election by the University of Akron's John C. Green showed Democrats holding a narrow lead in partisan identification among Catholics and trailing only slightly among mainline Protestants, but facing a 56 percent to 27 percent Republican edge among evangelical Christians. Evangelicals in the South are not merely more numerous, but doctrinally and politically more conservative than non-southern evangelicals. Not surprising, 2004 exit polls reported that nearly 4 in 5 self-described white evangelicals voted for George W. Bush. The top eighteen states in terms of their share of white evangelicals—which, of course, include every southern state—went for Bush. The evangelical chorus in the South wears red, sings with a decidedly conservative tenor, and votes righteously.

Two partisan features of the South further diminish any hope that Democrats harbor about a regional resurgence.

The first is the rising share of southerners who reached political maturity since Richard Nixon's successful use of the "southern strategy" in 1968. Born during the latter stages of the New Deal and coming of age after the Great Society, this postboomer generation of southern Republicans share no familial or historical connection whatsoever to the New Deal–era Democratic Party. Southerners under the age of 50 in some states have never seen a Democrat capture their state's electoral votes. As tough as it may be to reconvert Republican seniors who once revered Franklin Roosevelt or supported Lyndon Johnson, it will be even tougher to attract young southerners who associate the national Democratic Party with Jimmy Carter and Bill Clinton and have never cast a Democratic vote in their lives.

Second, the South is the region with the fewest swing voters and independents, as the recent presidential campaigns of John McCain, Ralph Nader, and Ross Perot made abundantly clear. Despite their glaring differences—a Republican who challenged his party from the inside; a Green who challenged the Democrats from the outside; and a Reform Party nominee who challenged both parties—all three candidates failed miserably in the South. In 1992, all ten of Perot's poorest showings were below the Mason-Dixon line. Nine of Nader's ten worst performances in 2000 were in southern states. And McCain? The humidity of the 2000 South Carolina primary quickly melted his tart tongue. The contemporary South extends almost no hospitality toward alternative candidacies. In partisan terms, it is a place where voters

Figure 1.1
Support for Ross Perot and Ralph Nader in South v. West

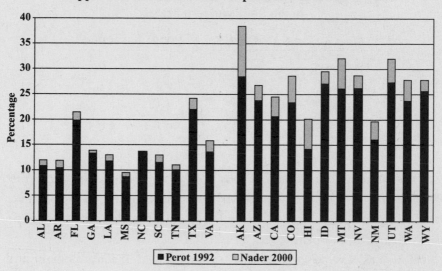

make firm commitments and stick to them, and insurgents and independents go to die.

As evident from Figure 1.1, Perot's 1992 performance revealed one place where soft partisans and disaffected independents are in play: the Interior West, where Perot got at least 20 percent of the vote in a wide variety of states including Arizona, Colorado, Idaho, Montana, Nevada, Utah, and Wyoming— several of which were also states where Nader performed better in 2000 than he did nationally. As Table 1.1 shows, the margins by which George W. Bush carried the southwestern states in 2000 and 2004 were far smaller than when his father won these states a few cycles earlier. Meanwhile, the Midwest remains the most competitive partisan region in the country. "The future Democratic coalition is going to be bicoastal, with the Midwest being the key and the Southwest being the opportunity," asserts Democratic pollster Paul Maslin. "And the South is gone."

For Democrats, electoral opportunities abound in places where the social and cultural hurdles are easier to clear. Indeed, demographic trends and the ideological preferences outside the South *favor* the Democrats, and thus any surrender to southern sympathies reinforces the very image of diffidence and dissension that turns off swing voters

Table 1.1
**Bush 41 v. Bush 43 Presidential Margins
in the Southwestern States**

State	1988	2000	2004
Arizona	21.2	6.3	10.5
Colorado	7.8	8.4	4.7
Nevada	20.9	3.5	2.6
New Mexico	5.0	-0.1	0.8

in other states and regions. The most foolhardy option is for Democrats to waste these new opportunities in a Sisyphean attempt to reconstruct an antiquated geographic coalition based on the notion that the party's southern wing can be revived.

Now let's reverse the partisan-regional question for a moment and ask, When is the last time anyone wrote a political analysis arguing that the Republicans need to somehow figure out how to restore *their* lost glory in the coastal states, or that the GOP's anti-northern posturing is turning off so many blue state voters that it prevents the Republicans from becoming a true, unchallenged national party? Such criticisms are rare, first, because the national media perpetuate the canard that the more regionally monolithic and racially monochromatic Republican coalition is somehow more "national" and "representative" than the Democrats' almost identically sized yet far more heterogeneous coalition. The second reason why this criticism is so rarely heard is more logical and therefore, legitimate: It simply doesn't make strategic sense for the GOP to focus primarily on trying to fill its partisan basket by reaching for high-hanging fruit in the bluest of blue cities and states along the coasts.

How, then, is it logical for Democrats to attempt to create a winning coalition by focusing first on the region of the country that will be hardest for them to reach? Strategically or operationally, it isn't. The pan-western states—in an arc from Ohio, west to Montana, and south to Arizona—are where the low-hanging and most ripe-for-the-plucking electoral fruit for Democrats is to be found. The party therefore must shelve its New Deal nostalgia and recognize that the South will be the last, not first, stop along the path to a new Democratic national majority. Efforts to recapture the South first will only imperil that future majority.

FUZZY (ELECTORAL) MATH

Doesn't the South's sheer size and rapid population growth make it too big for Democrats to concede? Actually, no. Here's a fact that might surprise lazy television pundits: Census data reveal that, in relative terms, the populations of several southern states are *stagnating*. During the 1990s, population growth in Alabama, Louisiana, and Mississippi was slower than the 13.1 percent national rate for the decade. The 2005 estimates further confirm that these three states—along with Arkansas and Tennessee, plus border states Kentucky and Oklahoma—have continued to grow more slowly than the rest of the country since the 2000 census. Half of the southern states have fewer seats in Congress than they did a century ago, when the Republicans dominated national politics with almost no support whatsoever from the South.

It's true that Florida, Georgia, Texas, and the Carolinas are rapidly gaining population, thereby increasing the South's total share of U.S.

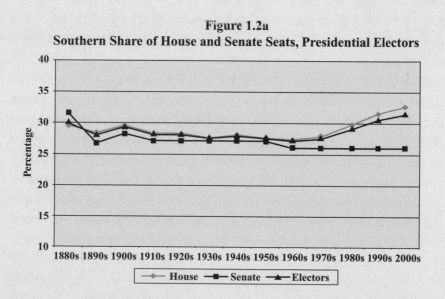

Figure 1.2a
Southern Share of House and Senate Seats, Presidential Electors

Figure 1.2b
Non-Florida Share of House and Senate Seats, Presidential Electors

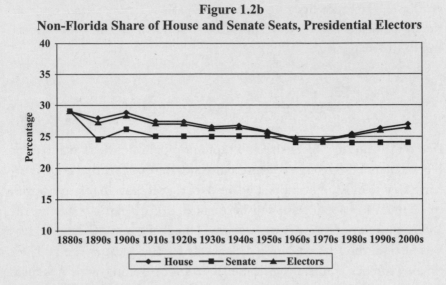

House seats and electoral votes slightly. But population booms in metropolitan areas surrounding Charlotte, Orlando, and Houston and other "new South" cities mask the fact that, relative to the rest of the nation, the rural red states of the old Confederacy are shrinking. Mississippi already lost a congressional district after the 2000 census, and Alabama is likely to suffer a similar fate in some future reapportionment. The five Deep South states had 38 of 310 House seats in the 1880s, but have just 37 of 435 seats today. The fact is the South today wields not much more electoral power nationally than it did a century ago.

Take a look at Figures 1.2a and 1.2b, which track, by decade, the political weight of southern states in the Congress—and, by extension, the Electoral College—since the end of Reconstruction. The first figure depicts the percentages for all eleven southern states; the second figure excludes Florida. Even with the rapid growth of the "Outer South" states like North Carolina, Virginia, and Texas, the region's share of House seats, Senate seats, and electoral votes is about what it was in the last quarter of the nineteenth century. Because of expanding statehood since then, the South has a smaller share of senators, and growth in the share of southern House seats, though not insignificant, has only increased from about 27 percent when Republicans were the majority party a hundred years ago to 32 percent today. If Florida—the most non-southern of the southern states—is excluded from consideration, southern power in the Congress and the Electoral College is actually *less* today than it was on the eve of the Republican realignment of the 1890s.

Based on census population projections, William Frey of the Brookings Institution forecasts a continuing, substantial shift in Electoral College voting power from the Snow Belt to the Sun Belt. Between 2000 and 2030, Frey projects, Texas (+8 House seats/electors) and Florida (+9) will receive the major windfalls, with Arizona growing at the fastest rate—catapulting from eight to thirteen House seats by 2030. Northeastern and midwestern states, bookended by New York and Illinois, account for most of the reapportionment losses to come. Some commentators cite Frey's study as proof that the Democrats need to fix their southern problem, noting that Bush-won states will gain seventeen electors during this period. "You can't get wiped out [in the South]," declares Democratic analyst Ruy Teixeira of the Center for American Progress. "These trends just put an exclamation point on that idea. You don't want to cede huge blocks of states to the other side—especially states whose electoral vote is increasing."

A closer look at Frey's projections, however, reveals that subtracting the western states (+12) from the eleven Confederate states (+19) results in a net gain of only seven electors in the next three decades. When highly competitive Florida is removed from the equation that margin disappears completely. And if Democrats can convert the Sunshine State, the net effect of the Snow-to-Sun Belt shift could actually *favor* the Democrats if they focus on capturing the Southwest. Moreover, part of the Sun Belt's new growth is occurring among demographic groups amenable to Democratic policy appeals. "The turbulent demographic change occurring in New America makes its political future much more up for grabs," writes Frey. "Two groups which favor Democrats, Hispanics, and Gen Xers, are a significant part of [its] recent growth."

The reason Bush won the White House in 2000 despite losing the popular vote is that many of the thirty states he carried were among the least populous. It wasn't just that Al Gore racked up huge margins in

California and New York. By a difference of 64,000 people, the twenty states plus the District of Columbia Gore carried actually *contained* more citizens than the thirty states Bush won. Because every state starts with two electors courtesy of its two U.S. senators, the smaller and more sparsely populated states upon which Republicans depend exercise disproportionate power in the winner-take-all Electoral College system. "This power imbalance has grown so large that 13 small states in Retro America with a population of more than 18 million have voting power equal to California with a 2004 estimated population of more than 35 million," writes John Sperling, in his comprehensive accounting of the differences in what he calls America's "metro" and "retro" states.

Republican power in the Senate today is similarly exaggerated. Following the 2004 elections, twenty-one states had two Republican senators, sixteen had two Democratic senators, and the remaining thirteen delegations were split. With the thirteen split-delegation states removed from the equation, those sixteen Democratic states are home to 120.9 million Americans, compared to just 116.9 million in the twenty-one GOP states. Blessed by winner-take-all elections and the exaggerated political power small states exercise in Senate and presidential elections, the Republican minority sheep is bleating loudly while dressed up in a majority wolf's disguise.

And remember: That sheep grazes in more crowded partisan pastures than the empty southern fields Republicans faced when they dominated American politics for seven full decades following the Civil War. That is, between 1860 and 1928, when Democrats won just four of eighteen presidential elections, the South was far more monolithically Democratic than it is Republican leaning today. If the GOP was capable of maintaining majority status for four generations with virtually *no* southern help, surely the Democrats can become a national majority with the support, however small or shrinking, they receive from southern states that today carry only slightly more electoral weight than they did a century ago—and *less* weight if Florida is removed from the scales.

This is especially true in the House, the place where the South's numerical clout has grown the most. The existence of a sizable African-

American population, coupled with Florida and Texas Hispanics and a core number of "yellow dog" white Democrats, guarantees that the Democrats will never be entirely shut out of the region the way the Republicans were during the late nineteenth and early twentieth centuries. Back then, the solid Democratic South took at least a fourth of U.S. House seats off the table, yet Republicans still managed to carve congressional majorities out of the remaining 75 percent of the nonsouthern seats. Because black, Hispanic, and "yellow dog" Democrats in the South are unlikely to ever account for fewer than 40 of the South's current 131 seats (they presently hold 49 seats), southern Republicans may continue to grow in number but are unlikely to ever reach 109 seats in the South—one-fourth of the House overall. At present, the southern Republicans make up 19 percent of the House. Surely the Democrats can build a majority from the remaining 81 percent if Republicans did exactly that a century ago with only 75 percent of the non-South chamber in play.

Being shut out in the Senate and the Electoral College, of course, makes for much more difficult Democratic tilling because these are winner-take-all elections in which African Americans add to the South's electoral clout but have insufficient power to swing states into the Democratic column. But again, even with Florida out of the mix— and certainly with Florida included—a non-southern Electoral College majority for the Democrats is very doable. Those who say it is impossible to win the White House without the South are conveniently overlooking the two most recent presidential elections. But for a few thousand votes in New Hampshire, Al Gore would have pulled it off while *winning* the popular vote; more astounding, but for the switch of about 60,000 votes in Ohio, Kerry nearly did so despite *losing* the popular vote. After surveying the American electoral landscape, partisan historian Todd Estes concluded:

[I]f there is a new political majority in the offing it is likely to belong to the Democrats. Republicans seem to have given it their all in 2004 and, with all those exertions, could produce the slimmest of majorities. . . . [T]hat Republicans need to win nearly all the states labeled as leaning Republican to win a simple Electoral College majority leaves them on dangerous ground. The loss of only a key state or two could drop them below the 270 [electoral] votes needed to win.

Anyone who claims that a non-southern majority is impossible is willfully ignoring either American political-electoral history, simple arithmetic, or both. Republicans won without the South when the region was not much smaller yet far more locked down than it is now, so certainly Democrats can build a national majority with little if any help from the South today.

BOXING IN THE REPUBLICANS

For a century, from the Civil War to the civil rights movement, the Democrats owned the South. For seven defeat-filled decades between 1860 and 1932, however, the solid South relegated the Democrats to the role of a regionally confined minority party. The party elected only two presidents, Grover Cleveland and Woodrow Wilson, neither of whom represented a southern state nor managed to win a majority of the national popular vote in either his election or reelection. The Democrats' favored strategy during this period was to nominate pro-southern northerners for president and hope for the best. Long-forgotten Democratic nominees such as James Cox, John Davis, and Alton Parker all captured the southern states yet failed to receive even 30 percent of the total electoral vote nationally. The South was unified, but in their unity southern Democrats mostly found themselves on the outside of American politics looking in.

That changed in 1932, when white southern populists joined northeastern ethnics to form the New Deal coalition, led by Democrat Franklin Delano Roosevelt. Thirty-two years later, Texan Lyndon Baines Johnson's landslide defeat of Arizona's Barry Goldwater in 1964 was the New Deal's apogee. LBJ's victory, though resounding, masked the growing frictions between the Democrats' southern conservative wing and its northern liberal wing. The South was about to become more pivotal to national politics than it had been at any time since before the outbreak of the Civil War.

Richard Nixon quickly grasped the new regional calculus Goldwater made viable by carrying the five Deep South states in 1960. Abandoning his earlier gestures toward racial reconciliation, Nixon in 1968 perfected Goldwater's "southern strategy" to narrowly win the White House. With that victory he irreversibly altered the partisan calculus in presidential elections, setting in motion a dramatic partisan transformation in which the Republicans—by fits and starts, including Ronald Reagan's presidential victories and the 1994 Republican takeover of Congress—gradually but inevitably converted the once solidly Democratic South into a Republican stronghold. GOP candidates have received 83 percent of all electoral votes cast by the southern states in the past nine presidential elections. In 1960, there was not a single southern Republican governor or U.S. Senator, but today the Republicans boast seven of the region's eleven governors and eighteen of its twenty-two senators. Capturing the South gave the GOP enough ballast, enough confidence, and enough momentum to begin envisioning itself as the dominant party.

Republicans cannot be a national majority party without the South, but neither can they do it *with the South alone*. Anyone who watched the last three Republican National Conventions realizes that, more than anything else, Republican operatives fear their party will become synonymous with its most radically conservative, southern-based elements. That's why Americans don't see the likes of Tom DeLay or Trent Lott paraded onstage for prime-time viewing. Indeed, the only fire-breathing southern conservative given a featured speaking role during the 2004 Republican convention in New York's Madison Square Garden was Georgia's Zell Miller—a disgruntled Democrat who supported Bush's reelection. And many regarded Miller's venomous speech as the convention's lowest moment.

With impunity from the media, Republicans brazenly mock Democrats for their ties to northeastern liberals, especially the "Tax-achusetts" variety. They depict Democrats as effete, permissive, "out of touch" snobs who "just don't get it." The GOP understands the power of us-versus-them politics, which requires that some ambiguous "them" be identified and subjected to abuse and scorn. To unify a Republican Party composed of both Wall Street bankers and heartland preachers—the profits-plus-pulpits coalition—the GOP has created the perfect foil: a ubiquitous and nefarious "liberal elite" that is somehow blamed for orchestrating America's cultural and spiritual demise. The Democrats need their own "them," and the social conservatives who are the bedrock of southern politics provide the most obvious and burdensome stone to hang around the Republicans' necks.

Democrats must therefore use political jujitsu on the Republicans to turn the solid South into a political-electoral albatross for Republicans in the same manner it was for Democrats for almost a century following the Civil War. Yet, despite polls showing Democratic advantages on a wide range of issues, from health care coverage to a living wage, Democrats make little attempt to depict southern resistance as out of step with the dramatic social, economic, and technological changes occurring in the country. If the GOP can build a national majority by ostracizing an entire region of the country, the Democrats should be able to run *outside* the South by running *against* the conservative South. Citing southern obstructionism as a continuing impediment to the investments and progress the country must make in the coming century, Democrats must not only resolve for themselves, but also send a message to the American electorate that they can offer something better than the retrenched, regressive, and sometimes revanchist southern way.

The Democrats' non-southern strategy must also utilize the same sort of tactics and coded language Republicans used to capture the region from Democrats. Because the majority party is in theory more susceptible to divide-and-conquer politics, the Democrats can use the South's social conservatism as the point of a wedge to split apart the pulpits wing from the profits wing. The Republicans want pro-life voters? Make them stand up at roll call and cast their votes for a constitutional amendment to outlaw abortion, something that President Bush and the Republican leadership in Congress know will destroy their chance of forging a more permanent majority. The GOP wants to secure cheap labor for American corporations? Make them defend the look-the-other-way border policies they support in one breath, while in the next bragging that they are the party to trust on homeland security.

Whenever possible, Democrats must also equate the Republican Party with its least-electable elements, many of whom have deep, long-standing ties to the South. This means forcing the GOP to either embrace or denounce people like Liberty University's Jerry Falwell and groups like the Alabama-based American Family Association. There's a reason Republicans keep what I call the "eyesore" and "black-eye" Republican elements within their coalition from public view—namely, because they frighten most Americans, as the Terri Schiavo right-to-die episode in Florida proved. The Democrats are regularly pilloried for their association with people like controversial filmmaker Michael Moore, even though Moore exercises little if any influence on the party. The Republicans, meanwhile, are far less often equated with their most radically conservative elements, despite the fact that the leaders of these movements are much more deeply embedded within the GOP's agenda-forming and decision-making apparatus. The Democrats must pull back the curtain behind which the "Michael Moores of the Right" are hiding, revealing a party that threatens the liberties that are dear to both eastern liberals and western libertarians alike. If Democrats do this, they can begin systematically to circumscribe and marginalize the Republicans as a party that dominates the South but *only* the South.

LET GO THE NEW DEAL COALITION

The first rule of electoral politics is, *Do not try to win the last election*. Yet far too many politicians and pundits continue to repeat the conventional wisdom that the Democrats must try to recapture the South. Their southern nostalgia is more than blurry sentimentality. It is a dangerously self-destructive form of political myopia that, left uncorrected, will only relegate the Democrats to minority party status for at least a generation. The notion that Democrats should pin their hopes for revival on the tail of a Southern donkey is no less absurd than witnessing the children's variant of the party game, for both involve desperate attempts to hit elusive targets while wandering around blindfolded.

Some region, by definition, must be the most politically and culturally conservative in the country. The South is that region, and the idea that Democrats ought to start rebuilding their national identity by trying to first restore its lost southern glory is what I call "extended ladder" politics—the stretching toward the treetops in a foolhardy effort to fill their partisan baskets when riper, closer-hanging fruit is at hand. That said, the time is long overdue for Democrats to let go of their electoral past and begin building a non-southern majority coalition. The party will need to develop the right messages and messengers to accompany this strategy—no easy chore, that. But before entertaining dreams of forty-nine-state Electoral College victories, the Democrats must first find a formula to win twenty-nine states. Rather than trying to compete in Alabama, the party should first figure out how to convert Arizona, or even Alaska. Only after making gains in other parts of the country—solidifying the coastal states, locking down the Midwest, converting the burgeoning Southwest, and stealing selected seats in the interior West—should the Democrats begin the arduous task of their own southern reconstruction.

Until then, the Democrats must whistle past their southern electoral graveyard. They must whistle past Dixie.

2

The Southern Transformation

Democrats everywhere are aware of their so-called "south-crn problem," the fact that most whites in this region used to vote for the donkey and now vote for the elephant.

—Former Democratic Congressman Glen Browder of
    Alabama

[T]he GOP's Southern base, the bedrock of its national election victories, is an illegitimate legacy from racist Dixiecrats.

—Conservative columnist Robert Novak

MORE THAN A FEW accounts of the Democratic Party's southern decline begin on the afternoon of July 2, 1964. At an ornate White House ceremony with some of the nation's top civic leaders assembled around him, President Lyndon Baines Johnson signed the 1964 Civil Rights Act. Though the racial democratization of the South was already under way, and there would be plenty of bloodshed and violence punctuating the battles for political equality to follow, the signing ceremony was a landmark moment. "We believe that all men are entitled to the blessings of liberty," said President Johnson in the nationally televised speech he gave that night from the East Room. "Yet millions are being deprived of those blessings—not because of their own failures, but because of the color of their skin." Later, off camera, Johnson privately wondered aloud whether he had just written off the South for the Democrats with the stroke of pen.

Johnson and the Democrats did not sign the South away. It was *taken* away. And the race-themed event that signaled the start of the Republicans' permanent seizure of the South occured not in the nation's capital in 1964, but sixteen years later in tiny Neshoba County, Mississippi, where former California governor Ronald Reagan gave his first major speech after accepting the 1980 Republican presidential nomination.

During the previous four presidential elections, Neshoba County appeared to be suffering from a severe case of electoral schizophrenia. After casting 95 percent of their votes for Republican Barry Goldwater in 1964, county residents voted 82 percent for American Independent Party candidate George Wallace in 1968 before promptly returning to the Republican fold in 1972 and giving 88 percent of their votes to Richard Nixon. Statewide, Mississippians also shifted in an identically erratic fashion, from Goldwater to Wallace to Nixon. What explained Neshoba's erratic voting patterns was, of course, race: Goldwater had denounced Johnson's civil rights initiatives; Wallace was America's most outspoken proponent of segregation; and, by the time he ran for reelection, Nixon's antidesegregation efforts and civil rights foot-dragging had calmed those same worried white southerners who had voted for Wallace.

Whereupon the next presidential election brought something of a surprise. By thirty-two votes, Democrat Jimmy Carter carried Neshoba County in 1976 and won statewide in Mississippi by roughly the same 2 percent margin by which he beat Republican incumbent Gerald Ford nationally. The former Georgia governor swept every southern state except Virginia. To Reagan's campaign strategists, Carter's election was a powerful reminder that the Republicans had not yet locked down the southern vote. Fresh from his coronation at the 1980 GOP convention in Detroit, on the advice of a young Mississippi congressman named Trent Lott, Reagan arrived in Neshoba County on a hot August afternoon determined to do something about it.

Neither Neshoba nor Mississippi was a national electoral barometer.

On matters of race, however, the county and state were southern bell-wethers. The fairgrounds were located just a few miles from the infamous spot where three young civil rights workers were murdered only two weeks before President Johnson signed the Civil Rights Act sixteen summers earlier. Students of southern history or those who saw the movie *Mississippi Burning* will recall that, of the various persons involved in the murders of civil rights activists James Chaney, Andrew Goodman, and Michael Schwerner, only a few were tried and ultimately convicted. Some of those who participated in those grisly murders—whether cleared initially or later released from short prison terms—likely attended Reagan's speech.

Not that it mattered who may have been in the crowd that day, for Reagan's message was aimed at a much larger audience. The former California governor had opposed the 1964 Civil Rights Act and espoused other southern-friendly positions. His campaign advisers realized that to capture the White House Reagan would need to send a strong, clear signal that the GOP presidential ticket of Reagan and George H.W. Bush would defend southern autonomy on racial issues. Under the famed tin-roof pavilion where so many important speeches had been given, Reagan pledged his support for "states' rights"—the familiar proxy term for opposition to federally imposed civil rights reform. From there, press coverage and word-of-mouth among white southerners spread Reagan's coded racial messages across the region.

Reagan was not the first Republican presidential candidate to use the southern strategy, a distinction that belongs to Barry Goldwater. Nor was he the first GOP nominee to win the White House using that strategy, as Richard Nixon did. As we will see, George W. Bush would later cement the Republicans' control over the South, garnering a much greater share of white southern support in 2000 than Reagan did in 1980, and about the same in his 2004 reelection as Reagan did twenty years prior to that. Still, the significance of 1980 is that Reagan perfected the southern strategy of luring away white southern Democrats. "Reagan was the first Republican presidential candidate to poll back-to-back landslide majorities from white southerners," note southern politics scholars Earl and Merle Black in *The Rise of Southern Republicans*. "[A]nd his vice president, George Bush, captured the presidency in 1988 by running on the strategy that Reagan had mastered: attracting substantial majorities from conservative and moderate whites, while implicitly conceding the votes of blacks and liberal whites." The Neshoba County Fair speech thus began the permanent Republican capture of the South. No Democratic presidential candidate has carried Neshoba County or the state of Mississippi since.

ELECTORAL TRANSFORMATION IN THE SOUTH

The Republicans now own the South. With each passing election cycle, the GOP continues to consolidate and solidify its control over the region. The South's partisan transformation in the span of just four decades is evident across all eleven states, and from the top to the bottom of the ballot. Though this realignment is most obvious in presidential election results, by fits and starts it has occured at the congressional and state levels as well, helping Republicans achieve their first national majorities since the New Deal. By the late 1970s, the once "solid" Democratic South emerged as a region in political flux. But the South is no longer America's swing region. It has swung, and is likely to remain solidly Republican for the foreseeable future.

What is the significance of this southern realignment? Although scholars of southern politics have been expansive in their focus, prognosticators and pundits have devoted much of their attentions to the electoral dimensions of the southern realignment. The fates of candidates and parties make for interesting story lines, and have understandably generated a surfeit of analyses about which politician ran for and won what seat, which chambers flipped control from one party to the other, or how much campaign cash was raised and spent. Electoral politics also offers many easy-to-quantify measures and fingertip-access databases to examine, from general trends like party registration rates or number of offices held, to zip code–level campaign totals and software-generated redistricting maps.

Elections won and governing majorities achieved are just the first of three related aspects of the southern partisan realignment, however. The second aspect is the myriad ways the Republican capture of the

South has changed national policy and politics, and the third is the significance of the South's capture of the Republican Party itself. I dedicate significant chunks of this chapter to these last two aspects of the southern realignment, because they are instructive to Democrats hoping to make electoral gains by reframing both themselves and their Republican opponents.

To understand the magnitude of the partisan transformation that unleashed these changes, I begin by chronicling southern electoral history during the past four decades.

The Presidency

Despite Nixon's adoption of a southern strategy in 1968, Alabama governor George Wallace carried four Deep South states that year. Since then, Republican presidential candidates have enjoyed a virtual monopoly on the South's electoral votes. In the nine presidential elections between 1972 and 2004, Democrats have sent one lamb after another to their southern slaughter. Jimmy Carter carried a total of eleven states during his two campaigns, and Bill Clinton won a combined eight states in 1992 and 1996. But Republican candidates won the remaining eighty of the ninety-nine winner-take-all victories during this period, often by wide margins. The Republicans won Virginia all nine times and carried Alabama, Mississippi, North Carolina, and South Carolina in every year except 1976. Of the 1,260 total electoral votes cast by the eleven southern states between 1972 and 2004, Republicans won 1,039 of them—almost 83 percent.

Table 2.1 shows the glaring—and growing—disparity in the regional performance of Democratic nominees during these nine presidential elections. The two-party advantage for Republicans was larger in the South than outside the region in every election except for 1976 and 1980, when Carter ran, and the GOP's average regional margin during the nine elections is more than 11 percent. Of course, along with Carter, who won the southern vote by more than 9 percent in 1976, Clinton was the only Democratic nominee to carry a plurality of southern votes during this period. But notice that Clinton did so *only* during his 1996 reelection, and then by the most razor-thin of margins: just 46.2 percent to 46.1 percent (+ 0.1).

The more startling lesson from Table 2.1 is how irreparable the regional breach has become, even when Democrats nominate a southerner. Carter did better in the South both in victory *and* defeat; he carried the region by 9.5 percent more than the rest of the country in 1976, and even in his failed 1980 bid for reelection still managed to post better numbers in the South than elsewhere (+3.7 percent difference). The opposite was true for fellow southerners Clinton and Al Gore: Arkansan Clinton did *worse* in his native region than outside the South in both his 1992 election and 1996 reelection campaigns (-9.5 percent; -11.6 percent), making him the only Democratic candidate since the Civil War to perform worse in the southern states than the non-southern states yet still win and retain the presidency. As for Tennessee's Gore, not only did he lose decidedly in the South, but his regional deficit (-15.6 percent) was larger than Clinton's—a disparity that, not surprising, widened further when Massachusetts senator John Kerry ran in 2004 (-16.7 percent). On the other hand, the Democrats have won the non-southern vote the past four elections, and on the strength of that support have finished first in the national popular vote in three of those four.

Table 2.1

Democratic Presidential Electoral Margins Inside versus Outside the South, 1972–2004

Year	Nominee	South	Non-South	Difference
1972	McGovern	-40.6	-18.8	-21.8
1976	Carter	+9.4	-0.1	+9.5
1980	Carter	-6.9	-10.6	+3.7
1984	Mondale	-25.2	-15.9	-9.3
1988	Dukakis	-17.4	-4.4	-13.0
1992	Clinton	-1.4	+8.1	-9.5
1996	Clinton	+0.1	+11.7	-11.6
2000	Gore	-10.8	+4.9	-15.6
2004	Kerry	-14.4	+2.3	-16.7
All		-11.2	-2.0	-9.2

Computed by author from data courtesy of www.uselectionatlas.org.

A state-by-state comparison of Clinton's election and reelection results confirms the Democrats' relative southern decline during
Clinton's presidency. Between 1992 and 1996, as Perot dropped 10 percentage points, Clinton's popular vote share grew by 6.2 percent nationally and increased in all fifty states plus the District of Columbia. In
the South, however, only in Florida (solidly, at +9.0 percent) and
Louisiana (barely, at +6.4 percent) did Clinton exceed his nationwide
benchmark. By contrast, in five southern states—Alabama, Arkansas,
Georgia, North Carolina, and Tennessee—Clinton improved by *less
than half* that 6.2 percent benchmark. In what turned out to be an ominous foreshadowing of Gore's 2000 home-state defeat in Tennessee,
Clinton's lowest popular-vote gain between 1992 and 1996—a measly
one-half of 1 percent—came in his home state of Arkansas. Overall, the
gap between Clinton's southern and non-southern vote share worsened
by more than 2 percent between 1992 and 1996. Despite a growing
economy, a listless 1996 opponent, an infusion of centrist policies courtesy of advisers Dick Morris and Al From, and two southern incumbents on the ballot, the Democrats made few gains in the South during
the 1990s under the Clinton-Gore banner. The region was solidifying
its Republican loyalties.

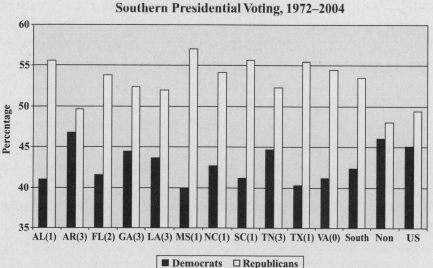

Figure 2.1
Southern Presidential Voting, 1972–2004

Coupled with Lyndon Johnson's 1964 landslide and Carter's narrow 1976 win, Clinton's election confirmed for many Democrats the belief that the party must nominate a southerner if it hopes to regain the presidency. Native sons always enjoy certain advantages, of course. But the undeniable fact is that Clinton won twice not as a result of a Democratic revival in the South but despite the absence of one. Clinton's performances in the South are not inconsequential and indicate a crossover appeal that helped him attract a sufficient number of non-southern voters to become president. Still, subtract the southern electoral votes from Clinton's totals and he still wins both election and reelection. Unlike Carter and Johnson, Clinton was a southern Democrat who won the presidency on the strength of non-southern votes. In that regard, he will be remembered as the first *northern* southern Democratic president, a fact which surely explains the hostility many southerners and southern politicians exhibited toward his presidency.

As Clinton's electoral performances demonstrate, the Democrats' southern problems are not uniform across all eleven states. Which states have proved most receptive to Democratic presidential candidates? Figure 2.1 depicts the partisan share of the vote in southern states between 1972 and 2004, with the number of times the Democratic candidate carried the state during the nine elections reported in parentheses. The figure reveals that the Deep South states that first broke away from the Democrats as far back as Goldwater's 1964 campaign—particularly Alabama (14.5 percent Republican advantage), Mississippi (17.1 percent), and South Carolina (14.5 percent)—have become virtually unwinnable. Most "Outer South" states like Texas (15.2 percent) and Virginia (13.3 percent) have been equally uncompetitive, although the historical results mask the fact that growth in the more liberal counties surrounding the District of Columbia has made Virginia more Democratic, while Texas in the George W. Bush era has moved beyond reach. Arkansas (2.2 percent) and Georgia (7.9 percent) have been most competitive—but misleadingly so, given the twin home-state victories by Carter and Clinton, respectively. Louisiana and Tennessee have also been relatively favorable southern states for Democratic candidates and, along with Arkansas and Georgia, are the only four states that Democratic nominees have carried three times in the past nine presidential elections.

As for Florida, made famous by the thirty-six-day 2000 recount battle, it is the one state in an otherwise rock-solid red region that is more "purple" today than historical trends indicate. Given how many of Florida's trans-populated residents moved there from other parts of the country, it is no coincidence that the region's lone swing state is the least southern in its historical, cultural, and political sensibilities.

In presidential elections, the simple truth is that the South has moved beyond the reach of the Democratic Party. "The creation of a Solid Republican South in most recent presidential elections has revolutionized the regional dynamics of presidential campaigns. Because of its southern gains, the Republican party has not needed northern electoral majorities to control the presidency," Earl and Merle Black concluded a decade ago. "Just as the South had traditionally functioned as a cheap and safe Democratic base in presidential politics, so the South today usually serves as an inexpensive and promising Republican stronghold." Their assessment of the two parties' presidential standing in the South rings even truer today.

Congress

Beyond presidential elections, the Democrats' situation is less gloomy, but not much. The party is more competitive the further one goes down the ballot, although less so with each new election. At every level—from the U.S. Senate and House of Representatives, down to governorships and state legislatures—the Republican takeover of the South, though lagging behind the presidential results, more or less parallels the partisan changes in presidential voting during the past four decades.

In 2004, five Senate Democratic incumbents retired—John Breaux of Louisiana, John Edwards of North Carolina, Bob Graham of Florida, Fritz Hollings of South Carolina, and Zell Miller of Georgia—and five Republicans were promptly elected to fill their vacancies: David Vitter, Richard Burr, Mel Martinez, Jim DeMint, and Johnny Isakson, respectively. In essence, Georgia's seat had already converted: Miller's increasingly conservative voting record, coupled with his endorsement of George W. Bush in 2004, only formalized his departure from a Senate

Democratic caucus he had long ago abandoned in spirit and at roll call. "That thing with Zell was a bunch of baloney," scoffs former South Carolina senator Fritz Hollings. "He said the party left him. I heard that from Strom back in '64. That was just opportunism." Whatever motivated Miller, his retirement and the five-seat partisan shift accomplished two things for the GOP. First, it more than accounted for the net national Republican gain of four Senate seats. Second, it gave Republicans eighteen of the South's twenty-two Senate seats, their largest share ever. In 1960, they had none.

Joined by Oklahoma's Tom Colburn and South Dakota's John Thune, the five southerners elected in 2004 are part of a Republican freshman Senate class some are already calling "the magnificent seven." Virginia Senator George Allen, who led the National Republican Senatorial Committee's 2004 election efforts and is viewed by many insiders as the party's alternative to John McCain in the 2008 presidential race, could hardly contain himself after the election. Allen promised that the Republicans' expanded majority would give it greater political leverage to cut taxes, enact tort reform, and confirm conservative judicial appointees. "I really believe with this strengthened majority we can get all of this done," he chirped. The southern Republican Senate delegation has come a long way since 1964, when the late Strom Thurmond switched parties to give the South its first Republican senator of the twentieth century.

Southern Democrats are more competitive in the U.S. House of Representatives, but their share continues to shrink. Following the 2004 election, 82 of the 131 southern House members, or 62.6 percent, are Republicans. As in the Senate, 2004 was also a big year for southern GOP newcomers to the House: fourteen of the twenty-four rookie Republicans in the 109th Congress came from the South. Only Arkansas and Tennessee now have majority-Democratic House delegations, with Mississippi's four-member delegation split two seats each. The remaining eight states have majority-Republican delegations, including lopsidedly Republican delegations in Georgia and South Carolina. In 1960 Republicans held just 7 percent of House seats in the South.

Republican dominance in southern House elections is partly a result of their ruthless packing of African American and Hispanic Democrats into a few, race-gerrymandered districts in order to create as many majority-white districts as possible. After Republicans took control of the Texas legislature in 2002, former Congressman Tom DeLay used this tactic to help the GOP gain five Texas seats in the 2004 elections— which, like the Senate gains, more than accounted for the net national increase of three seats for the Republicans. Rare is the Democratic candidate who can win in the remaining majority-white districts because, as data guru Mark Gersh of the National Committee for an Effective Congress discovered, some southern Democratic congressional candidates are capturing as little as 30 percent of the white vote.

Governors

Sonny Perdue is the Republican governor of Georgia. Repeat, Sonny Perdue is the *Republican* governor of Georgia. To understand how amazing this development is, consider that Perdue beat an incumbent Democrat in 2002 to become Georgia's first Republican governor since the nineteenth century because the Republicans failed to elect a single governor during the *entire* twentieth century. After just one election so far this century, it's the Democrats who are winless in Georgia.

Table 2.2
Southern Governors, 2006

State	Name (Party)	Elected
Alabama	Bob Riley (R)	2002
Arkansas	Mike Huckabee (R)	1998
Florida	Jeb Bush (R)	1998
Georgia	Sonny Perdue (R)	2002
Louisiana	Kathleen Babineaux Blanco (D)	2003
Mississippi	Haley Barbour (R)	2003
North Carolina	Mike Easley (D)	2000
South Carolina	Mark Sanford (R)	2002
Tennessee	Phil Bredesen (D)	2002
Texas	Rick Perry (R)	2001
Virginia	Tim Kaine (D)	2005

The Republicans had no southern governors until 1966. Today seven states have Republican chief executives, including every Deep South state but Louisiana. In addition to Perdue, many of these governors won comfortably in states where Democrats enjoy either a numerical advantage among registered voters, a majority in at least one state legislative chamber, or both. The fact that Arkansas has two Democratic U.S. senators and Democratic majorities in both state legislative chambers did not prevent Republican Mike Huckabee from winning election in 1998 and reelection four years later. Haley Barbour, a former Republican National Committee chairman and longtime Washington lobbyist with no prior elective experience, capitalized on the support of nearly four in five white voters in 2003 to become governor of Mississippi, the state with the highest share of African Americans. And Florida governor Jeb Bush, the Bush brother expected to win in 1994, recovered from his initial, stinging loss that year to beat incumbent lieutenant governor Buddy MacKay by almost 10 points in 1998, then cruised to reelection in 2002.

The rising number of Republican governors, not to mention their often-comfortable margins of victory, confirms that the electoral dissonance many southerners experienced during the 1970s, 1980s, and 1990s in voting for Republican presidential candidates but Democrats in their statewide elections has been resolved by the emergence of straight-ticket Republican voting. Consequently, the Republican brand name for gubernatorial candidates has gained the same currency that GOP presidential nominees reached in 1980 with Reagan's precedent-setting win. If trends continue, the moment may not be too far off when Republicans hold nine, ten, or even all eleven of the southern governorships, as the Democrats once did. There are Democratic bright spots, of course, most notably the back-to-back Democratic victories in Virginia by Mark Warner in 2001, and Warner's heir apparent Tim Kaine in 2005. Along with Democratic governors in North Carolina and Tennessee, any partisan reconversion of the South will have to begin in the same "Outer" southern states, like Virginia, which first turned Republican four decades ago.

State Legislatures

The Republicans reached another electoral milestone in 2004. For the first time since Reconstruction, and by just five seats, the GOP now holds a majority of the 1,335 seats in the southern state legislatures. The Republicans are approaching a majority of state senate seats, too, with Democrats holding on to a narrow, seven-seat edge (232 to 225). Overall, the Democrats control both chambers in five southern legislatures, the Republicans control five, with Tennessee split between a Republican senate and Democratic house. The southern state legislatures are deadlocked.

The Republicans have come quite a long way to reach parity. According to the National Conference of State Legislatures, at their high-water mark after the 1974 elections the Democrats controlled both chambers in thirty-seven legislatures, the Republicans controlled four, and eight states had divided legislatures—yielding a sixty-six-chamber Democratic advantage. Thirty years later, the Republicans control nineteen state legislatures, the Democrats nineteen, with the remaining eleven either divided or tied in one chamber, and many of the converted chambers are in the South. During the 2003 and 2004 election cycles, these trends continued as the GOP compensated for a net loss of legislative seats outside the South by picking up seats in the South.

The Solid (Republican) South

Figure 2.2 chronicles the dramatic change in the partisan share of southern congressional seats, governorships, and state legislators between 1960 and 2004. Although the conversion of the South did not proceed as quickly down-ballot as it did in presidential contests, the gradual decline of the Democrats' once "solid South" is clear. The Democrats have enjoyed momentary reversals, notably in governor and U.S. Senate races during the late stages of the Reagan-Bush era. Because House legislative seats in Congress and state lower houses are more numerous and thus less sensitive to isolated victories, their rates of decline better depict the Democrats' steady decay.

Obviously, a political party's presidential fortunes are connected to

Figure 2.2
Democratic Decline in the South, 1960–2004

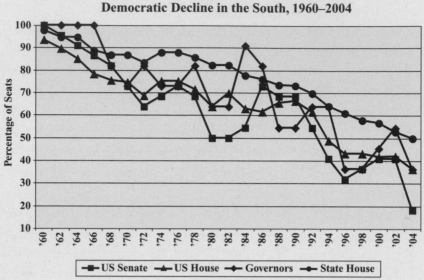

its performance elsewhere on the ballot. The conventional wisdom is that the gradual partisan conversion of lower offices in the South was a by-product of the much quicker reversal in the parties' presidential fortunes beginning in the 1960s. "At the same time, one should not assume that the partisan change was a completely top-down process with Republican success at the presidential level trickling down to the local level," cautions American University political scientist David Lublin. "Republican victories at the local level may have helped produce greater gains at the state and national level even if Republicans achieved majority status at the national level first."

The Democrats' down-ballot decline is thus a direct political consequence that indirectly affects presidential politics. Why? Because local and state party leaders legitimize a party's brand name and, as surrogates for presidential nominees, provide legitimacy and generate resources for the party's nominee. With fewer and fewer Democratic partisans able to provide endorsements and organizational support, the party's presidential prospects in the South will continue to diminish as the Republicans' new southern dominion expands. In other words, the GOP's political control over the South is not merely widening, but *deepening,* and there's little evidence that these partisan trends in the South have stopped or even slowed, no less begun to reverse. The Warner-Kaine victories in Virginia have garnered so much attention precisely because Democratic wins in the South have become about as common as the Bush administration admitting its mistakes.

Taking the fuller view, the South is a place where voters tend to make commitments and stick firmly to them and, as we saw in the opening chapter, where independent and third-party insurgents are treated inhospitably. These realities were true of the South for decades after the Civil War, and will continue to be true for decades in the post–civil rights era, too. The widening and deepening control Republicans now exert over the South, coupled with the region's xenophobic resistance to partisan outsiders, have put the region beyond reach for Democratic presidential candidates and most statewide Democratic nominees.

Although the Democrats can make small, isolated gains in parts of the South, the truth is that more fertile partisan soil for tilling can be found almost in almost every non-southern state except Idaho, Utah, or Wyoming. John Kerry learned this lesson the hard way in 2004, when he gambled $3 million in hopes of stealing Virginia's thirteen electoral votes—money that on Election Day he surely wished he had instead sunk into Ohio. Despite the investment, Kerry's performance was worse than Al Gore's four years earlier as Democrats lost Virginia for the tenth straight time.

SOUTHERN REPUBLICANS CAPTURE NATIONAL POLITICS

It took four decades for Republicans to capture the South. This transformation unfolded in different ways, across different elected offices, and at differing rates in the eleven southern states. The partisan changes are not necessarily irreversible, but neither is it clear that they have fully run their course yet. The South is likely to become more Republican in the decades ahead.

Have Republican electoral gains in the South translated into demonstrable political and policy impact? Yes, but not perfectly so. Electoral changes in the South did not always yield immediate changes in national policy. In fact, the partisan morphing of the South during the 1960s and 1970s occurred as American policy makers were rebuking southern preferences. Like the phasing effect in the physical world, in which the speed of light brings images to the eye before the comparably glacial speed of sound delivers audio to the ears, the sight of rising southern Republicanism—witnessed on the campaign trail and apparent from election night tote boards—was always heard at some later moment in the growing noise made by southerners in national policy debates. And, just as the phasing effect is magnified at greater distances but becomes practically imperceptible to the human ear at close range, across the past four decades the sight-then-sound lag between Republican electoral gains in the South and political responses has diminished. That is, as the GOP has moved closer and closer to becoming a majority party—not only in the South but, by consequence, nationally as well—the delay between the GOP's latest victories and the demands for political paybacks from the southern wing of the party that helped produce those victories has vanished.

It wasn't always this way. In the late 1950s and early 1960s, as the national conservative movement began to congeal, southern Republicans were still too few in number to bother counting, and their impact on presidential politics was far from pivotal. Franklin Delano Roosevelt's New Deal depended upon southern votes, but those votes were so reliable that the South was often taken for granted. Roosevelt and his Democratic successor, Harry Truman, understood the dangers of upsetting the party's southern base by meddling with southern autonomy. Because the Republicans posed so little threat in the South—because the region simply was not yet "in play"—southern demands during the New Deal were not always heeded. That began to change when postwar conservatives discovered an iconic politician who would do as much as segregationist presidential candidates Strom Thurmond or George Wallace ever did to initiate the rise of southern Republicanism. Ironically enough, the conservatives' new darling wasn't even a southerner.

Barry Goldwater and the Southern Pivot

The Republican Party of 1960 would be hardly recognizable to today's generation of partisans. Proudly linked back to its first president and greatest icon, Abraham Lincoln, the postwar Republican Party clung nobly to its abolitionist tradition and continued to command the loyalty of many African Americans. Its leaders were moderates, many of them from northeastern states, including governors Nelson Rockefeller of New York, Theodore McKeldin of Maryland, and Bill Scranton of Pennsylvania, and senators such as Margaret Chase Smith of Maine and Henry Cabot Lodge Jr. of Massachusetts. Richard Nixon, then the incumbent vice president and heir apparent to President Dwight D. Eisenhower for the 1960 Republican nomination, was a former senator from California—a state that would later serve as the cornerstone of the late-twentieth-century Democratic electoral coalition.

First elected to the U.S. Senate in 1952, Arizona's Barry Goldwater was a different kind of Republican. He infused edgy, unapologetic, frontier-style ideas into a moribund party based in the urban, eastern establishment. Goldwater rattled the cages of Republican moderates with his book *The Conscience of a Conservative*. Published in the spring of 1960 as Nixon was coalescing support for his presidential bid, the book was embraced by Goldwater acolytes as a political manifesto—a clarion call to challenge the party's orthodoxy, to shake its prevailing hierarchy, and to chastise its leaders for growing too comfortable with their minority status.

The Goldwaterites could not prevent Nixon from parlaying his institutional advantages into the 1960 presidential nomination, but they made their presence felt at the Republican National Convention in Chicago that summer. Delegates from Goldwater's home state, plus Louisiana and South Carolina, bucked the party's national leadership by pledging their support for the Arizona maverick. They warned that Nixon would lose. They were right, if barely so: In one of the closest elections in American history, Massachusetts senator John F. Kennedy beat Nixon by less than two-tenths of a percent nationwide.

Four years later, Goldwater and his flock would not be denied. Old-guard party leaders again favored moderate candidates like Rockefeller and Scranton, believing that the GOP's emboldened, defiant conservative wing was still too small to be relevant. Again, the moderates were wrong. Tapping into anticommunist zeal and racial antipathies, Goldwater's red-baiting and black-baiting positions attracted devotees from

frustrated groups on the radical right like Young Americans for Freedom and the John Birch Society. The more virulent Goldwaterites labeled President Kennedy a "nigger lover" and a communist. This toxic
mix of antiestablishment disdain, defense of states' rights, and asser-
tion of American military power won the hearts of millions of white
southerners, so much so that voting Republican in parts of the South
quickly went from being heretical to acceptable. "In the [1963] Mississippi governor's race the Democrat Paul Johnson won only because he
convinced the electorate he hated John F. Kennedy more than the Republican candidate did," writes Rick Perlstein in *Before the Storm,* his
authoritative account of Goldwater's ascendancy.

Opponents in both parties and the media depicted Goldwater and
his devotees as reactionary and racist, even fascist. But in trying to undermine Goldwater, many underestimated him and the intensity of his
followers. Perlstein describes the mind-set that emerged among leading
Democrats by late 1963:

> The Democratic National Committee had filled two filing cabinets
> with Goldwater intelligence. At the Western States Democratic
> Meeting, [Idaho Senator] Frank Church devoted his keynote to a
> new wedge issue. Goldwater had stated that America should con-
> sider nuclear retaliation against any Soviet territorial encroach-
> ment, Church noted. "Any American president," he answered,
> who "tampers cavalierly with the delicate balance of terror upon
> which the peace presently depends, might well be the last Ameri-
> can president." At the Midwestern States Democratic Meeting,
> [Democratic National Committee] chair John Bailey said that the
> GOP was "infiltrated by right-wing fanatics and fear mongers
> who think former President Eisenhower is a Communist dupe."
> Only Nebraska's loudmouth governor Frank Morrison spoke a
> certain fear aloud—predicting that Goldwater would carry every
> state west of the Mississippi.

It is striking how the Democrats initially misjudged the long-term
threat posed by the Goldwater conservatives. The incendiary comments by Church and Bailey about Goldwater were no doubt rhetorical,

intended as much to demonize him and the Republicans as to dismiss them. Yet future Republican candidates would successfully deploy refined versions of Goldwater's anticommunist insinuations to reverse voters' perceptions about which of the two parties should be associated with a strong military and muscular foreign policy. Indeed, the origins of almost every term of scorn and derision leveled against Democratic candidates by Republican operatives during the past half century— from "soft on crime" to "big government," from "freedom hater" to "race apologist"—can be traced back to this formative period in partisan politics.

As for Governor Morrison's worried prediction about Goldwater's western appeal, the Nebraskan was wrong in the short term—or maybe he was just thinking a step ahead in terms of where the conservative movement would expand to next. In fact, Goldwaterites established their first foothold in the South. Shut out in every western state except his own Arizona, Goldwater flourished in the heart of the Confederacy, winning all five Deep South states and narrowly losing two other southern states. Goldwater's fifty-two, mostly southern electoral votes were both symbolically meaningful and a portent of changes to come.

Ironically, Goldwater's presidential bid was also snuffed out in the South—specifically in Dallas, on November 22, 1963. The horrific, televised images of Kennedy's assassination altered the 1964 presidential campaign in two fundamental ways. First, it created a temporary backlash against the radical elements within the conservative movement. Second, Kennedy's death replaced a northern president with a southerner. It's tempting to speculate about how well Goldwater might have fared against Kennedy in 1964; before his death, Kennedy himself joked nervously to Vice President Johnson that they might carry only their home states. "In Republican circles that fancied themselves polite, the conclusion was drawn quietly," writes Perlstein. "The press, less courtly, didn't let a decent interval pass: Lee Harvey Oswald had cut down Barry Goldwater's chances as surely as he had John Kennedy's life. Dixie would never reject one of their own for President in the voting booth. And without a member of the Eastern Establishment as his opponent, it was thought, Goldwater lost much of his appeal."

Like the Republican moderates who ignored the threat from brazen Goldwaterites within their ranks, the Democrats misheard the sound of the fury heading their way. Conservatives made significant gains as early as the 1966 midterm elections, electing ten Republican governors, including California's Ronald Reagan. Those gains in turn allowed national Republicans to slow somewhat the Great Society's social programming, bolster the filibuster-dependent southern segregationists in the Senate Democratic caucus, and support the state-level reform efforts of newly elected Republican governors. With solid Democratic majorities in both chambers of Congress and Johnson in the White House, the GOP's southern conservatives had to assume a mostly defensive posture on civil rights. Significant advances on tax, welfare, legal, and cultural reforms remained well beyond the grip of fist-pumping conservative Republicans and their new southern converts. But soon enough, the phasing effect would become evident in the policies of a string of Republican presidents berthed by the partisan conversion of the South.

Richard Nixon

In 1968, Richard Nixon resurrected his political career by invoking the kind of race-loaded rhetoric he had purposely avoided eight years earlier. Nixon's win was thin: He and Wallace split the ninety-two electors in the ten southern states lost by Democrat Hubert Humphrey, who won Texas's twenty-five electoral votes as a Johnson legacy. (Had Wallace carried all ten states, the three-way split would have thrown the election into the Democrat-controlled House of Representatives.) More telling is the fact that Nixon became the first elected president in American history to enter the White House without his party capturing either chamber of Congress. The era of dealignment, hallmarked by no major dominant party and divided national government, had begun. And it was this unsettled state of partisan affairs gave the South more political clout than it had in a century.

In office, Nixon encountered resistance to his attempts to scale back the burgeoning Great Society bureaucracy he inherited, and even dared to expand environmental and occupational safety regulations—policies that would be considered heretical to today's unabashedly business-friendly Republicans. Nor were Nixon's problems limited to Beltway battles between the Republican White House and the Democratic Congress. Within a month of Nixon's inauguration, Republican Party chairs from the eleven southern states were already complaining that Nixon had betrayed them on race matters. Thurmond adviser Harry Dent wrote Nixon a memo to appraise the president of the situation:

> I asked why they (Southern Chairmen) can't see the President and hold a news conference at the White House like [NAACP chairman] Roy Wilkins, Dent reported. They say "we supported him and Wilkins fought him." With "southern fever running high" and "Tricky Dick" editorials appearing in the region's newspapers, Dent stressed school desegregation as the most pressing issue. Strong enough, perhaps, to spark a second southern revolt in another four years. Unless convinced "that this will not be a wild Administration on the subject of guideline implementation," Dent reiterated, all eleven states represented at the Atlanta meeting might cast their votes in 1972 for George Wallace.

Nixon got the message. To undermine desegregation and other civil rights legislation passed by his predecessor, Nixon urged bureaucratic footdragging at the U.S. Department of Health, Education, and Welfare, and the civil rights division of the Department of Justice. "Nixon further strengthened his credentials as a racial conservative when his administration sought in 1969 to weaken the Voting Rights Act," write Thomas Byrne Edsall and Mary Edsall in *Chain Reaction*. "The bid of the Nixon administration to eliminate provisions in the act requiring officials in the South to obtain 'preclearance' from the Justice Department for local election law changes, although ultimately unsuccessful, served to demonstrate to the concerned electorate that a Democratic Congress, rather than the Nixon administration, was behind the singling out of the South as the target of the most stringent enforcement provisions." Nixon also earned plaudits for twice attempting to use his first Supreme Court appointment to put a southerner on the bench.

For movement conservatives, especially the southerners who began to switch their affiliation to the Republican Party during the Nixon era, the paralysis created by race issues provided a welcome drag on civil rights reform. But solid Democratic majorities in Congress meant that tax cuts and business deregulation would have to wait. Nixon's resignation under threat of impeachment was a major setback, of course. Still, southern conservatives inched forward during the eight years of the Nixon and Ford presidencies, grooming a new cohort of southern Republican leaders, policy wonks, campaign consultants, and future elected officials. They had to sit out one presidential cycle, but they would be back.

Ronald Reagan

Ronald Reagan moved the Republicans another big step closer to a national majority. He carried ten southern states and his coattails swept a Republican majority into the Senate in 1980, allowing Reagan to pass the tax cuts inspired by California's now-famous Proposition 13 property tax reforms. Reagan expanded American military power through dramatic increases in defense spending, and engaged in petty wars in Grenada and Nicaragua to compensate for his cowardly retreat from Lebanon after a 1983 terrorist truck bomb killed 239 U.S. Marines in Beirut. On race, the "Great Communicator" paid lip service to affirmative action and supported tax credits for segregated school districts. Fewer than 2 percent of his appointees to the federal bench were racial minorities.

Though he conveyed support for many social positions dear to southern hearts, Reagan's conservative credentials—like Reagan himself—were more symbolic than substantive. It is often forgotten, for example, that Reagan quickly retreated on taxes (both income taxes and payroll taxes) and balked at several agenda items precious to orthodox conservatives. "A sober review of Reagan's presidency doesn't yield the seamlessly conservative record being peddled today," former *Washington Monthly* editor Joshua Green reminds forgetful Reagan revisionists. "Federal government expanded on his watch. The conservative desire to outlaw abortion was never seriously pursued. Reagan broke with the hard-liners in his administration and compromised with the Soviets on arms control. His assault on entitlements never materialized; instead he saved Social Security in 1983. And he repeatedly ignored the fundamental conservative dogma that taxes should never be raised." In regional terms, Reagan became the second California Republican elected twice on the strength of southern votes, and the fourth non-southern Republican president (counting Michigan's Ford) to serve in the postwar period—none of whom chose southerners as vice presidential running mates. The South was putting Republicans in the White House, but not southern Republicans.

Of course, there just weren't yet many seasoned, credible southern Republicans to run for national office. During Reagan's tenure, however, the first group of southern Republicans rose to positions of power in Congress. Tennessee's Howard Baker was Senate majority leader for four years before leaving to serve as Reagan's chief of staff. Jesse Helms of North Carolina—who once referred to the 1964 Civil Rights Act as "dangerous" and called Martin Luther King Jr. a "pervert"—became a prominent voice on the Senate Foreign Relations committee. The southern Republicans could not yet elect a president, but they had moved another step closer to taking over national politics.

George H. W. Bush

If official residence for voting purposes were the standard, George H. W. Bush would be counted as a Texan. But judging by either his biography or his policies, Bush cannot be regarded as the first southern Republican president. Raised in Connecticut and schooled at Andover and Yale, as a young congressman in the late 1960s Bush visited shantytowns on the National Mall and supported reproductive choice before it became fashionable. (His wife and daughter-in-law, both First Ladies, still do.) Like Nixon in deed, but unlike Reagan in word, Bush believed the federal government, rather than being the problem, could use its powers for good. He signed two landmark pieces of regulatory legislation: the Americans with Disabilities Act and the Clean Air Act Amendments of 1990.

Bush arrived in the White House two decades after Nixon, however, and was expected to behave in a manner befitting an heir to Reagan's mantle. What he failed to realize is that the southern conservatives in the party had crossed a patience threshold and were no longer willing to wait for results. When Bush pledged "no new taxes" in his acceptance speech at the 1988 Republican National Convention in New Orleans, conservatives intended to hold him to it. Instead, Bush did what a throwback Republican from the dying, moderate-dominated, northeastern-midwestern patrician wing of the GOP was to be expected to do—that is, the prudent thing: He raised taxes in order to put the country back on sound fiscal footing. "You can say Bush was politically naive, even suicidal, to break his tax promise, and you can say the promise was irresponsible to begin with," writes columnist Jonathan Rauch, in clarifying which president from the twelve-year Reagan-Bush reign was the real fiscal conservative. "But you can't deny this fact: It was Bush's budget deal that broke the deficit's back."

The tough fiscal choices made by Bush and then Bill Clinton helped stabilize the American economy, setting the stage for the expansion of the late 1990s—as if that mattered to rabid conservatives, for whom no good-deeder must go uncrucified on the altar of tax cuts. The political fallout from Bush's pledge cost him dearly during the 1992 campaign. Clinton and Ross Perot gleefully mocked Bush's "read my lips" pledge, further irritating already disgruntled conservatives. Coupled with his appointment of moderate David Souter to the Supreme Court, Bush was facing a full-scale partisan revolt by the time Republican National Convention delegates arrived in Houston in 1992.

Four years earlier, campaign strategist Lee Atwater used surrogates to run the infamous "Willie" Horton television ads that successfully stoked white fears about "soft-on-crime" Democratic nominee Michael Dukakis. By 1992, however, Bush's "carping liberals" complaints on the campaign trail rang hollow in conservative ears, especially in the South where his overall margin dropped 16 percentage points from 1988. Bush was often parodied by late-night comedians—especially *Saturday Night Live*'s inimitable Dana Carvey—for his malapropisms and his penchant use of the word "prudent." Prudence, of course, was the operative principle of the once-powerful but now crippled moderate wing of the Republican Party from which Bush came. Bush's Rockefeller Republicanism was no longer acceptable to southern conservatives, who demanded that their votes be properly rewarded with immediate, authentic results.

George W. Bush

Immediacy—and southern authenticity—is precisely what the southern conservatives finally got with George W. Bush. Political observer Michael Lind, a native Texan, explains the historical precedent set by Bush's election:

> George W. Bush is the first Southern conservative to be elected president of the United States since James Knox Polk in 1844. In the intervening generations, there have been Southern presidents and there have been conservative presidents. But the Southern presidents have not been conservative, and the conservative presidents have not been Southern . . . Bush's political ancestors [in West Texas] are not the Southern presidents of the twentieth century, but reactionary Southern senators and representatives who dominated the Democratic Party from the early nineteenth century until the New Deal, and who took over the Republican party in the 1990s. While George W. Bush is far more conservative than previous Southern presidents, he is also far more Southern than previous conservative presidents.

Bush's southern disposition swept into the Oval Office an elite-oriented, pious, secretive, culturally self-righteous form of corporate governance. Massive tax cuts for those who least needed them topped Bush's first-year agenda—and the post–September 11 agendas in his second and third years, too. The budget deficit ballooned, a problem the administration has solved by raising the national debt ceiling four times (thus far) so the government could pay its bills through further borrowing. The 2002 Farm Act added $139 billion in new agribusiness subsidies, while sunny labels were appended to policies expanding logging rights ("Healthy Forests") and permissive pollution standards ("Clear Skies").

On social issues, Bush signed an executive order the week he took office banning the use of federal monies to fund international planned parenting programs; he faithfully initiated (even if only for symbolic purposes) a faith-based initiative, complete with a new government administrator charged with shepherding public dollars away from social programs and into churches; and he compromised on a major "culture of life" issue by lying about how many stem cell lines were active. The administration prioritized missile defense, and continued to push for it after the September 11 attacks despite its uselessness in combating the type of borderless, target-poor "shadowy network" brand of terrorism exported by Osama bin Laden and others. Bush's neoconservative advisers stovepiped national security information around the Central Intelligence Agency and directly into the White House via the vice president's office to justify a preemptive strike against Iraq because it supposedly possessed stockpiles of weapons of mass destruction and had links to the al Qaeda terrorist network—two claims later proved to be false.

The undemocratic nature of the Bush presidency is the feature that most smacks of a southern-styled autocracy. After conservatives complained for years about the secrecy of the Hillary Clinton–led health care task force, Vice President Dick Cheney met secretly with energy industry executives to formulate an energy plan. Bush has held the fewest solo press conferences of any modern president, and almost invariably takes questions from a predetermined list of mostly fawning reporters. His first week in office, Bush invoked executive privilege to violate a 1978 law and seal the Reagan-Bush presidential papers that may have shed light on his father's involvement in the Iran-Contra scandal. His press staff has literally altered the transcript of White House press briefings to change answers they did not like, and they permitted a security-risk gay prostitute with Republican business connections and no legitimate press background to attend White House press briefings so press secretary Scott McClellan would have a safe reporter to call upon when the questioning got too tough. Most egregious, the Bush campaign traveled around the country in 2004, racking up huge overtime bills for the added security provided by local police departments during Bush and Cheney "public" campaign stops, but allowed only locals who signed loyalty pledges or who had volunteered on the campaign to attend, with any protestors who dared to sneak in removed.

With the arrival of a true-red southern conservative at 1600 Pennsylvania Avenue, the South's long winter had finally ended. Shut out of presidential politics for the first seven decades after the Civil War, the South was a silent second partner in the New Deal coalition. During the post-1968 era of partisan dealignment, at best the South could provide the crucial votes to elect non-southern Republicans. Not anymore. Bush's presidency stands as the crowning moment in the South's slow rise to national prominence. Provincial and pious, evangelical and exclusive, and decidedly dismissive of dissent, the Bush administration has finally elevated to the Oval Office all of the worst aspects of the old, one-party style of southern rule.

Most fitting, Bush became president despite losing the national popular vote in 2000. He entered the White House as a minority president who then governed as if he were instead crowned with an inherited mandate. And why not? For the first time in American politics, southern Republicans held the top positions across the elected branches: Bush in the White House; Mississippi's Trent Lott as the Senate's since-deposed majority leader; and behind the curtain of Dennis Hastert's speakership the lever-pulling hands of the since-resigned Texan Tom DeLay. (And let's not forget that the congressional revolution that swept Republicans into power in 1994 was orchestrated by Georgia's Newt Gingrich.) Bush governed brazenly from the start, as if riding high on a landslide and unchallenged Republican majorities in Congress. Four years later, after he added just a few southern-produced congressional seats and a paltry fifteen more electoral votes than his 2000 total, Bush trumpeted his newly won capital the day after the election.

Is this really a surprise? For decades, southern conservatives came to expect that they should exercise power beyond their numbers when *obstructing* the federal government. Why would they be inhibited about exercising power beyond their numbers when *controlling* it? Bush's reelection reduced the phasing effect to virtual imperceptibility. Now the sight of even the smallest, southern-produced gains reports like an immediate roar.

The Impatient, Moral Minority

Following the 2000 elections in which Democrat Al Gore won the national popular vote, Republicans controlled the Senate only because

Vice President Dick Cheney's tie-breaking vote was decisive in a chamber split fifty seats each. When Vermont's James Jeffords defected from the Republican caucus in April 2001, the Democrats led by South Dakota's Tom Daschle suddenly found themselves in the majority. Almost as vexing for Republicans as their battles with the Democrats were the intraparty machinations necessary to keep the GOP coalition together. Congressional reporter Michael Crowley recalls the mood on Capitol Hill at the time:

> It's hard to remember now, but back in the spring of 2001, the fate of the Bush administration seemed to hinge on the Senate's hearty moderate band. After Vermont Sen. Jim Jeffords dashed across the political DMZ and declared himself an independent, evenly splitting the Senate between the parties, it seemed as if the threat of a Jeffords repeat—[Rhode Island's Lincoln] Chafee, for one, began making noises about defection—could stop the GOP's lurch to the right. Conservatives who had sneered at their party's moderates started sucking up to them. Then–Senate Majority Leader Trent Lott magnanimously gave Pennsylvania centrist Arlen Specter a special seat at his leadership meetings. Some moderates said alarmed conservatives went so far as to shower them with physical affection.

The 2002 elections, the first following the September 11 attacks, gave the conservatives some wiggle room. Republicans gained two seats and a fifty-one-seat majority, mooting Jeffords's switch and ending all the superficial hugging within the Republican caucus. But the moderates still held some sway.

The 2004 election results ended all that. The GOP expanded its majority by four seats to fifty-five, a net gain more than accounted for by the five southern pickups. The southern delegation's share of the GOP caucus rose from a fourth to a third of all seats. Buoyed by these gains, the eighteen southern Republicans led by their new majority leader, Bill Frist of Tennessee, began to flex their newfound muscles on both sides of the partisan aisle. Within the caucus, the fragile détente between northern-based moderates and southern-based conservatives was shattered.

Just ask Arlen Specter. A pro-choice Pennsylvania senator who narrowly avoided defeat in the 2004 Republican primary to a staunch conservative, Specter was in line to become the chair of the Senate Judiciary Committee. Just one day after his reelection, Specter made the near-fatal blunder of suggesting that Bush needed to compromise on judicial appointments and that hard-line conservative appointees might have a hard time being confirmed. Back home, the conservative *Pittsburgh Tribune-Herald* went ballistic: "President Bush and the GOP extended their hands to pull Specter to a fifth term. In thanks, he has extended his middle finger. Senate leadership should respond—by denying Arlen Specter the chairmanship he so covets and is so prepared to abuse." Emails and phone calls from marauding moralists across the country flooded Washington, demanding that Specter not be made Judiciary Committee chair. The website NotSpecter.com was quickly launched by a prodigy of Richard Viguerie, the man who founded the now-defunct, Virginia-based Moral Majority. Cowed by the mounting pressure, Specter began to retreat and apologize. Although President Bush and fellow southern conservatives in the Senate could have twisted the knife, they chose instead to let Specter stay on as an admonished and weakened chair. They know he won't dare defy them again.

Specter is not alone. Once pivotal, the quartet of Republican moderates Crowley calls the "Fantastic Four"—Chafee, Maine's Susan Collins and Olympia Snowe, and Arizona gadfly John McCain—suddenly find themselves marginalized in the 109th Congress. "Given that only the Fantastic Four are reliable dissidents, Frist is almost never under the 50-vote mark," says Crowley. "Other GOP senators make occasional cameos as single-issue moderates: Ohio's George Voinovich on the deficit; Pennsylvania's Arlen Specter on abortion; Oregon's Gordon Smith on health care; Nebraska's Chuck Hagel and Indiana's Richard Lugar on foreign affairs. But it's rare for more than one of these senators to gang up with the Fantastic Four." Rarer still is finding a moderate Republican—what conservatives pejoratively refer to as RINOs, or "Republicans in Name Only"—who is a southerner. None of the Senate's four single-issue moderates, nor any of the "Fantastic Four," hails from the South.

The disappearing cadre of Republican moderates is being targeted for extinction either by the Democrats or angry conservatives. Chafee already infuriated Republicans when he said on the eve of the 2004 election that, as a symbolic statement, he planned to write in the name of former president George H. W. Bush, and was even rumored to be considering a switch to the Democrats. With one of the most liberal voting records of any Republican senator, Chafee now faces a primary challenger in 2006 who is supported by conservative groups like the Club for Growth, and his seat is one of seven the Democratic Senatorial Campaign Committee headed by New York's Chuck Schumer is targeting for pickup in the midterm election. Having shunted moderates like Chafee aside, the Senate's southern delegation is the keeper of the keys.

But the southern-led Republican majority, though formidable and decidedly conservative, is still frustrated because the GOP remains five seats short of a more magical threshold in the chamber: sixty senators, the number needed to end a filibuster. A lone senator can filibuster a measure and prevent it from reaching a floor vote—except if a supermajority of sixty senators triggers the cloture rule, thereby bringing closure to debate and forcing a vote. For decades, this was the very device southern senators—all Democrats in those days, led masterfully by Georgia's Richard Russell—relied upon to thwart civil rights progress, the most memorable moment of which was Strom Thurmond's 24-hour, 18-minute filibuster of the 1957 Civil Rights Act. That southern senators today dare to depict the filibuster as an anachronistic, undemocratic, majority-thwarting device—no less justify their opposition by appealing to historical precedent—exceeds even the normal bounds of Washington hypocrisy. But opposition among southern Republicans to using the filibuster to exploit minority rule appears illogical and ahistorical only to those unfamiliar with southern political history. If anything, a sense of natural entitlement to the exercise of power beyond its numbers conforms perfectly with the South's history and southern political sensibilities dating back to the very bargains struck to form the Constitution itself.

Southern-Style Rule

The South has long been the outlier region in American politics. Politically, the South was kept—or, rather, kept itself—at arm's length from Washington and the rest of the country. This distance allowed the region's highly undemocratic practices to perpetuate, as Democrats flouted the Civil War amendments for almost a century through the systematic use of poll taxes, grandfather clauses, literacy tests, convict leasing, intimidation, and violence—all of which were perpetrated as part of the successful campaign to subjugate blacks and many poor whites. The price the South paid for self-autonomy and the paranoid need to maintain its regional "heritage" was a disassociation from national affairs. The "solid South" retained control over regional matters, but at the expense of being excluded from national affairs—until Washington started meddling with southern home rule, that is.

The solid Republican South is something altogether different, for the South now forms the core of a truculent governing majority rather than backbone of a vigilant, racist minority. Southern politicians no longer must react and retrench, obstruct and oppose. They can preempt and demand, lead and propose, flexing their political muscle to set precedents they like and overturn those they do not. But to what end, exactly? "The South has twice sought to shatter the union, first and most tragically by secession and civil war, and then in our own time by its shameless defiance of court-ordered school desegregation," writes Leslie Dunbar, former director of the Southern Regional Council. "One might think George W. Bush, widely and accurately accepted as a Southerner, ought to be therefore acutely sensitive to the needs of national unity. He has not been. If he and his administration are much longer in office, the economic interests they respond to in Pavlovian predictability much longer ascendant, the essentials of unity will be under heavy stress. And again from a Southern-led party."

Yes, one might *think* the southern-dominated GOP would want to live up to Bush's "uniter, not a divider" pledge. But the days of the thinking man's Republican Party are gone. Stripped bare of the platitudes and catchphrases, the southern-based Republican majority stands naked as a ruling cohort no longer interested in limited government, in states' rights, in judicial review, in consensus-building filibusters, or any of the other measures of restraint that once informed the political philosophies of movement conservatives. They aren't much interested in national unity, either. The civil rights reforms that began in the middle of the twentieth century ended the Democratic South's one-party hegemony and regional autonomy. The Republican potentates who took over the postreform South realized that if America would no longer permit southerners to *divorce* themselves from Washington, their only recourse was to *dominate* national politics.

SOUTHERN REPUBLICANS CAPTURE THE GOP

You probably hadn't noticed until recently, but liberal activist judges are destroying America. Legislating from the bench, these black-robed, lifetime-appointed judicial terrorists are hell-bent on ratifying the radical homosexual agenda, undermining the American family by somehow both encouraging abortions and condom use, finding privacy rights where none exist, helping plaintiffs shake down helpless corporations for undeserved millions, and in general wielding their gavels in a concerted, systematic effort to shred the Constitution in the name of a Hollywood-inspired, campus-driven godless socialism.

The conservative rage toward the federal judiciary knows no bounds. Judges are now to be blamed for almost everything that's wrong in the country. Traditional Values Coalition president Lou Sheldon complains that dastardly liberals prefer "judicial tyranny" over constitutional government. Focus on the Family president Dr. James Dobson compares judges in black robes to Ku Klux Klan members in white sheets. Televangelist Pat Robertson wonders aloud on a Sunday morning talk show whether the "gradual erosion" in American culture fostered by liberal judges is worse than "a few bearded terrorists who fly into buildings." Eagle Forum's Phyllis Schlafly calls for Supreme Court associate justice Anthony Kennedy's impeachment because he referenced international law in ruling with the majority to ban the death penalty for minors. Ann Coulter "jokes" that somebody ought to

poison Justice John Paul Stevens's crème brûlée. "The Court has become increasingly hostile to Christianity, and it poses a greater threat to
representative government—more than anything, more than budget
deficits, more than terrorist groups," exclaims Tony Perkins, president
of the Family Research Council, summarizing the general mood among
reactionary conservatives. Suddenly, it seems, Supreme Court justices
have transformed from regular old judicial tyrants to full-fledged
America-hating terrorists.

Forget for a moment that Republican presidents appointed a majority of current U.S. Court of Appeals judges (about three in every five), a
majority of Supreme Court justices (seven of nine, including Justice
Kennedy), and the past two chief justices. Forget that, by any of the
conventional measures of what constitutes judicial activism on the
Supreme Court—the number of times the court gets involved in "political questions" between the executive and legislative branches; how
frequently justices ignore *stare decisis* to reverse earlier Supreme Court
rulings; and, most especially, the number of congressional acts the
court deems unconstitutional—the Supreme Court during Chief Justice William H. Rehnquist's tenure is the most activist *conservative*
court in American history. Forget, too, that "liberal, activist judges" is
a focus group–tested phrase Bush strategist Karl Rove long ago discovered works like all-purpose political catnip for tort reform tigers,
culture-of-life lions, pro-family panthers, and cages brimming full with
a variety of sharp-clawed conservative fat cats.

Pay no mind to any of that, because the southern-led conservative
wing of the Republican Party, its Supreme Court–selected southern
cowboy president, the army of Christian crusaders who embolden
them, and the talking-point pontiffs on television and talk radio who
parrot their messages have convinced themselves that the federal
judges they appointed are somehow undermining all the efforts of the
elected branches they elected. Because the southern-based evangelical
movement is convinced it delivered the 2004 election to George W.
Bush and the congressional Republicans, the time for preaching has
ended and the moment for a rapturous accounting has arrived. Pointing to the exit polls showing that 22 percent of Americans cited "moral
values" as the most important issue in the election, they believe they

are *owed*. They're not about to wait another minute for their votes, their shoe-leather canvassing, their dollars—and, of course, their prayers—to translate into the political clout they seek because, after all, pay-backs are heaven.

With the presidency and Congress already captured, the assault on the federal judiciary is the final, brazen attack on the one branch of the national government the southern-led Republican majority cannot bend as easily to its will as the elected branches. In targeting the courts for assault, the dominant southern face of the Republican Party finally revealed itself to the nation, however. And with that revelation the moderates who prevail in the rest of the country realized that a small, unrepresentative, intense, and dangerous regional minority now runs the country.

The Good Ol' Boys Network

George W. Bush likes his vacations. His disposition was perfectly suited for governor of Texas, where the state's lieutenant governor has greater responsibilities than the chief executive, and the legislature only meets every other year. That left Bush plenty of time for leisure, for baseball games, and most especially for making plans to run for president. Bush's regimen changed little when he reached the Oval Office. Count-ing the time he spent at his Crawford ranch, at Maryland's Camp David, or elsewhere beyond the Beltway, the *Washington Post* determined that Bush spent roughly 40 percent of his first term outside Washington, and by January 2006 he had spent a year's worth of days—a fifth of his presidency to that point—just in Crawford. Given the growth in fed-eral spending during his first four years in office, apparently when Bush preaches about reducing government he means the time the chief executive himself actually spends governing.

Bush bought his Crawford ranch in 1999 to provide a staged back-drop for his presidential campaign. His vacations there have been espe-cially leisurely, and in general are not to be interrupted. The president reminds his critics that the job can come to him, that advisers and cab-inet secretaries can work from Crawford, and notable persons both do-mestic and foreign are expected to make respectful pilgrimages so he need not budge. Bush didn't return to Washington in the summer of

2001 after reading language in presidential security briefings that was anything but historical ("planning" is not a past-tense verb), and referred to both New York City as a target and hijacking airplanes as a method. He didn't return to Washington in the summer of 2002 as the Adelphia, Enron, and Worldcom financial scandals—which cost Americans hundreds of billions of dollars in stock value and postponed millions of retirements—were unfolding. Nor did he return in the summer of 2003, five months into the Iraq war and with no weapons of mass destruction to be found. And he certainly didn't spend much time in Washington in the summer of 2004, while Fallujah continued to rage beyond the control of coalition forces a year and a half after the invasion: The Republican National Convention was approaching, and the Bush-Cheney reelection campaign was gearing up for the final push toward November. (Interestingly, the eventual assault on Fallujah, which became the deadliest period since the "end of major combat operations" in May 2003, began one week after Bush won reelection.)

But in late March 2005, a president reelected with what he claimed was newly earned political capital flew back from a vacation in his beloved Crawford in the middle of the night to sign a single act of Congress that applied to one American citizen: Terri Schiavo. We'll have to take the president at his word that his actions were motivated by a desire to protect a helpless woman, even if that meant violating her husband's wishes and the Florida law that empowered him to decide his wife's fate. We'll also have to take Bush's word about his veneration for the "culture of life," despite the fact that during the middle of the Schiavo controversy a four-month-old boy named Sun Hudson, over his mother's objections, had his medical life support removed by order of a Texas judge based on a 1999 state law Bush signed as governor that gives medical authorities more power than parents to decide which lives are worthy of cultural saving.

Whatever Bush's motivations, and however inconsistent and duplicitous they may be, what's clear about the response to the Schiavo controversy by the president and congressional Republicans is that all the finger-pointing extremism and precedent-reversing hysterics were choreographed by conservative politicians on behalf of America's true governing minority—the southern-based culture warriors who pull the strings of the Republican Party. Indeed, what's most fascinating about the culture war is how it inverts the normal political hierarchy. Culture warriors didn't take their cues and marching orders from the three southern men who were then running the country: George Bush, Bill Frist, and Tom DeLay. They gave them.

At the moment the Schiavo case burst upon the national stage, Senate majority leader Bill Frist, of Tennessee, and his fellow Republicans were in the process of carefully building the public case against the filibuster. They complained that the filibuster historically applied only to legislation, not the confirmation of presidential nominees—a fair enough point, were it not for the fact that the Republicans during the 1990s blocked six times as many of Bill Clinton's judicial appointees from getting an up-or-down vote by simply burying the nominations in the Senate Judiciary Committee. But any momentum Senate Republicans were gaining on the filibuster question was suddenly reversed by the overzealousness of conservative leaders during the Schiavo episode, starting with Frist himself.

Frist is a heart surgeon. Second only to his close relationship with President Bush, Frist's medical background is the root of his informal credibility and, by extension, his formal power within the Senate. But Frist is not a neurosurgeon, had never met Terri Schiavo, and never served as her personal physician or an expert witness in the various court cases involving Schiavo that had been adjudicated during the fifteen years she was trapped in a vegetative state. Yet, after watching just a few selectively edited minutes of a videotape made by Schiavo's parents, Frist blithely abused his position of public trust as a licensed physician and tarnished his national reputation by offering his expert "diagnosis" that Schiavo was not in a persistent vegetative state.

Frist aspires to succeed Bush in 2008, and the White House has let it be known that the president deems the Tennessean a suitable heir. Frist saw what South Carolina conservatives did to John McCain in 2000: Operatives within the supposedly patriotic, family-values party questioned the patriotism of a fellow partisan who had served as a prisoner of war, then spread rumors that his adopted Asian daughter was a mixed-race bastard child. No dummy, Frist recognizes that a decidedly pious, unrepresentative subset of southern conservatives have veto power over the 2008 Republican nomination and will exercise that veto in South Carolina if they want. So the Schiavo case presented Frist an early opportunity to begin the bent-knee groveling southern Republicans expect. By leaping blindly into the Schiavo controversy, Frist proved he understands that indiscretion is the better part of conservative valor.

Not to be outdone, then-House majority leader Tom DeLay of Texas entered the Schiavo fray by opening his ten-gallon mouth and inserting into it both of his cowboy boots. "This loss happened because our legal system did not protect the people who need protection most, and that will change," DeLay said, ominously. "The time will come for the men responsible for [Schiavo's death] to answer for their behavior." For good measure, DeLay also promised that the Congress would be taking a long, hard look at an "arrogant and out-of-control judiciary that thumbs its nose at Congress and the president." DeLay later backtracked somewhat, offering a public semiapology in which he artfully described his earlier comments as "inartful." Apparently, even DeLay's advisers recognize that the vast majority of Americans don't take too kindly to members of Congress making thinly veiled threats against federal judges.

DeLay typifies today's southern Republicans. As the owner of a small pest control company in Sugar Land during the 1970s, he became interested in politics because of his frustrations with business regulations. So DeLay ran for and won a seat in the state legislature, where he fought against government regulation almost as heartily as he partied. (His nickname in Austin was "Hot Tub Tom.") Known more for political skills than policy mastery, in 1986 the ever-ambitious DeLay won election to the U.S. House of Representatives. The west Texan soon became an adjutant to Newt Gingrich, a suburban Georgian whose political star was rising in the House. When Gingrich shepherded the Republicans out of their forty-year minority wilderness into control of the House following the 1994 elections, DeLay emerged as a top party whip. He shed his Austin nickname for a new, Washington moniker— "The Hammer"—that betrays his reputation in Congress as a ruthless, disciplined, and disciplining power player.

DeLay was already incensed about judicial tyranny before the Schiavo episode. On March 1, 2005, the Supreme Court's ruling in *Roper v. Simmons* extended the existing prohibition against the death penalty for persons aged 15 and under to all minors. At the time of the decision, twenty states had death penalty statutes for 16-year-olds and 17-year-olds, including almost every southern state. Of the seventy-two teenagers on death row at the time of the decision, all but seven were in southern prisons. With twenty-nine, Texas alone accounted for more than a third of death-row teenagers, followed by Alabama's fourteen. (No other state had more than five.) Justice Kennedy—a Reagan appointee on the bench since 1988 and, apparently, a justice nearly indistinguishable from a terrorist, by Reverend Robertson's accounting—provided the decisive vote and wrote the majority opinion in *Roper*.

On Fox News Radio, DeLay let host and future White House press secretary Tony Snow know that a target had been placed squarely on Kennedy's back. "We've got Justice Kennedy writing decisions based upon international law, not the Constitution of the United States," he said. "That's just outrageous. And not only that, but he said in session that he does his own research on the internet? That is just incredibly outrageous." Asked a few weeks later by the editorial board of the conservative *Washington Times* if he was in favor of pursuing the impeachment of judges, the suddenly cautious DeLay offered a curious nonreply. "I'm not going to answer that," he said.

Actually, DeLay doesn't blame judges for their supposed activism. He faults Congress—by which, of course, he means congressional liberals. "I blame Congress over the last fifty to a hundred years for not standing up and taking its responsibility given to it by the Constitution," says DeLay. "The reason the judiciary has been able to impose a separation of church and state that's nowhere in the Constitution is that Congress didn't stop them. The reason we had judicial review is because Congress didn't stop them. The reason we had a right to privacy is because Congress didn't stop them." DeLay's remarks moved *New Yorker* commentator Hendrik Hertzberg to write:

So there you have it, the DeLay agenda: no separation of church and state, no judicial review, no right to privacy. Next to this, the President's effort to repeal the New Deal social contract by phas-

ing out Social Security is the mewing of a kitten. DeLay may stay
or DeLay may go. But the real danger is not DeLay himself. It's
DeLay's agenda. It's his vision. It's his "values."

Following his indictment for criminal conspiracy in the re-redistricting
of the Texas House map, DeLay had to surrender his position as majority leader in 2005 and resigned his seat in June 2006. But DeLay's
agenda and his values still reflect the prevailing worldview of today's
southern Republicans.

Because of their prominence and coalition-building responsibility,
one might expect Frist and DeLay to take more centrist positions as
caucus leaders. The reverse is true: Not only are Frist and DeLay ideological outliers within their respective Republican caucuses, but they
are even *more conservative* than their decidedly conservative southern
cohorts. According to *National Journal*'s annual ideological scoring of
members of Congress, the composite conservative score (on a scale of 0
to 100) for the seventy-six southern GOP House members during the
108th Congress (2003–04) was 79.8, with DeLay earning an eye-
popping 93.3 score. The average for the 138 non-southern Republican
representatives was 70.2. Including Frist's 77.0 rating, the average conservative score for the thirteen southern Republicans in the Senate was
76.5, compared to 72.7 for the non-southern Republicans. What's
more, four of the five new southern senators (Florida's Mel Martinez
excepted) served in the House for six years before winning election to
the Senate. Their lifetime House ratings—David Vitter (Louisiana,
89.2); Jim DeMint (South Carolina, 88.6); Richard Burr (North Carolina,
76.6); and Johnny Isakson (Georgia, 73.1)—suggest that the southern-
versus-non-southern voting cleavages within the GOP caucus will only
become more pronounced in the future.

There's little doubt that the southern members like DeLay and Frist
drag the party's congressional caucuses rightward, and will continue to
do so. It will be interesting to see if Ohio's John Boehner, who beat out
DeLay protégé Roy Blunt to replace DeLay as majority leader, will take
the House Republicans in a new direction. Some Republicans who worried about the dangers of DeLay's ideology as well as his aggressive
political style privately expressed relief that he was taken down and

are hoping the House will move in a different direction now that DeLay is gone.

It may be too late, because the damage is already done. If the Democrats reap a windfall among Americans who are turned off by the moral crusading of the southern-led Republican majority, the thread that will be remembered as the one that unspooled the GOP was the gross political miscalculation by Bush, Frist, and DeLay in the Terri Schiavo episode. Shortly after Schiavo died a *USA Today*/CNN/Gallup poll revealed that the vast majority of Americans were disturbed that Congress and President Bush meddled in the end-of-life controversy. Only one in five Americans said it was extremely important how "federal courts handle moral issues." At least twice as many cited terrorism, health care costs, the economy, and even gas prices as extremely important. "Here's the troubling thing: That 20 percent is running the country, and they're now pressing for such changes in the way the courts decide cases," warns *Salon*'s Farhad Manjoo. "While most Americans are apparently indifferent to the long-term implications of the Schiavo case, many religious conservatives see it as having lasting political utility. Its most important outcome, they say, is in highlighting an unsettling flaw in American governance. They call this flaw 'judicial tyranny,' though most of the rest of us know it by a friendlier name, 'checks and balances.' "

Bush's late-night flight across the country, Frist's back-of-the-videotape-box diagnosis, and DeLay's brooding impeachment threats—each of these was a desperate effort to pacify the insatiable, southern-fried ruling minority that now controls national politics and does not like to wait for results.

Eyesore Republicans and Black-Eye Republicans

By 1998, just four years after he led the Republicans to their first majority in the House of Representatives since 1952, Speaker Newt Gingrich of Georgia had worn out his political welcome. Despite Bill Clinton's impeachment, and quite possibly in response to it, Republicans lost seats during the 1998 midterm elections. Gingrich's government shutdown and wacky public comments had soured too many Americans. It was time for him to go.

DeLay was on the short list to succeed Gingrich as Speaker. But DeLay's abrasive style worried many Republicans. Although "The Hammer" is precisely the sort of person Republicans want organizing their power-hungry ascent, having him as the public face of the party is another matter. A white male with socially conservative attitudes, a taste for aggressive political tactics, and cozy relationships with myriad corporate sponsors from whom he has raised tens of millions of dollars, DeLay is what we might call an *eyesore Republican*.

Eyesore Republicans are not party outcasts. They chair committees and subcommittees, mark up legislation, broker deals, and cajole colleagues. They build coalitions and political networks, form candidate and leadership PACs, develop strategy and talking points, and host cocktail party fund-raisers in Washington and around the country to raise money for the party. But eyesore Republicans hurt the party when they become too visible or make national headlines. Fearing that voters will equate the party with its worst elements, GOP leaders and strategists work diligently to keep eyesore Republicans from public view.

At the party's quadrennial national conventions, for instance, they are often assigned to less-noticed activities like cavorting with top donors on private cruises and golf outings. Meanwhile, more palatable and telegenic substitutes—women, racial minorities, and social moderates especially—are paraded one after the other to the podium to deliver speeches to the multitudes. Republican conventions have devolved into televised minstrel shows in which the skills of Soviet-era Kremlinologists are required to divine who holds power, but with an inverted twist: Aside from the obligatory appearances by the president and vice president, to determine who at the Republican conclave is powerful one starts by drawing up a list of those *not* featured prominently. Former Clinton adviser Sidney Blumenthal described the disconnect between what happened onstage during prime time at the 2004 Republican National Convention at New York's Madison Square Garden and what occurred offstage:

In the afternoon, a radical conservative platform against stem cell research, abortion rights and gay rights was approved by the convention without a murmur of dissent. Once, the moderates of the Northeast repelled right-wing insurgencies, sending them back into their dark woods to nurse their resentments. In 1960, New York Gov. Nelson Rockefeller compelled presidential nominee Richard Nixon to accept his provisions for the platform, an agreement called the Treaty of Fifth Avenue, long recalled with bitterness by conservatives as evidence of pragmatic betrayal. Under Bush, the first Southern conservative American president (since Jefferson Davis), the moderates are a nonentity, and the appearance of [New York mayor Rudy] Giuliani and McCain was testament to the decline of this historical wing of the party. The moderate remnants that filled appointments in the Bush administration—former New Jersey Gov. Christine Todd Whitman as Environmental Protection Agency administrator and corporate executive Paul O'Neill as secretary of the treasury—have left in disillusionment, and Secretary of State Colin Powell has become the invisible man. While the true powers of the party, like House Majority Leader Tom "The Hammer" DeLay, are like hidden imams in New York, Giuliani and McCain assumed the stage.

The Republicans learned their lessons after the ugly, divisive public battles and vitriolic rhetoric on display at their 1992 Houston convention. Never again would they intentionally reveal the party's true face, especially those white southern males who scare the jeepers out of moderate, suburban voters (especially women). "Republicans have a race problem," Faye Anderson, a former vice chair of the Republican National Committee's minority outreach committee, confesses. "The white swing voters will not support a party that appears harsh, so they use black and brown faces to appeal to white voters." Notice, too, that the white faces the GOP does promote in prime time tend not to be affixed to red necks.

For years, DeLay was the Grand Wizard of Eyesore Republicanism. He had proved especially adept at keeping himself out of the public spotlight, a rare politician with a remarkable knack for wielding power without the benefit of a pulpit, a public persona, or a personal following. "After 20 years in Washington [DeLay] is commonly said to be the most powerful legislator on Capitol Hill, owing to a rare blend of bold aggressiveness and quiet maneuvering," observed *Vanity Fair*'s Sam Tanenhaus in 2004, before DeLay's indictment changed his national profile. "Apart from a brief burst of publicity during the ancient days of the Clinton scandals, DeLay has hugged the shadows tightly. While his colleagues and rivals can be almost comically self-aggrandizing, DeLay has become a study in the ever lowering profile. He dispenses interviews stingily, even to the home-state Texas press, and largely absents himself from the evening cable free-for-alls and Sunday-morning gabfests, where you might expect to find the second-ranking House Republican."

DeLay's public comments about judicial tyranny, coupled with news of his ethics battles stemming from involvement with a suspicious corporate lobbyist, forced him out of the shadows. He became the subject of television talk shows and a punch line for late-night comedians. Suddenly, more than three in every four Americans could identify him. "Nobody knew who Tom DeLay is. Now they do," a worried Mark Souder, Republican congressman from Indiana, told *Time* magazine, prior to DeLay's indictment and resignation. "The stage is different now . . . He's got to control his anger. It's got to be a friendlier face." Tom DeLay had to go because he evolved from being a regular eyesore Republican to that rare, but rapidly reproducing subspecies: the *black-eye* Republican.

What does a black-eye Republican look like? Think Mississippi Senator Trent Lott. The same man who convinced the Reagan presidential campaign to come to Neshoba County in 1980, Lott was one of a handful of southern Republicans elected during the early 1970s. By comfortable margins, he was reelected seven times. Then, in 1988, Mississippi Senator John C. Stennis, a legendary Dixiecrat, retired after forty-two years of service. Lott ran unopposed in the GOP primary and beat Wayne Dowdy in a tough general election fight to take Stennis' seat. Reelected easily in 1994, by 1996 Lott rose quickly to the Senate's highest perch: His fellow Republicans chose him to be their majority leader, the most powerful position held by an independently elected federal official other than the president. Reelected again in 2000, Lott lost his majority leadership after Jim Jeffords's party defection but remained the Senate's top Republican. That is, until he made a fatal error during the retirement party of another senate legend and former Dixiecrat, Strom Thurmond.

Lott committed what pundits call a Washington blunder: He accidentally revealed his true feelings. "I want to say this about my state: When Strom Thurmond ran for president, we voted for him," said Lott. "We're proud of it. And if the rest of the country had followed our lead, we wouldn't have had all these problems over all these years, either." In other words, Lott was saying, the South may have lost the battle over desegregation, but southerners were right and the country would have been better off had it not gone through the important, if painful process of enforcing civil rights laws to end lynching, segregated facilities, and the wholesale disenfranchisement of African Americans. It's one thing to be wrong at the critical moments of history and realize it later. It's another to still believe you were right all along.

Lott soon found himself at the center of a media firestorm. Democrats howled, and many prominent conservative columnists denounced him in print and on television. A few days and several apologies later—including a pride-swallowing interview with Ed Gordon on Black Entertainment Television's *BET Tonight,* in which a smiling, oleaginous Lott expressed his support for affirmative action—it was all over. The interesting twist is that *Republicans* whacked Lott like some Joe Pesci character at the end of a mob movie, and the hit was rumored to have been ordered by none other than Karl Rove, the president's consigliere. For removing the carefully constructed mask behind which the lingering racism of southern Republicanism hides—even if he did so unintentionally, in a heady moment at an informal and celebratory event—Lott got the garrote.

Republicans have made significant political advances on race matters. But most of the changes are cosmetic and superficial. They've learned how to talk (or not talk) publicly about race in ways that convey racial sensitivity despite policies that tend to denigrate and handicap those who benefit most from civil rights protections and wars against poverty. History works in their favor, too, as memories of the segregation-era party switching that converted Thurmond, Jesse

Helms, and other paleo-racist Democrats into neoracist Republicans fade from the nation's collective memory. "Removing the segregationist stigma from Southern politics ironically opened the door for advancing the influence of Southern politicians from both parties," says southern politics expert Augustus Cochran. "Partly because of the new influence of Southern politicians, but more as a consequence of how issues of class, race, and gender have interacted with partisan politics in the last political generation, the South has liberalized while the nation has moved sharply to the right." Put another way, in order to maximize their political power, southern Republicans must be simultaneously able to racialize politics and use race-coded messages, yet avoid being stigmatized publicly as a racist party. For example, you won't hear Republican National Committee chairman Ken Mehlman—who regularly implores African Americans to "gives us a chance and we'll give you a choice"—mention the recent study which showed that congressional districts with greater degrees of bias against African Africans "systematically produced" more Bush votes, because appearing to be racist makes it harder for Republicans willfully to ignore the economic disparties that exist in the South and elsewhere.

With racial road bumps removed from their path, the GOP majority can move forward more quickly and efficiently in its campaign to exacerbate further the prevailing economic and political inequities. "[T]he South has proven to be the native home of American poverty. It continues to sustain the highest poverty rate and the lowest average income of any section of the country," laments Gene Nichol, dean of the University of North Carolina at Chapel Hill Law School. "Yet, ironically, we frequently elect public officials who pander to the wealthy and cripple the social structures of the poor. Southern leaders often seem to specialize in undermining democracy while giving the back of their hands to meaningful equality. We produce more poverty and more politicians who are untroubled by it than the rest of the nation."

Maintaining a blasé attitude while undermining the economic welfare of your own constituencies is a tough act of political legerdemain to execute, but the trick is made even harder when politicians like Lott reveal the racial secrets of the southern Republicans' magic. That was

Lott's real offense—he said openly what Republicans today know they must imply but never quite state openly: We are the party of choice if you want to vote against America's racial minorities.

FAIT ACCOMPLI IN THE SOUTH

At the height of the civil rights movement the South was the nation's decisive electoral region. By fits and starts—including, most notably, Ronald Reagan's presidential victories, the Newt Gingrich–led 1994 Republican takeover of Congress, and Tennessee Democrat Al Gore's total southern collapse in 2000—the once-solidly Democratic South peeled away from the New Deal coalition forged by Franklin Roosevelt seven decades ago. It is an increasingly hostile territory for Democrats. "The national image of the Democratic Party does not sell well in the South," says Democratic Congressman Harold Ford Jr., of Tennessee, understating the matter. The southern strategy invented by Barry Goldwater, accelerated by Richard Nixon, and perfected by Ronald Reagan—all non-southerners—has reached full fruition, and the Republicans now dominate the South. National Republicans not only draw important votes and leaders from the region, but ideas and inspiration, resources and organizational support. Their control of the region has given them congressional majorities they otherwise could not attain and has provided the votes to put the first southern Republican in the White House.

At first, the Republicans merely aspired to capture the South. As the twenty-first century opens, the GOP's fortunes in the South have evolved from ascendancy to symbiosis: The Republicans have captured the South but so, too, has the South captured the Republican Party. With the benefit of four decades hindsight it is clear that the very term "southern strategy" is an understatement. In policy terms, the southern strategy has reached far beyond the initial, race-baiting politics of segregation, busing, and voting rights during the postwar period to the backlash of welfare reform and resistance to affirmative action. Linguistically, it is evident in the steady replacement of edgier terms like "nigger lover" and "hippie radical" with more subtle, coded language like "liberal elite" and "judicial activism." Institutionally, it has taken root in the creation and expansion of an emboldened conservative media and think tank culture, and the funding of right-wing reactionaries. Demographically and geographically, its initial appeal to rural southerners has expanded to the suburbs and exurbs, and to states outside the South. By morphing into new forms and expanding its reach during the past four decades—adding new adherents, new issues, new messages, and new messengers along the way—the southern strategy has become both a fait accompli and a misnomer, for it has engulfed much more than the South and has taken on a meaning and proportions that far exceed a mere strategy.

Because Republicans run the country and the South runs the Republican Party, the southern Republicans are now running the country. As frustrating as that reality may be for Democrats, accepting it as truth is a crucial admission and precondition for Democrats to start pushing back with a non-southern majority of their own.

3

Blacklash and the
Heavenly Chorus

Some Republicans gave up on winning the African-American vote, looking the other way or trying to benefit politically from racial polarization. I am here today as the Republican chairman to tell you we were wrong.

> —Ken Mehlman, Republican National Committee chairman, apologizing at the 2005 NAACP national convention for the GOP's race-based "southern strategy"

This Republican party of Lincoln has become a party of theocracy.

> —Congressman Christopher Shays (R, Connecticut), in the aftermath of the Terri Schiavo controversy, lamenting the state of his political party

IT'S ELECTION DAY 2005 in Virginia, and voters are being treated to gorgeous weather—clear, blue skies and a warm blanket of sun ruffled intermittently by cool, autumn breezes. Outside the East District Center in a mostly African-American section of Richmond, former governor and current Richmond mayor Douglas Wilder is doing a lunch-hour voter meet-and-greet at Precinct 707 in support of his friend and former Richmond mayor Tim Kaine, the Democratic nominee for governor.

At 74, Wilder looks extraordinarily young and fit for his age. His slicked-back white hair and cherry-red tie gleam brightly in the noonday sun. Chatting with his constituents, Wilder's jowly face periodically breaks into a wide smile. He is man clearly comfortable in his skin and with his skin color—and so were enough Virginia voters in 1989 when they elected him the first and, to date, only black governor in American history. A small but growing cadre of black candidates have won other statewide offices since, and a few have tried to duplicate Wilder's feat. But none have succeeded. The grandson of slaves, a product of racially segregated Richmond public schools, and a military veteran, Wilder is *sui generis*—a politician literally in a category all his own.

After he completes a few obligatory stand-ups with local television reporters, I pull Wilder aside to ask him what has transpired—or, rather, *not* transpired—since his pathbreaking, 1989 victory. Is he surprised that, sixteen years later, there has yet to be another African-American elected governor? "I am surprised because I thought it *should* have happened, and disappointed because I haven't *seen* it happen," he laments. I press him to reveal what is the secret, if any, to propelling black candidates to victory in statewide elections, especially in the South where African Americans form such a large portion of the electorate. Though Wilder says he recently spoke about that very subject with Columbus's black mayor Michael Coleman (who, at that point, was a candidate for the Ohio Democratic gubernatorial nomination), it is apparent that Wilder long ago pondered this question at great length. "Don't run to make history as an African American candidate, run to be the best qualified candidate for that job," he said, without hesitation. "I think some of the mistakes have been people saying they're 'running to make history.' You can do it by going to the people as a qualified candidate, by not talking about race and history, but by talking about what people care about most."

Though nobody can challenge his authority on the subject, Wilder's prescription is harder to fill than his simple, eloquent logic suggests.

As I discuss later in the second half of the book, talking about the is-sues people care most about may be necessary, but it's hardly sufficient for Democratic candidates, black or white, to win statewide or nation-wide. And in the South, removing race from the equation to focus on the issues is unusually tricky because race—along with religion—are the fundaments of southern politics.

Southern politics is not solely bound up with race and religion, but almost every issue or controversy has some racial or religious element beneath the surface. The dual power of race and religion in southern politics will make it extraordinarily difficult for Democrats to recapture the South.

RACE TO THE BOTTOM

The significance of race in southern politics can be neither overstated nor fully understood. Racial themes and subthemes have been woven into every major episode of southern political history in the past four centuries. Though labor and economics were key factors in the two great constitutional crises of American history, the Civil War and the civil rights movement, at bottom these social upheavals were race-oriented conflicts. From the child labor disputes to Prohibition, from women's suffrage to welfare reform, race was an underlying current in many southern skirmishes that, on the surface, might otherwise seem race-neutral.

The favorite attack method for southern conservatives was to vilify social or political reformers by infusing race into any issue, pooling their opponents in with the "niggers," and casting aspersions on them jointly. A top Reagan White House official explained how race baiting progressed during the second half of the twentieth century:

You start out in 1954 by saying, "Nigger, nigger, nigger." By 1968 you can't say "nigger"—that hurts you. Backfires. So you say stuff like forced busing, states' rights, and all that stuff. You're getting so abstract now [that] you're talking about cutting taxes, and all these things you're talking about are totally economic things and a by-product of them is [that] blacks get hurt worse than whites. And subconsciously maybe that is part of it. I'm not saying that. But I'm saying if it is getting that abstract, that coded, that we are doing away with the racial problem one way or the other. You follow me—because obviously sitting around saying "We want to cut this," is much more abstract than even the busing thing and a hell of a lot more abstract than "Nigger, nigger."

The only other target so demonized was the communists, but they were always in far shorter supply and a bit too remote to be maximally effective. Of course, long before the Red Scare reached its McCarthy–era zenith, southern conservatives were already lumping the "commies" in with the "niggers," too.

Today, the racializing of southern politics is less overt and more sophisticated. It's subtextual and sublime, ubiquitous if often silent. The power of race has been most evident in presidential politics, but is also infused into congressional and state elections. Though not always conspicuous—like it has been in several recent Confederate flag controversies—race is ever-present in southern politics.

Strangers in a Familiar Land

As mentioned in the opening chapter, the great irony of partisan geography in the United States is that the South—the nation's most politically conservative and Republican region—is home to almost half of all African Americans, the most loyal block of Democratic voters. The nearly 18 million African Americans living in the South make up about one-fifth of the region's population. From a low of 12 percent in Texas to Mississippi's high of 37 percent, the share of African Americans in every southern state is in double digits. Outside the South, however, only about 1 in 10 citizens is an African American, and in all but ten of the thirty-nine non-southern states their population share is in single digits. The majority of local, state, and national black elected officials are southerners and, with a handful of exceptions, Democrats. The South is home to about half of the nation's nearly six hundred black state legislators, several of whom have risen to the highest positions within their state legislative hierarchies. The South has sent more black members to Congress than any other region, including all twenty of the black Republican congressmen during Reconstruction and a roughly proportional share (nineteen) of the forty-one Congressional Black Caucus members serving in the House of Representatives today.

Yet only a third of black members of Congress elected since Reconstruction are southerners, despite the fact that the South contained an even greater share of African Americans at the beginning of the twentieth century than the half it does today. Virginia's Wilder remains the only black candidate elected to a southern governorship or Senate seat. And in the forty years since Lyndon Johnson's 1964 landslide, the only African American–preferred presidential candidate to capture a majority of the South's electoral votes was Jimmy Carter, in 1976. All of which raises an obvious question: Why doesn't the power of African American votes translate into more victories for black candidates or, at the very least, white Democratic candidates preferred by African Americans?

It's not because African Americans are undermobilized in the South. As the first two columns of Table 3.1 indicate, because they are younger as a group, African Americans constitute a smaller share of the South's age-eligible citizenry than they do its total population. But the real surprise is the table's final two columns, which dispel any notion that African Americans in the South fail to register and vote at sufficient rates to flex their electoral muscles. In six southern states (Alabama, Georgia, Mississippi, North Carolina, Tennessee, and Texas), and in the region as a whole, African Americans account for a *higher* share of registrants than they do age-eligible voters. And in four of those six states (Tennessee and Texas excepted), strong turnout among African Americans made them an ever greater share of 2004 Election Day *voters*. Look at Mississippi in 2004, a non-swing state with no competitive statewide contest on the ballot: Political participation was so high among African Americans that they comprised a larger share of voters (36.9 percent) than their total population—even when under-18, voting-ineligible African Americans are included (36.8 percent).

In a speech to progressives at a Boston hotel during the 2004 Democratic National Convention, former presidential aspirant Jesse Jackson rattled off state-by-state totals of the thousands of African Americans in the South who in 2000 were unregistered or didn't vote—proof, in

Table 3.1

**2004 African-American Percentage of Southern Population,
Eligible Voters, Registrants, and Voters**

State	Population	Age 18+	Registered	Voted
Alabama	26.4	24.0	24.1	24.8
Arkansas	15.8	14.7	14.2	12.7
Florida	15.7	13.9	11.7	11.1
Georgia	29.6	26.6	27.4	27.6
Louisiana	33.0	29.8	28.7	29.3
Mississippi	36.8	33.5	35.2	36.9
North Carolina	21.8	19.9	20.4	21.5
South Carolina	29.4	27.3	26.6	26.2
Tennessee	16.8	14.8	15.2	14.4
Texas	11.7	10.6	11.8	11.7
Virginia	19.9	17.9	16.0	15.2
South	**19.8**	**17.9**	**18.0**	**17.9**
Non-South	**9.7**	**8.8**	**8.4**	**8.4**

Source: Computed by author from U.S. Census Bureau 2004 estimates.

Jackson's view, that the Republican domination of the region is an eminently if not imminently solvable problem. Jackson's solution might work if African-American registration and voting rates far, far exceeded those of southern whites. Overall, however, the problem is not underperformance by African Americans: Their share of actual voters and the age-eligible electorate is an identical 17.9 percent. Ironically, it is *outside* the South where the African-American share of registrants and voters (8.4 percent each) lags behind the African-American share of eligible voters (8.8 percent).

If comparatively low registration and turnout rates for African Americans cannot explain the lack of black governors and U.S. senators in the South, what does? One factor is the short list of black candidates nominated to run in the first place. On this score, Democratic leaders have some explaining to do. After all, the vast majority of African

Americans *are* Democrats. Southern black politicians do not shy away from complaining to party leaders about what they perceive as a neglectful taking for granted of the African-American base vote, and their complaints have a certain, undeniable legitimacy. In defense of frustrated national (white) Democrats, black Democratic candidates running statewide in the South face serious difficulties. All of the noble and earnest efforts to register and mobilize African Americans in the South during the four decades since the Voting Rights Act cannot overcome the reality that too many white southerners simply refuse to vote for black candidates. Indeed, because African Americans are correctly associated with the Democratic Party by southern whites who harbor racial antipathies, it is difficult for white Democrats to win statewide in the South because they are conveniently tagged as too liberal on social issues like affirmative action and economic issues like welfare spending.

The unfortunate reality is that African Americans are electoral strangers in a familiar land. When 90 percent of African Americans cast their votes for Democratic candidates, they often do so in vain. Consider the best-case scenario of Mississippi: If African Americans, who are 37 percent of voters, cast 90 percent of their votes for the Democratic nominee, that means Mississippi Democrats begin any statewide campaign with about 33 percent of the vote—or two-thirds of the way to a majority. Yet the Republicans control the state's governorship, both U.S. Senate seats, and have carried Mississippi in the last seven presidential elections. In effect, Mississippi Democrats start the dash to midfield victory at the 33-yard line but, because of the overwhelmingly Republican white vote, still finish second.

Race for the White House

As a way to win millions of white votes, especially those of white southerners, presidential candidates of both parties have used racial imagery and themes to signal opposition and even hostility toward African Americans. What's fascinating is not the fact of racialized presidential campaigns, but the manner in which visual and verbal tropes have evolved during the past four decades.

Historians tend to paint the Kennedy brothers with gentle brushes, but the crowns of Camelot are not untarnished. In 1960, when the partisan fidelities of African Americans still remained mixed—the Republicans *were* the party of Lincoln, after all—the Kennedy campaign tried to play both sides of the race card, cozying up to emergent civil rights leaders while distributing photos in Virginia's white communities showing Richard Nixon smiling with black leaders and noting that he'd been an "NAACP member for over 10 years!" In office, John Kennedy mostly took the black vote for granted. "John and Robert Kennedy remained civil rights minimalists for the whole thousand days, holding as best they could to the basic rules learned in the Massachusetts politics of the 1940s and 1950s: Cultivate the handful of people who could deliver the black vote, make an occasional symbolic gesture, never risk any political capital on behalf of anyone's civil rights," says author Kenneth O'Reilly, in *Nixon's Piano,* his book about race and the presidency. "To the extent that the Kennedys pushed the envelope on minority hiring, voting rights, federal housing, and combating segregationist violence, they did so because the civil rights movement forced their hand."

Neither a son of the Confederacy nor someone who countenanced racism, Barry Goldwater proved an unusual icon for southern racists during the 1960s. Goldwater's first, 1960 foray into presidential politics, followed by his 1964 Republican nomination, were watershed moments for many white southerners. The maverick Arizona senator became an unwitting vessel into which southern whites, angered by the increasing race liberalism of the national Democratic Party, poured their venom. As the national Republican leadership relaxed in 1963 and early 1964, blithely confident that either New York governor Nelson Rockefeller or Massachusetts senator Henry Cabot Lodge Jr. would quash the Goldwater insurgency, Goldwater operatives were negotiating in back rooms to line up Republican delegates. Goldwater got trounced in the 1964 New Hampshire primary, but no matter: Southern delegates from Georgia, North Carolina, and South Carolina were already pledging themselves for "AuH$_2$O."

Goldwater's full-throated defense of states' rights meant something different passing from his lips than it did upon arrival in southern ears. For the Dixiecrats who had rallied to Strom Thurmond's candidacy sixteen years earlier, however, it was close enough. Outside the 1964 Republican National Convention at San Francisco's Cow Palace, a man with a flattop haircut in a conservative business suit held up a home-made sign that read, "Be with Barry when they burn the crosses." The cross burners were there with him on Election Day, that's for sure: Besides Arizona, Goldwater's only victories over "Landslide Lyndon" came in the five states of the Deep South. Clif White, Goldwater's back-room wheeler-dealer, conceived the "southern strategy" one election cycle ahead of its time.

The Goldwater storm also swept away the economic dispositions of white southerners, who until the 1960s trailed only Jews and African Americans in their degree of economic liberalism. "Goldwater's success demonstrated that conservative ideology provided a new avenue for the Republican party in the South, an avenue that permitted the GOP to carry the most anti-black electorate in the nation without facing public condemnation," conclude Thomas Edsall and Mary Edsall in *Chain Reaction*. "For a substantial segment of the white South, conservatism became a cloak with which to protect racial segregation." As an economist might put it, the demand for racial control was so inelastic that southern whites were willing to pay almost any price for it, including the abandonment not only of their century-long Democratic attachments, but their own economic ideals and interests.

Nixon tried to honor his party's commitment and connections to black Americans in 1960, but he was a fast learner who understood the long-term significance of the 1964 campaign. Thurmond protégé Harry Dent picked up where White left off, fashioning a "southern strategy" for Nixon sufficient to triangulate between the liberal, northern challenge of Hubert Humphrey and segregationist George Wallace's third-party candidacy. Spiro Agnew—who attracted Nixon's attentions in the spring of 1968 by falsely accusing Baltimore's black leaders for inciting riots after Martin Luther King Jr.'s assassination—became "Nixon's Nixon" and was dispatched to "out-Wallace Wallace" on race issues. Humphrey's dismissive criticisms of Wallace as a racist drove southern white Democrats away, and Agnew shepherded them into Republican pastures. As Jeremy D. Mayer writes in *Running on Race*, Nixon's racial strategy had changed dramatically in just eight short years:

For example, in 1960, if Nixon had been able to win just 40 percent of the black vote, instead of 32 percent, he would have beaten Kennedy decisively. Eight years later, Nixon was able to write off all but the smallest fraction of black support (he received at best 12 percent) and win the White House. That a candidate could, in a three-way race, surrender the black vote and win, validated the Republican strategy of "the hell with them."

The southern strategy had claimed its first presidential victory for the GOP.

Nixon easily won reelection, and after Jimmy Carter's rude, post-Watergate interruption of the emerging Republican hegemony, Ronald Reagan restored the southern jewels to their proper owners. The Gipper's use of racial language was more sophisticated than Nixon's. The future embellisher-in-chief had a knack for latching on to an apocryphal story and repeating it incessantly as an all-purpose parable to explain his views on one issue or another. In the sordid tale of Linda Taylor—a woman who created a series of fictitious identities to defraud the welfare system—Reagan found his perfect racial foil. No matter that Taylor's case was an extraordinary one of illegal abuse: Reagan used her to inject the term "welfare queen" into the nation's electoral bloodstream as if her behavior were commonplace. Reagan didn't say welfare queens were black and he didn't need to. The appeal of speaking in code is that listeners know how to translate without much help.

Carter and his surrogates desperately attempted to remind the public and the press about Reagan's racial transgressions. They quoted statements Reagan made on busing, affirmative action, the 1954 *Brown v. Board of Education* decision, and his reaction to the riots that followed Martin Luther King's assassination. They pointed out that Reagan once signed a race-restrictive covenant on his California home, and that his 1980 candidacy had been endorsed by the Ku Klux Klan. The campaign's constant complaining about Reagan's efforts to racialize the election not only failed, but probably backfired. "By quoting Reagan at every opportunity," O'Reilly concludes, "the Carter campaign helped the rival campaign spread its southern strategy message." To southerners, as well as to national Democrats and President Carter himself,

Reagan's Neshoba County speech declared that a Republican ticket pairing a former Hollywood movie star with a blue-blooded Connecticut senator's son was not about to let even a native southern Baptist incumbent president stand between the GOP and the South's gold mine of electoral votes. That November, Reagan swept every southern state except Jimmy Carter's own Georgia to become America's fortieth president.

In 1988, Reagan's far less beloved heir apparent, George H. W. Bush, was staring at a 17-point deficit in the polls when Lee Atwater, a Thurmond-Dent apostle baptized in South Carolina's grand tradition of slaughterhouse politics, took a piece of opposition research unearthed by Andrew Card (the candidate's son's future chief of staff) and turned it into electoral dynamite. During the Democratic primaries, southern favorite son Al Gore had attacked the eventual nominee, Massachusetts governor Michael Dukakis, by criticizing the state's weekend-pass prison furlough program. After learning that five furloughed prisoners had committed heinous crimes, Atwater immediately knew which of the five to pick from the lineup: William Horton, the only African American. Though Horton never went by the name "Willie," Atwater applied the desultory moniker for added effect, and through a surrogate group ran television ads telling voters that Bush supports the death penalty and Dukakis opposes it. After showing a darkened picture of a bearded Horton and describing his stabbing of a young man and rape of the man's girlfriend, the ad closes with the tag line, "Weekend prison passes—Dukakis on crime."

In 1992, Bill Clinton finally broke the Republican string of victories by defeating Bush, but to do so he had to shake off the Democrats' "Jesse Jackson problem." Jackson had run two strong campaigns in 1984 and 1988, earning the Rainbow Coalition leader prime speaking slots at the Democratic National Convention. Clinton counter-scheduled as a way to keep his distance from Jackson in 1992, but the key moment that year was Clinton's criticism of female rapper Sister Souljah at a Jackson-headed Rainbow Coalition event on June 13. The rebuke stunned Jackson, and for good measure later that day Clinton informed both Jackson and the press that the reverend would not be a candidate for Clinton's vice president. "What Clinton got out of the Sister Souljah affair were votes, particularly the votes of the so-called Reagan Democrats like the North Philadelphia electrician who said 'the day he told off that fucking Jackson was the day he got [mine],' " writes O'Reilly.

Jackson ran for president twice. Shirley Chisholm, Barbara Jordan, Al Sharpton, and Carol Moseley Braun have also made their bids for the Democratic presidential nomination. Many believe the day is near when a black candidate, perhaps Condoleezza Rice or Barack Obama, will finally win the Oval Office. But the African Americans who figured most prominently in presidential politics in recent elections were not candidates, but racial avatars whom history might otherwise have overlooked: Linda Taylor, Willie Horton, and Sister Souljah. None was ever directly on the ballot, but each was present indirectly.

Unholy Alliances

The vast majority of black legislators in America represent majority-minority districts, about half of which are in the South. Racial gerrymandering has benefited the Republican Party tremendously, which is why Republican leaders happily colluded with black politicians in the early 1990s to forge an "unholy alliance" intent on packing as many African-American voters into as few districts as possible.

The impact of this unholy alliance was evident in 1992, a year in which African Americans were elected in record numbers to state legislatures and the U.S. House of Representatives. One-seventh of black members ever elected to Congress were part of the 1992 freshmen class; almost as if on cue, the next freshman class gave the Republicans their first House majority since the 1952 elections. Likewise, as recently as the 2001, about one in seven incumbent black state legislators first won their seats during that same, historic 1992 election cycle; in the decade since, the GOP has gained hundreds of southern legislative seats, plus control of legislative chambers in states like Florida, Georgia, North Carolina, and Virginia, which Democrats had dominated seemingly forever. By 2002, and for the first time since the New Deal, the GOP controlled a majority of state legislative seats and chamber majorities, and majorities in both chambers of Congress. Racial gerrymandering does not entirely account for rising Republican fortunes in the South and nationally, but it surely aided their cause.

For southern Republicans, redistricting strategy hinges upon the same, powerful premise on which most every other element of the southern strategy turns: Whenever and however possible, make Democrats pay for their support of racial minorities. Benjamin Ginsberg, who had to resign as counsel to George W. Bush's 2004 campaign because of his involvement with the Swift Boat Veterans group, was a key strategist for the Republicans during the 1990 round of redistricting. Ginsberg has referred rather unapologetically to the effort by Republicans to expand their share of southern congressional seats by ruthlessly packing minorities into a few districts as "Project Ratfuck."

Racial gerrymandering has thus reduced southern Democratic legislators to two, essential types.

The first are conservative whites who skillfully distance themselves from the national Democratic brand name by staking out socially conservative positions, capitalizing on local goodwill, or both. In a case study of congressional special elections in the South during the 1980s and 1990s, Tufts University's James Glaser discovered that Democrats can win in majority-white districts in the South by tapping into anti-Washington resentment—but with a revealing twist. "The outsider image that southern Democrats had was doubly effective as they disassociated themselves from *both* national parties," Glaser concluded. "They played an us versus them game, and 'them' included both the Republicans and the national Democrats." Think about that for a second: Southern white Democrats therefore must run not only against Congress but against their *own party's delegation* in Congress.

The second group of Democrats, of course, is the new generation of black and Hispanic legislators elected from race-gerrymandered districts. As *The New Yorker*'s Jeffrey Toobin points out, beyond increasing their share of seats, for Republicans the added benefit here is that the steady replacement of white Democrats with black and Hispanic Democrats reinforces in white voters' minds the Democrats' identity as the party of minorities.

There is a long tradition of candidates "running for Congress by running against Congress." Because of racial gerrymandering, the southern delegations are now comprised of white Democrats who survive by denigrating the national party and black Democrats who often complain that they are marginalized by the national party. Why should Republicans bother to vilify Democrats when Democrats will do this dirty chore for them?

The Resiliency of Race

Despite their increased numbers in the U.S. House of Representatives, southern black candidates continue to hit an electoral glass ceiling at the U.S. Senate. There has never been an elected black senator or, aside from Wilder, governor. The track record for electing black candidates to statewide office is not much better in the non-southern states, of course. Still, given the number of African Americans living in the southern states, racial geography ought to make the South the *most* electable region for black candidates. So why isn't it? The short answer is that, despite the best efforts of Republican spinmeisters to depict American conservatism as a nonracial phenomenon, the partisan impact of racial attitudes in the South is *stronger* today than in the past.

Conservative ideology is a strong predictor of Republican voting, but no more so in the South than other parts of the country. Attitudes on abortion and national defense no longer predict Republican voting of southern whites, either. What does? Racial attitudes do. "[R]acial issue opinions have become more strongly linked to vote choice in the South than the North and West in the 1990s, which was not true in the 1980s," conclude Nicholas Valentino and David Sears, who studied National Election Survey results between 1990 and 2000. Valentino and Sears confirm that overt racism, which is less useful and more prone to backfiring politically, has been replaced by "neoracist" attitudes. This new racism is most prevalent among southerners and can be measured in at least four ways:

- *Symbolic racism:* agreement/disagreement as to whether progress among African Americans was impeded by slavery and political discrimination;

- *Negative black stereotyping:* belief that African Americans are lazy, less intelligent, less hard-working;

• *White-black feeling thermometers:* scaled responses that measure racial affect toward blacks and whites; and, finally

• *Jim Crow racism:* support for keeping African Americans out of white neighborhoods, or opposition to racial intermarriage and miscegenation.

As Figure 3.1 shows, on all four measures white southerners harbor more racist attitudes than other white Americans, with profound differences between the five Deep South states (Alabama, Georgia, Louisiana, Mississippi, and South Carolina) and the six Outer South states (Arkansas, Florida, North Carolina, Tennessee, Texas, and Virginia).

In a similar study, political scientist Jonathan Knuckey found that racial attitudes correlate with Republican voting in the South, but discovered something else: In the past decade, racial resentments have come to explain not only the partisan *behavior* of white southerners, but their partisan *identities*. And that means Republicans don't need to play the race card in the South anymore because racially resentful white southerners don't just vote Republican—they *are* Republicans:

Figure 3.1
Regional Difference in Racial Attitudes

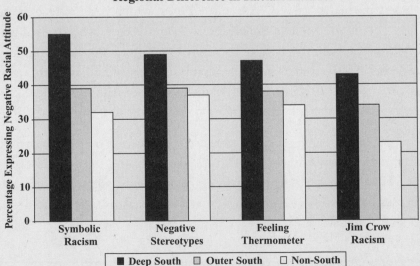

Prior to the 1990s, and since Nixon's "southern strategy," southern Republicans used race and racial issues as "wedge issues" to appeal to Democrats and independents in order to win elections. As the most racially resentful southern whites are also now Republican identifiers, this strategy is no longer necessary. Instead, a Republican candidate need now only make an appeal on the basis of partisanship.

This is why Republican National Committee chairman Ken Mehlman, in the quote at the start of this chapter, had the luxury of apologizing in 2005 for his party's relentless use of race to win southern (and many non-southern) votes during the previous four decades. Because they own the white South, the Republicans need not pay the region's racial rents any longer.

In the South, the electoral effects of race are most evident in comparisons of voting patterns in Deep South and Outer South states. In a *Claremont Review of Books* essay praised widely by conservatives, political scientist Gerard Alexander argued that it is a "myth" that Republicans used race to convert the South. In supporting his claim, Alexander notes that the six Outer South states began to elect Republicans to the U.S. Senate and vote for Republican presidential candidates before the five Deep South states did. Because the indisputably more racist states of the Deep South turned Republican later, goes the logic, the GOP's southern ascendancy must be attributed to factors such as the "new South's" economic and demographic changes, which are most prevalent in the affluent suburbs of the Outer South.

To be sure, suburbanization and economic development are partly responsible for the Republicanization of the South. The problem with the Outer-first, Deep-second argument, however, is that it ignores the difference between state-level threshold effects and the overall magnitude of a state's partisan conversion. That is, smaller partisan changes flipped the Outer South states first *because they were more party-competitive in the first place*—not to mention they had the ironic advantage of smaller African-American population shares. The blacker, more solidly one-party Democratic states of the Deep South underwent

Table 3.2

Increase in Republican Presidential Support, Outer South versus Deep South Between 1960 and 1988

	Presidential Year		Increase	
	1960	1988	Absolute %	Relative %
Outer South				
Arkansas	43.1	56.4	13.3	30.9
Florida	51.5	60.9	9.4	18.2
North Carolina	47.9	58.0	10.1	21.0
Tennessee	52.9	57.9	5.0	9.4
Texas	48.5	56.0	7.4	15.3
Virginia	52.4	59.7	7.3	13.9
Deep South				
Alabama	42.2	59.2	17.0	40.3
Georgia	37.4	59.2	21.7	58.1
Louisiana	28.6	54.3	25.7	89.8
Mississippi	24.7	59.9	35.2	142.8
South Carolina	48.8	61.5	12.7	26.1

Compiled by author from data courtesy of Dave Leip's Atlas of U.S. Presidential Elections.

much larger partisan shifts, a fact that is immediately obvious when comparing the 1960 and 1988 presidential results.

The Democratic capture of the African-American vote did not fully begin until 1964, so the Kennedy-Nixon matchup in 1960 provides a good benchmark for two-party southern voting prior to the civil rights revolution. Because each of the following six presidential elections included either a southerner on the Democratic ticket, a significant third-party candidate, a reelection landslide, or some combination of the three, the best post–civil rights era benchmark is the 1988 Bush-Dukakis contest. In other words, comparing 1960 with 1988 not only captures the partisan effects of race in the South during the critical quarter century between, but juxtaposes two open-seat elections wherein non-southern candidates competed without any interference from significant third-party candidates.

What do we find? As indicated in Table 3.2, the biggest absolute increase in Republican voting for any of the Outer states (Arkansas, 13.3 percent) is about the same as the smallest absolute change in any of the Deep South states (South Carolina, 12.7 percent). The magnitude of the relative changes between 1960 and 1988 are even more damning to the "race myth" theory. The shifts in Louisiana and Mississippi astound, but even when these two states are held aside the Republican gains were demonstrably higher in the Deep South. So the Outer South swung majority-Republican *first*, but the Deep South swung much, much *further*. And this trend persists: Other than the exceptional case of George W. Bush's Texas, the Deep South states have continued to vote more Republican since 1988. If the agreed-upon assumption is that the Deep South states are the most racialized, then the "myth of Republican racism" in the South is itself mythical.

Flag Burning

Mississippi's 2003 election epitomized the persistence of racial voting in the South. In the governor's race, Mississippi Republicans nominated Haley Barbour, a former Washington lawyer-lobbyist and national party chairman, to challenge Ronnie Musgrove, the Democratic incumbent. Musgrove served eight years in the state senate and four years as lieutenant governor before being elected governor in 1999. In 2001, Musgrove alienated many white Mississippians by establishing a commission to replace the state flag, which was (and still is) modeled on the Stars and Bars of the Confederate flag. Forebodingly, in April of the election year 65 percent of voters rejected a referendum to replace the old flag. Seven months later Barbour, a party operative with no governing experience, beat Musgrove, 53 percent to 46 percent. Though both nominees were white, 77 percent of white voters backed Barbour.

In that same election, two black Democrats faced white Republicans in statewide contests. The Democratic candidate for lieutenant governor, Barbara Blackmon, received just 37 percent of the vote against Mississippi's incumbent lieutenant governor Amy Tuck. Some believe that Blackmon made the already-tough task of unseating an incumbent tougher by asking Tuck to sign a pledge affirming that Tuck had never had an abortion. If Tuck's victory can be chalked up to incumbency advantages and Blackmon's blunder, Democrat Gary Anderson's fate in the open-seat contest for state treasurer cannot. As the state's former fiscal officer, Anderson, 47, was credited with helping the state work its way out of a $10-billion deficit—no small sum for one of the nation's poorest states. His opponent, Tate Reeves, was a white 35-year-old bank manager with no governmental experience. Yet the neophyte Tate bested Anderson, 52 percent to 47 percent.

Barbour is not the only Republican gubernatorial candidate in recent years to raise the Confederate flag. Georgia's 2002 governor's race might have turned on any number of local or national issues. It was the first election following the September 11 attacks, and the state was facing stagnant job growth. But Republican nominee Sonny Perdue led his campaign charge by pointing the staff of the Confederate flag directly at incumbent Democratic governor Roy Barnes's political gut.

Barnes was vulnerable to Perdue's attacks. Like Musgrove, Barnes formed a commission to consider changing Georgia's state flag which, since 1956, featured the Stars and Bars of the Confederate flag on the right two thirds, with the state emblem on the left third. The commission produced a new flag, featuring a larger state emblem in the center with a small string of five flags—the three previous Georgia state flags flanked by two American flags—boxed inside a rectangle beneath the emblem. The Confederate symbol had been shrunk to the level of near-imperceptibility, a slight that was not going to be unanswered. Soon angry Georgians were appearing at campaign events with banners and T-shirts that read, "Change the governor, keep the flag." The voters changed their governor. Georgia Republicans, who did not win a single gubernatorial election during the twentieth century, won the first election of the twenty-first. The controversy did not end there, however. After taking office, Perdue backtracked on his pledge of allegiance to the old Georgia flag and now finds himself in the same political stew as Barnes and Musgrove. Furious with "Pinocchio Perdue," members of the Georgia Heritage Council are leading the "punt Perdue" movement.

Almost 150 years after the Civil War ended, the Confederate flag retains great symbolic power. It is a racial symbol to many, of course, but more generally represents the southern tradition of resistance and defiance. "The Confederate flag's meaning in the late 1960s was logically and historically consistent with its meaning in the 1860s—as a symbol of opposition to the employment of the federal government to change the South's racial status quo," John M. Coski, library director for the Museum of the Confederacy in Richmond and leading authority on the flag, says. "There could be no more fitting symbol for this opposition than the Confederate battle flag." The flag burnings of Musgrove and Barnes are cautionary tales for politicians of both parties about the resiliency of Confederate memories.

Crawl, Jesse, Crawl

Like no other national political figure of his generation, North Carolina senator Jesse Helms embodied the tradition of steadfast southern resistance to racial equality. Helms used racist appeals to get elected and reelected, made racially inflammatory remarks in the Senate, and abused his senatorial courtesies to prevent the appointment of black judges to the federal circuit that included his home state. Helms never won by wide margins, but "the last prominent unabashed white racist politician in this country," as columnist David Broder called him, became the longest-serving senator in North Carolina history.

The legendary days of a united cabal of southern segregationist senators had faded by the time Helms arrived in the Senate in January 1973. Helms did, however, get a taste of racially divisive politics during his younger days. In segregationist Willis Smith's 1950 senate campaign, Helms personally cut-and-pasted together photos for a campaign flyer showing the wife of Smith's opponent dancing with a black man. Later, as a television commentator for WRAL in Raleigh, Helms criticized the lunch counter sit-ins by African Americans, derided Martin Luther King Jr. and his associates as communists, and proudly reprinted his commentaries in *Citizen,* a publication of the White Citizens' Council. The most infamous moment of Helms's career was the "Hands" television ad scripted by consultant Alex Castellanos in the final days of the senator's 1990 reelection campaign.

Trailing by 10 points to former Charlotte mayor Harvey Gantt—who in 1963 became the first African American to integrate Clemson

University—the campaign ran an ad showing a married white man in a black-and-red flannel shirt seated at a table. With foreboding music playing in the background, the man crumples a job rejection letter in slow motion as the narrator intones.

> You needed that job, and you were the best qualified. But they had to give it to a minority because of a racial quota. Is that really fair?
>
> Harvey Gantt says it is. Gantt supports Ted Kennedy's racial quota law that makes the color of your skin more important than your qualifications.
>
> You'll vote on this issue next Tuesday: For racial quotas, Harvey Gantt; against racial quotas, Jesse Helms.

Capitalizing on racial fears, the "Hands" ad helped Helms beat Gantt in yet another narrow victory. "[Helms] has a view of a fundamentalist Christian society in which everyone is not welcome," Christopher Scott, North Carolina AFL-CIO president and longtime Helms critic, says. "If you could pick up the [apartheid] South Africa of twenty years ago and transplant it to America, that's what he would do."

Four years later, and after voting to confirm Clarence Thomas to the Supreme Court, Helms played his part in the high-tech lynching of America's first "black president" (to borrow Toni Morrison's label), Bill Clinton, whom Helms had already warned "better watch out if he comes [to North Carolina]—he'd better have a bodyguard." Helms prevailed upon Chief Justice William Rehnquist to give David Sentelle, a Helms protégé, supervision of the Whitewater independent counsel investigation. Sentelle promptly replaced Robert Fiske, a Republican with prosecutorial experience and no partisan axe to grind against the Clinton White House, with Ken Starr, a Republican partisan with no prosecutorial background but ample partisan connections to people like "Arkansas Project" director Ted Olson. Though the independent counsel was assigned to investigate illegality in the Whitewater land deal, thanks to Helms's big assist, four years and $40 million later Starr produced a salacious, 3,183-page report about Clinton assignations that mentioned the word "Whitewater" just four times.

Helms also systematically frustrated Clinton's dogged efforts to put the first black judge on the U.S. Court of Appeals' Fourth Circuit. Considered the most judicially conservative circuit in the country, the Fourth has the highest share of African Americans, about 22 percent. Despite vacancies and a 1990 request from the Circuit's judges to fill them, Helms wouldn't budge. "Senator No," as Helms came to be known, said he might relent if the president also appointed a nominee his Republican predecessor, George H. W. Bush, was unable to get confirmed. Initially, Clinton refused. But after repeated stonewalling by Helms, Clinton finally agreed—only to have Helms renege on the deal. None of Clinton's four black nominees were ever granted a hearing before the Senate Judiciary Committee, no less a floor vote. With less than a month to go in his presidency, a beleaguered Clinton recess-appointed Roger Gregory. Because recess appointments are not permanent, it fell to Clinton's successor, George W. Bush, to make Gregory's appointment permanent which, to his credit, President Bush did. Thirty-five years after passage of the Voting Rights Act of 1965, the federal appeals circuit that is home to more African Americans than any other finally had a black judge.

Helms's congressional career was a testament to willpower exercised in the pursuit of bringing government to a crawl when it served his regenerate ideas and racist philosophies. As either chairman or ranking member on the Senate Foreign Affairs committee, Helms used his "truncheon" style of politics to batter fellow senators as well as presidents until he got his way in foreign policy. He attempted to block passage of the Chemical Weapons Convention, and was the chamber's strongest defender of South African apartheid. The man who once sang "Dixie" within earshot of his sole black colleague, Carol Moseley Braun, in the hopes of "making her cry," abused the senatorial courtesy in the judicial confirmation process, and gave Clinton haters a critical kick start just when the Whitewater investigation was about to fizzle.

Many senators improve the institution through their service. As the last of a dying breed of neo-segregationists, Helms improved it by finally retiring. What's most telling about his career is its longevity, and the fact that Helms continued to serve into the twenty-first century.

Race's Reach

Barack Obama is the Democrats' newest political superstar. In 2004, Obama became the first African-American male Democrat—and only the third African American overall—to win a seat in the U.S. Senate since the Seventeenth Amendment established the direct election of senators. The other two were Republican Edward Brooke of Massachusetts, who served during the late 1970s and early 1980s, and Carol Moseley Braun, who was elected in 1992. Both Obama and Moseley Braun hail from Illinois, where about one-sixth of the state's residents are African Americans.

Few political handicappers would dare predict that, say, Georgia will elect an African-American Democrat to the Senate anytime soon—even though Georgia's African-American population share is *twice* that of Illinois, and Georgia also boasts the nation's largest black state legislative caucus, the very farm system that has already produced many Congressional Black Caucus members, including former state senator Obama. Why, then, hasn't Georgia elected a black senator while Illinois has done so twice? The answer is that there is less racial crossover voting in the South, where the white populace is smaller in share but more monolithically Republican than it is in northeastern or midwestern states, like Illinois. These are the modern realities of racial voting in America.

Race does not operate in isolation, of course. It is spooled along with other threads of southern political identity, including the region's exceptionally strong militarism, misogyny, and mistrust of government. Southern women in the pre–New Deal South who dared to agitate for labor reforms and to remove children from factories and put them into schools were castigated by their fellow southerners as "negrophiliacs." White southerners also invoked racism to oppose integrating the military and ratifying the women's suffrage amendment. Nor did the demise of Jim Crow racism and the rise of African-American empowerment end the political "blacklash" against southern Democrats, both white and black. Today it is seen in the Republican attempts to reduce and marginalize the effectiveness of the African-American vote, such as the attempt in Georgia law to require those without a driver's license (i.e., urbanites, especially poor African Americans) to pay $20 to get an ID if they want to vote—the equivalent of an indirect poll tax, something outlawed in 1964 by the Twenty-fourth Amendment. It's also visible in South Carolina governor Mark Sanford's support of private school vouchers, what one state political observer in an off-the-record conversation labeled "segregation by other means."

Meanwhile, the GOP continues its invidious demonizing of the Democratic Party using the same, time-tested method that has worked for generations—that is, by simply lumping Democrats in with those "niggers" and cast aspersions on them both. The language is not so obvious or coarse; terms like "inner city youths" and "these people" are substituted for the kind of words that now end political careers. But as University of Alabama historian Glenn Feldman nicely summarizes, in myriad ways race continues to be inextricably bound up with the southern Republican agenda during the past four decades:

> With the base of racism taken from Dixie's old conservative Democrats and planted firmly in the soil of a new Republican South, the southern GOP has been able to make itself invincible by fusing together different strains of traditional southern culture and values: white supremacy, anti-federalism, xenophobia, anti-liberalism, laissez-faire economics, religious fundamentalism, traditional gender roles, super-patriotism, isolationism and jingoism, traditional moral conformity, and so forth. The party's strategists have been able to fuse these elements onto the central adhesive of race.

Apologists can claim otherwise, but the Republican national chairman has already conceded the point: The GOP manipulated racial attitudes to win the South. Race provided the electoral turnkey Republicans used to unlock the South and become the majority party nationally. In *The Emerging Republican Majority,* Kevin Phillips stated rather plainly that the GOP no longer needed to court "Negro" voters. Indeed, not only could Republicans "build a winning coalition without Negro votes" but, because "Negro-Democratic mutual identification was a major source of Democratic loss," the Republicans should welcome the Negro's new participatory rights:

Maintenance of Negro voting rights in Dixie, far from being contrary to GOP interests, is essential if southern conservatives are to be pressured into switching to the Republican Party—for Negroes are beginning to seize control of the national Democratic Party in some Black Belt areas.

Phillips knew of what he spoke when he took the full measure of race's power in the South forty years ago, just as he understands today that only religion rivals race in terms of impact on the political identity and partisan behavior of southerners.

GIVE 'EM THAT NEW-TIME RELIGION

"Now that the GOP has been transformed by the rise of the South, the trauma of terrorism and George W. Bush's conviction that God wanted him to be president, a deeper conclusion can be drawn: The Republican Party has become the first religious party in U.S. history," says Kevin Phillips today.

The South is, indeed, America's most religious region. On almost every possible measure of personal piety or public practice, southerners lead the nation: praying; reading the Bible and believing it to be the literal word of God; church attendance and volunteerism; listening to Christian radio and talk shows. According to 2004 presidential exit polls, 51 percent of southerners attend church at least once per week, compared to just 38 percent of Americans in the rest of the country. Among religious donors, southerners are most likely to give to Christian Right organizations and least likely to contribute to secular left causes. The now-defunct Moral Majority and the still-powerful Christian Coalition were both founded in the South. African-American Methodist and Baptist congregants flood southern pews each Sunday. From Houston to Atlanta, the region is home to sprawling mega-churches that draw worshipers from a variety of economic and ethnic backgrounds. Not surprising, the sixteen largest Christian-oriented consumer markets in the United States are located in southern states.

The evangelical explosion is the key development in American religion during the past century, and its effects can be seen everywhere but especially in the South. In *The Transformation of American Religion,* Alan Wolfe, director of Boston College's Boisi Center for Religion and American Public Life, explains the lure of modern evangelism:

> [T]hose who fear the consequences for the United States of a return to strong religious belief should not be fooled by evangelicalism's rapid growth. On the contrary, evangelicalism's popularity is due as much to its populistic and democratic urges—its determination to find out exactly what believers want and to offer it to them—as it is to certainties of faith. The biggest challenge posed to American society by the popularity of megachurches and other forms of growth-oriented Protestantism is not bigotry but bathos. Television, publishing, political campaigning, education, self-help advice—all increasingly tell Americans what they already want to hear. Religion, it would seem, should now be added to that list.

By focusing on the New Testament rather than the Old, emphasizing Jesus' role as spiritual savior and personal redeemer, and appealing to congregants through charisma rather than ceremony, evangelical churches during the past half century have opened their doors to millions of disaffected Christians who had grown tired of the stodgy traditions of liturgical, mainline Protestantism and Catholicism.

The growth of evangelism has continued unabated, fostering a new Christian pluralism and the parallel emergence of thousands of more accessible churches. In the past three decades alone, the number of evangelical private schools, bible seminaries, summer camps, radio and television stations, books and booksellers, and audio and video recordings has increased by several magnitudes. Evangelical churches are taking up residence in strip malls or temporarily renting conference spaces in local hotels until they can raise sufficient funds to buy property and build freestanding buildings. Feeling the crunch of declining congregations and competitive pressure from the burgeoning evangelical movement, some liberal Protestant denominations have taken the unusual step of running television ads to attract new members. For example, a creative ad campaign by the United Church of Christ targeting alienated gay Christians quintupled the number of hits on UCC's national website.

The South is home to more evangelicals than any other region, and the differences are stark: Whereas less than a third of Americans identify themselves as either evangelical or born-again Christians, 58 percent of Deep-state southerners and 49 percent of Outer-state southerners do. Yet evangelism actually arrived late in the South, says historian Christine Leigh Heyrman, after first making inroads to the Northeast and Midwest in the late 1700s. Southern evangelism began to blossom during the first half of the nineteenth century at the same time the national abolitionist movement was gaining adherents, especially in the North. Undaunted by abolitionist finger-wagging, southern evangelicals rallied to slavery's defense. By the time South Carolina senator John C. Calhoun called in 1828 for nullifying federal power to protect slavery, southern evangelicals had already compelled the three major evangelical denominations—Baptist, Methodist, and Presbyterian—to reverse to their earlier opposition to slavery. To reduce dissonance in the pews, congregants clung to the southern tradition of passive resistance. "[S]outhern Evangelicals intoned a kind of litany," writes Donald Mathews in *Religion in the Old South*. "Slaveholding is a civil institution; *and we will not interfere*. The character of civil institutions is governed by politics; *and we will not interfere*. Politics are beyond the scope of the church; *and we will not interfere*."

Meanwhile, southern clergymen bullied from their pulpits. They echoed southern politicians' claims about the risk of disunion, the inviolate sanctity of states' rights, and the need for southern self-determination. They peppered their Sunday sermons with scriptural interpretations purporting to divine biblical justification for slavery. Without a hint of irony, they complained that the growing abolitionist movement was creating strife in southern churches by undermining the clergy's moral authority. Some clerics and congregants were abolitionists, of course. (The Quakers were a notable and courageous, if small, minority.) But what's most fascinating about the moral equivocating of antebellum evangelical clergy and their southern congregants is how sharply their insistence on separating church from state contrasts with the uninhibited and unapologetic political involvement of today's southern evangelicals.

Lost Causes and Fundamentalist Foundings

Sociologist Mark Shibley attributes modern evangelism's strong southern following to two significant events: defeat in the Civil War and the fundamentalist-modernist dispute that erupted within Protestantism in the 1920s. "The first event was decisive because it intensified evangelism in the South," says Shibley, "the second because it marginalized evangelism everywhere except in the South." Though Shibley overstates the second point, it is worth pausing to take a closer look at these two, pivotal moments.

Defeat in the war instilled in many southerners a "lost cause" mentality mixed of equal parts resignation and resentment. As a crucial component of post–Civil War southern culture, evangelism allowed southerners to disconnect any notions of moral failure from the military capitulation at Appomattox. "The defeat of the Confederacy created such chaos, especially in values, and for the ministers it activated the fear of even greater moral anarchy if traditional Southern values died," asserts Charles Wilson Reagan in *Baptized in Blood: The Religion of the Lost Cause, 1865–1920* "The myth of the Crusading Christian Confederates enabled the clergy to assert that the Confederacy's values survived the war and would be a stable basis for Southern society." Reagan continues:

> A Southern political nation was not to be, and the people of Dixie came to accept that; but the dream of a cohesive Southern people with a separate cultural identity replaced the original longing. *The cultural dream replaced the political dream: The South's kingdom was to be of culture, not of politics.* Religion was at the heart of this dream, and the history of the attitude known as the Lost Cause was the story of the use of the past as the basis for a Southern religious-moral identity, an identity as a chosen people.

Southerners had always exhibited strong religious beliefs, and their piety fueled the growth of Methodist and Baptist churches prior to the

Civil War. But before the war, southern faith was typically not displayed in very public ways. "A private introspectiveness that even the colonial Puritans had never known became the hallmark of southern righteousness," says religion scholar Samuel S. Hill. "[W]hen southern evangelicals thought about or spoke of religion directly, they meant the inner life." Defeat and decimation in the Civil War changed all that.

The second turning point in southern evangelical history was the challenge to fundamentalist orthodoxy by "modernist" Christians following World War I. With more tolerant practices gaining acceptance and science providing new explanations for cosmic mysteries long regarded as God's sole dominion, a rift emerged within the evangelical movement between the liberalizing mainline Protestant denominations and fundamentalists clinging to "that old-time religion." Leading fundamentalists during the previous one hundred years, including John Nelson Darby, Dwight L. Moody, J. Gresham Machen, and Billy Sunday, dedicated their lives to the vigorous promotion of fundamentalism's key principles and assumptions: scriptural inerrancy; the virgin birth, resurrection, and human redemptive power of Christ; and the speedy conversion of as many souls as possible before the "rapture"— the seventh and final dispensation. The modernist challenge to scriptural literalism has been particularly threatening because so many other assumptions derive from a strict reading of the Bible, including the creationist account of the origins of man. Evolutionary theory thus shook fundamentalists to their core, for if the Bible could no longer be taken literally on issues like mankind's origins, what else in its pages could be doubted?

A key turning point, of course, was the Scopes "monkey" trial of 1925. With the prompting and financial support from the American Civil Liberties Union, a 24-year-old general science teacher from Tennessee named John T. Scopes agreed to challenge the state law that prohibited teaching of evolution in schools. Headline-seeking local prosecutors in the small town of Dayton quickly arrested Scopes. The specific details of the law, Scopes's purported violation of it, and the young teacher's legal and personal fates—none of these, nor even the state's school curriculum, were of primary concern. What mattered to both sides was the public spectacle, the clash of competing arguments about the role of God and science in human affairs. The ensuing "Trial of the Century" pitted two of the nation's most prominent figures against one another. Clarence Darrow was the sage of the secularists, a legal giant who had made recent headlines with his insanity defense of Chicago teenage murderers Nathan Leopold and Richard Loeb. The fundamentalists were represented by the legendary populist and three-time Democratic presidential nominee, William Jennings Bryan.

Bryan subscribed fully to the biblical account of creation. Yet, according to Pulitzer Prize winner Edward J. Larson in *Summer for the Gods*, the "Great Commoner" had even greater faith in the infallibility of majority will. Bryan believed evolutionists were wrong on the merits and contemptible for daring to tell taxpayers how to design their local curricula. He had little doubt that the campaign to pass antievolution statutes being waged by the World's Christian Fundamentals Association would succeed, and for the most part, he was right. In the South, where the county system of state legislative representation assigned disproportionate power to the less-populous rural counties, antievolution statutes passed easily.

The sudden fury over school curricula came in response to the dramatic rise in the number of children attending public school beyond the elementary level. William Bell Riley, who cofounded the WCFA in 1918 in search of more than statutory victories, stoked parental fears in the hopes of igniting a major dispute. Riley called evolutionists atheists and, for good measure, likened them to convenient boogeymen of the day. He specifically warned of "an 'international Jewish-Bolshevik-Darwinist conspiracy' to promote evolutionism in the classroom." Bryan and Riley received warm receptions in the southern states, where teaching evolution was unpopular. One man sought adulation, the other a public confrontation. Both men got their wish in Dayton.

Though Dayton is in eastern Tennessee's Rhea County, one of but a handful of southern counties Bryan never carried in his three presidential bids, Bryan and the creationists easily prevailed in the strict, legal sense: The jury found Scopes guilty. But Darrow's devastating interrogation of Bryan, who took the stand to defend biblical creationism, merely confirmed many southerners' fears that Dixie would be depicted

as a backwater region filled with rubes too ignorant to understand science—and too frightened of modernity to bother trying. The Scopes
trial sent the fundamentalists into retreat, but they "did not go the way
of the dinosaur," say evangelical historians Robert H. Krapohl and
Charles H. Lippy. "Increasingly forced out of mainstream American culture, they directed their energies inwardly and created a robust subcul-
ture of churches, colleges, Bible institutes, para-church organizations,
and publishing houses." These actions, as Mark Shibley explains, were
a response to outside threats and challenges to southern ways:

> The South's peripheral standing in American culture—its
> poverty, its rural population base, the Civil War defeat, and re-
> lated factors—conspired to insulate Southerners from the corro-
> sive effects of the new intellectual currents and social changes
> that threatened religious authority. But more importantly, be-
> cause evangelism was by then part of the very fabric of southern
> life—evangelical piety and conventional morality being synony-
> mous—the challenge to fundamentalism by northern intellectuals
> in the opening decades of the twentieth century was another at-
> tack on the integrity of southern culture, turning the South fur-
> ther inward and intensifying southern religion by forcing it into a
> defensive posture. Not merely Christian doctrine but the southern
> way of life was being challenged.

Eight decades later, the South is less under siege and more exposed
to "new intellectual currents and social changes." Yet the cultural-legal
battles that southerners initiated in Dayton continue. In many ways,
the stakes are even higher than they were in 1925, because the struggle
for cultural definition is occurring on a national rather than regional
battlefield, and the South today is more influential than ever in national politics. Only the circumstances, combatants, and scale of the
struggle have evolved since Bryan and Darrow clashed in Dayton.

Religious Exceptionalism

Why is the South so exceptionally religious and why are the religious
attitudes of beliefs of southerners so exceptional? The short answer is

that social class is a strong determinant of religious attitudes, and the evangelical ranks are filled disproportionately by Americans of lower socioeconomic status. "In contrast to the mainline pattern, evangelical churches—whose members came primarily from rural areas, were less educated, and were less likely to pursue professional careers—have generally been viewed as representing the marginalized and alienated," writes Alan Wolfe. As evidenced by their denomination affiliations and doctrinal belief systems, southern evangelicals—and especially lower-class whites—are more fundamentalist than non-southern evangelicals. They are more likely to affiliate with charismatic or Pentecostal churches, to believe the Bible to be literally true, and foresee a period of glorious Christian rule followed by the rapture.

Migrating southerners have exported their religious and cultural beliefs to other parts of the country, resulting in a certain "southerniz-ing" of American religion. Yet regional disparities persist. By the late 1980s, survey results revealed that 66 percent of southern white Protestants described themselves as evangelicals, 10 percent were self-described moderates, with the remaining 24 percent calling themselves liberals. By contrast, only 46 percent of non-southern Protestants were self-described evangelicals, with a majority identifying as either moderates (23 percent) or liberals (31 percent). Even Catholics, as few as they are in the South, are more conservative than fellow Catholics from the Northeast and Midwest. The religious conservatism of southerners is quite ecumenical, so to speak.

Religious-based conservatism among southerners runs so deep, in fact, that it overwhelms generational effects. Southern evangelicals are more likely than non-southern evangelicals to oppose homosexuality (+8, 92 percent to 84 percent), legalized abortion (+5, 76 percent to 71 percent), eliminating school prayer (+13, 74 percent to 61 percent), premarital sex (+9, 58 percent to 49 percent), and women working out-side the home (+12, 36 percent to 24 percent). As expected, older southern evangelicals (aged 40+) are more conservative on these five cultural issues than their non-southern age cohorts, and likewise for younger evangelicals inside and outside the South. But as Table 3.3 in-dicates, *young* evangelicals in the South are more conservative than *older* non-southerners on three of these issues (homosexuality, abor-

tion, and school prayer), and almost as conservative on whether
women should work outside the home. Only on the issue of premarital
sex are young southerners more liberal.

Table 3.3
Southern Attitudes on Social Issues (by Percentage)

Percentage Supporting conservative position on:	South		Non-South	
	Old	Young	Old	Young
Homosexuality	95	89	87	81
Abortion	80	71	70	71
School Prayer	79	68	64	57
Premarital Sex	71	41	55	43
Working Women	45	25	29	18

Source: Adapted by author from Shibley (1996), Table 7.5.

As the most salient and divisive cultural issue of the day, abortion
offers a useful window on how religion affects the policy positions of
southerners and non-southerners. In September 2005, SurveyUSA's
poll of all fifty states showed that only thirteen states had a higher
share of citizens describing themselves as "pro-life" than "pro-choice."
Of these thirteen, five are in the South (Alabama, Arkansas, Louisiana,
Mississippi, and Tennessee), compared to only eight pro-life pluralities
among the remaining thirty-nine states. Using 2004 census state population estimates to weight the results, SurveyUSA calculated that pro-
choice Americans exceed pro-lifers by an 18-point margin, 56 percent
to 38 percent.

Table 3.4 reports the state-by-state and regional breakdowns for the
South, plus totals for the non-South. A population-weighted average
for the eleven southern states reveals a curious result: Thanks to solid
pro-choice majorities in the four largest states—Georgia and Texas (+9
percent each), Virginia (+15 percent), and Florida (+22 percent)—as a
region the South is slightly pro-choice by a margin of six points (50
percent to 44 percent). Non-southerners are pro-choice, however, by a
stunning 22-point margin (58 percent to 36 percent). Later in the book
I discuss the special case of Florida, but for now notice that estimated

support for reproductive choice among Floridians is both a clear exception in the region and, at +22 percent, identical to support among Americans who live outside the South.

Table 3.4
Southern Support for Abortion Rights

State	Pro-choice	Pro-life	Difference
Louisiana	36	57	-21
Alabama	36	54	-18
Arkansas	40	55	-15
Mississippi	39	53	-14
Tennessee	42	51	-9
North Carolina	47	44	+3
South Carolina	47	43	+4
Georgia	52	43	+9
Texas	52	43	+9
Virginia	54	39	+15
Florida	58	36	+22
South	**50**	**44**	**+6**
Non-South	**58**	**36**	**+22**

In the post–*Roe v. Wade* era, abortion has been a critical issue in the political maturation of religious conservatives. "Without the unifying and galvanizing drive to end legal abortion, the Christian Right would not have become a social movement formidable enough to swing elections," writes religious historian Sara Diamond. "Certainly, opposition to gay rights and secular humanism in the public schools would have fostered their share of skirmishes. However, on such issues alone, the movement would have floundered and withered." The electoral utility of abortion politics is not limited to the South. For opponents of reproductive choice, however, the regional differences on abortion limit the issue's galvanizing effect to a handful of non-southern states—a fact that augurs well for Democrats hoping to build a non-southern national majority by running proudly as the pro-choice party. In fact, when the Christian Coalition decided to follow the lead of the Republican Party's 1994 *Contract with America* by producing its own *Contract with the American Family* in 1995, extensive focus-group testing revealed that a too-strident abortion stance would backfire and so the Coalition toned down the language in its contract. Even the most conservative elements within the Republican coalition know they are losing the choice issue, a fact that some Democrats too often forget.

Southern Religion and the GOP

Evangelism grew steadily during the middle decades of the twentieth century, and by the late 1970s and early 1980s emerged as a powerful political force. Evangelicals helped put Jimmy Carter in the White House, then just as quickly discarded him for Ronald Reagan in 1980. Since then, the rapid political maturation of the Christian Right has helped realign the two-party system, especially in the South. Religious conservatives in the South register and vote; they talk to their friends and neighbors about politics; they contribute money to and volunteer for campaigns; and they provide millions of names and dollars to a variety of interest groups in the conservative constellation. They have become the Republican Party's crucial base of support in the region, the political sextant by which the GOP charts its course and, increasingly, a serious problem for the party. "[C]onservative Christians are to the Republican Party what blacks were to the Democrats in the 1970s: its most loyal troops, the source of its most talented activists, its moral core," writes conservative *Weekly Standard* editor Christopher Caldwell. "For that reason they are also the main source of radicalization and overreach."

Ministers helped to accelerate the South's partisan transformation. Though survey data do not exist for 1976, circumstantial evidence suggests that clergy from the Southern Baptist Convention—the region's largest and most influential evangelical denomination—supported Carter's presidential candidacy that year. By 1980, however, SBC ministers were already supporting Reagan over Carter by a margin of 56 percent to 42 percent. Since then, they have given every Republican nominee at least 78 percent of their votes. In 2000, SBC ministers preferred George W. Bush over Southern Baptist Al Gore, 88 percent to 12 percent. Writes religion scholar James L. Guth:

[O]ver the past two decades, the Southern Baptist clergy has become an important factor in the growing Republican strength in the formerly Democratic Solid South. They increasingly identify as Republicans, vote overwhelmingly for Republican presidential candidates, and work for Republican tickets, at least in presidential elections. And all the evidence suggests that their propensities increasingly affect "down ticket" races for U.S. Senate and House, gubernatorial elections, and even state legislative seats.

Guth has also documented the significant increases since 1980 in the number of Southern Baptist clergy who engage in election-year "bully pulpit" activities, from talking about issues during their sermons to publicly endorsing candidates to contacting public officials. Southern clergy have become to the Republican Party what labor leaders are to the Democrats: opinion leaders, political gatekeepers, and supervisors of formidable retail voter and volunteer delivery machines.

Beyond rank-and-file clergy, a generation of televangelist leaders catapulted to national prominence during the television age, and most either reside in or derive much of their following from the South. Billy Graham, a North Carolina native, is an American icon who has millions of followers and the stature to counsel a variety of American presidents; his son, Franklin, has since established a following of his own. Three decades ago, conservative activists Richard Viguerie and Howard Phillips convinced Lynchburg, Virginia, preacher Jerry Falwell to create the Moral Majority. Fellow Virginian Pat Robertson, whose father was a U.S. senator, founded the Christian Coalition and runs a powerful media empire headlined by the *700 Club* show he hosts; like Graham, his son is following in dad's footsteps. The Reverend James Kennedy presides over Fort Lauderdale's gleaming Coral Ridge Presbyterian mega-church. The Reverend Dr. James Dobson is a regional outlier who built his Colorado-based Focus on the Family into an empire. Some of these ministers have amassed enough capital to form affiliated legal and lobbying organizations, including the Alliance Defense Fund and the American Center for Law and Justice. Wherever founded or headquartered and whatever their mission, Christian Right organizations find their roots in the South and receive much of their funding from southerners: 38 percent of "religious right" donors are southerners, compared to just 8 percent of "secular left" and 22 percent "religious left" donors.

In George W. Bush, the southern-based Christian Right finally put one of their own into the Oval Office. Many Christian conservatives (including the president) believe his selection was divinely inspired. Though Bush abandoned his commitment to faith-based initiatives during his first term and showed no inclination to spend any of his post–September 11 political capital pushing a constitutional amendment to ban abortion, he continues to receive the political blessings of evangelicals and born-again Christians. When Bush infuriated millions of conservatives by appointing Harriet Miers to the Supreme Court, notice who rushed to the president's defense: evangelical leaders like Dobson and Robertson. To many evangelicals on the Christian Right, legal qualifications and constitutional experience were matters secondary to the policy positions of a woman who Bush let be known was legitimate, in part, because she is an evangelical.

Southern evangelicals certainly have every right to believe Bush owes them. The sheer size of the evangelical/born-again voting block gave the Texas governor a nearly insurmountable advantage in the South during his two presidential runs. Based on 2004 exit polls, Table 3.5 reports the share of self-described evangelical/born-again Christian (EBA) voters, the percentage of these voters who supported Bush or Democratic nominee John Kerry, and the net advantage Bush gained from their support. That is, the final column represents the lead—or head start—Bush enjoyed even *after* the much smaller share of EBA voters who supported Kerry are subtracted out.

For Democrats, the results are disheartening. On the high end, about seven of every eight Mississippi evangelicals and born-again Christians (EBA) voted for Bush in 2004. Because they comprised almost half (48 percent) of Mississippi voters, Bush's built-in head start was 36 percent. Put another way, Kerry would have needed to capture almost the same seven-eighths share of the remaining 52 percent of Mississippi's nonevangelical voters to beat Bush, a virtual impossibility. Even on the low end, EBA voters in Louisiana provided Bush a 19 percent head start—greater than his overall advantage in any other *region*. Overall, southern states gave Bush a 20 percent lead, a far bigger net advantage than he enjoyed among midwestern (13 percent), western (11 percent), and, especially, eastern voters (5 percent).

Table 3.5
The Republicans' Southern Evangelical Advantage (by Percentage)

State	EBA share	For Bush	For Kerry	Head Start
Alabama	43	88	12	33
Arkansas	53	71	29	22
Georgia	35	84	16	24
Louisiana	27	85	15	19
Mississippi	48	88	12	36
North Carolina	36	84	16	24
South Carolina	30	88	11	23
Tennessee	51	74	26	24
South	**33**	**80**	**20**	**20**
Midwest	**25**	**76**	**23**	**13**
West	**19**	**79**	**20**	**11**
East	**10**	**72**	**27**	**5**

Source: Computed by author from 2004 Edison/Mitofsky
National Election Pool data. All cell entries are percentages.
The NEP did not report results for Florida, Texas, and Virginia.

The margins by which Bush carried the southern states (again, Florida excepted) gave Republicans the luxury of redirecting their resources elsewhere. With churches providing the surrogate grassroots and communication infrastructure, the GOP did not have to invest as much in its state parties or design elaborate get-out-the-vote field campaigns. Because southern Republicans churn churchgoers into voters with an efficiency that would make Boss Tweed or George Meany blush, the GOP ultimately pays a very cheap price-per-vote to win the southern states. Even Tammany Hall and the Rust Belt union machines during their heyday could not hold a votive to the southern evangelical's Republican juggernaut today.

The South in a Secularized America

To the chagrin of Christian conservatives, Americans have become increasingly secular. Comparative results from the American Religious Identification Survey conducted in both 1990 and 2001 reveal that the percentage of adult Americans who identify with no religion has almost doubled, from 8 percent to 14 percent. Though still a vastly majority-Christian nation, the share of self-identified Christians dropped from about 86 percent to 77 percent during the same decade.

Generational differences are driving these changes. Whereas only 14 percent of Americans aged 35 and over now describe themselves as "secular" or "somewhat secular," fully 23 percent of the 64 million Americans between the ages of 18 and 34 do. As they gradually replace their parents and grandparents, the younger and more secular generations will make America more liberal on issues such as premarital sex, abortion, and homosexuality. Evangelicals will be dismayed, for example, to learn the results of a 2004 survey of "Generation Y" attitudes conducted by the polling firm Greenberg Quinlan Rosner. GQR found that a majority of Gen Y'ers—who, incidentally, are only 61 percent white, compared to 86 percent for the GI Generation—support gay marriage and an even larger majority support reproductive choice. "Overall, these results suggest that the American political landscape could change fundamentally as this generation becomes a greater proportion of society," says Anna Greenberg, summarizing her findings. "The cultural divisions in our politics may become less powerful as issues of sexual preference and racial and ethnic diversity become less salient wedges in our political discussion." Whatever one thinks about the Christian Right's public hand-wringing over the declining role of religion and faith in American society, generational trends confirm their worst fears.

The respective roles of governmental and religious institutions only heighten their anxieties. Christian churches and their affiliated "parachurch" organizations (e.g., relief agencies and spiritual works foundations) have benefited from a massive infusion of philanthropy, and yet the ratio of church spending to government spending continues to shrink. In 1870, church income constituted one dollar for every $211 of

GNP. By 1926, that ratio doubled to about one dollar for every $119 in GNP and, except for a slight dip during the Great Depression, has remained about the same since. But rising tithes have been offset by a massive expansion in federal government spending. At its closest point, in 1916, for every dollar of church income there were two dollars in federal receipts. By 1997 that ratio had increased more than ten-fold, to $23 in federal receipts for every dollar of church income. Though government growth in the eight decades since the fundamentalist-modernist split is partly explained by rising defense costs for two world wars and a variety of Cold War–era conflicts, from a strictly fiscal standpoint the complaints of religious leaders that governmental social spending has eclipsed the financial clout of churches are as difficult to miss as they are to dismiss. Bush's faith-based initiative is a puny, mostly symbolic effort to rebalance this situation, but his token efforts will accomplish little more than provide a sop to his religious base.

As discussed in the previous chapter, the Terri Schiavo controversy typifies the southern takeover of the Republican Party, and it may be remembered someday as the moment when the party's southern culture vultures finally initiated the GOP's undoing. Recognizing the dangers of the GOP's response to the Schiavo case, some principled conservatives and libertarians raised their voices. So did a few courageous Republican politicians. In the quote that opened this chapter, Connecticut Congressman Christopher Shays lamented that his party was turning into a theocracy. Former Republican senator John Danforth of Missouri, an Episcopal priest who is more conservative than Shays and hails from a more conservative state, did Shays one better by voicing his concerns on the *New York Times* op-ed page:

> By a series of recent initiatives, Republicans have transformed our party into the political arm of conservative Christians. The elements of this transformation have included advocacy of a constitutional amendment to ban gay marriage, opposition to stem cell research involving both frozen embryos and human cells in petri dishes, and the extraordinary effort to keep Terri Schiavo hooked up to a feeding tube.
>
> Standing alone, each of these initiatives has its advocates,

within the Republican Party and beyond. But the distinct elements do not stand alone. Rather they are parts of a larger package, an agenda of positions common to conservative Christians and the dominant wing of the Republican Party . . .

During the 18 years I served in the Senate, Republicans often disagreed with each other. But there was much that held us together . . . But in recent times, we Republicans have allowed this shared agenda to become secondary to the agenda of Christian conservatives. As a senator, I worried every day about the size of the federal deficit. I did not spend a single minute worrying about the effect of gays on the institution of marriage. Today it seems to be the other way around.

A few months later, Danforth told an audience of graduate students at the University of Arkansas's Clinton School of Public Service that the takeover of his Republican Party by the Christian Right is "divisive for the country," and hoped it was not permanent.

Though policies like immigration have the potential to split apart the Republicans' pulpits-plus-profits coalition, the evangelical-inspired Republican obsession with "body issues" like abortion, stems cells, homosexuality, and end-of-life decision making threatens to undo the GOP's tenuous majority. "Republicans think this new [secular-religious] fault line in American politics will systematically favor the GOP, just as the old fault line, running along economic lines, favored Democrats," wrote former Clinton Labor secretary Robert B. Reich, in his political autopsy of the Schiavo episode. "They may well succeed, but it's a dangerous gamble. Most Americans consider themselves religious, to be sure, but when it comes to politics they are decidedly secular—they don't want politics to be dominated by religious belief."

True to Reich's assessment, almost half of *Republicans* surveyed said the interference by Congress and the president on Schiavo's behalf was wrong; 18 percent said they lost respect for Bush, and 41 percent said they lost respect for Congress. (Dissatisfaction among Democrats and independents was greater.) "Even many evangelicals, who otherwise embrace the culture of life, grow queasy when politicians in Washington start imposing solutions from afar, based on abstract principles rather than concrete particulars," scolded conservative *New York Times* columnist David Brooks.

What Hath God Wrought?

Some conservative intellectuals have found comfort in the self-deluding notion that evangelicals can be dismissed as unserious hangers-on—little more than a pack of undesirable party crashers knocking over the furniture and mucking up the carpets of what is otherwise a more thoughtful, composed, and secular conservative leadership running the Republican Party today. A decade ago, in his book *Dead Right*, conservative intellectual and future presidential speechwriter David Frum sneered at the very "pseudo-menacing" fundamentalists who eventually helped put him behind a desk at George W. Bush's White House:

> Churchgoers occupy the same place in the conservative intellectual's imagination that the proletariat once did in the imagination of the revolutionary intellectual: a mass that will muscle the intellectual's theories into power. But like the proletariat, American churchgoers will almost certainly disappoint the intellectuals who trust them . . . If fundamentalist America is too poor and weak to bear out secularist fears, it shares too many of the sins of secular America to sustain conservative hopes. Fundamentalists will go on giving conservative Republicans their votes, but it is not from them that the conservative movement of the future will draw its ideas.

Really? While Frum may find solace in the belief that fundamentalists' electoral brawn can be leveraged without accepting any intellectual contribution from the millions who troop from pew to poll, the truth is that modern Republican Party is fueled by the ideas as well as the votes of its fundamentalist wing. Sentiments like Frum's, normally voiced only in safety and privacy of cocktail parties and policy salons, will inevitably catch up with the neoconservatives who snigger behind the backs of the fundamentalists every November after the final voting returns are tallied. For the sake of the Democratic Party and the nation, *that* moment of final dispensation cannot come too soon.

The Democratic South was the outcast region for seven long decades of Republican rule following the Civil War. During the New Deal, or at least until the partisan disruptions of the civil rights era, the South was the silent partner in cahoots with the urban-ethnic chieftains who ran the Democratic Party from the North. Today, however, the South is the anointed region within the Republicans' governing coalition. No longer must southerners channel their ire and energies toward thwarting the imposition of progressive changes upon them: Instead, they can initiate and aggressively push an agenda of conservative change upon others. By encouraging religious conservatives to disregard their historical aversions to political activity, the GOP set into motion the capture of its party by its southern wing. The South's religious conservatives now make demands of their party and the federal government, make them publicly, and quickly grow impatient when their demands are unmet.

Ignoring the fundamentalists is the preferred option, as Frum let slip, but that tactic will only work for so long. On the other hand, paying the fundamentalists back too handsomely or too publicly introduces another set of problems for the Republican Party. Michael Lind, author and resident scholar at the New America Foundation, puts a rather fine point on the matter:

Hostile to the world and encapsulated in its own subcultural network of institutions, Southern Protestant fundamentalism at the beginning of the twenty-first century had hardly changed from the 1920s, when it took on its present form. Beginning in the 1970s, Jerry Falwell's Moral Majority and later Pat Robertson's Christian Coalition mobilized the so-called religious right—really the Southern Protestant fundamentalist right, most of whom in previous generations had been conservative Democrats. Although genuine fundamentalists amount to no more than around 5 per-

cent of the U.S. population, the high turnout of religious-right activists in Republican primary elections allowed them to capture
the Republican Party by the 1990s. As these ex-Democratic
Southern fundamentalists hijacked the GOP, growing numbers of
Republicans in the Northeast, Midwest, and West Coast quit the
party in disgust, becoming Democrats or independents.

This is the point where the Republican Party's ability to pacify simultaneously its evangelical Christian base, its non-Christian conservative
elements, and the millions of moderates breaks down—and the opportunity for Democrats to forge a non-southern begins.

The media made much of the 2004 exit polls, in which a plurality of
voters—22 percent, to be exact—cited "moral values" as their most
important issue, and that 9 in 10 voters who listed "religious faith" as
their most important candidate trait chose Bush over Kerry. But a closer
look at the numbers tells a different story. Pundits are quick to note
that three-fifths of American voters who attend church at least once a
week chose Bush. Far fewer mention that the reason Bush's national
popular vote margin was less than 2.5 percent is that 55 percent of
Americans who attend sporadically—less than weekly, if at all—voted
for Kerry and also slightly outnumber regular churchgoers. What's
more, given the higher church attendance rates and wider margins by
which Bush won in the deeply religious South, it is easy to surmise that
religious habits had either no effect or had a *negative* impact on Bush's
support outside Dixie.

Bush may have captured the South thanks in part to "righteous"
voting, but the reason he won reelection is that he exploited his advantages over Kerry on national security and terrorism. The truth is that
the conservative social agenda so firmly rooted in southern culture is
losing public favor. Even Richard Cizik, who lobbies for the 30-million-
member National Association of Evangelicals, worries that evangelicals
will be viewed as "modern-day ayatollahs" because of their sometimes
strident conservative views.

Christian fundamentalism also bears some odd resemblances to fundamentalist movements in other parts of the world, says Jimmy Carter,

himself a Southern Baptist who speaks with more authority than any Democrat and almost any American on this subject. "There has been, indeed, a disturbing trend toward fundamentalism in recent years, among political leaders and within major religious groups both abroad and in our country, and they have become intertwined," Carter writes in his latest book, *Our Endangered Values,* adding that the three words that "characterize this brand of fundamentalism [are] rigidity, domination and exclusion." The rigidity, says Carter, derives from an inability to compromise or negotiate with anyone who does not share the same doctrinal beliefs. The domination is usually perpetrated by authoritarian men upon women and other believers. And its exclusiveness demands that anyone who thinks differently be treated as "ignorant and possibly evil."

Rather than ignoring the power of evangelicals, faith-based organizations, and religious leaders, Democrats must use wedge politics to counterattack on moral issues. By making Republicans—especially moderates from blue states and districts—cast votes on controversial issues like a national amendment to ban abortion, the Democrats could force Republican politicians to choose between the religious conservative watchdog groups who monitor them and the far more moderate constituencies who elect them. As shown by the party infighting that ensued following President Bush's selection of Harriet Miers for the Supreme Court, there are deep fissures within the Republican coalition. The sharp point of the dividing wedge must be a broader, more systematic effort to point out the glaring inconsistencies between Republican policies and Christ's life, deeds, and teachings—and the disconnect between southern religious and political values and those to which most other Americans subscribe. "If the Republicans are daily improving their reputation on race, it is less clear whether they can control their religious wing," write John Micklethwait and Adrian Wooldridge in *The Right Nation: Conservative Power in America.* "[T]he Republicans' stands on various social issues have brought them a legion of Christian footsoldiers in the South. But Southerners are atypically culturally conservative . . . [and the] Southern wing's aggressive moralism does not scare off just independents; it also alienates other Republicans."

As Jim Wallis argues in his widely praised book, *God's Politics,* these values do not reflect the true Christian spirit. For example, says Wallis, there are more than three thousand biblical calls to support the poor. That call is at best a whimper from the South where, as we shall see in the second half of the book, the gap between the Republican votes of the richest and the Democratic votes of the poorest is wider than in most every other part of America. The deep tradition of Christian-based progressivism in America, especially in the Midwest and far West, provides Democrats a far better opportunity to recapture the mantle of faith through their deeds, not words. "The religious Right's grip on public debates about values has been driven in part by a media that continues to give airtime to the loudest religious voices, rather than the most representative, leaving millions of Christians and other people of faith without a say in the values debate," writes Wallis. "The truth is that most of the important movements for social change in America have been fueled by religion—progressive religion. The stark moral challenges of our time have once again begun to awaken this prophetic tradition."

Such an awakening is long overdue. If and when it occurs, however, the South will undoubtedly be the last region to rise from its collective slumber. In the interim, the South's strong religious commitments, coupled with the highly mobilized electoral power of the regionally based Christian Right, make it virtually impossible for Democratic presidential candidates and many state-level Democrats to win elections down in Dixie. Many white evangelicals and born-again Christians can be found outside the South, and there are secular progressives living in the deepest of Deep South precincts. But the cultural identity of the "lost cause" continues to deliver congregants to southern pews each Sunday morning and Republicans to southern poll locations each November. The South's heavenly chorus sings loudly and in two-party harmony—the voices in the higher octave exalting the superiority of southern values as the lower octaves chant for the Republican takeover of national politics.

REPUBLICAN COCKTAIL PARTY

The South is different. As a region, it is not as different from the rest of the country as it once was. Immigration into and out of the South, coupled with a steady homogenization of American society resulting from borderless markets for commodities and cultures, is beginning to erase some of the region's unique identity. But the South remains exceptional, and not just because of the region's food, music, art, literature, dialects, and customs. Southern politics are also distinct, and the two factors that most contribute to that distinctiveness are race and religion. Shaken and regularly stirred, together they produce a politically volatile cocktail in southern politics.

It would be convenient to just dismiss the South as the most racist and pious of America's regions, but also unfair. Central as they may be to the South's political identity, race and religion do not explain the entirety of southern politics. Geography, economics, social class, culture, climate, labor, and technology each played a role in the history of the South, and each has interfaced with race and religion in the formation of the South's political identity. It *is* fair to say that race and religion color the southern political experience more than they do in other parts of America, and will continue to do so for the foreseeable future. The more assimilated the South becomes with the rest of American culture, the better it will be for the Democrats and, dare I say, for the country. Full assimilation seems a distant reality, however, and one that southerners will continue to resist with the same, proud defiance they have exhibited from the time of the American founding to the latest Confederate flag skirmish. Unless Democrats are prepared to abandon their commitments to racial justice, women's rights, economic populism, and secular governance, the pre-assimilated South will continue to remain out of reach.

The expressed need among southerners, past and present, to affirm and impose their racial and religious attitudes within the South is one thing. But it is quite another when the South controls the Republican Party and, by extension, southern Republicans use their newfound powers to impose southern values on those in the rest of the country. Though conservatives might have us believe otherwise, the fact of southern control does not mean that southern political attitudes are any more representative of the rest of the nation today than when the South was trapped on the outside of the governing coalition with its nose pressed against the majority's window. The rest of America doesn't share the same attitudes toward race and religion that southerners do. The South is different, as Dorothy Parker might put it, because it's still full of southerners.

4

Go West, Young Democrats

Arizona, Colorado, Nevada, New Mexico are clearly the future of our party. The growth of these states presents a huge opportunity for us.

—Terry McAuliffe, former Democratic National
Committee chair

If we don't expand our base and cling to our limited base of support, I don't know how we win a presidential election. We have to build up the West.

—Democratic Senator Dianne Feinstein of California,
three weeks after Kerry's defeat in the general election

FOR CONSERVATIVES, the early 1960s were dark days. Although Republican Dwight Eisenhower won the presidency twice the previous decade, the war general and hero was not a movement conservative. Unified Republican control of the White House and Congress lasted just two years. The Democrats took back the Congress in 1954, expanded their majorities throughout the remainder of the decade, and then John Kennedy eked out a win over Richard Nixon in 1960. In some ways the situation the Republicans faced in January 1963—eight years without control of Congress, followed by a bitterly close presidential defeat for the incumbent vice president—mirrors the situation the Democrats were staring at forty years later in January 2003.

For the first six decades of the twentieth century, the roots of the Republican Party were in the Northeast-Midwest corridor, buffeted by pockets of support in the Far West. This regional configuration essentially dated back to the realigning election of 1896, won by Republican William McKinley in his first of two consecutive defeats of Democrat William Jennings Bryan, the Nebraska populist who carried the entire South and much of the Mountain West that year and again in 1900. There is an eerie resemblance between the 1896 and 1900 electoral maps and those from George W. Bush's 2000 and 2004 presidential victories, but with a very notable difference: The maps are reversed—blue states for red, red for blue. Republicans now rule where Democrats once did, and vice versa. The only reason McKinley's winning geographic coalition was ever-so-slightly insufficient for Al Gore or John Kerry to beat Bush is that the states of the Northeast and Midwest cast significantly fewer electoral votes today than they did in the 1890s.

During the Eisenhower era, the putative formula for a Republican presidential victory was to start by carrying the nation's two biggest

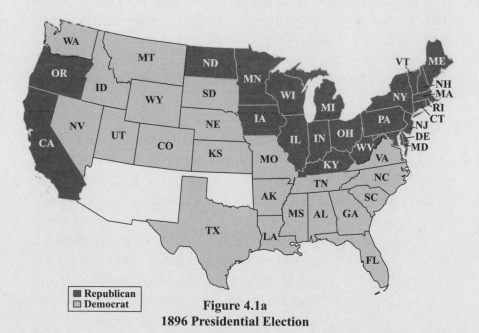

Republican
Democrat

Figure 4.1a
1896 Presidential Election

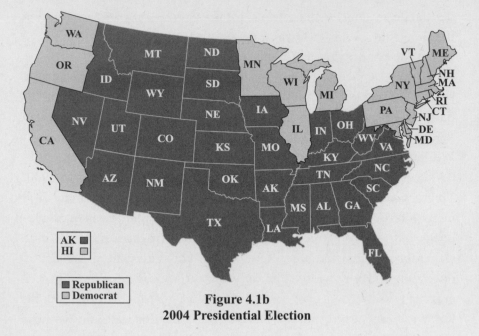

Figure 4.1b
2004 Presidential Election

states, New York and California, and build toward an electoral majority from there. But in a seminal 1963 article in the conservative *National Review,* publisher William Rusher presaged a different route to the Oval Office. After diagnosing the political shortcomings of Nelson Rockefeller—the New York governor and presumptive 1964 GOP torchbearer—Rusher set his sights on a new geographic Republican majority:

> [T]he Republican Party is at last within measurable distance of becoming what it has never been since Reconstruction: a truly national party, with a powerful state-by-state organization and successful local candidates in the South as well as elsewhere.
>
> And what are the Republicans of this new South saying? What will they be arguing, as they foregather with their fellow Republicans of the North and West in the convention of 1964? "Nominate Rockefeller?" Far from it. With a unanimity that cannot fail to impress, they are calling for a conservative GOP and a conservative presidential candidate. . . .

Rusher continued, wondering aloud—nine months before Kennedy's assassination, as it were—if the gathering storm clouds of 1964 might produce a silver lining:

> For what if, despite everything, 1964 is fated to be a Democratic year? How can the Republican convention, then, best build for a successful future? By turning its back on the new, conservative and increasingly Republican South and gumming blintzes with Nelson Rockefeller? Or by nominating a candidate who—win or lose—will galvanize the party in a vast new area, carry fresh scores and perhaps hundreds of Southern Republicans to unprecedented local victories, and lay the foundations for a truly national Republican Party, ready to fight and win in 1968 and all the years beyond?

Within a decade of Rusher's prognosis, a resurrected Nixon won the presidency twice, including a forty-nine-state reelection romp in 1972 that even Rusher dared not imagine a decade earlier. What has unfolded in "all the years beyond," of course, is near-total GOP domination of the White House, and rising Republican numbers in the Congress, among state governors, and in the state legislatures.

The early 1960s are an imperfect partisan analog to today. The American states are far more polarized now, especially in presidential elections. In the 1960 Kennedy-Nixon contest, only fourteen states were carried by one party or the other by at least 10 percent, with just six of these carried by more than 20 percent; in 2000, Bush or Al Gore carried a remarkable twenty-eight states by at least 10 percent, fourteen of those by 20 percent or more. This bifurcated electoral situation is worsening: The share of "landslide" counties won by either party with at least 60 percent of the vote jumped from 36 percent in 2000 to 44 percent in 2004. All but a few dozen of today's congressional districts are carefully gerrymandered to give one party a clear advantage, making the congressional turnover rates of the 1950s and 1960s seem like a hula hoop or other quaint period artifact to be marveled at from behind a glass case in a modern art museum display.

Partisan segregation in America today also has a self-fulfilling quality to it. That is, as each party writes off more states and districts, and abandons them earlier in the electoral cycle, the partisan divergence widens and the electoral map becomes less fluid. Only three states flipped between 2000 and 2004: Iowa and New Mexico from Gore to Bush, and New Hampshire from Bush to Kerry. That's the fewest state changes in consecutive presidential elections since 1792, when George Washington won a second unanimous term—and in Washington's time there wasn't popular voting for president yet. The point is that anyone who predicts the sort of tectonic shifts in the coming decade that Rusher foresaw forty years ago ought to be scheduled for a CAT scan.

Still, Democrats must dream big dreams, question what is possible, and abandon the sort of retrospective thinking that has stalled their progress of late. Despite the rigidified electoral map, the partisan situation is loose enough for Democrats to construct a thin majority in the short term, then work toward a more substantial and stable majority in the longer term by systematically converting and mobilizing voters in newly targeted parts of the country. The challenge facing Democrats in January 2003 is different from the one that confronted Republicans forty years earlier in one very important respect: The incumbent party again won the presidency the next year, but George W. Bush's measly 51 percent of the vote in 2004—the lowest percentage for any reelected Republican in American history—was not the landslide Lyndon Johnson and congressional Democrats posted in 1964. The hill Democrats need to climb is much less steep today. Much as the Rusher-led Goldwater Republicans looked at the electoral terrain with fresh eyes in the early 1960s, to ascend that hill Democrats must let go of the burden of trying to recapture their old, southern-based majority and instead press ahead toward a new winning geographic majority that awaits them at the summit.

Of course, giving up the South is an awful lot of electoral turf to concede. Just because a non-southern majority is numerically possible and the best option for Democrats hardly makes it inevitable. What would a non-southern Democratic majority look like and how can it be constructed? In the remainder of the book I unfurl the blueprint for a non-southern majority. Each of the next three chapters is dedicated to one of the three interrelated components of the non-southern strategy:

This chapter charts the geographic map of the states and regions that will form that majority; the next chapter describes the demographic coalition Democrats will need to assemble within these states; finally, chapter 6 prescribes the policy platform for attracting that winning coalition. What follows, respectively, are the "where," the "who," and the "why" of the future Democratic majority.

Starting with the "where," it is essential that the Democratic campaign to build a non-southern majority be fought simultaneously on two fronts. Battles on both fronts will be fierce, and must be waged with intensity and efficiency on both the state and national levels. The first, more familiar battle will occur *within* the blue states, where Democrats need to maximize their electoral control but have yet to do so—especially in the Northeast. The second, less familiar battle will be to solidify support or convert voters in a group of pan-western swing states contained in the odd-shaped polygon formed by drawing a line west from Cleveland, Ohio, to Helena, Montana, southwest toward Las Vegas, Nevada, down to Tucson, Arizona, and back up to Cleveland. During the second half of 2005 I toured five of these states, each of which will be crucial to the Democrats' revival: Arizona, Colorado, Montana, Ohio, and Wisconsin. Before moving to terra nova, let's begin in the blue states where Democrats already do well but simply must do better.

MAKING BLUE STATES BLUER

In theory, the Northeast is the most Democratic region of the country, a notion from which Democrats ought to draw little comfort. "Throughout American history, national parties too closely identified with New England have repeatedly been marginalized. This has been the fate of the Federalist Party, the Whig Party, and the old Republican Party at its nadir, between the 1930s and the 1960s," writes Michael Lind, senior fellow at the New America Foundation. "And it is the fate that threatens the Democratic Party today—unless it takes conscious and aggressive steps to constitute itself once again as a regionally diverse coalition of interests that can become a majority party."

Lind's observation, though astute, does not mean Democrats should abandon New England and their northeastern base. Quite the opposite, in fact: They must *maximize* their electoral control of the Northeast, yet not allow themselves to be defined by, or confined to, the region. As the recent, highly sanitized Republican conventions have made abundantly clear, this dominate-without-being-defined-by approach is precisely the regional posture the GOP takes toward its southern base. The Democrats, however, are unfairly burdened with the label of being a northeastern party when, in fact, their domination of the region is overstated.

Much of this misperception is the by-product of recent presidential elections. In the dozen states comprising New England, the Atlantic seaboard and northern Appalachia, the Democrats have lost only three times in forty-eight attempts during the past four presidential elections. In both 1992 and 1996, Clinton carried all twelve states; in 2000, Gore carried ten of twelve, losing New Hampshire and West Virginia; and four years later, Kerry took back New Hampshire to make it eleven. Moreover, some of the largest victory margins posted by these three Democratic nominees came in the Northeast. The six states where the Clinton-Gore ticket increased its victory margins the most between 1992 and 1996 were, in order: Massachusetts (+14 percent), Maine (+12.8 percent), Rhode Island (+12.7 percent), New Jersey (+10.7 percent), Connecticut (+10.6 percent), and New Hampshire (+10.4 percent). Yet Democrats have made almost no progress expanding their down-ballot control over the Northeast, specifically by eliminating as many as possible moderate Republicans in Congress and electing more Democratic governors.

Congress

The Democrats control sixteen of the twenty-four northeastern senators, but their only net "gain" since 2001 is the party defection of former Republican James Jeffords of Vermont, who often votes with the Democrats but stubbornly remains an Independent. Democratic senators surely appreciate the thoughtful spirit of bipartisan compromise that Jeffords and Republican moderates like Rhode Island's Lincoln Chafee or Maine's Olympia Snowe bring to the Senate; in strictly ideological or policy terms, Democrats would rather negotiate with these familiar, if sometimes unpredictable centrists than, say, a reliably conservative newcomer like South Carolina Republican Jim DeMint. Chafee made headlines in the final weeks of the 2004 campaign when he said he would cast a write-in vote for President Bush's father, causing some to speculate that he might leave the Republican caucus and join Jeffords. (He didn't.)

But no matter how these moderate Republicans voted on the Iraq war or the Federal Marriage Amendment, the first vote they cast when a new Congress is convened every other January is for Senate majority leader. *Any* Democratic senator is preferable, even to those more palatable, moderate opponents derided by conservatives as "Republicans in Name Only." Pennsylvania's Rick Santorum is arguably the most ideologically misplaced senator of the entire region. Should Santorum survive his 2006 reelection—as his more liberal state counterpart and fellow Republican, Arlen Specter, did in 2004—and should Democrats also fail to unseat Chafee, the election cycle will rightly be judged a failure for New York's Chuck Schumer, chair of the Democratic Senatorial Campaign Committee.

Democratic control of northeastern House seats has also stagnated. During the past four years, the Democrats netted three seats. But these gains are mostly attributable to the fact that the region lost five districts after the 2000 reapportionment, with Democrats dropping one seat (down from fifty-nine to fifty-eight) while Republicans lost four (forty to thirty-six). Though much attention has been paid to the evaporating *number* of northeastern seats—declining from 122 to 95 as a result of the last four reapportionments—few have noticed that the Democratic *share* of seats is no higher than it was four decades ago. In fact, some will be surprised to learn from Table 4.1 that the Democratic share of House seats today (62 percent) is less than what it was in the late 1960s when the Republicans were just beginning to transform into a southern-based party—and this, despite the fact that 1968 Democratic nominee Hubert Humphrey carried fewer northeastern states (eight) than Clinton, Gore, or Kerry did. Although Republicans control a greater share of House seats (63 percent) and a much greater share of Senate seats (82 percent) in the South today than Democrats do in the

Table 4.1

Partisan Share of Northeastern House Seats, 1968 versus 2004

State	1968		2004	
	Dem	*Rep*	*Dem*	*Rep*
Connecticut	5	1	2	3
Delaware	0	1	0	1
Maine	2	0	2	0
Maryland	5	3	6	2
Massachusetts	8	4	10	0
New Hampshire	0	2	0	2
New Jersey	9	6	7	6
New York	27	14	20	9
Pennsylvania	14	13	7	12
Rhode Island	2	0	2	0
Vermont	0	1	1*	0
West Virginia	5	0	2	1
Total	**77**	**45**	**59***	**36**
Percentage	(63%)	(37%)	(62%)	(38%)

Tabulated from data maintained by the Clerk of the House of Representatives.

* For purposes of visual clarity, Vermont's Bernie Sanders is counted as a Democrat.

Northeast, the GOP is much less frequently depicted by the media as a southern-based party. If talk-show conservatives and Republican presidential candidates are going to malign Democrats as a bunch of northeastern liberals anyway, the party may as well control at least 70 percent of the region's congressional seats.

This task is not as difficult as it may seem. *The Cook Political Report*—namesake of Washington's preeminent election handicapper, Charlie Cook—publishes a "partisan voting index" (PVI) for all U.S. House districts based on district-level presidential voting. Republican-voting districts have a positive score, Democrats a negative score, with higher absolute values indicating more partisan districts. In the extremes, for example, Utah Republican Chris Cannon's 3rd District is the most Republican (PVI = +26.2), while José Serrano's 16th District in the Bronx is the most Democratic (-43.4). Not surprising, the PVI score in the vast majority of districts (381 of 435) matches the partisanship of its House member—i.e., positive scores for Republican congressmen, negative for Democrats.

The remaining fifty-four districts—the fewest in the past half century—are far more interesting because these are the ticket-splitters: twenty-nine have +PVIs with a Democratic House member, with twenty-five the other way around. Of those twenty-nine House Democrats from Republican-leaning presidential districts, sixteen are in the South—confirmation that some Democrats are still capable of winning in southern districts that vote Republican for president. But Democrats have essentially maxed out in Dixie with their combination of race-gerrymandered seats held by members of the congressional Black and Hispanic caucuses, plus a handful of white conservatives. What's worse, those sixteen survivors are the most obvious candidates for national Republicans to target as part of their ongoing campaign to rid the South entirely of white Democrats. In handicapping the 2006 midterms, *Hotline* editor Chuck Todd lists seven endangered House Democrats—four of whom are southerners, including Georgians Jim Marshall and John Barrow. If they must invest in Dixie, the Democrats' main priority should be defending these members.

By contrast, notice how few vulnerable Republicans there are in the South. Table 4.2 lists fifty-nine Republican incumbents who represent those twenty-five Democratic leaning districts (-PVIs), plus another thirty-four members from narrowly Republican districts (+PVIs < 3.0). The regional breakdown is astounding. If Kentucky and Oklahoma are included with the eleven former Confederate states, a mere eight of the ninety-one Republicans in these thirteen southern and border states are potentially vulnerable—and half of them are Floridians. Amazingly, twenty-five of the thirty-six GOP House incumbents who ran unopposed in 2004 were southerners.

Why are southern Republicans so electorally secure? Gerrymandering is a key reason, but Republican party-line voting is also on the rise. Previous generations of southerners voted Republican in presidential elections but still split their tickets often enough to elect Democrats to

Congress and to state and local offices. Southerners today are more in-clined to cast party-line ballots, thereby reducing the number of vul-nerable Republicans in Congress and imperiling most of the South's conservative Democrats. Indeed, upon their deaths or voluntary retire-ments or bids for other office, those Democrats not already targeted for defeat have been steadily replaced by Republicans. The result, ob-serves Capitol Hill reporter Jeffrey McMurray, is the virtual extinction of southern white congressional Democrats:

Look around Congress these days and you'll find few conservative Democrats in the mold of the late Sen. Howell Heflin or Rep. Tom Bevill. Those who remain are almost as likely to represent the Mid-west or Great Plains as the once-solid South . . . According to *Con-gressional Observer Publications,* only one current House member voted against his party at least a third of the time last year. That was Democratic Rep. Collin Peterson of Minnesota . . . In 1998, there were 13 in that category, including eight Southerners, and three of them opposed Democratic leaders more than half the time.

A perfect example of this replacement phenomenon was the sudden, tragic death in March 2001 of Virginia's Norm Sisisky, a nine-term con-servative Democrat from the Norfolk area whose seat was promptly filled by Republican Randy Forbes, who narrowly won the special elec-tion to replace Sisisky but has easily won reelection twice since. Vir-ginia has elected two consecutive Democratic governors, and yet the eleven-member House delegation has eight Republicans to just three Democrats.

Table 4.2
Potentially Vulnerable Republican House Districts

State	Member	PVI	State	Member	PVI
Northeast (24)			Midwest (20)		
Connecticut 2	Simmons	-7.6	Illinois 6	Hyde*	2.9
Connecticut 4	Shays	-5.4	Illinois 10	Kirk	-3.6
Connecticut 5	Johnson	-3.7	Illinois 11	Weller	1.1

State	Member	PVI	State	Member	PVI
Northeast (24)			**Midwest (20)**		
Delaware At-large	Castle	-6.5	Iowa 1	Nussle*	-4.8
New Hampshire 1	Bradley	0.1	Iowa 2	Leach	-6.9
New Hampshire 2	Bass	-2.7	Iowa 4	Latham	-0.4
New Jersey 2	Lobiondo	-4.0	Michigan 6	Upton	2.3
New Jersey 3	Saxton	-3.3	Michigan 7	Schwarz	2.5
New Jersey 4	Smith	0.9	Michigan 8	Rogers	1.9
New Jersey 7	Ferguson	0.6	Michigan 9	Knollenberg	0.1
New York 3	King	-2.1	Michigan 11	McCotter	1.2
New York 13	Fossella	-0.8	Minnesota 1	Gutknecht	0.9
New York 19	Kelly	1.5	Minnesota 2	Kline	2.7
New York 20	Sweeney	2.5	Minnesota 3	Ramstad	0.5
New York 23	McHugh	0.2	Ohio 1	Chabot	0.5
New York 24	Boehlert*	0.6	Ohio 3	Turner	2.9
New York 25	Walsh	-3.4	Ohio 12	Tiberi	0.7
Pennsylvania 3	English	1.6	Ohio 14	LaTourette	2.2
Pennsylvania 4	Hart	2.6	Ohio 15	Pryce	1.1
Pennsylvania 6	Gerlach	-2.2	Wisconsin 1	Ryan	2.2
Pennsylvania 7	Weldon	-3.6	**South/Border (8)**		
Pennsylvania 8	Fitzpatrick	-3.4	Florida 8	Keller	3.0
Pennsylvania 15	Dent	-1.6	Florida 10	Young	-1.1
Pennsylvania 18	Murphy	2.2	Florida 16	Foley	2.4
West/Southwest (7)			Florida 22	Shaw	-3.6
Arizona 1	Renzi	2.2	Georgia 11	Gingrey	2.7
Arizona 8	Kolbe*	1.4	Kentucky 3	Northup	-2.4
California 11	Pombo	3.0	North Carolina 8	Hayes	3.0
Colorado 7	Beauprez*	-2.3	Virginia 11	Davis	0.6
Nevada 3	Porter	-1.1			
New Mexico 1	Wilson	-2.4	
Washington 8	Reichert	-2.3	

Negative PVIs are Democratic-voting districts; positive PVIs are Republican-voting. Asterisks indicate open seats created by retirements.

Turning to the rest of the country, Table 4.2 reveals where the Republican-held seats that vote either Democratic or narrowly Republican in presidential elections are located: in the Northeast and the Midwest. Setting aside the Midwest momentarily, notice that the Northeast has fourteen Republicans from Democratic-voting districts and another ten from marginally Republican districts. New Jersey, New York, and Pennsylvania alone account for eighteen of these twenty-four members. Of New York's nine Republican-held House seats, in either 2000 or 2004 Bush carried only one of them by more than 55 percent of the vote district-wide. In Connecticut, several handicappers list Chris Shays and Rob Simmons as possible 2006 casualties.

Roll Call's Louis Jacobson correctly pegs Pennsylvania—a swing state with twelve Republican members to only seven Democrats, despite the fact that both Gore and Kerry won it—as the most intriguing state for competitive House races in 2006. It is the only state with four Republican congressmen—Charlie Dent, Jim Gerlach, Michael Fitzpatrick, and Curt Weldon—elected from districts Kerry won in 2004. Gerlach will again face Democrat Lois Murphy, the same woman he barely defeated in 2004 in a district he won with just 51 percent of the vote in each of the past two elections. Meanwhile, Fitzpatrick and Weldon are among a handful of Republican congressional incumbents likely to be challenged in the general election this fall by Democratic nominees who are military veterans. "While the Congressional realignment in southwestern Pennsylvania was mostly carried to fruition by the GOP-led redistricting after the 2000 Census, the Philadelphia area remains ripe for further Democratic gains," writes Jacobson. "That accounts for much of Pennsylvania's No. 1 ranking on our list."

Based on recent reelection results and the quality of their 2006 opponents, some Republican incumbents are obviously more at risk than others. But what's equally obvious is that Democrats must set their sights first on the Northeast during the 2006 midterms.

Governors

Governors are an even more glaring example of Democratic underperformance and disappointment in the Northeast. Republicans currently control seven of the twelve northeastern governorships, and their control is neither new nor fleeting: Remarkably, the GOP has held the office for at least eight of the past twelve years in seven northeastern states. Republicans Jodi Rell of Connecticut and Jim Douglas of Vermont are among the nation's most popular governors, and New York's George Pataki won three consecutive terms in a state with a significant Democratic registration advantage. As the expected Republican nominee in 2006, Hall of Fame Pittsburgh Steelers wide receiver Lynn Swann may spoil Pennsylvania Democrat Ed Rendell's reelection bid.

Democrats expect New York attorney general Eliot Spitzer to recapture Albany in 2006, and Maryland's Bob Ehrlich is an extremely vulnerable Republican up for reelection. Nevertheless, the past decade has been very disappointing for Democratic gubernatorial candidates in the region. "Republicans who win statewide office in the Northeast . . . most often hold views clearly at odds with the national GOP," writes Trinity College's Kevin J. McMahon. "Typically, successful Republicans in the Northeast prevail in statewide races by promising to keep the lid on spending, taxes, and crime while also proclaiming a liberal attitude on issues like abortion and gay rights." That many of these Republicans win by distancing themselves from the national Republican Party—in the mold of Christine Todd Whitman, New Jersey's popular former governor—is about as much consolation to Democrats as having Senator Chafee cast his futile vote against confirming Judge Samuel Alito to the Supreme Court.

Now compare the underwhelming partisan situation for northeastern Democrats with what's happened in the other solidly blue region in presidential elections: the Pacific Coast states of California, Oregon, and Washington, plus Hawaii. The reason there are so few vulnerable Republicans listed in Table 4.2 from these four states is that Democrats have already done a good job of maximizing electoral control there. The Democrats boast seven of the eight U.S. senators and hold 66 percent of U.S. House seats, including thirty-three of California's fifty-three-seat delegation, both Hawaii seats, and strong majorities in Oregon (5D/1R) and Washington (6D/3R). The Democratic duos of Dianne Feinstein and Barbara Boxer in California, and Washington's Patty Murray and Maria Cantwell, are just two of three cases in Senate history of two women representing the same state simultaneously. (Republicans Susan Collins and Olympia Snowe, the third duo, currently represent Maine.) California's seventeen female House Democrats are almost as many as the twenty-three *total* House Republican women nationwide, and the female-led California delegation includes minority leader Nancy Pelosi—the highest-ranking woman in the history of congressional party leadership.

The Democrats still have some work to do in state-level races in the Pacific Coast states. After a contentious recount, in 2004 Washington Democratic governor Christine Gregoire won the closest election in state history to give the Democrats six straight gubernatorial wins since 1984. Washington State Democrats have a solid house majority and a newly won, albeit thin senate majority. Although Oregon's Ted Kulongoski is considered one of the more vulnerable Democrats up for reelection in 2006, he is also the fourth consecutive Democrat to hold that office, dating back to 1986. Republicans control the Oregon house, but Democrats broke a 15–15 seat tie in 2004 to become the majority party in the senate. Mirroring the mid-1980s partisan switch in governors, after voting Republican in all four presidential elections from 1972 and 1984, Oregon and Washington backed the Democratic nominee in each of the previous five elections. In a 2002 surprise, Linda Lingle became the first Republican elected governor in Hawaii since 1958—but the Aloha State has not voted Republican for president since 1984.

California is similar to its Pacific neighbors in presidential voting, but strikingly different in statewide elections. Republicans George Deukmejian and Pete Wilson together won four straight elections in the 1980s and 1990s before Democrat Gray Davis snapped the GOP's streak in 1998. In a bizarre political turn of events after his 2002 reelection, Davis was recalled by voters in 2003 and replaced with movie star Arnold Schwarzenegger. Schwarzenegger's initial popularity has plummeted since his unlikely ascension, however. If Democrats can terminate the Terminator, with solid majorities in both state legislative chambers, they can reassert unified state-level control in 2006.

Electoral Efficiency

Becoming a majority party requires Democrats to not only minimize losses in places where Republicans dominate, but maximize their electoral grip on the states and regions where Democrats have an advantage in partisan registration, presidential voting, or both. The Republican strategy of systematically targeting red-state moderate Democrats has succeeded, and Democrats must conduct a similar purge in the blue states by putting to the fire the feet of every Republican elected from Democratic-leaning districts or states. Persuading southern voters who gave George W. Bush double-digit statewide victories to cross party lines to elect Democrats to Congress, governor, and state legislatures is a lot to expect. But it is unacceptable that Democrats do not dominate down-ballot more in states where Clinton, Gore, and Kerry all prevailed, often by wide margins. Put another way, there are plenty of reasons why Senator Jeff Sessions wins comfortably in Alabama, but absolutely none why his fellow Republican, Rick Santorum, ought to feel safe in Pennsylvania.

Building an electoral majority in this era of divided, calcified partisanship also requires a heightened attention to intrastate partisan efficiency. For example, having a scattered majority of the fifty governors is always good, but controlling twenty-four state houses in key Democratic-leaning or swing states might be preferable. It mattered little to John Kerry in 2004 that there were Democratic governors in some rather unlikely places, like Kansas or Wyoming, or that his own state's governor, Mitt Romney, was a Republican. What *did* matter is that in Ohio, the most pivotal swing state of the 2004 presidential election cycle, Democrats didn't have a single statewide elected official, were the minority party in both chambers of the state legislature, and held only six of the state's eighteen U.S. House seats and neither of its Senate seats. Perhaps Kerry never had a chance to overcome the field plan strategist Karl Rove and the Bush-Cheney team set into motion three years before Kerry even secured the nomination. Yet once Kerry arrived in Ohio, and despite the millions of dollars his own campaign and the constellation of left-liberal "527" groups eventually spent there, no amount of resources could substitute for the one priceless commodity Republicans enjoyed: a far larger and more credible fleet of in-state party surrogates to promote the president's reelection, raise money for the highly organized and well-funded state Republican Party, and generate legions of in-state canvassers and other volunteers. *New York*

Times Magazine's Matt Bai described the Bush-Cheney campaign's precinct-by-precinct field model as a sophisticated electoral version of an Amway pyramid marketing program, and concluded after the election that out-of-state Democratic canvassers brought into Ohio by America Coming Together and other groups were poor substitutes for the more native and organic volunteer operation the GOP assembled. Having a greater number of elected Democrats across the state might have rectified this imbalance.

A variety of new national organizations, most notably Progressive Majority, have dedicated themselves to focusing on the election of liberals and progressives to state and local offices. These are inspired grassroots programs that will produce more local and state Democratic elected officials and provide ballast for the party in future "up-ballot" races for governor, Congress, and president. The tragedy for Democrats is that these organizations were not founded and funded a decade ago.

DIAMOND IN THE ROUGH

It's difficult to look at the 1976 presidential electoral map without doing a double take. Former Georgia governor Jimmy Carter carried every southern state but Virginia, yet lost five northeastern states. Meanwhile, President Gerald Ford won the Pacific Coast states, key pockets of the Midwest, plus states like Connecticut and New Jersey that vote solidly Democratic today. The 1976 election was the New Deal's last gasp, a throwback election to a bygone partisan era and a Democratic coalition that no longer exists.

For all the attention paid to the territory Democrats have ceded since Carter's victory, often forgotten is how much terrain Republicans have surrendered. California, Oregon, and Washington were once the western backbone of the Republican Party, but now vote Democratic in presidential elections. Many of the Republican-leaning northeastern and midwestern states also tilt, slightly or in some cases decidedly, to the Democrats. With the South beyond reach for Democrats for the foreseeable future, what remains up for grabs are a group of swing states in the pan-western polygon formed by connecting Ohio, Montana, Nevada, and New Mexico. In the spirit of optimism, I'll call this region the *Democratic Diamond*—or "the Diamond," for short.

Not every state contained within the Diamond is realistically in play. A very Republican Idaho is generally out of bounds, and Utah and Wyoming remain snowball's-chance-in-hellish for Democratic presidential nominees and most of the party's candidates elsewhere down the ballot. Though Wyoming's current governor is a Democrat, neither Utah nor Idaho has had a Democratic chief executive in the past ten years. All six state legislative chambers in these three states are controlled by overwhelming Republican majorities, and all six U.S. senators are Republicans. In fact, 1970 was the last year either Wyoming or Utah elected a Democrat to the U.S. Senate, and the party's drought goes back almost as far (1974) in Idaho. Nebraska, Oklahoma, and both Dakotas—all of which have Republican governors and solid Republican state legislative majorities—are tough but not impossible states for Democrats.

The rest of the states show some promise, and many that were once reliably Republican are now very much up for grabs. The Midwest continues to be the country's most competitive region. The burgeoning southwestern states have become more "purple" in the past decade. Even certain pockets of the Mountain West are poised for a Democratic renaissance. After a general overview of the political-electoral situation in the Midwest and interior West, I tour through five states that will be crucial to a future Democratic majority: Arizona, Colorado, Montana, Ohio, and Wisconsin.

MIDWEST: THE BATTLEGROUND

The Midwest has long served as the critical crossroads of American politics and culture. Until the rapid expansion of statehood in the second half of the nineteenth century, what is now called the Midwest was still regarded as "the West." Hardened by cold weather, blessed with Great Lakes shipping routes, and anchored by Chicago's meatpacking mecca, the region has produced some of the nation's most colorful leaders and dynamic political movements. Indeed, the home of America's auto in-

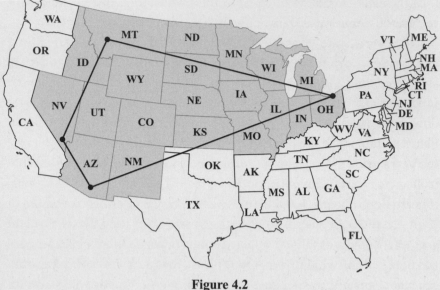

Figure 4.2
The Democratic Diamond

dustry and dairyland berthed William Jennings Bryan's farmer populism, Joseph McCarthy's anticommunism, and Paul Wellstone's fiery liberalism. The Midwest has some of the nation's best-performing public school systems, and its many prestigious state universities have graduated scads of notable American politicians, including President Gerald Ford and a majority of the region's current U.S. senators. The Midwest produces smart politics and smart politicians, and any party that ignores what's happening in the region is just plain foolish.

Lately, globalization has debilitated midwestern economies, forcing natives young and old to abandon their factories and families for new-growth job markets and warmer retirement locales. The relative rate of population decline during the past hundred years has been greater in the Midwest than the Northeast. As indicated in Table 4.3, in 1904 the dozen Midwest states cast thirty-seven more electoral votes than they do now, and every state save Michigan has fewer House seats and electoral votes today than it did a century ago. Notwithstanding its economic woes and stagnating population base, the Midwest continues to leverage sufficient political clout to retain its reputation as the most crucial region in American politics. Between Iowa's January caucuses and Ohio's role as quadrennial November bellwether, the Midwest usually has the first and last say in presidential elections. No Republican has ever won the White House without carrying Ohio, and the only Democrats in the past century to win without the Buckeye State are John F. Kennedy in 1960 and Franklin Roosevelt in 1944. Had Al Gore spent more time and resources in Ohio during the late stages of his 2000 campaign, "hanging chad" might still be a term familiar today only to election board supervisors.

Along with Ohio—site of the most ferocious, most sophisticated ground and media war in American campaign history—Iowa, Michigan, Minnesota, and Wisconsin were among the dozen target states in 2004, and all five were among the nine states decided by less than 4 percent. (Kerry edged Bush by about twelve thousand votes in Wisconsin, and Bush flipped Iowa by fewer than ten thousand votes.) In fact, the Bush campaign's backup plan for getting to 270 electoral votes in

Table 4.3
Midwest as Presidential Battleground

State	Electors		Recent Presidential Elections				
	1904	2004	1988	1992	1996	2000	2004
Illinois	27	21	D	D	D	D	D
Indiana	15	11	R	R	R	R	R
Iowa	13	7	D	D	D	D	R
Kansas	10	6	R	R	R	R	R
Michigan	14	17	R	D	D	D	D
Minnesota	11	9	D	D	D	D	D
Missouri	18	11	R	D	D	R	R
Nebraska	8	5	R	R	R	R	R
North Dakota	4	3	R	R	R	R	R
Ohio	23	20	R	D	D	R	R
South Dakota	4	3	R	R	R	R	R
Wisconsin	13	10	D	D	D	D	D
Totals	160	123	8R/4D	5R/7D	5R/7D	7R/5D	8R/4D

case Kerry somehow won Ohio was to snag New Mexico's five electors along with the seventeen from two midwestern states: Iowa and Wisconsin. The GOP succeeded in the first two states and, if not for the field wizardry of Democratic strategist Teresa Vilmain, might have won Wisconsin, too.

There is partisan diversity within the Midwest, of course. Plains states like Kansas, Indiana, Nebraska, and the Dakotas are more conservative, and have voted for the Republican candidate in every election since 1968. On the other hand, Minnesota and Wisconsin in the "upper" Midwest are the region's two most liberal states. (Thanks to Walter Mondale's home-field advantage in 1984 and the state's Democratic-Farmer-Labor Party tradition, progressive Minnesota is the only state Democrats have carried in each of the last eight presidential elections.) Overall, the region's 2004 exit polls most closely approximated the national results, making the Midwest the closest thing to a national microcosm. Michael Lind summarizes the region's importance: "For Democrats today, the Midwest is the key to the White House, for the same reason it was crucial a century ago: Its location at the confluence of the major cultural regions of the United States means that its politicians must appeal to more than one tradition."

Congress

Given the general parity within the region, the Democrats have done surprisingly well in securing midwestern Senate seats. They presently command a 14–10 advantage and boast at least one of the two U.S. senators in every state except Kansas, Missouri, and Ohio—and in Ohio, Republican incumbent Mike DeWine faces a much tougher reelection fight in 2006 than his twenty-point drubbing of political legacy Ted Celeste in 2000. In 2004 the Republicans finally unseated then-Senate minority leader Tom Daschle of South Dakota, and are hoping to knock off Democrat Tim Johnson there next. Conversely, to the continued frustration of national Republicans, both of North Dakota's senators, Kent Conrad and Byron Dorgan, are Democrats. In 2006, Michigan's Debbie Stabenow, a first-term Democrat, should survive her first reelection. No regional roll call would be complete without mentioning Illinois's Barack Obama, the Senate's lone African American, and

Indiana's Evan Bayh. Obama became an immediate national star after his 2004 win, and the former two-term governor and son of Birch Bayh is likely to run for president in 2008. If Bayh is not the nominee, he and Obama will surely be on the short list of potential vice presidential running mates.

What's most bizarre about the partisan control of midwestern Senate seats is the fact that Republicans hold two seats that might otherwise be in Democratic hands were it not for the tragic plane crashes that killed Minnesota incumbent Paul Wellstone in 2002 and challenger Mel Carnahan in Missouri in 2000. Both crashes came just days before the election, paving the way for Republican Norm Coleman to replace Wellstone and Republican Jim Talent to take the seat the very popular Carnahan won posthumously against incumbent John Ashcroft. In a November 2002 special election, Talent edged Jean Carnahan—the former governor's widow appointed to fill the seat for two years—by fewer than 22,000 votes, but in 2006 he will have to beat popular state auditor Claire McCaskill to win a full term. Coleman, who was trailing Wellstone on the eve of the 2002 election, will be up for re-election in 2008 and should be considered one of the Democrats' top targets that cycle in this blue-leaning state. Along with DeWine's Ohio seat, Democrats will unseat all three of these incumbent Midwest Republicans only if 2006 is a landslide. But two out of three would set the table for Democrats to recapture the Senate in 2008.

The need for Midwest Democrats to expand their seat share is greater in the U.S. House, and there will be ample opportunities. Returning to Table 4.2, the region has twenty districts with potentially vulnerable House Republicans, including almost half (sixteen) of those thirty-four districts that tilt slightly Republican in presidential elections. As Charlie Cook has observed, Ohio and Michigan are prime targets, with five Republican congressmen from districts that voted narrowly for Bush. Illinois, Iowa, and Minnesota each have another three Republicans potentially at risk. Political analyst Chris Bowers tabs Iowa's open 1st District as perhaps the Democrats' "best chance at a pickup in the entire nation." After sixteen terms, Republican Henry Hyde, scourge of the Clinton impeachment era, is also retiring, opening another seat Democrats covet. Ohio's Bob Ney and Steven LaTourette have been both implicated in the widening probe involving corrupt lobbyist Jack Abramoff and his Indian tribe clients. Wisconsin's 8th District seat will be tough to swing, but incumbent Republican Mark Green's gubernatorial bid opens the kind of seat that might turn if 2006 produces a Democratic surge. Election handicapper Stuart Rothenberg lists Republican incumbents John Hostettler and Mike Sodrel of Indiana among his top ten most endangered incumbents.

Combined with the twenty-four potentially vulnerable northeastern Republicans, it is clear that the fight to recapture the House of Representatives must be waged in the dozen or so states located within the rectangle formed by New Hampshire and Delaware to the east, and Iowa and Minnesota to the west. Fittingly, Illinois Representative Rahm Emanuel, the flinty but aggressive former Clinton White House staffer leading the Democrats' campaign to retake the House in 2006, lives smack dab in the middle of this rectangle. Emanuel has promised to "minimize our defensive posture [of protecting Democratic incumbents while] maximizing our offensive posture." That's the proper spirit. What remains to be seen is who—and where—these newly offensive, Emanuel-led Democrats will target and with what candidates and resources.

Governors

Just five of the twelve midwestern governors are Democrats. Four of them—Iowa's Tom Vilsack, Illinois's Rod Blagojevich, Michigan's Jennifer Granholm, and Wisconsin's Jim Doyle—represent the more liberal states in the region, with Kathleen Sebelius of Kansas a surprise 2002 winner in a reliably Republican state. The most likely 2006 Democratic pickup is in Ohio, where Congressman Ted Strickland, a moderate Democrat from a rural district in the state's southeast Appalachian corner, will be very competitive in the race to replace the nation's least popular governor, Republican Bob Taft. Doyle and Granholm will face tough reelection battles in 2006 but should survive if there is a general tailwind for Democrats in the midterm cycle.

Increasing the number of midwestern Democratic governors will not only help the party's 2008 presidential nominee, but will give Democrats needed leverage in the redistricting battles that commence after the 2010 census, especially in Michigan and Ohio. If speculating about the post-redistricting legislative races of 2012 seems far off, consider that gubernatorial candidates who win in 2006 and are not term-limited will run for reelection in 2010 in the usually stronger position of incumbents—and winners *that* year will supervise the drawing of lines for the new state and U.S. House legislative districts for the coming decade. The fight for control over the House of Representatives in the next decade begins on November 7, 2006.

THE INTERIOR WEST: THE OPPORTUNITY

If the Midwest is the primary battleground, the states of the interior West present new opportunities for Democratic growth. This is especially true in the burgeoning Southwest, but there are increasing signs that Republicans are losing favor in parts of the Mountain West, too.

The southwestern states have been trending Democratic since the late 1980s. Although George H. W. Bush won Arizona and Nevada by more than 20 points over Michael Dukakis in 1988, his son's margins were in the low single digits. New Mexico, for example, went consecutively for Nixon twice, Ford once, Ronald Reagan twice, and the first President Bush once, before Clinton carried it twice, Gore once, and Kerry lost it narrowly. The twenty-nine combined electoral votes cast by Arizona, Colorado, Nevada, and New Mexico—all states that Clinton carried in either 1992 or 1996—are two more than Florida and two fewer than New York. As Figure 4.3 shows, the five southwestern states have been volatile but highly competitive during the past five presidential cycles.

More critical to the Democrats' national partisan calculus is the growth of the southwestern states. The 2000 reappointment added two congressional seats in Arizona, and one each in Colorado and Nevada. Since 2000, Nevada's 19.7 percent population increase makes it the fastest-growing state in the nation, Arizona (15 percent) is not far be-

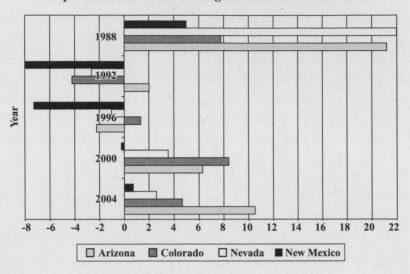

Figure 4.3
Republican Presidential Margins in Southwestern States

hind in second, and Colorado's population (7.8 percent) has grown more than half again as fast as the rest of the country (5 percent). Clark County, home of Las Vegas, is one of America's fastest-growing counties; in 1940, Clark contained less than a third of the Nevada's residents but now accounts for more than two thirds. In Arizona, Phoenix recently surged past Philadelphia into fourth place among the nation's largest cities.

The Southwest's rapid growth is fueled by migration both international and domestic. Rising Hispanic populations—especially the massive immigration of Mexican Americans—are complemented by an influx of Americans who moved from the Midwest and California to these southwestern hot spots. The full impact of the Hispanic vote has yet to be realized because Hispanics, who recently surpassed African Americans as the nation's largest ethnic minority, have a greater share of under-eighteen or voting-ineligible citizens. "The new path to the White House runs through the Latino Southwest, not the former Confederacy, especially for a Northern nominee," argue Democratic consultant Steve Cobble and former Clinton White House deputy political director Joe Velásquez. "Hope blooms as a cactus flower, not a magnolia blossom."

Congress

Three of the eight southwestern senators are Democrats, and Ken Salazar's election in Colorado was one of the party's major highlights of 2004. When Daschle's defeat the same day opened the Senate minority leader's position, Democrats tapped Nevada's Harry Reid to replace him. Since 1983, New Mexico Democrat Jeff Bingaman has served alongside Republican Pete Domenici. President Carter's son Jack will try to unseat rookie Nevada Senator John Ensign in 2006. Should the 74-year-old Domenici opt to retire in two years, there may be a chance for Democrats to snap up his seat in 2008—the same year Colorado Republican Wayne Allard, who won with just 51 percent of the vote in 2002, is next up for reelection.

In the House, Republicans hold two-thirds of the twenty-one seats in the four delegations, including 2-to-1 advantages in Nevada and New Mexico. Flustered Democrats have been gunning unsuccessfully for Republican Heather Wilson's 1st District in New Mexico; Wilson won with only 55 percent and 54 percent of the vote in her 2002 and 2004 reelections, and this time she faces her toughest foe yet: state attorney general Patricia Madrid. Nevada's newly created 3rd District, represented by Republican Jon Porter, votes narrowly Democratic in presidential elections—and Porter won his first reelection in 2004 with just 56 percent of the vote. Colorado Republican Bob Beauprez's bid for governor opens another Democratic-leaning seat the party will target in 2006. Likewise, the pending retirement of moderate Republican Jim Kolbe has made Arizona's 8th District (PVI = +1.4) a prime pickup opportunity for Democrats in 2006.

Governors and State Legislatures

The Democrats bucked national trends in 2002 by electing governors in both Arizona and New Mexico. Secretary of state Janet Napolitano won by a wisp in Arizona, while former congressman and Clinton Energy Secretary Bill Richardson posted the biggest victory margin in any New Mexico governor's race since 1964. Courtesy of his chairmanship of the 2004 Democratic National Convention, stewardship of the Democratic Governors Association, and frequent appearances on na-

tional television, Richardson—the nation's only Hispanic governor—
has a bigger national profile. But the extremely popular Napolitano has
foiled her critics with solid fiscal management and aggressive support
for educational reforms. In August 2005, the two governors made national headlines by declaring state emergencies and demanding that
the federal government do its job to secure the U.S.-Mexican border.
Both are well positioned to win reelection in 2006. Meanwhile, University of Virginia election specialist Larry Sabato considers the 2006 contest between GOP Congressman Jim Gibbons and whomever the
Democrats nominate to replace Kenny Guinn, Nevada's term-limited
Republican governor, a "toss-up" race.

Table 4.4:
Partisan Control of Southwestern States

State	Governor	State legislature		Congress	
		House	Senate	House	Senate
Arizona	Janet Napolitano (D)	63.3 R	60.0 R	6R, 2D	2R
Colorado	Bill Owens (R)	53.8 D	51.4 D	4R, 3D	Split
Nevada	Kenny Guinn (R)	61.9 D	57.1 R	2R, 1D	Split
New Mexico	Bill Richardson (D)	60.0 D	57.1 D	2R, 1D	Split

State legislative control also reflects how evenly the four southwestern states are divided. Republicans have a chokehold on the Arizona
state legislature, Democrats enjoy comfortable majorities in New Mexico, and the Nevada legislature is split, with Democrats controlling the
house and Republicans the senate. Thanks to an aggressive recruitment
program, in 2004 Democrats converted both chambers of the Colorado
legislature into thin majorities. Of these four southwestern states,
therefore, only New Mexico's governor and legislature are unified
under the same Democratic banner.

The mountain states of the interior West, plus Alaska, will be
tougher than the Southwest for Democrats to crack, but recent elections
have exposed GOP weaknesses here, too. Although Bush improved his
popular vote by 3 percent nationally, his reelection numbers dropped in

sixteen states, including ten states he won both times. All but two of these twice-carried states are west of the Mississippi River, and include not only southwestern states like Colorado and Nevada, but Alaska, Idaho, Montana, and Wyoming. This is not to suggest there is much hope in the short term for Democrats to carry Mountain states in presidential elections. (Though Clinton won Montana in 1992.) But it does suggest a certain undercurrent of dissatisfaction with the Republicans.

These currents have already swept key Democrats into office. There was not a single Democratic governor in the interior West in 2001, but in addition to Arizona's Napolitano and New Mexico's Richardson, Democrats elected Dave Freudenthal in Wyoming in 2002 and Brian Schweitzer in Montana in 2004. Schweitzer's victory sent shockwaves across the country, drawing reporters from a variety of eastern media outlets westward to find out how he won in one of the reddest presidential states in America. If the Democrats can capture Colorado's open seat in 2006, it will be possible to run a finger down the map along the eastern edge of the Rocky Mountains from Canada to Mexico without touching a Republican-governed state.

As for the Senate, the big news may again come from Montana, where Republican Conrad Burns is knee-deep in the Abramoff scandal and already running neck-and-neck with Jon Tester, the Democrat trying to unseat him. Even in Alaska there may be hope for Democrats in the medium term: Political legacy Lisa Murkowski, who was appointed in 2002 by her father to the Senate seat he resigned to become governor, narrowly won election to a full term in 2004 and will be a ripe target in her reelection. If the unbeatable octogenarian Ted Stevens decides to retire in 2008, Democrats will have a decent shot at his seat as well. Meanwhile, the big news is that popular former Democratic governor Tony Knowles, who lost to Lisa Murkowski in 2004, will challenge her faltering father in his 2006 reelection for governor. "With the Northeast, South, Plains and West Coast states increasingly set in their electoral ways, and with the Midwest becoming a harder sell each year, the shifting demographics of the interior West, long written off as a Republican bastion, are starting to look more attractive," writes John Yewell, a regular *Salt Lake Tribune* commentator.

In 1992, Bill Clinton peered across America's western landscape and envisioned new possibilities. With seven western Democratic governors in tow, Clinton barnstormed through several western states in late October. "We want to win the West," Clinton told a crowd during a stop in Pueblo, Colorado. "The Republican Party has taken you for granted too long." The Republicans still do and it's long past time for Democrats to start making the GOP pay for its repeated neglect.

FIVE STATES, FIVE FATES

During the last six months of 2005 I traveled to five states—Arizona, Colorado, Montana, Ohio, and Wisconsin—that will be critical to the Democrats' non-southern majority. I interviewed politicians, party operatives, pollsters, and pundits to get a sense of the challenges and opportunities facing Democrats in each state.

The states provide an interesting political-electoral mix. Heading into the 2006 midterm elections, three have Democratic governors, two have Republicans. Three have Republican majorities in both state legislative chambers, Colorado has Democratic majorities, and but for the deadlocked state house the Democrats would have both chambers in Montana. Only one state—Ohio—has unified control of all the branches, and the rock-bottom popularity of Republican Governor Bob Taft threatens to undo the Republicans' lock on the Buckeye State.

The states' congressional delegations—and thus, their electoral prizes—range from at-large Republican Congressman Denny Rehberg and Montana's three electoral votes to Ohio's eighteen-member delegation and twenty electors. Arizona and Ohio have two Republican U.S. senators, Wisconsin has two Democrats, with Colorado and Montana split one each. In total, there are a combined thirty-three Republicans and only nineteen Democrats in their five congressional delegations, a much more disparate ratio than nationally. Bush carried four of the five states in both his election and reelection, losing Wisconsin twice. While the president's winning margins increased in Arizona and Colorado, they shrunk in Ohio and Montana, and his loss in Wisconsin was slightly worse in 2004 than the 5,708 votes by which Al Gore edged him in 2000. These five states, then, present something close to a microcosm for the Diamond: a mixed partisan bag with a decided, but not insurmountable Republican advantage. In keeping with the spirit of the book's broader theme, I start in Ohio and move west and south from there.

Heartbreak in Ohio

In no state have Democrats experienced greater grief and disappointment during the past ten years than Ohio. Losing statewide in Utah or South Carolina is one thing; being completely shut out from statewide elected office, both state and federal, while holding a meager six of the state's eighteen U.S. House seats, is another. There's no way to sugarcoat matters: During the past decade, Ohio Democrats have been an embarrassment and a failure.

The party's troubles in Ohio began with the back-to-back retirements in 1994 and 1998 of veteran Democratic U.S. senators John Glenn and Howard Metzenbaum. When Metzenbaum yielded his seat in January 1999 to then-departing Republican Governor George Voinovich, the Democrats had been already out of the governor's office for Voinovich's two terms and were watching Republican Bob Taft succeed Voinovich for what turned out to be another eight years. Democratic consultant and former Glenn adviser Dale Butland recalls the void created in the mid-1990s by the Glenn and Metzenbaum departures. "In retrospect, that was the mistake that the [state] party made. We did not build a farm team, so when they retired, we didn't have anyone there to step in," says Butland. "As a consequence, the walls came tumbling down."

The Democrats' tumble is particularly galling because Ohio—home to more American presidents than any other state—is not a place where Republicans have a clear partisan advantage. In fact, one pollster who knows Ohio well says that, despite the recent run of Republican governors and other statewide officials, the state remains the partisan and political bellwether it has always been:

Ohio is like the epicenter of what's going on in the country, but what's going on in Cleveland and Chillicothe are totally different. Because Ohio has six different media markets, and because it doesn't have a single dominant urban media market, it's difficult to get a handle on the state, and there's a lot of cultural and economic disparity within the state. Winning in Ohio forces you to win in urban, suburban, and rural districts.

Unfortunately, the Democrats don't seem to be winning the way they should in any part of the state, and no matter the media market. "Ohio Democrats have shown an extraordinary capacity to screw up," says John C. Green, director of the University of Akron's Ray C. Bliss Institute of Applied Politics. "The state Democratic Party basically collapsed in the 1990s and they've had no end of trouble since then. Here in Ohio it has been very difficult to unify the Democratic coalition, to get the labor unions, the environmentalists, the civil rights community, the black community—all on the same page."

The tide may finally be turning, however—if only because the Republicans are screwing up worse. By mid-2006 Bush's net approval rating among the states he carried in 2004 was lowest in Ohio, and the fact that the White House is no longer concerned about the political situation on the ground in Ohio should worry state Republicans in 2006 and 2008. As the nation's only governor with an approval rating in the teens, Taft has become an even bigger liability for Republicans. Meanwhile, DeWine is ranked among the least popular senators in the country, and he has so angered the National Rifle Association and Gun Owners of America that they gave him an "F" for his Senate voting record. The sad irony for Ohio Democrats is that their most encouraging news comes from state Republicans, 65 percent of whom in a poll earlier this year agreed that Ohio is going in the wrong direction.

The Democrats will have strong candidates at the top of the 2006 ticket. Seven-term, Akron-area Representative Sherrod Brown is running against DeWine for Senate, and fellow congressman Ted Strickland from southeast Ohio is running for the open governor's seat. Though their politics and voting records are similar, Brown and Strickland come from different parts of the state and will face different challenges. Strickland wins in one of the state's most rural, conservative House districts. Stir in the Democratic base vote in Columbus and Cleveland, and Strickland's appeal to small-city and rural voters should serve him well in his expected matchup against Ken Blackwell, the African-American secretary of state likely to be the Republican nominee. "For a Democrat to win in Ohio, he or she has definitely got to win down south, and has definitely got to win rural counties," says Paul Hackett, the Iraq war veteran who made national headlines in 2005 by almost winning the special election in Ohio's 2nd District in the southwest corner of the state.

State Democratic Party communications director Brian Rothenberg disagrees. "The fact of the matter is that Bush gained more votes in the urban counties than the rural counties, so you can't go by county-level won-loss outcomes," says Rothenberg. "He closed his deficits significantly in blue-collar Catholic areas like Parma. In some white-collar suburban areas, like Solon [Cuyahoga County], Kerry actually did better. It's real simple to say we have to go to these rural counties, but it's not correct." As a comparison of the 2000 and 2004 presidential results attests, however, the impact of the rural counties cannot be discounted. The top four jurisdictions where Bush's vote share increased most—and seven of the top ten—were small counties clustered along the western border Ohio shares with Indiana: Shelby (up 5.8 percent), Van Wert (+4.9 percent), Mercer (+4.8 percent), Darke (+4.3 percent), Miami (+3.3 percent), Auglaize (+3 percent), and Paulding (+2.6 percent). Combined, Bush mined 24,578 more votes from these seven counties in 2004, while Kerry gained just 2,426 over Gore's 2000 totals. The net Bush gain of 22,152 votes may seem a pittance, but these votes amounted to almost one-fifth of Bush's statewide margin—even though these seven counties combined cast just 3 percent of all votes statewide. Not surprising, the seven counties are represented by Republican congressmen: Michael Oxley, Paul Gillmor, and John Boehner, who was chosen in 2006 to replace Tom DeLay as House minority leader. Wapakoneta, Sidney, Piqua, and other small cities scattered along Interstate 75 thus played a big role in Bush's reelection. Because the demographics in this part of the state are more akin to neighboring Indiana than the big cities and neighboring suburbs of Cleveland or Columbus, it's only a slight exaggeration to say the Bush campaign won Ohio in part by figuring out a way to win Indiana twice.

In the Senate race Brown may have a tougher time than Strickland,

and for two reasons. First, no matter how badly DeWine has struggled, as an incumbent he will be well financed. Second, Brown will have to prove he can win outside the northeastern portion of the state anchored by his Akron-based, west Cleveland suburban district. "Everything in Ohio has fallen short [for Democrats]," shrugs Brown. "The Republicans have had a lot more money, that's the first thing. Second, they have had the power of incumbency. Third, we've had a particularly inept Democratic Party." But Brown predicts 2006 will be remembered as the year Democrats turned things around. "You're going to see better recruitment and more money, and we're going to have good candidates for governor and Senate." It's hard to imagine the situation getting any worse. At this point, the only direction Democrats can go is up.

Wisconsin Twice by a Whisker

Americans may associate Wisconsin with bundled-up Cheeseheads rooting heartily for their beloved Green Bay Packers on the windswept "frozen tundra" of historic Lambeau Field, but lately the turf most frozen in Wisconsin is the partisan playing field. Wisconsin was the third closest state in the 2000 presidential race and the closest in 2004, with Gore and Kerry each winning it by a few thousand votes. Ohio and Florida get more attention because of their bigger electoral prizes, but their state governments are uniformly Republican whereas Wisconsin is divided between a Republican legislature and a Democratic governor. Even Wisconsin's eight-member U.S. House delegation is split, with Republicans and Democrats each holding four seats. From top to bottom, the Badger State is a purple state.

Wisconsin has produced some outsized political figures, from the steely progressivism of "Fighting" Bob La Follette in the early decades of the twentieth century to Joe McCarthy's Red Scare megalomania of the 1950s. Between 1910 and 1960, the German-American communities of Milwaukee elected three socialist mayors who collectively ran the state's largest city for thirty-eight years. (No other major American city has elected even one.) Republican William Proxmire, the state's longest-serving U.S. senator and one of Washington's most storied gadflies, will be remembered for his early opposition to the Vietnam War and the "Golden Fleece" awards he issued in recognition of especially wasteful and ridiculous government boondoggles. More recently, Republican Tommy Thompson won an unprecedented four terms as governor on the strength of his welfare-reform agenda. The only U.S. Senator to vote against the Patriot Act and the Iraq war, Democrat Russ Feingold has emerged as the natural heir to Proxmire's maverick legacy and is a favorite among his party's liberal base.

In 2004, Feingold received more votes than any other candidate in Wisconsin history, and won twenty-nine counties that Bush carried in the presidential race, including several counties in Republican Congressman James Sensenbrenner's 8th District, which covers the northeastern quadrant of the state. Democrat Herb Kohl, the state's senior senator and scion of the department store chain of the same name, won reelection in 2000 with a bigger share of the vote than Feingold did, and he is virtually untouchable again in 2006. Democrats dominate Milwaukee urban politics, where former state senator Gwendolyn Moore in 2002 became the state's first African American elected to Congress, and only the state's second woman. The first was Tammy Baldwin, whose base of support is Madison's Dane County, another Democratic stronghold. The dean of Wisconsin's House delegation, Democrat David Obey, has kept his district in northwestern corner of the state—which stretches across twenty counties from Stevens Point to Lake Superior—from trending too far Republican. State Democrats are convinced that Paul Ryan, the young, articulate and popular Republican congressman from the Milwaukee suburbs will immediately throw his hat into the ring as soon as either Feingold or Kohl retires. Though Ryan's district voted only narrowly for George W. Bush in 2004 (PVI = +2.2), and Feingold carried it by about 7 percent, most Democrats believe the only way they can defeat Ryan is if he abandons his seat to run for higher office or his district lines are redrawn for 2012.

What's the winning statewide electoral combination in Wisconsin? On the map, Wisconsin is shaped like a left-handed mitten, a fitting symbol for a Great Lakes progressivism presently weathering a Republican storm whipped up by Thompson's strong headwinds. Steve Kean, the former chair of the Wisconsin Democratic Party, puts his left hand palm-down on the table and maps out the parts of the state where the partisan battles are taking place:

As you look at Wisconsin, in terms of swing voters you have pro-choice Republican women in the Milwaukee suburbs. Then you have business-wealth suburbs to the west and north of Milwaukee County. The suburbs south of Milwaukee, like Kenosha and Racine, are white ethnics, including a lot of hunters.

Kean pauses a moment, then points to the junction of his thumb and forefinger.

This area, from Green Bay down to the Milwaukee suburbs—the Fox River Valley—is a key to the state for Republicans. If Democrats keep it close, split it close to 50–50, they can win in Madison, Milwaukee, Eau Claire, and Lacrosse.

Wedged between the cities of Milwaukee and Madison, Jefferson and Waukesha counties are especially pivotal, and voters there are fed a steady diet of Milwaukee-based conservative talk radio. Democrats need not win these counties, but to compete statewide they must do well enough among these suburbanites—many of whom either moved out of Milwaukee or moved into the state from nearby cities Chicago or St. Paul. Another crucial battleground is the Minneapolis–St. Paul suburbs in the western counties along the Minnesota border in Obey's district. Burnett, Polk, and St. Croix are among the fastest-growing counties in the state; St. Croix alone is expected to grow almost 70 percent by 2030. "Many work in Minnesota, most root for the Vikings, and they don't often see Wisconsin television," says George Aldrich, a Feingold adviser, in describing these border-county commuters. In these three areas—the Milwaukee suburbs, the Fox River Valley, and the Minnesota border communities—Democrats must persuade independents and soft partisans to support their agenda.

In 1986, Thompson was elected to the first of his four, record-setting terms, and he quickly proceeded to rebuild the state GOP and make Wisconsin more competitive for statewide Republicans and congressional candidates. He remains the most important figure in modern Wisconsin politics, and still casts a long shadow over state politics. So when Democrat Jim Doyle edged Scott McCallum—who succeeded

Thompson in 2001 after Bush tapped Thompson to be his secretary of Health and Human Services—to win the 2002 governor's race, Democrats were ecstatic. Doyle's win was no landslide, however: In a strange twist, he won with just 46 percent of the vote because Ed Thompson, the former governor's younger brother, skimmed 11 percent of the vote off the top as a Libertarian candidate with an unusually powerful surname.

Still, Doyle's victory breathed new life into the state Democratic Party, and he has worked doggedly to build his political support across Wisconsin. One of his outreach efforts is the so-called Capital for a Day program, wherein Doyle hauls himself and as many of his cabinet members and top administrators as possible to a county or two that he has designated as the surrogate state capital. The program is the brainchild of Doyle adviser Kirk Brown, who methodically charts Doyle's movements across the state to ensure that the governor spends time in the counties commensurate with their electoral power. In early November 2005 at the Sentry Insurance campus in Stevens Point—the last of Doyle's seven stops on a daylong tour through designated co-capitals for the day Wood and Portage counties—the governor talked about "the values of hard work and focusing on our families and communities." At one point, Doyle reflected on the divisive politics he confronts with the Republican-controlled legislature:

> That's why it's so helpful for us as a government to come here and touch base with you here a little bit. Because, believe me, in Madison we'll fight over one issue or the other. I get very frustrated with the legislature—not the legislators here today [laughter]— but some of the others that would choose to do nothing but just pick fights with us, to figure out what it is that divides us. I guarantee you that there are two or three issues I could mention right now that we could divide this room right down the middle, we could go to opposite sides and we could spend all our time fighting and arguing with each other without one side ever convincing the other.

Though Doyle was inspecific, he was probably alluding to clashes with Republican legislators earlier that autumn over legislation that would allow citizens to carry concealed weapons, and another bill that would have given doctors the right to cite religious or personal reasons to refuse treatment to certain patients. Both issues are part of the broader Republican effort to use wedge politics to energize social conservatives and dampen Doyle's reelection chances.

Refusing to cave to the conservative elements within the Republican Party trying to malign and unnerve him, a gutsy Doyle vetoed both bills. Those vetoes will be part of the showdown this November when Doyle stands for reelection. A win would continue the Democrats' state-level party revival, especially if Doyle carries along into office with him some new state legislators. Doyle's reelection will also provide ballast for the party's 2008 nominee. In America's most competitive state, that might make all the difference.

The Montana Miracle

Montana was a rare bright spot for Democrats in 2004. Democrat Brian Schweitzer capitalized on the scandals plaguing his Republican predecessor, Judy Martz, to beat secretary of state Bob Brown in the governor's race. Democrats also captured the state senate, forced a tie in the House, and won statewide races for attorney general, state auditor, and superintendent of public education. Given Bush's easy victory over Kerry the same day, it's clear that enough Montanans had grown disgusted with Martz and the state GOP to cross party lines and vote for state-level Democrats. "We ran a good race and had good candidates," boasts Brad Martin, the former executive director of the Montana Democratic Party who now runs the western desk for the Democratic National Committee. "One thing that became clear was the impact of the presidential race on the state races. Essentially, our statewide candidates made up a 25-point deficit. That means about 20 percent of Bush's voters were crossing over and voting Democratic in one of those races."

Schweitzer, a self-employed rancher who speaks Arabic and has a degree in soil science, surprised the state political community four years earlier by nearly upsetting Republican Conrad Burns in the 2000 Senate race. At one point, he had an armored truck back up to the State Capitol in Helena and deliver a satchel of cash, which Schweitzer promptly dumped out on the steps in front of reporters in order to make a point about all the money Burns had taken from pharmaceutical companies. Schweitzer lost, but admits he never stopped running: He merely redirected his sights from Washington to Helena. In the governor's race, he drove to all fifty-six counties in a pickup truck and kept the GOP off balance with the surprise pick of Republican state senator John Bohlinger as his running mate. His brash campaign style is so rare as to be nearly extinct in today's world of cautious, overmanaged politicians. In fact, Schweitzer didn't even hire a campaign manager until March 2004, when Eric Stern approached Schweitzer about becoming his campaign manager. "Brian likes to do things himself and he wanted to run his own campaign," says a too-modest Stern, who is now the governor's counsel. "And he essentially did."

The state legislative results were also cause for Democrats to celebrate, and a testament to organizing on a statewide level. State senator Jon Tester and state representative Monica Lindeen toured Montana throughout 2004, talking to citizens while they scoured the state for quality Democratic candidates to run for the legislature. "We did town hall meetings everywhere—east, west, north, south, central, big towns and small town," says Tester. These efforts paid off handsomely: He's now running for U.S. Senate against Burns in 2006; she's taking on Republican Denny Rehberg in the state's at-large U.S. House race.

Montana is America's seventh least-populous state. With just shy of a million people, Montana is actually growing faster than the country as a whole, yet lost one of its two congressional seats after the 1990 reapportionment. Only about one in three of the state's counties have more than ten thousand residents, and the only more sparsely populated states are Wyoming and Alaska. Montana has voted Republican in every presidential election since Lyndon Johnson won it in 1964, with one exception: In 1992, Clinton carried Montana by about 2 percent over George H. W. Bush. It was a strange result. Perot received 26.2 percent of the vote statewide and beat Clinton in nineteen counties, yet drew down Bush's 1988 vote enough to allow Clinton to squeak past Bush and win. Clinton deserves credit, however, for at least making Montana a second-tier target. His late-October stop in Billings was the biggest campaign rally most Montanans have ever seen.

Unlike neighboring Idaho, Montana voters are more inclined to vote

Democratic in statewide elections. The state has a long progressive tradition, something state auditor John Morrison—whose grandfather, Frank Morrison, was a progressive Democratic governor in Nebraska in the 1960s—knows by heart. Morrison almost runs out of fingers as he counts off the progressive Democrats who have represented Montana in the Senate, from Thomas Walsh to Burton K. Wheeler to Max Baucus, the Democratic incumbent who won his record-setting fifth term in 2002. "This state has always been a progressive state, and it's always been a Democratic state until recently and mostly in presidential elections. Conrad Burns is the first Republican ever to be reelected to the Senate," Morrison, who lost to Tester in the senate primary, reminds anyone who dares to forget the state's rich Democratic history. "We have the senior senator, the governor, and most other statewide elected officials. The Republicans have the junior senator, the congressman, and the secretary state—and that's it."

Though Morrison's correct about the long-run history, until 2004 the state Republicans were enjoying a great, recent run. Much of their success was a credit to the popularity of two-term Republican governor Marc Racicot, who was elected in 1992. Two years later, Racicot helped the Republicans regain the majority in both houses of the state legislature, then won reelection in a romp in 1996. Mike Dennison, capital bureau chief for the *Great Falls Tribune,* says the GOP's dominance of state politics during the 1990s—and particularly their surge during the 1994 midterm elections—was a case of the partisan planets aligning perfectly for the GOP. First, the 1990 round of redistricting was skewed to the Republicans' advantage. Second, Racicot was a huge campaign asset. Finally, 1994 was a strong Republican cycle nationally.

Since then, the partisan heavens realigned. The Democrats stalled the 2000 round of state redistricting until the Supreme Court intervened to select the fifth and decisive member (a Native American female Democrat) for Montana's redistricting commission, giving Democrats a 3–2 commission majority and a chance to draw fairer maps. They were also blessed by Racicot's parting gift—the blunder-prone Marks, whom Racicot chose to replace Denny Rehberg, his lieutenant governor, on the ticket in 1996 when Rehberg decided to challenge Baucus in the Senate race that year. (Rehberg lost, but subsequently was elected to Montana's at-large House seat.) Finally, in Schweitzer the Democrats had a dynamic candidate at the top of the 2004 ticket. "I haven't seen Democrats this optimistic since I've been here," says Dennison, who has covered state politics since 1977.

Those newly optimistic Democrats convened in July 2005 in Great Falls for their first statewide meeting after the 2004 victories. Baucus was on hand, and the senior senator conveyed the reaction from Washington to the news emanating from Montana. "When I'm in Washington people say, 'Gee, Max, what's going on out there in Montana? What kind of water you drinking back there? It's the only bright Democratic spot in the nation,' " Baucus told the assembled partisan faithful. "I say we're getting our act together. We're listening to people. There's no magic to it."

The Colorado Comeback

Colorado in 2004 provided an encouraging glimpse at the Democrats' southwestern future. The Democrats won majorities in both chambers of the state legislature, elected the Salazar brothers to Congress, and reduced George W. Bush's winning margin by almost 4 percentage points. Though Bush escaped with Colorado's nine electors, 2004 was a strong Democratic year. "We had a lot of resources in Colorado, and we had a big turnout driven by the presidential and Senate election," says Denver-based Democratic strategist Mike Stratton. "We had very good candidates down-ballot with well organized campaigns. From the top to the bottom of the ballot Democrats were active and organized like they never were before." Colorado is crucial because it is growing: The state ranked behind only Nevada or Arizona in total population growth during the 1990s, and was home to eight of America's eighteen fastest-growing counties last decade.

Bush's margin not only declined from 8.4 percent in 2000 to 4.7 percent in 2004, but his two-party share of the vote dropped in a majority of Colorado's counties. Kerry improved Democratic performance in large jurisdictions, including Denver city and Boulder and Larimer counties. (To be fair, some of Kerry's "gains" must be attributed to the return of Ralph Nader's voters; in 2000, Nader received 5 percent of the vote statewide and reached double digits in eight Colorado counties, thanks mostly to votes from the college town of Boulder, the state's environmental voting bloc, and assorted "Trustafarians" scattered across a variety of remote ski towns.) Attorney general Ken Salazar beat beer magnate Pete Coors to replace Ben Nighthorse Campbell in the Senate. Although Coloradans cast 30,000 fewer votes in the Senate race than they did in the presidential contest, Salazar got about 80,000 more votes than Kerry and outpolled his new colleague from Massachusetts in all but two counties.

Salazar's older brother, John, a one-term state legislator who still runs the family's seed potato farm near the New Mexico border, was elected to the U.S. House from the 3rd District. That district covers all or parts of twenty-five counties, making it one of the largest and most rural House districts in the country represented by a Democrat. With the benefit of the Salazar brothers on the ticket, the rural counties in the southwestern corner of Colorado were among those where Kerry made the greater relative gains over Gore's 2000 performance. Democrats also swung enough seats to capture both chambers of the state legislature, thereby elevating Andrew Romanoff to the position of House speaker and Joan Fitz-Gerald as the new Senate majority leader. "Having a guy like Ken Salazar at the top of the ticket made it safe to be a Democrat in Colorado," says Romanoff. "It showed that you could have a moderate, mainstream candidate with a 'D' after his name at the top of the ticket. Republicans helped in some cases by nominating folks pretty far out to the right, and in some cases to replace moderates who were term-limited out."

The rural successes of the Salazar brothers notwithstanding, statewide elections in Colorado are won in the cities and suburbs in the densely populated north-south Interstate 25 corridor along the eastern edge of the Rockies that most Coloradans know simply as the "Front Range." Colorado political experts Thomas Cronin and Robert Loevy explain the basic electoral calculus in the state:

> Partisan elections in Colorado tend to be battles to win votes on the Front Range. Republicans work to get out as large a vote as possible in El Paso County (Colorado Springs) and also hope to

turn out a large vote in Arapahoe and Jefferson counties. Democrats, on the other hand, work to turn out as large a vote as possible in Denver and Pueblo counties and also hope to pick up support in Boulder and Adams counties. The central arena of competition between the two major political parties, therefore, is the Denver suburbs.

Those suburbs are growing, and many of the voters who live there are among the third of the state's voters (33.2 percent) who register as "unaffiliated"—a group that actually outnumbers registered Democrats statewide (30.2 percent). "As the Denver/Boulder area stretches into previously remote rural communities mixed with a military and defense industry presence, it resembles a dynamic not unlike southern California. And central Colorado and southern California gave Bush an almost identical slight majority in 2004," explains political scientist David Rankin. "Such geographic space is in play for Democrats and Republicans, in between urban and rural, astride inner and outer suburbs, where cultural diversity clashes with social conservatism, and economic individualists meet environmental activists."

During the past two generations, Colorado voters have chosen an eclectic group of Democrats for statewide office. Senator Gary Hart was leading the field in the 1988 contest for the Democratic presidential nomination, and he might have spoiled George H. W. Bush's presidential bid had Hart's "monkey business" episode with Donna Rice not derailed his campaign. In the early 1970s, a young, relatively unknown state representative named Dick Lamm parlayed antigrowth and environmental irritations with the International Olympic Committee's selection of Denver as host site for the 1976 winter Olympics into statewide notoriety and a successful run for governor in 1974, the first of his three record-setting terms. (Amazingly, Denver rallied behind Lamm and refused to host the Olympics—an outcome almost unfathomable in today's environment of corporate-sponsored, dog-eat-dog competition to be a host site.) Fellow Democrat Roy Romer followed Lamm with three terms of his own. Tim Wirth won Hart's old Senate seat in 1986, and Native American Ben Nighthorse Campbell, running as a Democrat, followed Wirth in 1992. That same year, Clinton carried Colorado in the presidential race. The Democrats were on a roll.

By the late 1990s, however, Democratic fortunes had reversed. Campbell changed his party affiliation after the GOP's 1995 takeover of Congress, and won reelection as a Republican in 1998, the same year Owens ended the Democrats' twenty-four-year grip on the governor's office. The state's other Senate seat passed from one Republican to the next, starting with Bill Armstrong's election in 1978 to three terms, to Hank Brown for one term and, since 1996, to Wayne Allard. Meanwhile, until 2004 the GOP controlled one or both chambers of the state legislature for what seemed like an eternity. Bob Drake, a veteran Democratic pollster from Boulder, put his state's partisan history in perspective:

> Colorado has traditionally been a default-Republican state—that is, if you know nothing about the candidates, you vote Republican. But the Democrats had a lot of offices at the top because the more people knew about the candidates, the more it negated the default lever. We put up guys like Gary Hart, Dick Lamm, and Tim Wirth, and they'd put up some schlock candidates and we'd kill them. So, in the 1970s and 1980s you had all these Democrats at the top and all these Republicans at the bottom. Then things shifted and you had all these Republicans moving in and moving up, and the Democrats lost their farm team. In 2004, two things changed. First, we started to get a better farm team coming up, better candidates. But the big thing that happened in 2004 is that the default button on the local level was no longer Republican.

Similar to Ohio's grassroots decline, Colorado is a case study in how the failure to build the party eventually leads to collapse. But in Colorado, Democrats have turned things around much more quickly, and if they can build upon their 2004 successes they could solidify their control over state government, unseat Allard in 2008, and make Colorado a blue state in presidential elections.

Abandoning Arizona

Arizona is exploding. It is the second-fastest growing state in the country, and Phoenix is the nation's fastest-growing major city. Arizona's population is concentrated in two jurisdictions—Phoenix's Maricopa County and Tucson's Pima County—the residents of which cast more than three of every four votes statewide in recent elections. South of Phoenix, the suburbs of Avondale, Buckeye, Chandler, Goodyear, and Queen Creek have nearly tripled in population since the 1990 census. The net effect is that Arizona jumped from six to eight U.S. House seats following the 2000 reapportionment, and is projected to add five more seats in the next three decades.

Arizona's recent growth is not the state's first experience with boomtowns. The 1877 Desert Land Act brought mining speculators and other settlers to the Arizona territory in search of new beginnings, including David King Udall, the Mormon pioneer and patriarch who moved west and spawned four generations of Arizona politicians. Because of neighboring New Mexico's disproportionate Hispanic population, Arizona opted against joint statehood and in 1912 became the last continental state to join the union. The population of Maricopa County at the time Arizona gained statehood was small enough to fit into the new barrel cactus–inspired stadium in Glendale that will serve as the home for football's Arizona Cardinals and site of Super Bowl XLII in 2008.

In the true western tradition, Arizona boasts its share of maverick politicians and Mormon legacies. The state has elected to public office a virtual fleet of Udall's sons, grandsons, and great-grandsons. To become John Kennedy's Secretary of the Interior, in 1961 Stewart Udall gave up his seat in the U.S. House of Representatives to his younger brother, Mo, who served until 1991. The family's reach today extends beyond Arizona, with Stewart's and Mo's sons, Tom and Mark, serving respectively as Democratic congressmen from New Mexico and Colorado. Gordon Smith, a distant cousin and partisan defector, is a Republican U.S. senator from Oregon.

In Barry Goldwater and John McCain, Arizona produced the two most iconic Republican senators of the past half century. The irony is that Goldwater bucked his moderate, Midwest-based party to blaze a new, western conservative trail—a path from which the defiant McCain, who has one of the most liberal interest group ratings of any Republican senator, now tends to wander. The most important politician in state history, however, is Democrat Carl Hayden, the longest-serving member in the U.S. Congress. Hayden's accomplishments during his seven House terms, followed by seven more in the Senate, are too many to recount. His lasting legacy will be passage of the Central Arizona Project, which provided the water necessary for the state's population growth in the second half of the twentieth century. Succeeded first by Goldwater and then McCain, together the state's three most famous senators held the same Arizona seat for a combined eighty years (and counting). Arizonans may like mavericks, but they prefer stability in the rebels they send to Washington. "Arizona has long had a candidate-centered rather than party-centered election system where party organizations play a central role, though the organizations in the modern era have been able to secure a niche for themselves," explains David R. Berman of Arizona State's Morrison Institute for Public Policy, adding that state voters have always shown "a streak of individualism . . . [and] reluctance to register with a political party."

As in other Southwest states, the party registration advantage Democrats enjoyed in the middle of the last century has steadily declined, with Republican registrants in Arizona overtaking Democrats by 1988. What's more remarkable is how the influx of new residents during the past decade, who arrive with no political connection to either party, are pushing the independent registrant share closer toward Colorado-like levels. In fact, between 1996 (when Clinton carried Arizona by 2 percent) and 2006, the share of independents jumped from 14 percent to more than 25 percent statewide. In theory, these new voters should make the state more competitive for Democrats, because many of them are transplants from the Northeast, Midwest, or California.

The problem for Arizona Democrats is that Al Gore and John Kerry abandoned the Copper State. Doug Wilson, who supervised both Clinton's 1996 and Kerry's 2004 campaigns in Arizona, says it is impossible to compare the two efforts:

The difference was almost entirely message and the success of conveying of that message. Kerry came to Arizona only a few times, almost always as a featured speaker at the convention of a constituency group. He never came and addressed Arizonans as Arizonans, as he did in so many other states. He went to Ohio 967 times. Had he come to Arizona three of those times, we might have had a different result.

When Kerry did come to the state for two days as part of his western train trip, he visited Williams, a small town along Interstate 40 just west of Flagstaff in the heart of Republican Arizona. Initially, Kerry was only supposed to change trains there, but the campaign cobbled together a last-minute event at which Kerry spoke to an estimated crowd of about five thousand. He "really connected with people," says Wilson. Later that night, Wilson was sitting in a nearby Wendy's fast-food restaurant when a man spied Wilson's Kerry button, approached with his young son in tow, and asked Wilson if he had attended the rally. Without identifying himself, Wilson nodded, and asked the man for his reaction. Wilson recalls vividly the man's reply:

I was there and I brought my son. I will tell you: I am a Republican and a Mormon and a big supporter of [Republican Congressman] J. D. Hayworth. But I'm going to vote for Kerry this time, because in this area the hospitals are terrible and you can't get in without going through all sorts of bureaucracy, my kid is not reading at the level he's supposed to be, and my job sucks. It's time for a change and I'm going to vote for him.

"This is the Arizona audience that John Kerry didn't pay attention to and didn't come back to," Wilson laments.

Williams is in Coconino County, home to the Grand Canyon and the largest county in the state and second largest in the United States. Almost 80 percent of the county's vast, underpopulated lands are either on Indian reservations or owned by the federal government. More than a fourth of Coconino residents are Native Americans, and the population is so young that only 7 percent are aged 65 or older. Williams and most of Coconino County are in Republican Congressman Rick Renzi's district, which had been considered a top House target until Renzi's 23-point victory in 2004 over Paul Babbitt, brother of Bruce Babbitt, the former governor and Clinton administration Interior secretary. Compared to Gore's 6.3 percent margin of defeat in 2000, Kerry lost to Bush statewide by 8.5 percent in Arizona and, despite the drop in Ralph Nader's support, his performance was worse than Gore's in thirteen of Arizona's fifteen counties. But one of the two where he improved was Coconino, which nearly doubled from a 6.6 percent Gore victory to a 12.8 percent margin for Kerry, and was also the only county in the 2nd District where Babbitt edged Renzi. One unplanned visit by Kerry and a thirty-minute speech cannot account for all of those gains, but they certainly contributed to Coconino's against-the-tide result. "I told the [Kerry] campaign over and over again that Arizona is not a typical Republican state," says Wilson. "It may not be Massachusetts, but it's not Wyoming or Utah, either."

As a warm-up to taking another crack in 2008 at Arizona's ten electoral votes, Democrats have two key races in 2006: Governor Janet Napolitano's reelection campaign, and millionaire businessman Jim Pederson's bid to unseat Republican Jon Kyl in the Senate. The state party was in shambles as recently until a few years ago, when Pederson stepped in as the new chair and infused the party with cash and new leadership—all of which Napolitano needed in her razor-thin victory into the 2002 governor's race. "Janet is going to win again because she has been able to maintain the fragile Democratic coalition we need to win, which is people of color—Latinos, African Americans, and Native Americans—and the rest of the coalition, including working folks, retirees, and women," predicts Tucson-area Democratic Congressman Raúl Grijalva, who also thinks Pederson has a chance against Kyl. Though Pederson's personal wealth and generous party investments will help (he still pays the rent on the party's Phoenix headquarters), a lot of things will have to break his way to defeat Kyl, who will have McCain's backing.

Kyl is a poor retail politician, however, and his support for the Iraq war is a potential liability, even in a state with several key military installations. If Napolitano runs strong and draws new Democrats to the polls, and immigration issues boil over, Pederson might pull close enough for a chance at a surprise upset. McCain is running for president in 2008, and if he's the nominee, Jesus would have a hard time taking Arizona's ten electors from the Vietnam War hero. If not, Democrats should work to pare down the GOP's winning margin from 2004, and put Arizona in position to be a blue state in the short term and a reliable Democratic state once McCain retires.

The Setting: Florida

The Democrats' future national majority can be found in the pan-western states of the Diamond. If there is a "setting" for that Diamond it is Florida, the one southern state that is competitive precisely because it is so misfit within the region.

Florida is the least southern of the southern states for a variety of reasons. Unlike any other southern state except Texas, it has a double-digit Hispanic population. It is full of northern transplants, including millions of retirees from other states. (The state's over-65 population share is about 5 percent higher than the national average.) Many of those who haven't moved to Florida visit the state: From the Orlando-area theme parks to the Kennedy Space Center at Cape Canaveral to Key West, Sunshine State attractions draw nearly 80 million visitors a year from across the nation and all over the world. Along with native Floridians, those who in-migrated from elsewhere in America, the Caribbean, or Latin America have turned Florida into something that rivals Disney's It's a Small World ride in Orlando. Political handicapper Chuck Todd, editor of *The Hotline,* says Florida offers visitors from almost every other part of America at least a little something that might look like home:

> Florida *is* America—the perfect microcosm. The Panhandle mirrors the Deep South. Northeast Florida is very "new South," that is, like Virginia, North Carolina and Tennessee. The Tampa-Orlando megalopolis mirrors the Southwest (i.e., it's gone from rural-to-exurb-to-suburb). Southwest Florida reflects the conser-

vative Midwest, southeast Florida is the Northeast, and Key West
is San Francisco.

Throughout the preceding pages, the evidence of this microcosmic effect have been evident in a variety of ways: The fact that Florida's support for reproductive choice mirrors the rest of the country; the fact
that Clinton's increase in Florida between 1992 and 1996 was similar to
his national performance; and, most of all, by the fact that it is the most
closely contested state of the region in presidential elections.

A hundred years ago Florida had only five electoral votes, but now
has twenty-seven, joining California as the only two states that quintupled their number of electors in the past century. Along with Ohio, it is
the most critical prize in presidential elections. Although the 2000 recount and its infamous 537-vote margin will be a staple of Electoral
College lectures in American Government 101 courses for decades,
2000 was not the first time Florida was competitive in a close presidential contest: It was the second-closest southern state in the 1960 presidential election and third-closest in 1976. As noted in the first chapter,
with Florida removed, the South as a region has less electoral clout than
it did a century ago, and the Snow Belt–to–Sun Belt changes of the future will increase the political clout of the West more than the former
Confederate states.

The Republicans have done a masterful job maximizing their political control over Florida. Governor Jeb Bush and the Republican legislature have so perversely gerrymandered the state to their advantage that
Democrats, despite winning slightly less than half the statewide popular vote in the past two presidential elections, control just seven of the
state's twenty-five House seats. The state legislature is not much better,
where Republicans enjoy exaggerated majorities in both the house and
senate (65 percent and 70 percent, respectively). Democratic efforts to
fully mobilize the vote in southeast Florida's Dade and Broward counties have been noble, but futile. Despite Dade County's rapid growth
during the past quarter century, Carter actually carried the county by
more votes than either Kerry or Gore did.

Dade is, of course, home to the largest concentration of Cuban
Americans, and the infamous Elián Gonzales episode only reaffirmed

Cuban Americans' traditional preference for Republicans because of their strident anticommunism and opposition to Fidel Castro. Indeed, one demographic feature of Florida that is not microcosmic of the nation's is its large Cuban-American population, which is more than 5 percent statewide but miniscule in the other forty-nine states. President Bush's strong Cuban support in Florida, meanwhile, has been declining, especially among younger Cuban Americans—not that Republicans are relying on the Cuban-American vote to win the state for them anyway. The key racial voting block is actually the Puerto Rican voters living along the I-4 corridor from Daytona Beach to Tampa to Orlando. "Both parties know if you win the non-Cuban Puerto Rican Hispanics, you're likely to set your party in good stead for the next ten years," says Susan McManus of the University of South Florida. "They're the most sought-after prize in politics."

"I think for the Republican Party to maintain its status, it needs to be in its ascendancy, which means we need to be constantly reaching out," says Republican governor Jeb Bush. "The demographics of Florida reflect what the future of the country looks like." Bush is spot-on: Aside from being home to twenty-five House seats and twenty-seven crucial presidential electors, as a bellwether state Florida is a place where Democrats therefore must continue to fight, because doing well there will continue to be a good indication that Democrats are doing well elsewhere. "It was not a good campaign for us down there in 2004," shrugs former DNC chair Terry McAuliffe, who blames the Kerry campaign for wasting too much time between securing the nomination and setting up its coordinated campaign in the state. "But I'm still a huge believer in Florida."

WHERE THE VOTES ARE

On paper at least, the Democrats are positioned to do well in the 2006 and 2008 election cycles. Historically, a second-term president's midterm cycle favors the out-of-power party. In 2008, the Republican presidential nominee then faces the difficult task of achieving what only George H. W. Bush has done in the post–World War II era—winning a third consecutive term for his party. And where will Democrats have the best opportunities to make gains between now and 2008? Not in the South, that's for sure. To summarize, let's map the electoral terrain from the top to the bottom of the ballot.

The Presidency

In the 2004 presidential election, as depicted in Table 4.5, the Democrats carried fourteen states, totaling 183 electors, by at least 5 percent. Republicans carried twenty-five states with 213 total electors by that margin, giving them a built-in advantage of 30 electoral votes. The remaining twelve states—and their 142 precious electors—split almost evenly: The Democrats won six states with a combined 69 electors, and the Republicans won the remaining 73 electors in the other six states.

Look at the geographic location of the twelve swing states: With the exception of regionally exceptional Florida, not one is in the South. Eight are in the Democratic Diamond, including five midwestern states, plus Colorado, Nevada, and New Mexico. In the medium-to-long term, Democrats will want to compete for some of the states in the Republican column of Table 4.5, especially Arizona, Kentucky, Missouri, and West Virginia, and even southern states like Arkansas, Louisiana, Tennessee, and Virginia. But, Florida aside, the low-hanging fruit is not in Dixie. It's in the Midwest and Southwest.

Congress

Without recapitulating the earlier analysis and list of districts from Table 4.2, it's clear that the Northeast and Midwest are where the majority of vulnerable Republican incumbents in the U.S. House reside. And the Senate? Look no further than the target list that Senator Chuck Schumer, the chairman of the Democratic Senatorial Campaign Committee, has announced for 2006: The top seven GOP-held Senate seats identified by Schumer are in Arizona, Missouri, Montana, Ohio, Pennsylvania, and Rhode Island—with the open seat in Tennessee courtesy of Bill Frist's retirement the only southern target.

That the Democrats are poised to do well in 2006 is especially encouraging because, despite being in the minority, they will be defending eighteen Senate seats (if James Jeffords is included) to just fifteen

Table 4.5
Electoral College Snapshot

Democratic	Competitive	Republican
14 states	*12 states*	*25 states*
183 electors	*142 electors*	*213 electors*
California	Colorado	Alabama
Connecticut	Florida	Alaska
Delaware	Iowa	Arizona
District of Columbia	Michigan	Arkansas
Hawaii	Minnesota	Georgia
Illinois	Nevada	Idaho
Maine	New Hampshire	Indiana
Maryland	New Mexico	Kansas
Massachusetts	Ohio	Kentucky
New Jersey	Oregon	Louisiana
New York	Pennsylvania	Mississippi
Rhode Island	Wisconsin	Missouri
Vermont		Montana
Washington		Nebraska
		North Carolina
		North Dakota
		Oklahoma
		South Carolina
		South Dakota
		Tennessee
		Texas
		Utah
		Virginia
		West Virginia
		Wyoming

for the majority Republicans. In 2008, however, the tables of the Senate's staggered election system turn: The GOP will be defending twenty-one Senate seats to just twelve for the Democrats. If Democrats can net two or three seats in 2006, there are several Republican seats that in 2008 may either open up because of retirements or feature imperiled GOP incumbents, including Wayne Allard (Colorado), Norm Coleman (Minnesota), Susan Collins (Maine), Pete Domenici (New Mexico), Gordon Smith (Oregon), Ted Stevens (Alaska), and John Sununu (New Hampshire). There's not a southern senator among them.

Governors

In gubernatorial races, California's Arnold Schwarzenegger and Ohio's Bob Taft are two of the three least popular governors in the country. Picking up these two governors plus what looks like a surefire win for Eliot Spitzer in New York, would shift control of three of the nation's seven most-populous states from the Republicans to the Democrats. Though a Democratic victory in the race to replace term-limited Jeb Bush in Florida will be tough, a win there would put Democratic governors in charge of six of the nation's seven biggest states. Again, the best source for a list of potential pickups is the person whose task it is to elect and reelect Democratic governors: Bill Richardson, the chairman of the Democratic Governors Association. "My prediction for governors—we have twenty-two right now—and I predict we'll get to twenty-six or twenty-seven," says Richardson, who then proceeded to list Maryland, Massachusetts, New York, and Ohio as the party's best chances in 2006, with decent possibilities in California and Colorado. "We could be the only Democratic entity—the governors—that have a majority [after the 2006 elections]."

Richardson disagrees with giving up on the South. Though it's not his fault, the fact is that the only southern state on the DGA's target list for 2006 is Florida, that familiar regional outcast. Meanwhile, there is not a single southern Republican governor in serious danger of losing reelection in 2006. Two of the region's four incumbent Democratic governors, however, may face tough reelection fights in the next two years (Tennessee's Phil Bredesen in 2006 and Louisiana's Kathleen Blanco in 2007), and a third, North Carolina's Mike Easley, is term-limited in 2008.

Blanco is about as popular in Louisiana as Schwarzenegger in California, and both Bredesen and Easley have approval ratings in the low 50s.

State Legislatures

Republicans headed into 2004 with a slight, sixty-four-seat national lead in the total number of state legislative seats—their first such edge since the 1920s. Amazingly enough, the Democrats netted sixty-three seats in 2004, creating almost perfect two-party parity nationwide. Thirteen chambers switched party control: Democrats captured eight chambers and deadlocked a ninth, while the GOP captured the other four. Where did the shifts occur? In addition to the four chambers in Colorado and Montana discussed already, Democrats took the Vermont house, and the Iowa, Oregon, and Washington senates. The North Carolina house was the Democrats' only southern pickup. Meanwhile, the Republicans converted two southern chambers—Georgia's house and Tennessee's senate—along with Indiana's and Oklahoma's lower houses. The disparate regional outcomes are glaring. Counting the 2003 off-year elections, in the 2002–2003 cycle Democrats netted sixty-seven house seats outside the South, but lost thirty-six inside the South. Meanwhile, the Democrats gained seven net senate seats outside the South, but lost eleven southern senators.

In short, the partisan record is becoming a broken record: few if any Democratic opportunities inside the South, but ample opportunities elsewhere. Recent election results point to this conclusion, the prognoses of political handicappers echo it, and the target lists created by the party leaders tasked with electing Democrats confirm it. The ineluctable conclusion is that Democrats need to win outside the South because the pickings are slim in Dixie. The Democrats must maximize control of the Northeast, fight hard to turn the Midwest from purple to blue, and begin to bleach some of the red out of the Interior West. Winning outside the South is the party's only chance to recapture one or both chambers of Congress, not to mention the White House. At that point, majority Democrats can prove to Americans that they are far better at leading the country toward a more safe and prosperous future. Then and only then will they have the momentum to begin thinking about how to restore their lost glory in the South.

5

Diamond Demography

For far too many women, the American Dream seems a million miles away, because when you've barely got time to sleep—who's got time to dream?

> —Democratic presidential nominee John Kerry, to an audience of mostly women in Milwaukee, one week before the 2004 election

The growth of the Latino vote presumably is the only thing keeping the Democratic leadership off Prozac.

> —John Pitney Jr., government professor at Claremont McKenna College and former Republican National Committee researcher

WHO AMERICANS ARE—what we believe, what we do for a living, where we live, and with whom—is a subject that keeps demographers busy and politicians busier. The paradox of American partisanship today is that so many remarkable demographic changes are occurring at the very moment the electoral map has rigidified. Observers such as David Brooks resolve this paradox by suggesting that Americans choose to live in proximity to people like themselves. Others, like Jonathan Rauch, dismiss this notion as more myth than fact. However pervasive this self-segregating phenomenon really is, it transcends racial and class distinctions. Immigrants from across Latin America settle where they can find suitable jobs, bringing them into communities with other Hispanics who immigrated a month, a year or a decade before they did, quite possibly from the same country or town. Young professionals starting their families depart the big city for bigger houses in better school districts in sprawling suburban communities already inhabited by other couples like them. Newly retired seniors from every race and occupational background put their houses on the market and yard-sale their furniture, then head for warmer destinations where squadrons of golf cart–riding grandmas and grandpas await. And so on.

From a strictly geography standpoint, we know *where* Americans are moving. The geographic migration is occuring from north to south, east to west, urban and rural to suburban and exurban. Sweeping demographic changes, however, are equally if not more important. Taking a step back to view the portrait of America in its most abstract outlines and hues, this is how the country looks:

• Racially and ethnically, the United States is becoming browner, not whiter—and Democrats win among every racial minority subgroup except Cuban Americans, who are largely confined to Miami's Dade County.

• Women are an ever-increasing share of workers, and are already a majority of single parents, recent college graduates, and voters—an advantage for Democrats, who historically draw greater support from females.

• Each year the percentage of U.S. citizens aged 65 or older expands—and poll after poll shows that seniors view Democrats as far more trustworthy on issues like Social Security and Medicare.

• The American family is becoming less nuclear, more multiracial, more likely to be reconstituted by divorce and remarriage, and increasingly involves the pairing (whether legally or not) or same-sex couples—all trends that intertwine with Democratic domestic policies and themes of social inclusion.

• The country is becoming more secular as the number of Americans who self-identify as religious and attend church continues to decline—yet another pattern that favors Democrats.

These transformations do not mean Democrats can relax and wait for demographic currents to sweep them into the majority. Quite the contrary: Other important trends, like rising suburbanization and declining unionization, are breaking against them.

What these changes do mean is that the traditional portrait of a heterosexual, married, white Protestant couple who take their three biological children to church every Sunday is being painted over with a more complex mural. One consequence of all this change is that middle-aged, married, white male Christians—the "default demographic," if you will—are increasingly anxious, even angry. Conservatives are by nature change-averse. But default-demographic conservatives surely feel the greatest discomfort, for they awake each morning to an America that looks a little less like them than it did the day before. Nobody—and certainly no Democrat—should be surprised by the reactionary politics and hoary rhetoric that follows. Conservative white men raise their voices precisely to compensate for their fears about their declining political and electoral clout. Sean Hannity, Rush Limbaugh, and Bill O'Reilly are some of the many by-products of this fear.

Unfortunately, the resulting cacophony prevents some Democrats from thinking clearly. To listen to some analysts, Task 1 on the checklist for restoring Democrats to national prominence is finding a way to reconnect with white southern men who watch NASCAR on Saturday, attend church on Sunday, and vote culturally on Tuesday. Others warn in foreboding tones that Democrats must figure out "solutions" to policies on which most Americans actually support them, like reproductive choice. Something is seriously wrong when Democrats are being advised to cave on majority positions in order to appease loud minorities that are shrinking as a share of the population and disinclined to support Democrats anyway. Would Democrats benefit from doing better among those guys in pickup trucks with gun racks and the Confederate bumper stickers on the back that Howard Dean famously mentioned? Sure—but not if it means passing over the heads of voters who are more open to Democratic messages and messengers.

Early critics of the Clinton administration noticed an unusual presidential reflex: Clinton was quicker to respond to his detractors and opponents than to his advocates and supporters. I submit that too many Democrats are gripped by a similarly backwards mind-set, the origins of which derive from an internal dissonance about the South. That is, many Democrats who essentially reject the South's core political values nevertheless feel some guilt-addled need to identify with, and justify themselves to, southern conservatives. Why? The 1992 and 1996 election results proved Clinton to be the first *northern* southern Democratic president. What separated Clinton from other Democrats was his uncanny ability to mask the disconnect between his public image and his personal ideology—and southerners quickly saw through this façade, as Clinton's smaller relative gains in the South between 1992 and 1996 confirm.

The point is not to criticize Clinton's unrivaled political savvy, but to caution Democrats against taking too much to heart the criticisms of conservatives who scold them for not acting more like Republicans on cultural issues or failing to "find religion," literally or figuratively. It is absurd and counterproductive to suggest that Democrats can find salvation in appealing more to those who identify with them little and regard them even less. Were Bush adviser Karl Rove to make a similar declaration—that to build a more durable majority the Republicans must start connecting with, say, unmarried, secular professional women of color in the Northeast, a demographic that is at least *growing*—he'd be rightly howled out of Washington and his own party.

As already demonstrated, not only is there a historical precedent for a non-southern majority, but the South exercises not much more electoral clout today than it did when Republican majorities ruled the country with no southern support whatsoever. In the previous chapter I argued that the states of the Northeast and the pan-western Diamond are where Democrats can build this majority anew. If that is the "where" of it, the next logical question is, "Who?" Among what sorts of voters can Democrats forge a winning demographic coalition inside the Diamond? This chapter provides some answers.

PERSUADING AND MOBILIZING THE NON-SOUTHERN MAJORITY

Beyond a party's core supporters, building a majority coalition involves attracting voters through one of two methods. Liberal Democrats tend to favor a *mobilization* (or *base-voter*) strategy, which entails getting to the polls as many likely supporters who are either unregistered or vote sporadically, because when they do turn out they vote reliably Democratic. Centrist Democrats emphasize the need for a *persuasion* (or *swing-voter*) strategy, in which uncommitted moderates and independents from among the pool of reliable voters are contacted in an effort to convert them into Democratic votes. The risk of mobilization is that some resources will be wasted on people who ultimately do not show up, whereas the risk of persuasion is that some resources will be spent on people who show up and vote for the other party.

Obviously, the two strategies are not mutually exclusive: A well-funded party mobilizes *and* persuades. Faced with scarce resources, however, choosing between the two strategies becomes a question of efficiency. Should the next dollar, campaign ad, phone call, or volunteer be allocated to mobilizing new voters or persuading likely voters? At first glance, persuasion seems more efficient because converting a potential Republican vote into a Democratic vote counts twice, whereas a newly mobilized Democratic vote counts once. On the other hand, if the per-voter cost of mobilization is less than half that of persuasion, mobilizing is more efficient. Either way, for a candidate or party to get to 50 percent, there must be a sufficient number of voters available to persuade or mobilize in the first place.

Whether by mobilization or persuasion, the feasibility of building a non-southern Democratic majority requires an understanding of the populations and demographic changes in the various states and regions. In their new book, *The End of Southern Exceptionalism,* Byron

Shafer and Richard Johnston argue that the South is becoming less distinct, which is certainly true. Even if future demographic trends were projected to be similar in the Diamond and the South, a weak case could still be made for a non-southern majority because Democrats start in a better relative position in the Midwest and Southwest. Still, the reality of a fully assimilated South remains at least a generation away, probably two. Surely the Democrats' strategy cannot be to sit back and watch thirty years of Republican rule from the sidelines in breathless anticipation of becoming the majority party in some future America where the South is somehow indistinguishable from the rest of the country, can it?

Actually, this question is moot because the current demography and future population trends in the Diamond are strikingly different from those in the South. Most of these differences are *favorable* to Democrats, and thus the strong case for a non-southern majority can be made: Mobilize and persuade voters in the pan-western states, because doing so is the most effective and efficient route back to power. The demographic equation for a non-southern Democratic majority is complex, and it varies from region to region, state to state. Yet, on virtually every criterion—from race to gender, from age to marital status—the opportunities in the Midwest and Interior West are more amenable to Democratic gains than they are in the South.

Race

The most dramatic demographic change of the past century is the country's increasing racial diversity. In 1900, only two American states outside the South had nonwhite populations of 10 percent or more; by 2000, twenty-six states did. Since 1900, the minority population share has increased in all but five American states, and these changes are accelerating. "If you look in the 1990s, in every one of the fifty states, non-Anglo Hispanic populations grew faster than Anglo populations," says University of Texas at San Antonio demographer Steve Murdock, adding that the country will be half racial minorities by 2050. "It's a very pervasive pattern."

Minority population growth is not uniform across all races and regions, however. The South contains the highest share of African Amer-

Figure 5.1
Black Population in the South, 1950–2000

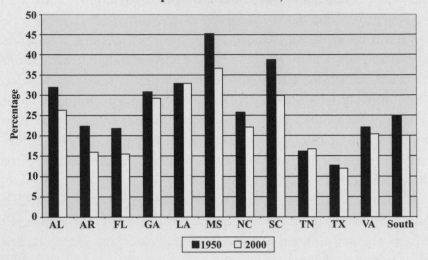

icans, but their state population declined across the twentieth century as African Americans migrated to other parts of the country to build a new future. In fact, as Figure 5.1 shows, since 1950 the percentage of African Americans has fallen in every southern state except Tennessee. In Louisiana it is about the same, although the displacement effects of Hurricane Katrina are sure to change that.

And those five states where the minority population share is lower today than it was a century ago? Sure enough, four are southern states—Alabama, Arkansas, Mississippi, and South Carolina. That's right: In a country where the single defining demographic pattern of the past hundred years is the rising number of people of color, parts of the South are actually *whiter* than they were a century ago. As discussed in chapter 3, polarized black-white voting in the South already makes it difficult for Democratic candidates to win there, even though African Americans in most states turn out in equal proportion to other southern voters. The catalog of injuries endured by African Americans over the centuries went from slavery to segregation to systematic vote suppression. The insult added to these injuries is that, just as African Americans were fighting and winning equal voting and participation rights in the South, their regional numbers were shrinking and whites began voting Republican with a vengeance.

Moreover, the southern white vote is increasingly distinct from the rest of America. Figure 5.2 depicts the white vote, by region, during the past eight presidential elections. The figure starts with 1976, an interesting year because in that election white votes were uniform across the nation: Democrat Jimmy Carter and Republican Gerald Ford split the white vote in the Northeast, with Ford edging Carter by almost imperceptible margins in the rest of the country. Since then, with the notable exception of 1992—when defections to Ross Perot brought western and southern white voters into rough parity in their shared dissatisfaction with Republican incumbent George H. W. Bush—white southerners have steadily diverged from the rest of the country. In the three most recent elections, the South has voted between 13 percent and 15 percent more Republican than the Midwest and Far West. This divergence is so dramatic that George W. Bush's share of the southern white vote in 2004 (70 percent), when he captured 51 percent of the national vote, was about the same as Ronald Reagan's 1984 share (71 percent) in an election Reagan won with 59 percent of the vote. Because white Americans in the "flyover states" of the Midwest and Far West vote much more like their northeastern than southern cohorts, that puts the South out of the mainstream of the country's white electorate—a fact rarely heard from national pundits who are too busy shouting over each other to (falsely) proclaim how "out of touch" northeastern liberals are.

The truth is that once the South is removed from the equation, Democrats are generally competitive among white voters. Though Republicans depicted the last two Democratic presidential nominees as radical liberals, Bush failed to win a majority of the non-southern white vote in 2000 and barely won a majority in 2004. Democrats don't have a white voter problem, as some suggest. What they have is a *southern* white voter problem, for a variety of reasons already chronicled in this book.

Turning to the Diamond, the eye-popping growth of Hispanic populations, especially Mexican Americans, has transformed the country

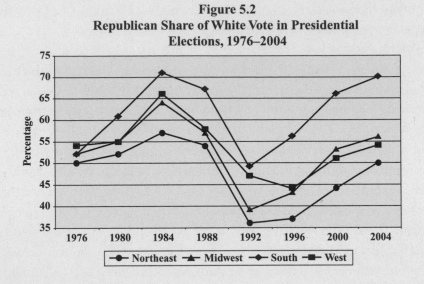

Figure 5.2
Republican Share of White Vote in Presidential
Elections, 1976–2004

and the Southwest in particular. The Hispanic population of the United States grew from 22.4 million in 1990 to 33.5 million by 2000, a 58 percent increase. As of 2004, thirteen states have double-digit Hispanic populations, a list that obviously includes the four states that border Mexico, but also surprises like Connecticut, Rhode Island, and Utah. Nevada, Arizona, and Colorado, which in order were the three fastest-growing states of the 1990s, owe their top-three rankings to surging Hispanic populations. On a related note, although only 3 percent of state legislators nationally are Hispanics, Arizona (16 percent), Colorado (10 percent), and New Mexico (39 percent) are among the five states with double-digit shares of Hispanic state legislators.

Hispanics remain severely undermobilized. The political clout of this "sleeping giant" of American politics is more latent than realized for three reasons:

• Millions of adult Hispanic immigrants have not established citizenship, which is the obvious precondition for voter eligibility;

• Some Hispanics who *are* eligible are hesitant to register and participate; and

• Newborns—the fastest-growing segment of Hispanics—are Americans by birthright but simply too young to vote yet.

And thus, despite surpassing African Americans earlier this decade as the largest ethnic minority in the country, at the polls Hispanics are still vastly outnumbered by African Americans. "In 2004, Hispanics outnumbered blacks by nearly 5 million in the population count, but blacks had nearly 7.5 million more eligible voters," reports Robert Suro of the *Washington Post*. "To put it another way, eligible voters made up 39 percent of the Hispanic population compared with 64 percent of blacks." Between 2000 and 2004 Hispanics accounted for 50 percent of new population growth in the country, but only 10 percent of new voters.

Obviously, Democrats cannot take Hispanic voters for granted. The Bush brothers have campaigned aggressively for their support. Though some question estimates that range as high as 44 percent, nobody disputes that George W. Bush in 2004 received a minimum of 40 percent of the Hispanic vote nationally, a jump of about 5 percent over 2000 and a shift that makes Hispanics one of the most coveted persuasion targets in the country. Florida governor Jeb Bush, whose wife was born in Mexico, is almost single-handedly responsible for his brother's stronger-than-expected support among Florida Hispanics (Cuban or not), without which there would never have been a recount in 2000.

Beyond their latent and long-term potential, Hispanic voters will be crucial to a non-southern Democratic majority for two additional reasons. First, with the exception of Cuban Americans, and despite Herculean efforts by Republicans to wrest them away, Hispanics still retain close historical ties to the Democratic Party. Second, although the Hispanic population explosion is beginning to reach into southern states other than Florida and Texas (more about that in chapter 7), the Southwest and key northeastern states are where Hispanics have the most electoral clout now.

Simon Rosenberg, president of the New Democratic Network, has tirelessly channeled his organization's resources toward opening new lines of political communication with Hispanic households. Rosenberg laments the fact that in 2004 Republicans, who mailed out a slick CD to

Figure 5.3
States with Double-Digit Hispanic Populations, 2004

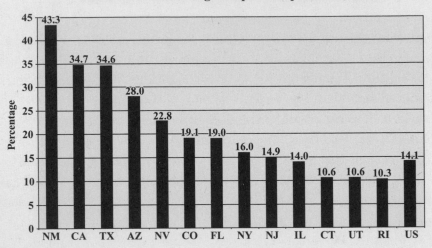

select Hispanic households during the final days of the campaign, were more sophisticated than the Democrats in their Hispanic outreach efforts. Complicating matters is the fact that, although the vast majority of Hispanic politicians are Democrats, most cannot speak conversational Spanish. This appalling deficiency creates problems on Univision and other Spanish-language media. (Rosenberg rates Univision second only to the Catholic Church in institutional importance within the Hispanic community.) Nor is this problem limited to national politicians: Phil Lopes, the Democrats' House minority leader in Arizona, confirms that state Democrats often scramble around to find fluent politicians to go on Phoenix-area, Spanish-language television. Because newer immigrants are less likely to speak English than earlier generations or native-born children of immigrants, speaking in conversational Spanish is important to establishing credibility with Hispanic audiences.

Though Hispanics are arriving from across Central America, South America, and the Carribbean, the largest proportion of immigrants are Mexicans who aspire to first be Mexican Americans but, ultimately, just plain Americans. Gregory Rodriguez, a senior fellow at the New America Foundation and contributing editor of the *Los Angeles Times,* puts Mexican assimilation into a wider historical context:

Throughout American history, countless other ethnic groups have been stripped of their foreignness and have achieved mainstream acceptance . . . Of course, while European immigrant experiences generally had a beginning and an end, Mexican immigration has been virtually continuous for the past century. This has made the process of Mexican integration a perpetual one. But this dynamic hasn't so much retarded assimilation as it has sown confusion in the formulation of political and cultural identities. Though the self-definition of European-American groups gradually evolved from an immigrant to an ethnic American identity as time passed, Mexican-Americans have always had to contend with the presence of unassimilated newcomers as well as cyclical waves of anti-Mexican sentiment. Consequently, Mexican-Americans have had to battle against the presumption of foreignness longer than other ethnic groups.

Because the continuous immigration of Mexicans during the past century shows little sign of abating in the coming century, Rodriguez's point applies prospectively as well as retrospectively. That said, the party that makes Hispanic voters (Mexican or otherwise) feel welcome and genuinely assimilated into the broader American culture—without ignoring or denigrating their unique cultural identities—will win the ultimate battle for their support. Republicans seem to understand this better than Democrats do. "They have been more assertive about appealing to Hispanic voters, especially first-generation Hispanics who have the same Democratic attachments that earlier generations do," warns Rosenberg, noting that the Bush campaign in 2004 communicated to Hispanics how much the GOP loves them—but did so at a whispered level, to avoid alarming white voters. "Among Hispanics the Democrats have the legacy, but the GOP in 2004 had a strategy. If Democrats get a strategy, they can make gains. The split is 60–40 [for Democrats], so we have to persuade as well as mobilize."

Another group of growing importance to the pan-western strategy is Native Americans, who vote 80 percent to 90 percent for the Democratic candidates. Like Hispanics, Native Americans are undermobilized, but for opposing reasons: Whereas most Hispanics arrived in the

United States after the voting rights battles of the 1960s, Native Americans have been on American soil for millennia but have met repeated resistance to their attempts to gain suffrage. In fact, after returning from World War II battlefronts—where they served in greater proportions than almost any other group of Americans—Native Americans still did not enjoy full voting rights. Consequently, though very active in tribal politics, until recently many Native Americans preferred to self-select out of participating in state and national matters. As a result of this insularity, not to mention their physical remoteness, Native American voters continue to be difficult to organize and mobilize.

Political involvement among Native Americans has accelerated rapidly in recent decades. Gaming in particular has altered the political complexion of Indian country. "In the legislative process [Native American influence] certainly has increased, where you have very, very rich gaming tribes who have dollars, and then you have large tribes in the West who have votes," says Anna Whiting-Sorrell, who directed Native American outreach for John Kerry's 2004 presidential campaign and now serves as a top policy adviser to Montana governor Brian Schweitzer. "The two things that matter are dollars and voters, and so in some of the western states the tribes are certainly the margin of victory." The first significant electoral victory credited to Native American voting clout was Democrat Tim Johnson's reelection victory by 524 votes over Republican John Thune in South Dakota's 2002 Senate race. (Thune got revenge two years later by ousting then-Senate minority leader Tom Daschle.) Republicans cried foul, claiming that Native Americans stuffed ballot boxes on the reservations. However legitimate those fraud charges may be, the very fact that Native Americans are significant enough to be involved in such a controversy demonstrates that they will have other chances to swing elections in prairie and southwestern states. "I think in certain, key states, especially the Dakotas and in the Southwest, the Native American political influence has grown by leaps and bounds ahead of what it was," says Robert C. Harmala, who lobbies on behalf of Native American tribes in Washington, DC. "They are electing local officials, like sheriffs, so it's very grassroots. The money has been there a while, and now the votes are coming along with it."

Table 5.1
Top Ten States, by Share of American Indians or Alaskan Natives (by Percentage)

State	1990	2003
Alaska	15.6	15.9
New Mexico	8.9	10.0
South Dakota	7.3	8.4
Oklahoma	8.0	8.0
Montana	6.0	6.5
Arizona	5.6	5.3
North Dakota	4.1	4.9
Wyoming	2.1	2.4
Washington	1.7	1.6
Idaho	1.4	1.5

Tabulated by author from U.S. Census Bureau data.

It's an open question how pivotal Native American votes are, but what's not in dispute is where their impact will be felt: in the West. According to census figures shown in Table 5.1, six western states, from Alaska to North Dakota (plus border state Oklahoma), have Native American statewide populations of at least 5 percent. Since 1990, their statewide shares have been growing in all but one of these six states, and the only reason that's not the case in Arizona is because the Copper State is such a magnet for in-migrating Americans from other parts of the country. Perhaps the best indication of the nascent power of Native Americans are recent Republican efforts to require physical addresses on reservations as a condition of voter eligibility. The transparency of these maneuvers signals that the GOP harbors little hope of luring Native Americans into its supposed "big tent." Given the damage done by Republican lobbyist Jack Abramoff, who took millions of dollars from tribal leaders while calling them "troglodytes" and "monkeys" behind their backs, the preferred Republican strategy seems to be to demobilize Native Americans by whatever means necessary. Democrats should continue to invest the resources necessary to activate the reservations, where almost every newly mobilized voter will be a Democratic voter.

Finally, even the Asian-American population is a growth demographic for Democrats. Asian Americans were 4.2 percent of the national population in 2000, and comprised a higher than average share in nine states, only one of which is southern: Hawaii (58 percent), California (12 percent), Washington (6.7 percent), New Jersey and New York (6.2 percent each), Nevada (5.6 percent), Alaska (5.2 percent), Maryland (4.5 percent), and Virginia (4.3 percent). Exit poll data for Asian Americans exist only back to 1992, when they voted 55 percent for George H. W. Bush to just 31 percent for Bill Clinton. The Democratic share has been steadily rising since. In 2004, John Kerry won Asian Americans by 17 points, 58 percent to 41 percent.

What's apparent from the racial and ethnic changes across the past century, and especially of late, is that the real opportunities for Democratic growth are west of the Mississippi, particularly in the Southwest. California, New Mexico, and Texas are already majority-minority states by virtue of their Hispanic populations, and Arizona, Nevada, and Colorado have significant Hispanic populations. The Pacific Coast states are magnets for Asian Americans. Meanwhile, in an otherwise ever-browning America, parts of the former Confederacy are whiter now than one hundred years ago—and white southerners are voting more and more Republican.

Gender

Might the Democrats' southern struggles be a gendered problem? Women are evenly distributed across almost every geographic unit, so the question of interest is whether gender gaps vary by region, a question that actually is twofold. First, do southern women vote more Republican than non-southern women? Second, is there a gender gap in the partisan behavior of women relative to men which varies by region? The answer to both questions is yes, and in both cases the data point to a non-southern Democratic majority.

Nationally, Kerry won among all women by 3 percent, a much lower margin than previous Democrats but a winning margin nonetheless. Because African-American women vote overwhelmingly Democratic, however, Kerry lost among white women by 11 percent. Women voters in the South do not even come close to these performance benchmarks.

The only southern state Kerry didn't lose among women in 2004 was Virginia—he broke even. Among white women only, the margins are mind-boggling. Even if the National Election Pool estimates are off a bit, in some of the states the votes of white women are the mirror image of the votes of black women: Bush carried white women in Mississippi by 79 points (89 percent to 10 percent), and won six other states— Alabama, Georgia, Louisiana, North Carolina, South Carolina, and Texas—by a net margin of at least 44 points.

Table 5.2
Gender Voting in the South, 2004

State	Democratic Margin Among Women		Performance Gap, Democratic W-M	
	All	Whites	All	Whites
Alabama	-14	-58	12.5	3.0
Arkansas	-1	-20	9.0	7.5
Florida	-1	-13	3.0	3.0
Georgia	-12	-52	6.0	0.0
Louisiana	-9	-49	6.0	2.5
Mississippi	-19	-79	0.0	-8.0
North Carolina	-8	-44	7.0	2.5
South Carolina	10	-56	8.5	0.0
Tennessee	-13	-29	1.5	2.0
Texas	-26	-52	-3.0	-3.5
Virginia	0	-29	9.5	8.0
United States	**+3**	**-11**	**7**	**7**

Computed based on data from Edison/Mitofsky National Election Pool results.

These high rates of Republican voting are also evident in the relative absence of a gender gap between female and male voters in the South, as the latter two columns of the table show. In fact, the gender gap is much smaller in the South. This is especially true for white southerners, among whom the 2004 gap was less than 3 percent in nine states, including all five Deep South states. The most extreme case was

Alabama, where women overall voted 12.5 percent more Democratic, but white women voted only 3 percent more Democratic than white men. Notice that there was no white gender gap at all in Georgia and South Carolina, and that white women in Mississippi and Texas actually voted *less* Democratic than men. That's four southern states where the gender gap did not favor Kerry. Outside the South, that was true in only three states: Missouri (-1 percent), Nebraska (-4 percent), and West Virginia (none).

Because southern male voters are more Republican to start, the tiny gender gap among the southern white majority is a huge obstacle for Democrats. A gender *chasm* of Grand Canyon–like proportions would have to open up in the South for white southern women to vote Democratic at the rates non-southern women do. Failing that, any effort by Democrats to mobilize low-turnout white women in the South is unlikely to help—and probably would backfire.

Bush made significant inroads with women voters between 2000 and 2004 by stressing homeland security and his credentials in the war on terror. "The Republicans have been very aggressive about targeting women voters and won the last election because of it," writes Democratic pollster Celinda Lake. "They particularly targeted segments of women voters around the security issue." The GOP's strong-on-defense profile may be losing some of its potency, however. By early 2005, polls revealed the shift:

> Homeland security and terrorism dominated the public's security agenda for several years following September 11th . . . However, the current focus appears to have shifted from safeguarding against terrorism to a stronger emphasis on issues that hit home financially. In dozens of recent focus groups among many different cohorts of women, concerns like retirement, health care, and economic security are trumping the sorts of homeland security concerns that dominated women's issue agenda before the last election.

The Democrats are at fault for losing their advantage over women. They will have to work hard to reassert their role as the party that women should trust to promote their interests. It can be done, and especially in

the post-Katrina and post-Iraq era of Republican incompetence, because women are less wary of big government. "The biggest difference
between men's and women's attitudes is around the role of government,
and you do find women more supportive of the role of government than
men and more likely to believe that someone in their family may need a
safety net program," says Lake. Not surprising, the South is also the region least likely to elect women to public office, particularly to the
state legislatures and Congress.

American women today are anxious. They may be worried because
they are raising a child in a fatherless home with limited resources and
without health insurance. They may be full-time working women living in the exurbs who earn as much if not more than their husbands
but worry about how good the local school district is and how much
private school might cost—and, either way, are concerned that their
kids return home every afternoon to find both parents away at work.
These worried women might also include 25-year-old college graduates
fretting over their job prospects, mothers fearful that their 25-year-old
sons fighting in Afghanistan or Iraq will not return, or lesbians who
have lived with their partners for the past twenty-five years and feel
that they are under increasing attack. Democrats need to listen and respond to these women, not only because they outvote men but because
they will have more influence than perhaps any other persuadable voting bloc in deciding the fate of the two parties in the decades to come.

But in the South, barring near-universal turnout among African
Americans and especially African-American women, the gender gap is
moot because white women vote Republican by the same, overwhelming margins their husbands, brothers, and sons do.

Age

America is aging, and until recently that was good electoral news for
Democrats. In 2000, Al Gore lost to George W. Bush among voters
under age 60, but won the national popular vote on the strength of his
4-point margin (51 percent to 47 percent) among those over 60. Bush
more than reversed that deficit in 2004, winning among 60+ voters by
8 points, 54 percent to 46 percent. The 18-to-29 age cohort, which Bush
lost in 2000, is the only group he lost again in 2004 to John Kerry.

Table 5.3
The Youth Vote in 2004

State	State %	Kerry	Bush	Difference
Alabama	18	41	57	-16
Arkansas	16	51	47	4
Florida	17	58	41	17
Georgia	19	47	52	-5
Louisiana	20	45	53	-8
Mississippi	20	63	37	26
North Carolina	14	56	43	13
South Carolina	18	48	51	-3
Tennessee	16	46	53	-7
Texas	20	41	59	-18
Virginia	17	54	46	8
South	**18**	**49**	**50**	**-1**
United States	**17**	**54**	**45**	**9**

Data from 2004 Edison/Mitofsky exit polls; region total calculated by author.

A bright spot for Democrats is that Kerry's 9-point margin (54 percent to 45 percent) among under-30 voters actually mattered in 2004. Normally, winning the youth vote is the Democrats' electoral booby prize, because under-30 voters turn out at such abysmal rates. But 2004 saw a dramatic surge in youth voting, jumping 9 points from 2000 to 47 percent, including higher turnout among white, Hispanic, and African-American youth. Internet-savvy young voters are providing more than votes, too: An estimated 80 percent of 2004 campaign contributions by Americans aged 18 to 34 were made online. Their votes and dollars were not enough to put Kerry over the top, but younger Americans provide a solid foundation for future Democratic nominees.

Younger voters are more tolerant than their elders on a range of social issues, including gay rights, racial equity, and immigration. "Moreover, youth support for equal protections for gays seems to cross partisan, ideological, and religious lines," concludes a recent report by the Center for Information & Research on Civic Learning & Engagement. "For example, majorities of Republican, conservative, and Born-Again Christian youth also support protections on housing, employment, and hate crimes, although they oppose gay civil unions, marriage, and adoption." These differences are to some degree a by-product of the fact that younger voters are more racially diverse (if not mixed-race) as a cohort: The percentage of younger citizens who are white has declined from 87 percent in 1972 to just 72 percent by 2004, with Hispanics increasing from 5 percent of young Americans in the mid-1970s to 12 percent now. These trends are not an exclusive function of ethnicity, however. "Today's young voters could be the core of a progressive majority in 2028," writes Ben Hubbard, who tracks the youth vote for the Center for American Progress. "Twenty-four years from now, today's youth will be middle-aged. And while old age, children, and a mortgage may tarnish their idealism, it's hard to believe that it will undermine their tolerance or transform their values. The party of the future will be the party that best reflects the values of this emerging majority."

Although Kerry won the youth vote nationally, he lost 18-to-29-year-olds in the South. Bush won six of the eleven southern states, and by wide margins in both Alabama and his home state of Texas. Curiously, despite losing Mississippi statewide by almost 20 points, Kerry won the youth vote by 26 points. That Kerry did well in Florida, North Carolina, and Virginia makes more sense, given that these states contain many of the South's new-economy opportunities that attract young, more liberal professionals.

Turning to the other end of the life cycle, Democrats also draw significant support from seniors, but must do better. Historically, the party's strong advocacy for Social Security and Medicare has earned the loyalty of millions of seniors. With cause, Republicans complain that Democrats try to scare older Americans by warning about potential GOP assaults on these two programs. Why are Democrats slipping among seniors? A major reason is that New Deal–era messages resonate less well as Baby Boomers replace their parents among the senior citizen population, as Robin Toner of the *New York Times* explains:

For years, Democrats counted on the over-60 vote to regularly return their party to power on Capitol Hill—the party of Franklin D.
Roosevelt, Social Security and Medicare, as Democrats were quick
to remind retirees. But that changed in the 1990s, when that vote
began tilting toward the Republicans. One reason for the change
was demographics—the passing of the New Deal generation and
its replacement with retirees whose political loyalties were formed
in a more Republican era. But it also reflected Republican success
in muting or neutralizing the longtime Democratic advantage as
the more trustworthy party on Social Security and Medicare. The
passage of the Medicare prescription drug law in 2003 was intended to be the crowning accomplishment of that strategy.

Indeed, Michael Dukakis lost the senior vote in 1988 by 1 point, and
Bill Clinton won it comfortably in 1992 before losing some ground to
Bob Dole in 1996. Then came the flip from Gore in 2000 to Bush in 2004.
Fittingly, although Bush won 60+ voters by 8 points, he won the subset of 65+ voters by only 5 points, 52 percent to 47 percent—a testament to the enduring Democratic attachments of many of America's
eldest voters.

The Democrats have a chance to make a comeback among senior citizens. Notice that Bush shrewdly avoided antagonizing seniors before
his 2004 reelection. The president waited until early 2005 before moving forward with his plan to reform Social Security, and his "crowning
accomplishment" Medicare drug benefit did not kick in until January
2006. Bush's privatization scheme quickly imploded, and when the
prescription drug program took effect it was such a disaster that governors were compelled to step in to solve the bureaucratic problems that
ensued. Suddenly, all those ominous warnings from Democrats about
trusting the Republicans with Medicare and Social Security seem more
accurate than alarmist. Bush's sly maneuvers give Democrats a huge
opportunity to exploit—and if they must play the fear card with older
Americans, so be it. It's not like Republicans have hesitated to manipu-
late fear for political gain.

To swing the pendulum back, Democrats will also have to focus on
Baby Boomers, a massive age cohort, the first wave of whom turned 60

in 2006. In *The Greater Generation: In Defense of the Baby Boom Legacy*, American University professor Leonard Steinhorn describes what makes Boomers different from their parents:

> Over the last four decades the Baby Boom has created, reinvented, invigorated, or sustained most of the great citizen movements that have advanced American values and freedoms—the environmental movement, the consumer movement, the women's movement, the civil rights movement, the diversity movement, the gay and lesbian movement, the human rights movement, the openness in government movement. In its wake the Baby Boom has left not a single institution unchanged for the better, from the workplace to the university to the press to the military to the basic relationship between men and women.

The Boomers may be less connected than their parents to the New Deal and Great Society programs championed by Democratic presidents and congresses, but they are also more liberal in their social outlooks. Because age tends to make people more conservative, these cross-pressured Boomers will be a key persuasion target.

As this massive Baby Boom cohort moves into retirement age, where will the future growth of senior populations occur? The 65+ population in the United States grew 63 percent during the Clinton years, and is projected to grow another 51 percent between 2000 and 2020. Now, the surprise: As Figure 5.4 shows, growth in the senior populations will actually be *faster* in the eight states of the interior West than in the South (64 percent)—slightly so in the four Mountain West states (Montana, Idaho, Utah, and Wyoming = 68 percent), and much faster in the four southwestern states (Arizona, Colorado, Nevada, and New Mexico = 78 percent). The real challenge for Democrats is figuring out how the out-migration of retirees from the Northeast and Midwest will affect the electoral calculus in the Rust Belt states that many seniors have abandoned.

If electoral margins among seniors continue to be like Kerry's in 2004, the Democrats will have a tough time forging a national majority. If they are more like Gore's in 2000, the Democrats will be tough to

Figure 5.4
Senior Population Growth, 1993–2020

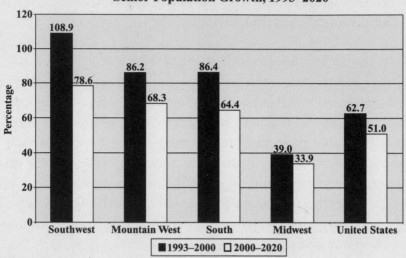

beat. Either way, this is one group where Democrats might be able to make some gains in the South, although much better opportunities loom out west.

Community of Residence

Americans are moving out of the cities to the suburbs and exurbs. Suburban flight has been so dramatic during the past half century that it has led, somewhat paradoxically, to urban renaissances in places such as Baltimore and Detroit, where young professionals are taking advantage of cheap housing to begin the process of regentrification. With cities hemorrhaging population and wealth—and much of the residual urban vote firmly in the Democrats' pocket—both parties have directed their attentions to suburban, exurban, and rural voters.

The suburbanization of American politics has created a new language for categorizing and labeling, as talking heads quibble over whether "soccer moms," "office park dads," or some other suburban target group is the next flavor-of-the-electoral-cycle. Berthed in California's famed Orange County during the Barry Goldwater era and nurtured on Reagan Revolution politics, the rise of these "suburban warriors," as Harvard University historian Lisa McGirr calls them, have branched out well beyond Southern California, and their votes have launched far more careers than Goldwater's, including some of the Republicans mentioned in the previous chapter: Arizona's J. D. Hayworth, Colorado's Bob Beauprez, and Wisconsin's Paul Ryan, to name a few. As metropolitan areas expand ever outward, their growing geographic footprint is changing the political landscape and giving rise to new policy concerns like sprawl and traffic congestion. The crowding of these suburbs has in turn led to growth in the exurbs—those McMansion-filled gated communities that ring the outer suburbs.

Denver-based Democratic consultant Mike Stratton is situated right in the middle of one of the most unprecedented suburban-exurban population explosions in American history. During the 1990s, eight of America's eighteen fastest-growing counties were in Colorado, including top-ranked Douglas County in the Denver suburbs. Stratton describes what he sees unfolding around him:

> You have suburban and exurban areas [in Colorado] that demonstrate the same demographics and behavioral patterns in most other states in the country. I believe Colorado is either first or second in terms of population turnover. More people ingress and egress than any state in the country. You have the phenomenon where people move to California from somewhere and then move back from California to Colorado. You also have a large number of people who have moved here from the Midwest—those Republicans are more progressive than Republicans here because they're Rust Belt Republicans, Gerald Ford Republicans. They are socially more progressive, and that makes them more akin to Democrats here than Republicans. They come here for quality of life, for clean air, clean water, and the Rocky Mountains. These are people moving here with their kids.

Such changes are transforming the West, which no longer is (if it ever was) a mythic land of tumbleweeds and cowpokes. To get a closer look at these changes, I visited Denver during the summer of 2005.

Being a mile above sea level provided no sanctuary from the heat wave that swamped the country during the third week of July 2005.

Triple-digit temperatures in Denver overheated cars, creating delays and gridlock on I-25 and I-225 where electronic "ozone alert" signs reminded drivers to fuel up at night. Local kids jumped into public fountains or hit the water slides at Six Flags amusement park to cool down. It was a hot week for Colorado politics, too. On July 18, the *Denver Post* released a poll showing the public split about a pair of state budgeting referenda awaiting them on the November ballot. That state-level controversy got far less attention than it might have because talk radio was buzzing about the remark the previous Friday by Tom Tancredo, Colorado's virulently anti-immigration congressman, that America ought to consider bombing Islamic holy sites. In other news of state interest, Eric Rudolph, the anti-abortion terrorist convicted of the 1996 Atlanta Olympics bombing, was headed for Colorado's maximum security federal prison in Florence.

At the state capital, I tracked down Representative Andrew Romanoff who, thanks to the Democrats' capture in 2004 of both chambers of the Colorado legislature, had just completed his first legislative session as speaker. (The Democrats had not controlled the House since 1975, "or as I like to remember it," the 39-year-old Romanoff likes to joke, "third grade.") Romanoff asked me to tag along with him on the short walk from his capital office to the nearby Wells Fargo building for an after-work cocktail reception sponsored by the Colorado Software & Internet Association. Hosted in a conference room on the twenty-fourth floor offices of the Fairfield and Woods law firm, three dozen business leaders from nanotechnology, photonics, biotechnology, and related industries chatted quietly while sipping on wine and Stella Artois beer. Through the floor-to-ceiling windows I could see below the steeples of the Cathedral Basilica of the Immaculate Conception where Pope John Paul II—who had died just two months earlier—stayed during his 1993 tour of the United States. Beyond that, stretching east to the horizon as far as my eyes could see, were the short-grass counties of Colorado's Great Plain.

Romanoff is slightly built, with closed-cropped brown hair and a frenetic personality. He had come to talk to CSIA members about Referenda C and D, which Colorado Democrats had put on the ballot to correct the state's TABOR law—the taxpayer "bill of rights" passed the previous decade by Republicans that was preventing this rapidly growing state from raising the revenues necessary to pay for educational and infrastructural improvements. To Denver's assembled tech leaders, Romanoff presented the two referenda as a clear, but stark choice:

> This is the most significant policy discussion in this state in this decade, and it will really help us answer the question of what kind of state we want to leave our kids. A state like the one we've got now, that has fallen to forty-eighth in high school graduation, forty-ninth in job growth, and fiftieth in child immunization? If that's the kind of state you're satisfied with, then you should vote "no" on "C" and "D" and stay the course we're headed on, and that's where we'll head—ranking somewhere between Mississippi and Louisiana for the distinction of last in the nation. That, in my view, is not good enough. We ought to be leading the nation in all of those categories, not lagging in them.

Romanoff then shared a conversation he had, shortly after becoming speaker, with an executive from Amgen, the biotech giant. Romanoff wondered what inducements the executive was seeking from Colorado's government to locate Amgen's facilities in the state. "Do you want some change in tax policy or some regulatory reform?" he asked, presuming the standard, antigovernment Republican orthodoxy. "No," Amgen's exec replied. "If you want more companies like mine to come to a state like yours, invest in education because that's where we go. Why would I go to a state that's in the process of de-funding education instead of a state that's upgrading it?"

During the question-and-answer period that followed, CSIA president Su Hawk told the group that scare tactics by referenda opponents had already begun. A push-pollster happened to call her home, falsely claiming that the referenda would give monies to the University of Colorado's athletic program. The tech leaders frowned. To them, the conservatives' virulent antitax, starve-the-government attitude—no less their heavy-handed tactics—have become passé. "I think the business community realized that we need both parties to help move the state forward," Dennis Oddy, a software accounting company executive and self-described Republican who attended the meeting, told me. "In Colorado, the software business has taken a hit. [These referenda] will encourage companies to take another look at Colorado because of the funding invested in higher education." A few months later, Romanoff and his fellow Democrats got half of what they wanted. In an off-year election, Colorado voters passed one of the two referenda, thereby loosening the fiscal handcuffs on state legislators.

In their influential book, *The Emerging Democratic Majority,* John Judis and Ruy Teixeira label urban communities such as the Denver-Boulder corridor progressive-centrist "ideopolises," which, they believe, are ripe for Democratic gains. Postindustrial America has "transformed the economic geography" of the country, say Judis and Teixeira, creating new-growth cities built upon some combination of light industry, soft technology, university and research centers, and growing retail and service sectors. The demographics of these areas provide a fascinating glimpse at the twenty-first-century American metropolis.

> Professionals and technicians are heavily concentrated in the workforces of these postindustrial metropolises . . . Plentiful, too, are low-level service and information workers, including waiters, hospital orderlies, salesclerks, janitors, and teacher's aides. Many of these jobs have been filled by Hispanics and African-Americans, just as many of the high-level professional jobs have been filled by Asian immigrants. It's one reason that the workforces in these areas we call ideopolises tend to be ethnically diverse and more complex in their stratification . . . than the workforce of the older industrial city . . . The ethos and mores of many of these new metropolitan areas tend to be libertarian and bohemian, because of the people they attract.

These cities are not the blue-collar, European ethnic melting pots that gave birth to the union-dependent, machine-style urban politics of New Deal Democratic strongholds like Richard Daley's Chicago or Erastus Corning's Albany. Today's major metropolitan areas are more dynamic and more independent in their political attachments. In other words, they are swing-voter havens.

Where are these ideopolises? Outside of Florida, Northern Virginia, and North Carolina's Research Triangle, by Judis and Teixeira's own accounting progressive centrism in the South is basically confined to a few college-based cities like Austin, Texas, and Augusta, Georgia. Ideopolitan growth is more prevalent in urban areas outside the South, especially those west of the Mississippi River like Seattle-Tacoma, Portland, San Francisco–San Jose, Phoenix, Las Vegas, Albuquerque–Santa Fe and, of course, Denver-Boulder. If southern exceptionalism is really disappearing, perhaps long-term economic and demographic changes will bring more ideopolises to the "new South," or expand the political clout of the few that do exist. Still, there are only so many places in the South that can replicate, in either scale or dynamism, what's happening in the Research Triangle formed between Raleigh, Durham, and Chapel Hill. Universities like Duke, North Carolina, and North Carolina State—which provided the infrastructure and human capital the Triangle needed to rise to national prominence—do not just pop up in a matter of decades, if ever.

Of course, southern ideopolises lure a disproportionate share of migrated non-southerners, the arrival of whom is not exactly cheered by southerners. Take, for example, the upscale bedroom community of Cary, outside of Raleigh, which is home to thousands of suburbanites working in the Research Triangle. As a sign of how well progressive centrism is being received there, sneering natives have invented their own acronym for Cary—*Contamination Area: Relocated Yankees.* Moonpies and RC Cola will make a comeback in the South before progressive centrism takes hold beyond a handful of places like central North Carolina and Northern Virginia.

The rural vote is a more dominant component of southern demography, and no political analysts understand rural America as well as Steve Jarding and Dave Saunders. In their book, *Foxes in the Henhouse,* Jarding and Saunders paint a sobering picture of rural poverty, especially its pernicious affect on children and seniors. Rural voters are less likely than other Americans to have health insurance, an automobile, or even a home telephone. "Lack of governmental investment, high unemployment, low-wage jobs, limited day care, scarcity of food, poor health care, lack of educational opportunities, and little mobility all contribute to an environment where the least among us are hurt the most," they lament. "This has got to stop. Republicans have neglected this gigantic problem, and they need to pay for their sins of omission."

Rural voters ought to be most receptive to Democratic messages, but the fact is Democrats are faring worse and worse among rural voters with each election cycle. "Rural Nevada beat John Kerry," said Harry Reid, whom Democrats later chose to replace Tom Daschle as Senate majority leader, about his home state after the 2004 election. "I believe where the Kerry presidential bid failed was in not selling itself to rural America." Overall, in 2004 John Kerry did 5 points worse (38 percent) than Al Gore did in 2000 (43 percent) among rural voters. "We put a lot of money behind the rural strategy," says former Democratic National Committee chairman Terry McAuliffe. "The point is to show these rural communities that you would be better off with a Democrat than a Republican because we've done more historically for rural communities and are not out of touch with rural communities." Others question how much effort national Democrats are really putting into rural strategies, but it's understandable why the party wouldn't: Rural voters are a difficult group for Democrats to persuade.

To find out what working-class voters in rural communities are thinking, pollsters Karl Agne and Stan Greenberg of Democracy Corps conducted extensive focus groups in 2005 with rural voters living near four small cities: Appleton, Wisconsin; Little Rock, Arkansas; Louisville, Kentucky; and Golden, Colorado. They found education level to be a powerful indicator of how voters rated the two parties:

> Particularly among non-college voters, cultural issues not only superceded other priorities, *they served as a proxy for many voters on those issues*. With most voters expressing little understanding of the differences between Democrats and Republicans on the relative merits of their positions on economic policy, health care, retirement security, and other issues, they felt it safe to assume that if a candidate was "right" on cultural issues—i.e., opposed to abortion, but most importantly opposed to gay marriage and vocal

about defending the role of faith and traditional Judeo-Christian values in public life—that candidate would naturally also come closest to their views on these other issues.

College-educated voters, on the other hand, were much more circumspect about the focus on cultural issues among many Republican politicians. They decried efforts by President Bush and others to use the resources of elected office to enforce their moral beliefs on others, with the Terry Schiavo case and opposition to stem cell research serving as the most noteworthy examples.

Here again we enter the world of the culture-credentialing filter and Thomas Frank's Great Backlash. These are the much-discussed "values voters," those less inclined—especially if they are not college educated—to even consider differences in the economic platforms of the two parties until and unless their social and cultural concerns are addressed. It doesn't take a cynic to see why Republicans are happy to slash education funding, especially for colleges and student loans: The fewer people who graduate college, the better the GOP's values-based messages sell.

Nobody can doubt the seriousness or moral authority of advocates like Jarding and Saunders when they call for the Democrats to address the problems and pathologies of America's appalling rural poverty. From a purely electoral standpoint, however, rural voters—and rural white southerners in particular—are too hostile to the Democratic Party to expect much in the way of persuasion opportunities. That hostility might be blamed on Democratic neglect. But as Jarding and Saunders concede, rural Americans vote Republican even though the GOP does worse than ignore them: Their policies perpetuate and exacerbate the problems of rural America. The fact that rural voters either know so little or care so little about Republican economic policies yet vote for the GOP anyway testifies to the degree to which rural voters view Democrats as illegitimate. The upside for Democrats is that the rural vote in America is shrinking and, although there are key pockets of rural voters in the Midwest, the most rural region in America is one that Democrats are losing badly anyway: the South.

A much bigger problem for Democrats is exurban voters, because this cohort is not only well educated but growing. "President Bush carried 97 of the nation's 100 fastest-growing counties, most of them 'exurban' communities that are rapidly transforming farmland into subdivisions and shopping malls on the periphery of major metropolitan areas," reported *Los Angeles Times* political analysts Ronald Brownstein and Richard Rainey, in a special postelection voting analysis. "Together, these fast-growing communities provided Bush a punishing 1.72-million-vote advantage . . . almost half the president's total margin of victory." Mark Gersh, data wizard for the National Committee for an Effective Congress, cites Florida as a perfect example of how Kerry's urban mobilization in 2004 was offset by the Republicans' superior exurban mobilization:

> In just five mainly exurban counties (Brevard, Polk, Hillsborough, Lake, and Pasco), Bush picked up a net 99,000 votes over his 2000 performance. The blowout was a combination of higher turnout, especially among Republicans. Despite his success in urban areas, Kerry's support dropped to 39 percent of the vote in Florida's exurban communities, compared with Gore's 43 percent . . . No turnout operation could possibly overcome these margins of defeat, especially given the fast-growing nature of the state's exurbs.

This lethal combination of rural and exurban mobilization also helped slay Kerry in Ohio in 2004, says *Columbus Dispatch* columnist Joe Hallett. According to Hallett, who has been covering state politics for two decades, political experts in Ohio on election night have always relied on three back-of-the-napkin calculations when trying to discern how well Democratic candidates—especially presidential nominees—are doing statewide. Did the Democrats carry Cleveland's Cuyahoga County by at least 150,000 votes? Did they keep Republican margins in Cincinnati-based Hamilton County below 60,000 votes? And, finally, did they break even in Columbus's Franklin County? In an Election Day trifecta, Kerry obliterated all three thresholds, winning Cuyahoga by 226,903 votes, keeping his losing margin in Hamilton to 22,937 votes, and winning Franklin outright by a whopping 48,548 votes. "If you looked at those three counties, based on tradition you thought for sure Kerry had won," says Hallett, recalling the early mood on election night. "In the big six urban counties Kerry won by 14 percent overall, but Bush swamped him in the other eighty-two counties, where he got 57 percent of the vote."

Exurban voters will be much easier to persuade than rural voters, however. Ruy Teixeira completed a comprehensive study of the partisan behaviors and political attitudes of these nascent exurbs, which take one of two forms. "True exurbs" are very far-flung and low-population counties so far from the urban centers that most of their physical geography is converted rural farmland. These areas comprise just 2 percent of the national population and voted for Bush by wide margins in 2004. The bigger, more pivotal areas are the "emerging suburbs" closer in, which comprise 13 percent of the country and voted only 53 percent to 46 percent for Bush over Kerry—and in competitive states, Kerry lost them by just a point (50 percent to 49 percent). "Public opinion data indicate that emerging suburban voters are tax-sensitive and concerned about government waste, but not ideologically antigovernment," says Teixeira. "Similarly, while they tend to be religious and family-oriented and hold some conservative social views, they are socially moderate in comparison to rural residents . . . And these voters worry more about concrete issues like public education than they do about whether politicians have the 'correct' stance on various values issues."

As for claims that the rural vote is somehow responsible for the gubernatorial victories of Democrats Mark Warner in 2001 and his successor Tim Kaine in 2005, that is simply not true. It is the rapid growth of the northern Virginia suburbs and exurbs that most account for the Democrats' improved fortunes in Virginia. Alexandria City and the bedroom communities outside of Washington, DC, provided hundreds of thousands more new Democratic votes for Warner and Kaine than they did for Don Beyer, the Democratic nominee who lost to Republican Jim Gilmore in 1997. Setting aside the sheer size of the vote difference, even the *rate* of Democratic gains between 1997 and either 2001 or 2005 was higher in northern Virginia than it was in many rural counties in Virginia. The reason Virginia, after Florida, is becoming the most competitive state for Democrats is that Virginia increasingly looks more like Maryland, its neighbor to the north, than West Virginia, its rural neighbor to the west.

The flight by Americans from cities to the suburbs and exurbs is a critical development in American politics in the second half of the twentieth century. If Democrats aspire to be the majority party in the first half of the twenty-first century, they need to fight for an appreciable share of the voters who are moving out of the cities and, by both literal and metaphorical extension, away from the Democratic Party. Although that fight will take place in pockets of Central Florida, Northern Virginia, and Central North Carolina, most of the key suburban-exurban battlegrounds are outside the South.

Occupation and Socioeconomic Class

The chasm between rich and poor is wider today than at any time since the 1920s. This bifurcation is depleting the middle classes, and the only reason matters are not worse is because the additional earnings of women working part-time or full-time jobs keep families in the middle class that would otherwise fall into poverty. "Income is now more concentrated at the very top of the income spectrum than in all but six years since the mid-1930s," writes Isaac Shapiro of the Center on Budget and Policy Priorities. Despite all their bluster about family values, the truth is that anti-union, anti–minimum wage, anti–health care Republicans do not really care that Americans are spending less time with their families as they work longer and harder to afford housing, utilities, food, tuition, and health insurance for themselves and their children. With tax cuts for the wealthiest Americans in a time of war and record-setting deficits, the Republicans have demonstrated that, no matter the political or economic situation, they are willing to fight on behalf of the richest and most influential Americans. Because money is time, what the GOP is really doing is redistributing family time from poorer citizens into leisure time and earlier retirements for wealthier ones.

More galling is the fact that Republicans whine about "class warfare" whenever Democrats dare to point to the countless studies that document the growing disparities in earnings and wealth in the United States. Liberal *Washington Post* columnist E. J. Dionne expresses the frustration many Democrats share when Republicans complain about class warfare:

> Class matters. Bush and the Republicans condemn "class war-fare"—and then play the class card with a vengeance. Bush has pushed through policies that, by any impartial reckoning, have transferred massive amounts of money to the wealthiest people in our country. Yet it is conservatives, Bush supporters, who trash the "elites," especially when it comes to culture. Class warfare is evil—unless a conservative is playing the class card . . . Why does the right wing get away, year after year, with this double standard on elitism and class warfare?

Dionne may find some comfort in the assurances of Paul Harstad, a Democratic media and polling consultant, who says Republicans do not always get away with it.

> What I do—and the way we win—is, candidly, by playing class warfare. Republicans scream bloody murder when we do it, and they do it for a reason: Because it works. I am relentless about it. There is not a survey I conduct that does not elevate class warfare . . . The Republicans vote against the middle class, day in and day out, with no embarrassment and with alacrity. The fact that they win as much as they do is a testament to the Democrats' incompe-tence.

Harstad has advised many candidates over the years, particularly in helping craft campaign messages for radio and television that tease out the most powerful visceral theme of all: "Whose side are you on?"

The decimation of middle-class America, especially among those without a college education, is partly a result of globalization. Biparti-san support for free trade, coupled with Republicans' incessant push for right-to-work laws, has replaced high-paying union careers that come with benefits and pensions, with low-paying, part-time and tem-porary jobs that offer little if any collective bargaining leverage. An undergraduate student of mine came to my office a few years ago to ask what recourse he had when United Parcel Service informed him that he had to take a pay cut at his part-time job. I suggested he pick up more hours at his other part-time job. Trouble was, the employer at his second job was . . . UPS! Imagine that: To avoid classifying him as a full-time employee even though he worked about fifty hours a week—for which he would otherwise be paid overtime—UPS hired him for two part-time jobs at the same location. (He even punched different time cards and received separate paychecks.) Welcome to the modern American labor market, where Wal-Mart locks its employees inside to work them off the clock and people can have two "part-time" jobs for the same employer.

The devastating effects of trade policies and globalization are most apparent along the stretch of the I-90 corridor connecting Boston with Detroit. Many Rust Belt cities in this corridor—Syracuse, Buffalo, Cleveland, Toledo—have been virtually hollowed out. Not coincidentally, these are among the cities where housing is most affordable because real estate demand is plummeting. In 2005, I toured through Ohio and Michigan during Halloween week, and the mood seemed fitting. To get to a poverty-themed event at a food pantry in East Cleveland headlined by U.S. Representatives Sherrod Brown, Stephanie Tubbs Jones, and Ted Strickland, I drove eastward along Euclid Avenue from downtown Cleveland—which has its own share of closed storefronts—past one vacated factory or boarded-up warehouse after another. The buildings looked haunted and, indeed, in several Ohio towns I noticed that a few of these shelled-out, abandoned facilities actually *had* been converted temporarily into for-profit Fright Night houses. But the scariest thing I saw during my travels was a sign tacked to a light pole on an exit ramp of I-71 in Columbus that might have made a great title for the next Farrelly brothers movie if it weren't a very serious plea for work: "Two Men and a Bobcat." The sign included the phone number to call if anyone needed earth-moving or other such tasks performed at their home or business. This is the level to which some of the desperate, unemployed Rust Belt laborers are stooping.

The following week, in Detroit, I attended a celebration in honor of Congressman John Dingell, Michigan's labor champion nonpareil, for his fifty years of service in the U.S. House of Representatives. Top labor leaders and politicians in the city and state gathered to pay him tribute in what was a bittersweet moment. A few days earlier, Delphi—a major parts supplier for General Motors that once employed tens of thousands of Ohio and Michigan union workers—announced major cutbacks and layoffs. Soon thereafter, General Motors announced it was letting another 30,000 employees go. The halcyon days for Dingell and his beloved United Auto Workers are gone. UAW's membership is half of what it was twenty-five years ago, and all the banquets in the world are no remedy for the Bobcat-wielding unemployed living in the post-globalization midwestern states like Ohio and Michigan.

Democrats will need to find new means and messages to communicate with American workers. At the end of World War II, about one in three American workers were unionized. Today, only about one in eight is, and most of these workers are government employees. Oddly enough, the share of Americans who live in union households has actually held rather steady over time, thanks in part to the millions of union retirees. Rick Weiner, a veteran Democratic strategist in union-heavy Michigan and the recently retired chief of staff to Governor Jennifer Granholm, suggests that union messages may actually be resonating stronger in today's postglobalization era:

I haven't seen anything that would lead me to believe that unions will be less effective. Yes, they are talking to fewer members—although they may not be talking to fewer members plus retirees. The more interesting piece is the degree to which the unions' message on public issues may have greater salience right now because the impact of constricting wages is relevant to both union *and* nonunion workers. I suppose 2006 and 2008 will test this theory. Ironically, it's possible that although the unions may be talking to fewer members, their electoral message may speak more to nonunion members.

A March 2006 poll confirms Weiner's instincts. Despite constant headlines about the Iraq war, the Dubai Port deal, the Jack Abramoff and Duke Cunningham lobbying scandals, and news that Republicans

would be raising the national debt ceiling for a fourth time during the
Bush administration, what did pollsters find was Americans' top issue
concern? Globalization and outsourcing.

Table 5.4
Unionized Labor Force in the South, 1964–2000

State	1964		1984		2000	
	Percentage	Rank	Percentage	Rank	Percentage	Rank
Alabama	21.1	34	15.2	28	9.8	29
Arkansas	15.0	43	10.0	42	5.9	45
Florida	14.0	46	9.6	45	6.9	40
Georgia	11.9	48	10.3	41	6.3	43
Louisiana	18.1	37	11.1	36	7.1	38
Mississippi	15.4	42	9.7	44	6.1	44
North Carolina	8.4	49	7.5	49	3.7	50
South Carolina	7.0	50	4.2	50	4.1	49
Tennessee	22.1	30	13.5	30	8.9	32
Texas	13.5	47	8.0	48	5.9	46
Virginia	15.8	40	10.8	38	5.7	48
United States	29.1	—	19.1	—	13.6	—

In 2004, Bush carried every single one of the twenty-three current
right-to-work states, which include all of the southern states, plus Kentucky, Oklahoma, and most of the Plains states. The South, of course, is
where unions have always been weakest. Table 5.4 reports the share of
the statewide labor force that was unionized in 1964, 1984, and 2000.
Union rolls have fallen everywhere, but what's telling is that no southern state during the past four decades has ranked higher than twenty-
eight, and most have been consistently at or near the bottom of the
rankings. North Carolina and South Carolina, America's textile jugger-
nauts, have battled for decades for the title of least-unionized state.
Non-college-educated white men generally don't vote Democratic, but
members of unions or union families are a notable exception. As al-

ready discussed, Democrats don't have a white voter problem so much as a southern white voter problem, and a key reason for this is the historical absence of a significant union presence in the South. As we'll see in the next chapter, however, the South's antilabor traditions are starting to catch up with local politicians.

Socioeconomic status operates in other, strange ways in the South. Consider this paradox: John Kerry ran strongest nationally among voters from families with incomes under $50,000 per year, yet did horribly in the South, the nation's poorest region. Cultural voting partially explains this paradox, because poorer white southerners support Republicans despite what ought to be more attractive economic messages from Democrats. As Columbia University statistician Andrew Gelman and his colleagues discovered, another curious reason for this paradox is that in the poorer, red states the rich vote much more Republican, whereas in the blue states the relationship between income and partisanship is weak, if it matters at all.

There are several ways to depict this finding, but the easiest may be to examine how voters in households with incomes over $50,000 and those under this threshold behaved nationwide, and compare the results with those of southern voters. To keep terminology simple, I'll call these two groups "high-income" and "low-income" voters. Nation-

Figure 5.5
Bush's High-Income Voter Gap, 2004

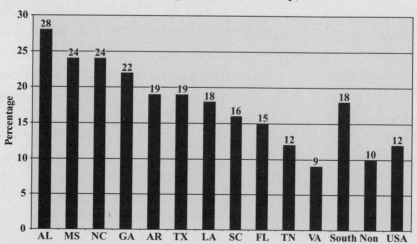

ally, Bush won 56 percent of high-income voters, but only 44 percent of low-income voters—a split of 12 percentage points. In the non-southern states, that split was only 10 points, with Bush winning 53 percent of high-income and 43 percent of low-income voters.

However, in the South the gap was 18 points. Low-income southerners were only slightly more supportive of Bush (47 percent) than their non-southern cohorts—but this is a by-product of the fact that the lower category includes the vast majority of Democratic-leaning African Americans. Meanwhile, high-income voters were *much more* supportive of Bush (65 percent) than non-southern high-income voters, especially in Alabama, Mississippi, North Carolina, and Georgia. In fact, Virginia was the only southern state where the high/low income disparity was smaller (9 points) than the non-southern average—and that's no surprise, given that Virginia is the highest-income southern state and the only one in 2004 where at least three of every five voters came from families with incomes over $50,000. Once the African-American vote is held aside in the South, the pattern is clear: Poor whites vote their cultural interests and rich whites vote their economic interests but, either way, the outcome is the same—millions of Republican votes.

A final, labor-related feature of the South that is often overlooked is the fact that southern states are home to almost half of American military service personnel. Despite having only 62.7 million eligible workers, 390,000 southerners were members of the U.S. armed forces in 2000, or about 1 out of every 160 workers; outside the South, the 409,000 total service personnel comprise just 1 in every 360 workers. These totals include neither military spouses nor extended families. The concentration of service personnel and their families can make an electoral difference, especially in close races when absentee ballots trickle in from overseas after the polls close. (During the 2000 Florida recount, at one point the certification of several thousand military ballots became a matter of dispute between the Gore and Bush camps.) Members of the military, especially officers, tend to vote Republican, so their southern residency turns out to be an indirect Democratic blessing, given that Republicans win presidential and many statewide elections there by comfortable margins anyway.

Family and Marital Status

Somebody needs to write an obituary because Ozzie and Harriet are dead. Although the nuclear family in America is still quite common, rising divorce rates, longer wait times before young people first marry, the increase in childless couples, and the demolition of taboos toward same-sex relationships have combined to reduce the prevalence of traditional marriage. At some point between 1990 and 2000, for the first time in American history single-parent households surpassed two-parent families with children as the most common family combination—and childless couples, gay or straight, are not far behind the traditional nuclear family in third place, as Figure 5.6 shows. Most astounding is the fact that half of adult Americans are currently unmarried. Only because they turn out at higher rates are married Americans still a majority of voters—at least for now.

Some election watchers foresee serious trouble for Democrats among married Americans. "Married white women are almost entirely responsible for the change in the Bush vote," argues Harvard University political scientist Barry Burden, noting that married white women favored Clinton by 5 points in 1996, were split in 2000, but by 2004 chose Bush by 9 points (55 percent to 44 percent). Among all married women, Bush increased from a 48 percent to 46 percent margin over Al Gore in 2000 to a 55 percent to 44 percent edge over Kerry four years later. "In the larger context of so much geographic and demographic stability, these are seismic shifts," Burden concludes. Should these trends expand to include Hispanics, the Democrats will have an even larger persuasion problem. "If Latino voters continue to move into the middle class, buy houses, and relocate to more conservative areas—in other words, if they replicate the patterns of white nuclear families who are leaving behind the childless city centers—Democrats may have a hard time holding on to them," warn political demographers Joel Kotkin and William Frey.

Families produce children, and a 2006 study by Phillip Longman of the New American Foundation further warns that, unless they start breeding more, Democrats face a possible "liberal baby bust" because heartland conservatives from blue states who attend church and vote

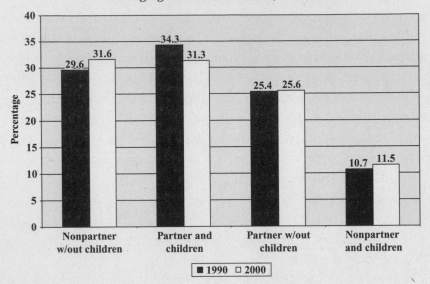

Figure 5.6
Changing American Families, 1990 to 2000

Republican are simply having more offspring. "In Seattle, there are nearly 45 percent more dogs than children," writes Longman. "In Salt Lake City, there are nearly 19 percent more kids than dogs." When it comes to married couples with children, despite the party's repeated emphasis on kitchen-table issues, Democrats have a serious persuasion problem.

As counterbalance, Democrats have a great mobilization opportunity among unmarried Americans. In 2003, 49.7 percent of American women were unmarried, and at some subsequent point unmarried women became the majority. Almost half of American men are unmarried, too. Kerry won unmarried women by a whopping 25-point margin over Bush, 62 percent 37 percent. This is no sliver segment of the population, mind you: Unmarried women cast one-fourth of all votes in the 2004 election. By 53 percent to 45 percent, Kerry also won unmarried men, one of the few subgroups of male voters that favor Democrats. Results from a recent survey for Women's Voices Women Vote reveal that by wide margins unmarried men (22 points) and women (56 points) see the country as moving in the wrong rather than the right direction. On specific issues unmarried men and women differ, but in general they are dissatisfied with Bush administration policies, foreign and domestic, as Table 5.5 shows. The combined effect is what some are calling a "marriage gap" in American politics.

Because younger voters are far less likely to be married, and gay voters are prohibited from marriage, to a certain degree Democratic success among the unmarried is an artifact of their age and sexual orientation. Still, as a group the unmarried also include divorced adults and other heterosexual adults who either delay marriage or choose not to marry. Because they may be the lone adult in their households and may also be raising children, the political-economic concerns of this

Table 5.5
Policy Views of Unmarried Americans
(by Percentage)

Issues	All	Women	Men
The war in Iraq was worth the cost in U.S. lives and dollars.	25	23	28
The war in Iraq was not worth the cost in U.S. lives and dollars.	70	71	68
It's best for the future of our country to be active in world affairs.	37	34	40
We should pay less attention to problems overseas and concentrate on problems here at home.	57	58	54
Government regulation of business is necessary to protect the public interest.	49	50	48
Government regulation of business usually does more harm than good.	42	40	46
The government should do more to help needy Americans, even if it means going deeper into debt.	61	62	59
The government today can't afford to do much more to help the needy.	32	29	36

Poll for Women's Voices. Women Vote., by Greenberg Quinlan Rosner, released February 27, 2006.

subset of unmarried Americans are often quite different from, say, unmarried gay professionals living together in upscale, two-income households without children. For unmarried single parents, the Democrats' kitchen-table policy messages should resonate—but only if these folks turn out. A whopping 22 million unmarried Americans failed to vote in 2004, providing an important base-voter target for Democrats to mobilize.

Interracial marriage is another American phenomenon on the rise. In 1990, about 1 in every 23 marriages was interracial, but by 2000 the rate had increased to about 1 in every 15 marriages. Not surprising, interracial marriage is least prevalent in the South. Figure 5.7 scatterplots each state's white population share against its percent of interracial marriages, with the national average (6.7 percent of marriages, 69.1 percent nonwhite population) dividing the chart into four quadrants. Most of the states in the upper-left corner have understandably few interracial marriages because the state populations are near-universally white. On the other hand, those in the bottom-right corner are Hispanic-dominated states whose diverse populations feature high rates of interracial marriage.

Figure 5.7
Interracial Marriage in the States, 2000

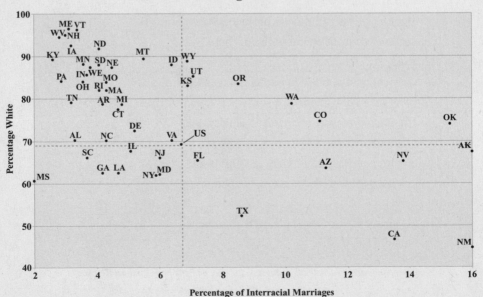

The two exceptional cases are in the top-right corner, where states with significant Asian American and/or Hispanic populations like Colorado and Washington have higher-than-expected numbers of interracial couples, and the bottom-left corner, where interracial marriage is unusually low given the high share of minorities statewide. The latter is where we find a cluster of mostly southern states. The combination of greater taboos and geographic segregation, plus a lower preference for interracial relationships, makes black-white marriages rare. "African-Americans are much rarer, despite the fact that blacks comprise a similar share of the U.S. population as Latinos, and are about three times more numerous than Asians," writes demographer William Frey. "Only about one in eight marriages involving African-Americans are of mixed-race. At the other end of the spectrum, nearly three of four marriages involving Native Americans, Eskimos and Alutes are interracial." Twenty-two percent of Americans say they have at least one interracial marriage in their family.

Religion

Having discussed in some detail in chapter 3 the regional differences in American religious attitudes—particularly the huge southern evangelical base that voted overwhelmingly for Bush in 2004—I pause briefly to revisit the subject of religion only to note that Americans are becoming more secular. In 2001, the City University of New York conducted 50,000 interviews for its American Religious Identification Survey, and compared the results with a similar survey conducted in 1990. In just over a decade the proportion of the population identifying with one or another religious group dropped from 90 percent to 81 percent, with self-described Christians falling from 86 percent to 77 percent. "[T]he greatest increase in absolute as well as in percentage terms has been among those adults who do not subscribe to any religious identification," reads the report's summary. "[T]heir number has more than doubled from 14.3 million in 1990 to 29.4 million in 2001; their proportion has grown from just 8 percent of the total in 1990 to over 14 percent in 2001."

Changes in religious identity may be occurring within generations, or as a result of immigration. But the key factor is generational replace-

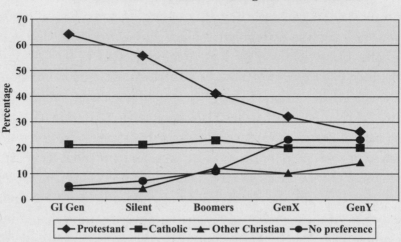

Figure 5.8
Generational Differences in Religious Identification

ment: Younger Americans with weaker religious attachments are re-placing older Americans with stronger identifications. Figure 5.8 depicts results, by generation, of a recent Greenberg Quinlan Rosner Research survey of religious self-identification. The share of self-described Protestants today is highest among the eldest, GI Genera-tion, then drops for each successively younger generation: the Silent Generation, the Baby Boomers, Generation X and Generation Y. The percentage within each of these generations that is self-described as ei-ther "no preference/atheist/agnostic" has risen to 23 percent among Gen X and Gen Y—higher than the percentage of Americans from the two youngest generations who call themselves Catholics. Younger Americans are not only less religious themselves, but are more tolerant of religious diversity for others. Even in Utah, the closest thing to state religion on American soil, Mormons are projected to be a minority of residents by 2030.

Summary

As with narrow victories in sporting events, an almost endless list of factors could be cited as decisive in a closely contested presidential elec-tion. In this chapter alone, one analyst or another deemed white voters, married voters, women voters, over-60 voters, rural voters, exurban voters, non-college-educated voters, security voters, or values voters as crucial if not decisive to George W. Bush's reelection in 2004. Obviously, these categories often overlap: Rural, non-college-educated, married, white women over 60 who voted on security and values were undoubtedly a tough demographic for John Kerry to crack.

Leafing through all of these electoral postmortems, one might wonder how Kerry managed to convince 59 million Americans to support him. Yet he did, and that support was good enough for 48 percent of the vote—the highest total against an incumbent president since 1980. Despite a variety of problems, the Democrats are hardly getting blown out in presidential contests. The Democrats won the popular vote in three of the past four elections, and Kerry came 2.4 percent short in the fourth. Though Democrats have plenty of work to do, fortunately there are ample persuasion and mobilization opportunities available for building a new national majority coalition. As we saw repeatedly throughout this chapter, most of those opportunities lie outside the South.

THE DISAPPEARING DEFAULT DEMOGRAPHIC

The demographic transformations occurring in America are many and profound, yet the national map remains mostly gridlocked. Few House seats have changed partisan hands in recent elections, and the presidential map barely budged between 2000 and 2004. Although there are some interesting electoral dynamics at the state level, it is as if partisanship on a national level is bottled up, ready to burst wide open. Despite all the breathless, this-changes-everything talk in our post–September 11 America, the partisan situation is very similar now to what it was in 2000. The horrific attacks perpetrated by al Qaeda simply did not reconfigure partisan politics in the United States the way the Civil War, the depressions of the 1890s and 1930s, or the civil rights movement did—and all four of those events predate the twenty-four-hour media age, when millions of Americans saw over and over again the images of the Pentagon ablaze and the Twin Towers crumbling to the ground.

Despite the chorus of voices mocking the Democratic Party's litany of problems, and the weaknesses of Democratic leaders from Al Gore to John Kerry to Nancy Pelosi to Howard Dean, a broader view suggests that the bigger failure was that in January 2005 George W. Bush and his fellow Republicans did not surge into office on the strength of a forty-state presidential win and newly insurmountable congressional majorities. In the 2004 elections, the GOP had control of all branches of government, plenty of campaign cash, and the bully pulpit. They not only knew who their nominee was three years before Kerry surfaced, but started building their field operation at least two years ahead of the arrival of the Democrats or their affiliate campaign groups. Most of all, Republicans had the powerful issue of terrorism to campaign behind. And the result? Bush carried a grand total of one more state than he did in 2000, and the net Republican gains in the House and Senate can be attributed entirely to the reredistricting of the Texas House delegation and the fortuity of having five southern Senate Democrats retire in a single election cycle.

Historically, partisan realignments result from the confluence of significant demographic changes and the sudden emergence of a dramatic political moment, which, taken together, obliterate the previous partisan arrangements and produce a new majority coalition. The Republicans were clearly given their moment on September 11—the first opportunity of such magnitude for either party since the Supreme Court's 1954 decision in *Brown v. Board of Education* put the solid Democratic South into play. That said, there are only two possible explanations for the GOP's failure thus far to realign America. The first is that Republicans lack the messaging skills, political leadership, electoral resources, think tank infrastructure, technical capacity, or sheer taste for the political jugular necessary to overtake American politics. The second is that gradual, underlying demographic changes are working against them. Since there seems to be not a single political analyst in America who would argue the former, there must be a lot of truth to the latter. If the Democrats are hamstrung by mealy-mouthed, infighting, and clueless leaders, and the always more politically savvy Republicans have the benefit of the biggest political-electoral opportunity of the past half century to exploit, the pull of these anti-Republican demographic currents must be very strong indeed.

Karl Rove, the president's political architect, says the Republicans are enjoying a "rolling realignment" in which they are making steady gains, cycle after cycle, as opposed to the tectonic partisan shifts made in the 1860, 1896, or 1932 elections. Rove may be right, but it's difficult to see such a rolling realignment based on a close inspection of demographic trends, which reveal a country becoming more racially diverse, less male dominated, more secular, and less traditional in its familial arrangements. Since the South—and especially the politically dominant rural white South—is moving at crosscurrents with many of these changes, it's even more puzzling that some Democrats still think the party should begin its revival in Dixie.

Although the share of Christian, white, married men from traditional families is declining, what's less clear is whether another default demographic will ever emerge to replace it. Indeed, a future Democratic majority would, by its very design, be so heterogeneous that it cannot possibly have a comparable core subgroup, which is why Democrats find it much harder to communicate simply and succinctly to their more diverse set of potential supporters than the Republicans, who can easily identify and mobilize their default demographic. Put another way, although Hispanics, women, religious seculars, the aged, westerners, suburban-exurbanites, and the unmarried are comprising larger and larger shares of the national quilt, we're a long way from a time when Unitarian, widowed *abuelitas* from the outskirts of Albuquerque are considered typical Americans, no less the political base of a national Democratic juggernaut. In the interim, the closest thing there is to a core Democratic voter is African-American women, and bless their souls for their continued fealty to the party—especially since half of them live in the South, where their votes for statewide office are almost always cast proudly in defeat.

What is clear, however, is that the overall demographic portrait of the United States today and in the near future—and thus, the "who" of any future Democratic majority—confirms that the "where" of that majority coalition must be constructed outside the South. The next question is: What policies and messages should Democrats use to persuade and mobilize this non-southern coalition?

6

A Non-Southern Platform

We have been in a reactive posture for too long. I think we have been very good at saying no, but not good enough at saying yes.

> —Senator Barack Obama, Illinois Democrat, describing his party

On issue after issue, they stand for nothing except obstruction.

> —President George W. Bush, describing the Democratic Party

A STOCK CAMPAIGN slogan frequently uttered in Democratic circles goes something like this: "When Democrats talk about the issues, we win." Obviously, this statement is patently false. Democrats talk plenty about the issues, more so than Republicans do. For all the sneering by Republicans that Democrats have no ideas, it is the Republicans who usually want to turn elections into discussions about the character of the candidates rather than substantive debates about the issues. Why? Because a purely policy debate would force Republicans to pervert their positions and mask their policies. As Jacob Hacker and Paul Pierson argue so powerfully in their book, *Off Center*, Republicans have become very adept at obfuscation—so much so that voters, who are no more but no less informed than they were in previous generations, are empowering politicians to enact a radically conservative agenda that does not approximate their own views:

> Agendas are painstakingly crafted and ruthlessly enforced. Messages are carefully calibrated to influence popular perceptions. Policies are expertly designed to exploit weaknesses in voters' ability to get and use information. Costs are hidden; benefits are structured in ways that confuse; policies are engineered with long lag times, confusing provisions, and ticking time bombs—all for one purpose: so that conservative elites, not ordinary voters, will set the future political agenda.

It is precisely because Republicans can't sell their agenda on its merits that they must convince voters that Democrats can't be believed or trusted—that they have zero credibility. After all, any policy platform, no matter how popular, when multiplied by zero is still zero.

Notice how Republicans characterized the past two Democratic presidential nominees. Al Gore, we were told, was a man who would say *anything* to get elected, whether he believed it or not. Four years later, similar voices claimed John Kerry was a man who would say *everything* to get elected, whether those statements contradicted one another. In 2000, Gore actually proposed a ten-year defense budget increase more than twice the size of Bush's proposal. Surely this fact sailed past many voters because it didn't square with theirs or the media's preconceived notions about which party is strong on defense. During the 2004 presidential debates, Kerry ripped all manner of holes in Bush's securing-the-homeland claims, again, mostly for naught. The Bush campaign didn't bother trying to out-propose Gore or Kerry to beat them among security-minded voters—they just personally discredited the Democrats to beat them among security-minded voters.

The point is that if Democrats won merely by talking about the issues, there wouldn't be a Republican in the White House, Republican majorities in both chambers of Congress, a Republican majority of state governors, or Republican control of a majority of state legislative chambers. No matter how thin these majorities may be, they are real. And they stand as proof positive that the phrase "Democrats win when they talk about the issues" is more of a wistful mantra than an operational strategy.

Why, then, is belief in this mantra so pervasive? The reason many otherwise clear-thinking Democrats believe that talking about the issues will win elections is that so many of the party's policies and solutions test well in polls. Responding to poll questions is not the same as voting, however. If the attitudes expressed to pollsters were translated directly and in an unfiltered way into votes by those respondents, then yes, Democrats would probably be winning a lot more elections. But a voter's decision calculus involves much more than his position on the issues or how well his positions square with the candidates and parties appearing on the ballot. This is such a fundamental point it deserves restating: The *political value* of issues is not the same as the *popularity* of issue positions. Understanding the issues—their policy content, their potential implications for the country, their pros and cons, who supports and who opposes what positions—is not the same as using issues to win elections.

As Hacker and Pierson demonstrate, Republicans clearly understand how to politicize issues. In almost Darwinian fashion, the Republicans *need* to develop clever and sometimes insidious ways to masquerade their policies because any honest and transparent accounting of their implications would cost the GOP dearly at the ballot box. For Democrats, the problem is the reverse: Falsely comforted by poll numbers telling them that they support the policies Americans want, they fail to politicize issues for maximum electoral advantage.

Take, for example, the current national controversy on immigration reform. If the Democrats are not careful they are going to blow one of the best policy-political opportunities in a generation. As a public policy question, immigration has almost too many dimensions to count. It is a race issue, an economic issue, a cultural issue, a social services and budgetary issue, a crime issue, a labor issue and, of course, a border and national security issue. Beyond its policy import, the issue of immigration offers a bevy of political opportunities for the Democrats.

The salience of the issue only seems to increase with each election cycle, and the Republicans would rather it just went away. Though it is a tricky needle to thread, if handled correctly a Democratic policy on immigration reform can unite the party, attract new voters to the Democratic coalition, and supply a powerful wedge for dividing the Republican Party against itself. Because of the security aspect of immigration reform, the Democrats can also use immigration to reinsert themselves in an aggressive way into the national security debate. Moreover, Democrats can gain politically from this issue while doing the morally correct thing by the estimated 12 million illegal aliens already in the country, by the already naturalized Hispanic Americans, and by the broader, native-born citizenry who reject the reactionary ideas of people like Colorado congressman Tom Tancredo and conservative pundit Pat Buchanan. Given the Hispanic population explosion in the Southwest, the issue is also a regional one with implications for the non-southern strategy.

Though a platform designed to appeal to a non-southern majority must include more than an immigration plank, I mention this issue to open the chapter because it provides a perfect case study for how policies can be used to win elections and build a party. A principled party sometimes must take stands that have little or no political benefit, but a party that neglects to consider the political aspects of policy choices—or, worse, does not have the stomach for politicizing policies—is destined for minority status if not extinction.

The two previous chapters outlined where and among which voters the Democrats can construct a non-southern majority. Before connecting the platform to the geo-demographic coalition of the non-southern majority, it is necessary to digress for an examination of how to use issues for political and partisan gain. Using issues for political advantage is so elemental that one might think every elected official and party knows how to do so. Of late, however, Democrats seem to have forgotten some of the basics. Though some of the discussion in the following section is not specific to regional politics or the non-southern strategy, as the second half of the chapter will make clear, a non-southern strategy allows Democrats to politicize issues for maximal advantage.

POLITICIZING ISSUES FOR PARTISAN GAIN

Let's start with the three features of every issue, and the fact that partisans, pundits, and politicians place far too much emphasis on just one aspect—the spatial positions of candidates or parties. We hear that this politician is too far left or that interest group is too far right. Arguments ensue about how big the middle is, where that middle is located, which party or candidate is positioned closer to it, and what motivates the pivotal voters who reside in this murky middle. The only restriction that would be more punitive to political pundits than banning baseball or boxing metaphors would be to outlaw left-right analogies.

Within the Democratic coalition there are significant left-right ideological disagreements, and these fights typically divide the moderate wing epitomized by the Democratic Leadership Council from the liberal wing that finds its home in places like the Campaign for America's Future or the online crowd at MoveOn.org. This internecine debate over the soul and future of the Democratic Party inevitably devolves into arguments about whether Democrats need to spend more attention trying to attract moderates and centrists (the DLC claim), or acknowledging and nurturing its liberal base (the CAF counterclaim). Sub-arguments ensue: Are the Democrats too weak on defense because they don't sound *more* like the Republicans or because they sound *too much* like the Republicans? Should the party invest more in persuasion efforts or mobilization efforts?

Though useful as a device for introspection, arguments between the liberal and conservative wings of the Democratic Party not only waste a certain amount of time and energy, but preoccupy Democrats so much that they tend to forget that not all issues fit along some single, left-right ideological axis in the first place. Based on his views of reproductive choice we may have a good idea about how a voter feels about gay rights, but can we intuit his views on the mortgage interest deduction? Not likely, because many issues operate in their own dimension, akin to the numerous spokes around a wheel hub rather than a single, horizontal left-right spectrum along which all issues are conveniently arrayed. In 2000 at the Wardman Park Marriott in Washington, on a panel of assembled political hotshots with academic backgrounds, including former speaker Newt Gingrich of Georgia, Norman Ornstein of the American Enterprise Institute, and the late senator Paul Wellstone of Minnesota, *Washington Post* columnist E. J. Dionne remarked that nobody had taken the Democratic Party farther to the left than Bill Clinton— but that nobody had tugged his party farther to the right, either. Dionne's observation attests not so much to Clinton's ideological schizophrenia but the simple fact that depicting the policy universe solely in left-right terms oversimplifies the matter.

If issues are about more than left-right positioning, what are the other two aspects that matter politically? The first is *salience,* or the priority a candidate or party assigns to an issue, and the second is *efficacy,* or the ability of a candidate or party to deliver on issue promises. The problem for Democrats is they too often get caught in saliency traps, push low-efficacy issues, or both.

Saliency Traps and Low-Efficacy Issues

Some issues are more important than others, and not just because of how many votes the party stands to gain or lose by advocating and fighting for its policy positions. For example, when forced to justify their support for eliminating what used to be called the "estate tax," Republicans began referring to the tax, first, as the "inheritance tax" and, eventually, as the more oppressive-sounding "death tax." (As if the homeless man who freezes to death inside a cardboard box will have that box and its possessions hauled away as a duty because everybody is taxed for the very act of dying.) For all the praise heaped on Republicans for their skillful use of semantics, the GOP would rather not make the estate tax a defining issue because it reinforces the party's justly earned image as a bunch of country clubbers. On the other hand, Republicans assign significant weight to income tax cuts—vaguely defined, and purposely so. After all, only a small segment of the population pays inheritance taxes, but almost everyone pays income taxes. The former issue has low saliency, the latter has high saliency.

Democrats too often get caught in salience traps. That is, they allow themselves to be defined by what should be low-salience issues, and abortion is a case in point. A growing number of myopic Democrats believe the party must change its position on abortion. But a majority of

Americans agree with the Democrats on choice; the party's *position* on abortion is not the problem. Rather, the problem is how prominently abortion figures in the public perceptions of the party. Shrewdly, Republicans invoke the issue of "partial-birth" abortion to goad Democrats into a semantic debate. As Democrats scramble around to defend the term "late-term abortion," Republicans are winning the larger saliency war because what many Americans take away from the flap is that the Democrats are the party obsessed with third-trimester abortions, no matter the label. This is a saliency problem, and a grave one indeed: In a recent Democracy Corps survey, the first and third highest sources of negative association with the Democrats are gay rights and abortion, with "no strong direction" (a nonissue, general image) cited second. Support for civil unions or reproductive choice are important planks in the Democratic platform, but not the foundations. Republicans have managed to convinced the public otherwise because Democrats have let them.

Republicans have become so adept at defining what the nation's most salient issues should be that we have reached the point where "responsible" Republicans are focused on real issues like taxes and defense while "silly" Democrats obsess over political correctness, assaulting Christmas, protecting transgender rights, and defending violent content in movies and video games. Within a month of Bush taking office in 2001, conservative columnist George Will condescended to assure the country that the new administration had revived "government by grown-ups." Thus the familiar, if false dichotomy of Republicans as the strong, protective, defense-oriented "daddy party" and Democrats as soft, nurturing, domestic-oriented "mommy party" has been eclipsed by a political household where Republicans are the only adults. Childish Democrats, of course, are to be seen and not heard.

Another manifestation of the Democrats' salience problem is the constant Republican harping about "moral values," followed almost immediately by the accusation that Democrats have none. Panicked and confused, Democrats rush to assure everyone that they *do* have values. How? By parroting whatever Republicans define as moral values. Recently, Democrats have begun to counterattack by talking about how budgets are moral documents that reflect a party's values, and here we see the influence of language consultants (especially George Lakoff of *Don't Think of an Elephant* fame), who have convinced Democrats that they can improve their fortunes by reframing issues. Semantic repackaging is useful, so far as it goes. But just like the framing of an actual painting or photograph, the menu of choice involves much more than wood or metal frames, single- or double-matting. Framing is also about *where* items are placed—how high or low, how prominently or not. What a home owner decides to mount with great care above the mantel in the living room and what she carelessly tacks on the wall of her renovated basement playroom tells you something about her. These are not semantic choices, but salience choices.

Democrats are justifiably proud of their domestic positions and performance. If they hope to restore their national majority, they will have to place defense and foreign policy frames above the mantel for all to see. As for cultural issues, it's long past time to cease the hand-wringing and take a cue from gutsy, no-nonsense politicians like Montana governor Brian Schweitzer or former Ohio congressional candidate Paul Hackett. Schweitzer solves the saliency problem on cultural issues by dismissing Republican attempts to emphasize culture issues with a "who cares?" wave of the hand. In effect, he zeros out any GOP advantages and returns the discussion to winning Democratic topics. As we will see later in this chapter, Hackett has an even more inventive solution when the subject turns to gun control.

If Democrats pay little attention to issue saliency, they pay almost none to issue *efficacy*—the degree, real or perceived, to which a candidate or party can deliver on its promises.

The issue of judicial appointments makes this oversight painfully clear. Karl Rove has said the reason "liberal activist judges" is such a powerful trigger for conservatives is that each of the different elements of the conservative coalition find their own aspirations in this loaded term—CEOs hear a defense of deregulation, small-business owners hear tort reform, and social conservatives hear an end to privacy rights. Beyond these constituency-pleasing benefits, the political allure of campaigning against activist judges is that Republicans can *actually deliver* the goods: They are constitutionally empowered to appoint and confirm the judges they please and claim credit for delivering on their promises to do so. Contrast this level of efficacy with, say, a major piece of legislation that, assuming it can be pushed through the legislative committee and subcommittee systems and over the objections of scores of interest groups to arrive finally on the president's desk, will, by the time it is enacted, have almost as many Washington fingerprints on it as the moon rock on display at the National Air and Space Museum.

If that legislation is a "jobs" bill, delivery is further complicated by the fact that no politician, including the president, controls the economy. I can't tell you how many Democrats around the country reflexively mention "jobs" as one of the top three issues facing the country or their state. I have no doubt that poll numbers and the politicians' street sensibilities confirm that jobs are a top priority for voters. It's easy to pound the jobs theme, but delivering newer or better jobs is much tougher. Even when new or better jobs *are* produced, this achievement is discounted by many voters who believe—or want to believe, even if it's not entirely true—that their personal economic fates are entirely beyond the control of decisions that politicians in their state capitals or Washington make. "The biggest reason Democrats' economic appeals to white, working-class voters fell flat *isn't* that they weren't passionate enough," observes the *New Republic*'s Noam Schieber, summarizing the party's performance in the 2004 election. "It's that Democrats have run up against the limits of what they—or anyone else—can do to create and protect good jobs, the top economic priority of working-class voters. And the political implications of that development are enormous."

Although a person's employment and earning status are more central to his everyday life and livelihood, promising jobs has low-issue efficacy whereas promising new judges is high-efficacy. Republicans attack the character of the Democratic Party and its candidates as a way to zero out the Democrats' inherent issue advantages. When Democrats promote low-efficacy issues, the effect is the same, but the damage is self-inflicted: Voters figure the Democrats can't deliver anyway, so all their marvelous-sounding, poll-tested promises get reduced to nothing.

A final point about issue efficacy deserves mention: Sometimes the vote or electoral outcome *itself* is the deliverable. Consider the eleven state ballot measures passed in 2004 to protect the sanctity of marriage.

It's doubtful that the passage of these referenda will alter the sexual lifestyles of homosexuals, or even the nonsexual elements of their lives—their home-buying, business-creating, and family-raising activities. My wife and I attended our first gay wedding in 2004, which I'm betting won't be our last. The lesbian couple who wedded that day— whether in the legal eyes of the state or merely ceremonially—is now raising a son together thanks to the artificial insemination of one of his mothers by a sperm donor. Passing ballot measures won't make American society less open or accepting of homosexuality in the future, and there won't be any fewer gay relationships, gay home owners, or gay parents because of their passage. Since same-sex marriage was already illegal in these eleven states, the Republicans really didn't change state policies so much as they clarified or codified them. Those eleven "victories" were essentially symbolic.

That's just fine with Republicans, because their objective is the political potency of the issue, no matter the policy impact or its potential for increasing turnout (which, by the way, the referenda didn't). By putting gay marriage on state ballots the Republicans gave their supporters something to savor the moment the results came in: The comfort of knowing that those dastardly liberals in Hollywood and on campus are stewing somewhere about it. As he puzzled over what's wrong with his home state in his widely acclaimed book, *What's the Matter with Kansas?*, Thomas Frank wondered how Republicans get away with talking a lot yet never quite delivering much when it comes to the promises they make on cultural issues. Frank concluded that Republican leaders never intend to deliver tangible policy changes, but instead want to perpetuate a cultural crusade that will forever keep battalions of warriors at the ready:

Their grandstanding leaders never produce, their fury mounts and mounts, and nevertheless they turn out every two years to return their right-wing heroes to office for a second, a third, a twentieth try. The trick never ages, the illusion never wears off. *Vote* to stop abortion; *receive* a rollback in capital-gains taxes. *Vote* to make our country strong again; *receive* deindustrialization. *Vote* to screw those politically correct college professors; *receive* electricity deregulation. *Vote* to get government off our backs; *receive* conglomeration and monopoly everywhere from media to meat-packing. *Vote* to stand tall against terrorists; *receive* Social Security privatization efforts. *Vote* to strike a blow against elitism; *receive* a social order in which wealth is more concentrated than ever before in our lifetimes, in which workers have been stripped of power and CEOs are rewarded in a manner beyond imagining.

Frank's observation is blisteringly accurate, if incomplete. The Republicans who stage-manage what he calls the Great Backlash often give their supporters policy-empty victories that are quite satisfying, either symbolically or emotionally. The eleven antigay ballot initiatives are a perfect example: *Vote* for a sanctity of marriage referenda, *receive* the satisfaction of passing that referenda. The win itself is the thing.

GOOD POLICY IS NOT ALWAYS GOOD POLITICS

Beyond the three features of issues, there are (at least) four political purposes an issue can serve for a candidate or political party. The first, of course, is the implicit, small-d democratic expectation that parties can claim credit for implementing policies that solve important public problems—the vaunted the notion that "good policy makes good politics." Though there will always be hypocrites who espouse positions they don't really believe will fix the country's problems, most politicians believe they have the right solutions for America. Democrats believe this more than Republicans do, which is why the GOP spends so much time developing catchy labels like "healthy forests" and "clear skies" for policies they know can't be sold on their merits.

Unfortunately, the "good policy makes good politics" mantra is often the self-deluding governing corollary to the misguided "we win when we talk about the issues" electoral axiom. Former presidents George H. W. Bush and Bill Clinton both had the courage to raise taxes and put the country on a course toward fiscal solvency. Their reward? Each was vilified by conservatives for doing the right thing. Meanwhile, Ronald Reagan and George W. Bush cut taxes and increased spending, thereby creating unprecedented deficits—and both smiled along to reelection. In politics, as in life, no good deed goes unpunished, and good policy sometimes translates into bad politics.

Setting aside arguments about which party has the right prescriptions for the country, and whether those policies make for good politics, the other three political purposes an issue can serve are to:

1. *Attract* some portion of the electorate (demographic, ideological) to vote for a party's candidates and/or against its opponents through micro-targeting;

2. *Create* or reinforce a party's brand, and/or negatively brand the opposing party; and

3. *Unify* heterogeneous elements within a party's coalition and/or *divide* the diverse elements in the other party.

A crippling problem for Democrats is that they focus too much on the first objective rather than the latter two.

In our heterogeneous society, getting to the mythical 50 percent threshold in a two-candidate contest is a daunting task. Democrats will survey the electoral landscape and do some back-of-napkin analysis (not to mention plenty of pricey, focus group—and poll-tested analyses) to figure out how to micro-target voters from specific subgroups. *If we say this, we can get 65 percent of the married white female vote. If we promise that, we can draw 58 percent of American-born Hispanics*—and so on. Done correctly, this approach may yield some success for specific candidates. But adopted universally, the micro-tailoring of issues to attract demographic subgroups risks defining away a party's essence. A party that tries to stand for everything stands for nothing and makes itself vulnerable to the type of flip-flopper frames and negative attack ads upon which Republicans rely.

Besides, it's always easy to find slight areas of disagreement to exploit. Imagine a hyper-simplified Divided America in which there are just ten policies, and every citizen's position can be reduced to either supporting or opposing each policy. Further assume that the public is split evenly, 50–50, on each of these ten dichotomized issues. The probability that a politician and a random voter agree on any policy is, of course, one-half. The chance that they agree on all ten, however, is one-half raised to the tenth power—or less than 1 in 1,000. If both are self-defined liberals (or conservatives) who tend to agree 90 percent of the time, the likelihood that they share the same view on all ten issues is still only 1 in 3. Thus, even in a simplified political world of just ten support-or-oppose issues, a liberal congresswoman and her liberal constituent are unlikely to be in total agreement. Of course, the actual public policy arena includes hundreds of issues, each of which offers a range of possible solutions. As I often tell my students, if you want to vote for somebody with whom you are in perfect agreement, be prepared to put your name on the ballot.

Because deft politicians understand these realities—not to mention the electoral damage their opponents can create by running negative ads built around a few unpopular votes—they spend an inordinate amount of time building trust. A few adroit pols like Arizona's John McCain even manage to establish for themselves the coveted "maverick" image. Politicians invest all this time and effort on reputation building because trust affords them the latitude to cast votes that will offend good portions of their constituents and yet still ask for—indeed, expect—their votes. The problem for McCain is that all of the recent pandering to the right-wing elements within his party whom he not long ago rebuffed is quickly destroying his long-built reputation.

Unfortunately, the individual wisdom of politicians does not always translate into the collective wisdom of political parties. A party that tries too hard to micro-tailor policies to attract specific sub-demographics risks losing its moorings, its very identity. It will become a party with no political discretion, no leeway either to make mistakes or enact needed but unpopular policies. Bill Clinton, who spent millions on polling, ably used "small ball" politics on policies like school uniforms and community college investments to nudge his popularity up, inch by inch. But figuring out where the 57 percent majority is on every issue and then moving to that position is no way to build a partisan brand name in the long term. This approach is the essence of followership, not leadership, and the support it generates, though a mile wide, is often only a foot deep. Clinton now seems to understand this, conceding that a significant number of voters will always find a certain allure in George W. Bush's "strong and wrong" approach. Why this most politically skilled and intellectually dexterous of politicians could not figure this out until after he left office is one of the great mysteries of Clinton's presidency—especially since the Democrats, based on the issue polling they so faithfully follow, have the potential to be both *strong* and *right* on so many issues.

How can the Democratic Party reinvent its brand and, in the process, begin to discredit the Republican identity? The best way to develop a brand is with what might be called *flag planting:* Taking a firm, nonnegotiable position on issues and affirming that position repeatedly. Doing so will always turn away some voters, but the resolve shown by planting flags and standing vigilantly to defend them not only helps unify and motivate the party's base but gains the respect of moderates and independents who, though perhaps disagreeing on the particulars of the policy defended, will show grudging respect for resoluteness.

Trade policy and the passage of the North American Free Trade Agreement (NAFTA) is a perfect example of how *not* to flag plant. Americans accept the fact that the domestic economy is going to be transformed by competition from foreign labor and the outsourcing of jobs once performed by Americans. The electoral problem created by the Clinton administration's support for NAFTA is that it eliminated the party's ability to differentiate itself sufficiently on labor and economic policies. Ohio congressman Sherrod Brown, who is running for U.S. Senate in 2006, is one of the staunchest critics of national trade policy:

> Democrats need to speak out about trade policy, and I will talk trade more than any statewide candidate in the country probably ever has. Trade is the reason that the city I grew up in, Mansfield, has lost so many jobs—it's not the only reason, but it's the primary reason. Trade policy is the reason so many of our young people have left the state. Trade policy has helped to bankrupt our local governments, in terms of police and fire protection. Trade

policy especially hurts minorities, who are the first to lose these jobs. Trade policy has cost our state over a million jobs.

The Democrats' identity as the working-class party is one of their few remaining brands. Support for NAFTA signaled to blue-collar workers, many of whom already felt uneasy about the Democrats' social policies, that they no longer needed to wrestle with the dissonance between the party's social and economic positions. If blue-collar workers perceive no difference between the two parties on job and pension security, they may as well troop angrily to the polls to vote against the "baby killers" and the "Hollywood homosexuals," for at least they know there's a branding difference between the parties on *those* issues. Though union workers are declining, the share of voters from union households (including retirees and spouses) has slipped only slightly in the past thirty years, and voters in those households have consistently voted 11 to 12 percentage points more Democratic than the rest of the country. When white union workers are putting "W" bumper stickers on their pickups—or, more audaciously, their *company* vehicles—it's obvious many are voting against some of the very Democrats their union leaders have endorsed.

Countless political analysts have grappled with the question of why Democrats are struggling among blue-collar white men. Many have concluded, as Republicans would prefer people believe, that the Democrats are simply out of step with the working classes. This is ridiculous. Democrats were more antiwar and pro–free love in the early 1970s than they are today. The difference is that thirty years ago the party differentiated itself sufficiently on labor issues, a fact that even Clinton's pro-trade national economic adviser Gene Sperling concedes in his new book, *The Pro-Growth Progressive*. Recalling a conversation with Federal Reserve Board chair Alan Greenspan during the 2004 campaign, Sperling writes:

When . . . Chairman Greenspan chided me because he felt one of Kerry's position was too protectionist, I told him that he "had no idea how hard it was to be a pro-trade Democrat." He whispered back, "You have no idea how hard it is getting to be to be a pro-trade Republican."

Indeed: By the time George W. Bush started pushing for the Central American Free Trade Agreement (CAFTA) in the summer of 2005, Republican congressmen in solidly red, low-unionized states like North Carolina were avoiding Bush during presidential visits. When Republicans are running *from* Bush trade policies, one has to wonder why some Democrats are running *toward* them.

According to results from twenty-one polls the Pew Research Center conducted since January 2004, as income disparities between rich and poor widen, "when it comes to partisanship and income, the key battleground in American politics is in the middle brackets. And there, after a long slow climb that has occurred mostly in the past two decades, the GOP has reached parity with the Democrats." The GOP's biggest gains of late have come in white households with incomes between $19,000 and $35,000—precisely the sort of families that were once the unionized bedrock of the Democratic Party. As political analyst David Sirota argues, the problem is not that Democrats are pressing for some radical, unpopular economic agenda: Majorities of Americans support progressive solutions to issues including corporate accountability, nationalized health care, scaling back tax cuts to balance the budget, and competitive pricing for prescription drugs. Yet in Brown's Ohio, which had one of the highest state unemployment rates in the country in 2004, the Kerry campaign and a constellation of liberal groups spent millions of dollars and countless hours in a failed effort to capture the state's twenty electoral votes for the Democratic nominee. Despite the fact that only 17 percent of Ohio voters said the job situation in their part of the state was better than it was four years earlier, Kerry did no better in Ohio among union members or union household voters than he did nationally. This is astounding and unacceptable.

The Democrats needed to plant a flag on trade policies during the 1990s. They are supporting CAFTA at much lower rates than they did NAFTA, but it's too late. The brand has faded, and restoring it will be difficult. The opposition to Bush's Social Security privatization scheme was a much better example of flag planting, and the immigration debate provides another great opportunity for Democrats to do the same.

Wedge Politics

In autumn 2005, each week produced another poll showing a new low in President Bush's approval rating and a new high in the percentage of Americans who considered the Iraq war a mistake. On November 17, Pennsylvania congressman and decorated war veteran John Murtha, who voted for the October 2002 Iraq resolution, criticized the administration's war management. The White House came unhinged. Its initial reflex, validated by so many earlier successes, was to attack Murtha personally. When that backfired, a desperate Republican National Committee resorted to counterattacking Democrats with its secret weapon . . . other Democrats!

The RNC created a four-minute web video showing a stream of selected clips from 1998 to 2003 of national Democrats—including Bill and Hillary Clinton, Jay Rockefeller, Nancy Pelosi, Howard Dean, Evan Bayh, and John Edwards—asserting either that Iraq had weapons of mass destruction or that action needed to be taken to remove Saddam Hussein from power. The clips were carefully edited for effect, and the video never mentions that Bush's October 2002 war resolution was supported by all but seven Republicans in Congress, compared to just 40 percent of House Democrats and 60 percent of Senate Democrats. In essence, the embattled administration's war defense had been reduced to "we were completely wrong, but so were half of our opponents." Still, the fact that almost half of congressional Democrats voted for the war testifies to the skill with which Republicans play wedge politics to divide Democrats against themselves and, in general, manage their politics the way the mob maintains its power: by getting the goods on as many people as possible, so nobody is clean enough to squeal. The video served its purpose of letting Democrats know that if they want to fault Republicans for Iraq, they should be prepared to share the blame.

How can Democrats play wedge politics against the Republicans? In our polarized political environment, it's tempting to try to split apart the GOP's moderate and conservative wings—and there are clever ways to do this. The better place to point the tip of the wedge, however, is *between* the "profit" and "pulpit" wings of the party's conservative base. The profit wing has ample financial resources but depends upon the pulpit wing's crusading armies for electoral ballast. Rich conservatives have little fear that their sexual lifestyles will be scrutinized, their entertainment censored, their kids' prep school curricula polluted by politically correct secularists, or their wives and daughters deprived of clinic access should they need abortions. So long as their business agendas are not interfered with, the profiteers are willing to suffer the largely ineffectual rants of the pulpit wing as the price paid for the rich bounty of votes they provide. But that price is getting steeper by the moment, especially now that Republicans control every branch of the national government. "[The Republican] party's split has become harder to gloss over, its disagreements harder to keep under control," says electoral handicapper Charlie Cook. "All Republican members of Congress will be pressured to choose sides or, more accurately, to establish priorities that risk alienating one faction or the other."

Cook's comment confirms that the phasing effect has reached the point of virtual simultaneity, as discussed in chapter 2. The pulpit-profit wedge issues are therefore a great way to split the Republicans' southern-based cultural wing that will no longer wait patiently for results from its more moderate, non-southern elements, which pick up the tab and are used to immediate results. Again, immigration is a perfect example here, because profit-wing Republicans want cheap labor and pulpit-wing Republicans want cultural purity through English-only laws and so forth. Make the GOP choose one part of its base or the other.

The pulpit-versus-profit Armegeddon is abortion—the ultimate wedge issue. Rather than wavering in their support for reproductive choice, congressional Democrats ought to lay down a marker and call upon Republicans who whine incessantly about "judge-made law" to settle the question once and for all by proposing a constitutional amendment to outlaw abortion. Because a majority of Americans oppose same-sex marriage but a minority support banning abortion, an abortion-ban amendment has far less chance of receiving the required two-thirds majorities of both chambers of Congress than the failed Federal Marriage Amendment. Notice that Republicans never make abortion bans a high-saliency issue because the last thing they want is a floor vote on the question. Why? Because their members will be exposed: Those who vote *for* it will be depicted as amendment-crazed radicals who already tried tinkering with the Constitution to ban gay marriage and are meddling with the national chart again; and those who vote *against* it will immediately become targets of the Christian Right.

More to the point, the profiteers ensconced in their K Street offices will start to worry that the millions they have pumped into Republican campaign accounts will go down the political drain as horrified Americans abandon the GOP. The added benefit of calling the GOP's bluff on banning abortion is that, from that point forward, whenever a Republican-appointed judge rules against reproductive choice Democrats can complain that *conservative* activists are trying to create judge-made law from the bench in opposition to the will of the public, as expressed by their national representatives in the floor vote on the constitutional amendment. Finally, the abortion issue also splits very dramatically along south and non-south lines, as we saw in chapter 3.

It's no mystery that Democrats are not only more ethnically diverse, but also exhibit greater toleration for homosexuals, the disabled, the poor, and the dispossessed. Yet there is ample diversity within the Republican coalition, which includes Wall Street financiers, intelligent designers, chamber of commerce small businessmen, subsidy-dependent agribusiness farmers, border-patrolling Minutemen, flat taxers, Second Amendment sharpshooters, corporate deregulators, right-to-lifers, country clubbers, homeschoolers, and many more. "Conservatives have thrived because they are split into feuding factions that squabble incessantly," says author and *New York Times* columnist David Brooks. "As these factions have multiplied, more people have come to call themselves conservatives because they've found one faction to agree with." Not all conservatives are Republicans, and vice versa. But that's precisely the point: Where Brooks sees strength in the absence of anything such as a garden-variety conservative, Democrats should see opportunities to use wedge politics to divide this loose coalition of social and corporate conservatives who make up the modern Republican party. Immigration and abortion are just the start.

Issues and Regionalism

What does issue saliency and efficacy, and the political use of issues to unify one's party and drive a wedge into one's opponents, have to do with regional politics? Part of the Democrats' issue failure has nothing to do with regionalism, or the South in particular, and everything to do with bad tactical use of issues to make partisan gains. Upon closer inspection, however, I submit that Democratic ambivalence and diffidence is as often as not rooted in a reflexive fear of alienating Americans who subscribe to southern ways of political thinking. When Democrats give the president authority to start a preemptive war in Iraq, they accede to southern bellicosity. When Democrats go soft on defending social policies, they lend credence to the southernized, "starve the beast" mentality of governance. When Democrats scramble around to declare that they, too, have moral values, they kneel in the pews of southern evangelism. This absurdist catering to the worst fitting, least supportive component of the Democratic coalition must cease. Few voices ever call upon Republican leaders to bow before their dwindling, mismatched, and marginalized northeastern wing. Why should Democrats be expected to appease southern voters who reject all Democratic presidential nominees and most statewide Democratic candidates? A glaring, almost insidious double standard is at work here.

Sadly, far too many Democratic leaders and their consultants have bought into Republican tropes about how Democrats are out of touch and need to talk and act more like Republicans to be competitive. We already know what that strategy yields: When Republicans get into a stew because of their bad policy ideas or poor management, they just cue the tape of Democrats agreeing with them and rub their noses in it. Democrats are trying too hard to be things they aren't and appeal to voters who are least likely to subscribe to Democratic philosophies and policy prescriptions toward the economy, military, civil liberties, and social insurance programs. This is not the result of failing to listen to southerners. If anything, it's a result of wilting in the southern heat. Unencumbered by the need to please a southern electorate that produces little support for Democratic candidates anyway, the party can be more aggressive and forward-looking in the fashioning of its national platform.

Parties are akin to products, and building market share requires product differentiation. That doesn't necessarily mean the Democrats have to lurch leftward, but it does mean that they should offer clear alternatives. Instead of bending to southern value systems and governing philosophies, the Democrats should promote a set of themes that will appeal to the true American majority of the future. Indeed, a non-southern Democratic coalition can go on the policy *offensive,* and all of the policy ideas the Democrats need are in right in front of their noses. Liberated from having to satisfy a southern-based conservative element that pays little attention to Democratic messages or messengers anyway, the Democrats can advance a progressive agenda that will attract a non-southern majority.

What's missing, of course, is the proper formulation—an easy-to-articulate policy platform that is sufficiently differentiated from what the Republicans offer, yet broad enough to include the party's panoply of center-left ideas and interests. What Democrats need is a simple, clear elevator pitch that will appeal first, and especially, to a non-southern majority and then, perhaps in the long run, to southerners who either decide to return to the Democratic fold or are persuaded to vote Democratic for the first time in the lives.

THE ELEVATOR PITCH

In the run-up to the 2004 election, Markos Moulitsas, America's most influential blogger, challenged readers of his website, the *Daily Kos,* to come up with the Democratic Party's "elevator pitch." The task for "Kospolitans" was to convey to a stranger in just thirty seconds—roughly the time of a shared elevator ride—what it means to be a Democrat. The Republicans more or less have their pitch down, claiming that they stand for limited government, low taxes, heartland values, and a strong defense.

The answers provided by *Daily Kos* readers varied widely. Some were good, others incoherent. Many lacked synthesis or could not be boiled down to achieve the brevity and simplicity inherent to any good elevator pitch. Democrats are a diverse, heterogeneous bunch, and it's difficult to develop a pitch that captures fully that diversity. But it can be done. Though some will take issue with my formulation, after surveying the principles, policies, and coalition partners comprising the Democratic universe, and with a non-southern majority coalition in mind, the simplest articulation of the elevator pitch is this:

Democrats believe in a strong defense but a smart offense, a culture of investment, and the exercise of inalienable liberties.

There is hardly a policy position or philosophical ideal—from environmental conservation to reproductive choice, from health care reform at home to promotion of democracy abroad, from immigration to Social Security—that cannot be subsumed within one of these three simple values. Let's look at each in some detail.

Strong Defense, Smart Offense

For almost four decades, the Republicans have enjoyed an advantage on issues related to the military, defense, and foreign policy. Seizing back that advantage should be the Democrats' long-term goal, but in the short term they merely need to draw close enough to the Republicans to win on domestic issues. There will be many legacies of George W. Bush's Iraq war: the fatalities and casualties, the veterans' hospitalization and rehabilitation bills, the burgeoning deficits fueled by war costs, the rupturing of historical alliances, the stagnating reenlistment and rising divorce rates among military personnel, and the general decline of global respect for the United States. From a purely political-electoral standpoint, Democrats must add to this list the image of Republicans as the party that has weakened America's defenses and proved recklessly unreliable on offense.

Now is the perfect moment to do so. Thanks to the Republicans' misleading actions before the war and their management of the war once we got to Baghdad, by late 2005 Americans rated the Democrats more trustworthy in handling Iraq, and by early 2006 more trustworthy in handling terrorism. Most Americans now believe the Bush administration misled the country into the war, and that the war itself was a mistake not worth the cost in lives and dollars. Postwar Iraq (if it can be called that) has been shoddily managed, and the theory of preemption is so thoroughly discredited that Vice President Dick Cheney and Secretary of Defense Donald Rumsfeld can't bring themselves to utter its name. The president speaks often of this or that turning point, but the facts are that average daily American fatality rates are higher since Saddam Hussein's capture than before, and higher since the purported "handover" of Iraqi sovereignty than before. The daily number of attacks on our troops and vehicles, neither of which have been properly fitted with armor, continue to rise. Iraq's borders are not secure, and but for the small, heavily guarded Green Zone in downtown Baghdad the interior is unsafe for military or political personnel to travel. In summer 2005 came news that oil was being rationed in Iraq—the equivalent of learning that Iowans had started rationing corn. Almost every prewar scenario about the difficulties of winning the peace was ignored, and most have come to pass: insufficient troop counts, domestic and civil-ethnic unrest, rising Islamic fundamentalism, an emboldened insurgency, evaporating global support, and an unfazed nuclear neighbor across the border in Iran.

It took Republicans four decades to establish their credibility on defense and foreign policy issues, and as they did they inched closer toward majority status. The only thing the party lacked was a major realigning issue, much as the Civil War in the 1860s or the depressions of the early 1890s and late 1920s shifted voters' partisan attachments and created new dominant parties. September 11 finally gave Republicans their long-awaited opportunity *and they blew it*. Thanks to the Cheney-Rumsfeld cabal's Iraqi idée fixe, the GOP risked all of its chips on an ill conceived, poorly planned, and incompetently executed preemptive war. In just five short years following the September 11 attacks, an impetuous Bush and his sand castle–smashing cronies have managed to destroy what the Republicans took forty painstaking years to build.

The first key for Democrats to winning on national security is magnifying the distinction between defense and offense and emphasizing homeland defense *first*. On this score, none other than 2004 presidential nominee John Kerry has already shown the way. Kerry was a flawed candidate who ran a very flawed campaign, but nobody can deny that the Massachusetts senator performed masterfully in the presidential debates, especially on the issue set where Bush was expected to dominate: security and terrorism. Kerry throttled Bush for failing to tighten America's borders, secure our seafaring ports, properly screen air cargo, and other security lapses. The first presidential debate, in Miami, was the highest moment of Kerry's campaign and the lowest for Bush, who stumbled repeatedly in trying to respond to Kerry's withering criticisms. Kerry put Bush on the ropes and kept him there with jabs like this:

> The president hasn't put one nickel—not one nickel—into the effort to fix some of our tunnels and bridges and most exposed subway systems. That's why they had to close down the subway in New York when the Republican Convention was there. We hadn't done the work that ought to be done . . . 95 percent of the containers that come into the ports, right here in Florida, are not inspected. Civilians get onto aircraft, and their luggage is X-rayed, but the cargo hold is not X-rayed.

Bush is no great orator, but he usually can repeat stock phrases and simplistic logic to hammer home his points. In the first debate and much of the second, however, Bush was a disaster. Even First Lady Laura Bush reportedly chided her husband for his diffident, surly performance.

For all the focus on his moody disposition and parrotlike repetitiveness, Bush's struggles were rooted in a more substantial deficiency: He simply didn't *have* many answers to Kerry's attacks about homeland security failures and oversights because, in its haste to get to Baghdad the administration spent far too little energy and money securing the homeland. Former presidential counterterrorism adviser Richard Clarke put matters into stark budgetary terms:

> Of all the new funding that went to national defense in the four years following 9/11, only 14 percent went to homeland security.

People concerned about readiness on the home front have taken to comparing the cost of specific projects to the "burn rate" of spending on the war, as in this analysis published in *Mother Jones:* security upgrades for all subway and commuter-rail systems, or tweny days in Iraq; security upgrades for 361 U.S. ports, or four days in Iraq; explosives screening for all U.S. passenger-airline baggage, or ten days in Iraq.

Alas, the problem is worse than that because, as the cochairs of the bipartisan September 11 Commission, former New Jersey governor Thomas H. Kean and former Indiana congressman Lee H. Hamilton, informed Americans in December 2005, the monies have often been spent in wasteful, uncoordinated, irrelevant ways:

> Billions have been distributed with virtually no risk assessment, and little planning. Nor has the federal government set preparedness standards to help state and local governments use the money wisely. The District of Columbia used part of its grant to buy leather jackets and to send sanitation workers to self-improvement seminars. Newark bought air-conditioned garbage trucks. Columbus, Ohio, bought body armor for fire department dogs.
>
> These are not the priorities of a nation under threat. The result of this disarray is that taxpayers have no guarantee that these billions have increased our overall level of national preparedness. The response to Hurricane Katrina suggests that we have not come far.

Tack on federal emergency response management and disease control—highlighted by the administration's bungled Katrina response and the avian flu scare—and you have a recipe for attacking Republicans at the very core of their policy stronghold: defending the homeland.

"Smart offense" should be the second half of the Democrats' new defense theme, and here the Republicans' political vulnerabilities are even greater. National Democrats thus far have adopted one of two basic approaches in response to the Republicans self-immolating Iraq policy. First, get out of the way and let them burn. Second, add some fuel to the fire now and again by citing the negative consequences of the Iraq war: the management failures and lack of planning, the insufficient armor and supplies for our troops, the declining enlistment rates and standards, the stretching thin of our active and reserve duty service ranks. Democrats need to go a step further and criticize the policy of preemption not only on the grounds of its cost, management, and execution, but also on its strategic merits, whatever they may be.

Bush repeatedly argues that we have to fight the terrorists "over there" so we don't have to fight them at home. That's a cute phrase for justifying the idea of preemptive war, but Americans just aren't buying it. A July 2005 poll by Hart Research read Americans two statements about how to fight the war on terror:

Statement A: There is no adequate or affordable way to prepare for all the possible ways that terrorists might strike us here in the United States. Instead of spending billions on homeland security measures that may or may not be effective, we should focus our efforts on capturing and killing terrorists before they strike us— both by attacking their bases and training camps overseas, and using strong law enforcement to identify and arrest potential terrorists in the United States.

Statement B: It is simply too risky to put all the focus of protecting America on the hope that we can capture or kill terrorists before they try to strike us. We also must invest in smart, tough measures such as strengthening our border and port security, installing detection devices that can find bombs hidden in cargo, stopping the spread of nuclear weapons, and increasing security at nuclear plants, chemical plants, and facilities where hazardous biological agents are stored.

Though many Americans would surely like to pair an aggressive offensive presence with a more defensive posture, the point of the question is to force respondents to choose, and Americans stated a clear preference: 68 percent supported Statement B either strongly (49 percent) or not strongly (19 percent), compared to just 26 percent who supported Statement A (19 percent strongly; 7 percent not strongly).

Americans know that the best offense is a good defense, and they want a strong defense to be based on—surprise!—actually strengthening our defenses. The GOP hasn't given it to them, and the Democrats should not allow the absence thus far of another September 11–style attack deter them from striking at the very heart of the Republicans' supposed strength by asserting that the GOP has left American vulnerable and at risk. Bush's fight-them-over-there mantra is wearing thin, as his declining approval on terrorism, depicted in Figure 6.1, shows. Fearful that taking a defensive posture toward terror will make them appear to be *on* the defensive, the Democrats have unfortunately been too scared to make Bush explain why he has put the nation at risk. Bush relied on fear to win reelection, and Democrats should fight fear with fear.

Democrats should not preclude the possibility of offensive action, but they must offer Americans an alternative vision for the use of U.S. force abroad that contrasts sharply with the neoconservative theory of preemption. Thanks to the administration's foolish discarding of a very workable doctrine (along with its inventor), the Democrats need not in-

Figure 6.1
Approval of Bush's Handling of Terrorism

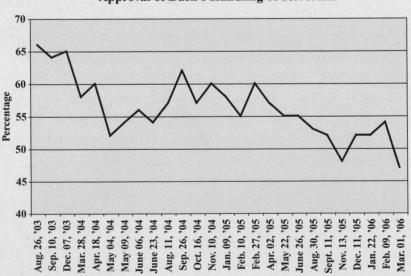

vent a set of principles for offensive military engagement because one already exists: the Powell Doctrine. The puissance of the former secretary of state's doctrine is that its premises are so compelling yet simple that they can be articulated in just a few sentences even by foreign policy novices, as a former colleague of Powell's proved a few years ago, when he argued that any military deployment of American troops abroad:

> . . . must be in the national interests, must be in our vital interests whether we ever send troops. The mission must be clear. Soldiers must understand why we're going. The force must be strong enough so that the mission can be accomplished. And the exit strategy needs to be well defined.

That colleague? George W. Bush, of course, who promised military prudence during the third presidential debate with Al Gore. Bush's about-face between October 2000 and the March 2003 invasion of Iraq would be laughable were it not for the fact that the number of Americans killed in Iraq is fast approaching the number killed on September 11, 2001. (This milestone, incidentally, is the one Republican congressmen most fear having to explain during the 2006 midterm election.)

It's difficult to imagine how much more thoroughly Bush could have ignored Powell or his doctrine. The president decided to preemptively invade Iraq with a cobbled-together U.S.-led coalition. He forged ahead without a two-front attack after Cheney failed to gain Turkey's permission to invade from the north. There was never a clear understanding of the mission in terms of winning the peace once Baghdad fell. Scoffing at Army Chief of Staff Eric Shinseki's warnings, Rumsfeld pressed ahead with forces insufficient simultaneously to control the border, protect the country's natural resources, instill domestic tranquility, and coordinate the political transition. Finally, of course, to this day instead of a clear exit strategy Bush offers yet another silly mantra about Americans "stepping down" when the nonexistent Iraqi army somehow steps up. Is it any wonder that Bush's policy has not only led to instability in Iraq but, as Figure 6.2 shows, a precipitous decline in his approval of the handling of Iraq?

Figure 6.2
Approval of Bush's Handling of Iraq

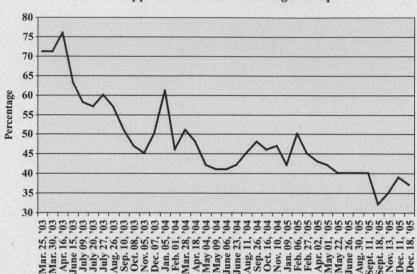

Had Powell's doctrine guided Bush's approach to Iraq, America either would never have gone to war or would have gone in under far different circumstances. To change the national debate on security, Democrats should pick up the Powell Doctrine discarded by the Cheney-Rumsfeld cabal, dust it off, and place it squarely above the Democratic mantel for all to witness. Democrats who say they cannot forgive Powell for his career-marring February 2003 testimony before the United Nations need to get over it. Unlike other Bush administration officials, at least Powell had the guts to admit his error. His doctrine now looks better than ever, and if Powell wants a second act in American politics Democrats ought to consider auditioning him.

In a profile of Delaware Democratic senator Joe Biden, a self-proclaimed foreign policy and defense hawk, *The New Yorker*'s Jeffrey Goldberg summarized the conventional wisdom about Democrats needing to "unbrand" themselves on national defense. "[N]ational-security Democrats try to distance themselves from the Party's post-Vietnam ambivalence about the projection of American power," says Goldberg. "In other words, they are men and women who want to reach back to an age of Democratic resoluteness, embodied by Franklin D. Roosevelt, Harry Truman, and John F. Kennedy." *New Republic* editor Peter Beinart subscribes to this view and laments that Democratic "softs" have overtaken the party's "toughs" who embody the party's Cold War—era reputation. But the resurrection by Beinart and others of stale, dove-hawk dichotomies is an oversimplification in a world where September 11 has "changed everything." It also defies political reality, given that majorities of Americans now view the Republican philosophies toward defense, their management of our homeland and borders, their prosecution of the war on terror, and their stewardship of the Iraq war as failures. As tempting as it may seem to try to beat Republicans to the policy center on a battleground the GOP has configured, the better way to undermine the Republicans' advantage on foreign policy and defense is to redefine that battleground by emphasizing defense over offense—pausing only long enough to remind Americans that Republicans have been reckless on offense, too.

It's been a long time since the GOP has been this vulnerable to direct attacks on foreign policy and defense. A Garin-Hart-Yang Research poll taken in spring 2006 showed the Democrats actually to be two points *ahead* of the Republicans when Americans were asked to base their vote in the 2006 congressional election solely on which party they "trusted more to protect America's national security." Given the public opinion trends, frustration with the Republicans over Iraq is hardly limited to the antiwar left and parents like Cindy Sheehan. During a nationally televised Senate committee hearing in 2005, Senator Lindsey Graham let Secretary Rumsfeld know that in South Carolina, "the most patriotic state I can imagine, people are beginning to question [the Iraq war]. And I don't think it's a blip on the radar screen. I think we have a chronic problem on our hands." When support for the president's war is waning among South Carolinians, the moment has arrived for Democrats to stop parroting the Republicans and start attacking them.

A Culture of Investment

The second component of the elevator pitch involves domestic and economic policies. Again, Democrats must dispense with tired dichotomies (i.e., big government versus small government) by fundamentally altering the way Americans view their government, the taxes they pay to it, and the programs those tax dollars support. The emphasis must be on government *investing* rather than spending—and that distinction must be more than semantic gimmickry or reframing. In terms of the policies emphasized, the way those policies operate, and the notion of fiscal management more generally, the Democrats must persuade Americans to view their government and its budgets in temporal rather than size terms, specifically by emphasizing long-term horizons as an alternative to the Republican philosophy of short-term plunder and interest-compounding debt creation.

Republicans complain incessantly about the size of government, and what hypocrites they are. The government has grown under every post–New Deal Republican president. Pork-barrel spending has nearly tripled since the Republicans took control of Congress in 1995, and non-defense discretionary budgets have ballooned by 35 percent under George W. Bush, who has never exercised his veto power on a spending bill but has increased the federal debt ceiling four times. Bruce Bartlett, author of *Reaganomics* and former adviser to the first President Bush, says Bill Clinton was better on fiscal policy than Bush, whom he dismisses as a conservative "impostor." Despite all the Republican bluster, comparatively speaking, the U.S. government is pretty small, operating on about 22 percent of the gross domestic product, lower than any other industrialized nation except Mexico's nineteen cents on a dollar. In other words, the U.S. government is a lot smaller than Republicans say it is, yet they protest its size while expanding it. Listening to Republicans whine about fiscal management is like taking etiquette lessons from John McEnroe, a comparison that insults the former tennis great.

Weekly Standard editor Fred Barnes excuses the exploding federal budget under Bush as "big-government conservatism." The *National Journal*'s Jonathan Rauch more ably defines it as "demand-side conservatism." Whatever the label, Republicans have become big spenders, and *wasteful* big spenders at that. What we are really witnessing, says *Slate*'s Jacob Weisberg, is "interest-group conservatism."

[A] variation on the old interest-group liberalism has emerged as the new governing philosophy. One might have expected that once in command, conservative politicians would work to further reduce Washington's power and bury the model of special-interest-driven government expansion for good. But one would have been wrong. Instead, Republicans have gleefully taken possession of the old liberal spoils system and converted it to their own purposes. The result is the curious governing philosophy of interest-group conservatism: the expansion and exploitation of government by people who profess to dislike it.

The Republicans moaned for years about unfunded federal mandates, and Bush gave the nation No Child Left Behind, a complicated, onerous, and widely criticized testing initiative that more than doubled federal education spending. They scowled at welfare recipients, yet Bush signed a 2002 farm bill that gives away more each year to agribusiness than the 1996 welfare reforms save, causing conservatives like *National Review*'s Rich Lowry to call the farm subsidies "scandalous" and "perverse." The biggest abomination has to be the 2003 prescription drug law, sold by the administration to Congress at a ten-year pricetag of $395 billion, even though Bush officials knew it would cost at least $530 billion and it is now expected to cost the country almost $800 billion   and when the program went into effect it was such an administrative disaster that state governors had to step in to fix it. "He's the biggest-spending president we've had in a generation," anti-tax conservative and former Club for Growth president, Stephen Moore, says of Bush.

The first part of establishing a "culture of investment" theme, therefore, is making the negative case against the big-government Republicans and their record-setting budget deficits. As Vice President Cheney let slip, the administration basically believes that "Reagan proved deficits don't matter." He's right, of course, if cynically so: By the time mounting deficits really start to threaten the economy, the Republicans' free-lunch tax policies have served their electoral purposes. After winning election and reelection and rewarding their political benefactors with tax cuts, deregregulation, and federal subsidies—who cares? Let the next sap in the Oval Office pooper-scoop the fiscal mess. Democrats who can successfully tap into the anger that fiscal-minded Ross

Perot voters west of the Mississippi River voiced in 1992 stand to reap huge political windfalls.

In making an affirmative case for their own domestic programming and fiscal philosophy based on smart, risk-averse, long-term investing, the Democratic message ought to be: We believe in a culture of investment, because investing your taxes produces better long-run payoffs for Americans and future savings for the country. Doing so shouldn't be hard, given the small-*c* conservative design of so many domestic programs the Democrats have initiated and supported over the years. Indeed, the dirty little secret of American government is not that Republicans don't have the stomach to reduce the size of the federal government, but that once the GOP got inside the gates they realized that the major government programs induce the very type of behaviors conservatives often espouse. This claim requires a bit of explanation.

Bush administration Treasury under secretary Peter Fisher has described the American government as essentially a "gigantic insurance company" with a sideline in defense and domestic public works. Now stop and answer this question: What kind of people buy insurance? In the generic sense of the term *conservatives* do, because insurance is the ultimate form of risk aversion—a means of planning for a potential misfortune or unfavorable episode in the future. To insure is to be prudent, a term once associated with the Bush family name. For all their blather about trying to instill values in Americans, it is curious how much Republicans abhor government programs that compel Americans to safeguard against the possibility of becoming unemployed, sick, incapacitated, or simply for reaching retirement age—precisely the sort of long-range planning and set-aside investing that honest conservatives ought to esteem. Granted, these behaviors are coerced, but coercion never seems to be a stumbling block when conservatives aim to prevent people from having abortions or gay sex.

Republicans say they trust Americans to manage their money better than the government can. But do Republicans really think the high school stock clerk or grad school waiter is going to set aside money for retirement or in case they lose their job? I'd bet a pair of presidential cufflinks that the Bush twins haven't saved a non–trust fund nickel for their own retirements, and their father is so-called conservative leader of the country. If Republicans really thought Americans would save their money and plan ahead, instead of privatizing Social Security for younger Americans President Bush would have simply proposed eliminating the payroll tax for everyone under 40, refunded them the monies they have paid in so far (adjusted for inflation, plus interest) and said, "See y'all at retirement!" Tellingly, he did not. One also never hears Republicans point out that the administrative overhead for Medicare and Social Security is between 1 percent and 2 percent, much lower than the overhead that private insurers in the magical "free market" take off the top to run insurance programs. The truth is that, dollar for dollar, not only is America's the world's most effective and efficient government, but the social programs Republicans bemoan are actually conservative in both their conceit and practical effects.

Bush learned these lessons the hard way in early 2005 during his failed attempt to "reform" (i.e., privatize) Social Security. The genius and popularity of Social Security is simple: Though it actually operates like a social insurance program, which spreads risk across and within generations, most Americans view it as a government-sponsored pension. To American taxpayers, one reason living a long life is so attractive is that they get back (or believe they do) all of those premiums they contributed during their working years. Other than insurance cheats, retirees are one of the few groups of people who experience the rare joy of filing an insurance claim. To convince people to support him, Bush needed to disabuse the public of a useful fiction—a decidedly against-type maneuver for an administration that relies on creating, not deconstructing, such fictions. In essence, the president would have had to inform millions of today's grandmas, many of whom are getting back more than they ever paid in FICA taxes that, in effect, they are a pack of lazy welfare queens.

Bush's Social Security debacle offers Democrats an important lesson on how best to present their domestic economic agenda, whether they are defending existing programs or proposing new ones: *Couch it in investment terms.* Republicans like to invoke Jefferson's "governs best that governs least" maxim, but Americans seem to prefer a stylized New Testament philosophy toward social programs based on the notion that government helps those who help themselves. Dozens of programs

Figure 6.3
Dissatisfaction Toward Government Taxes and Spending

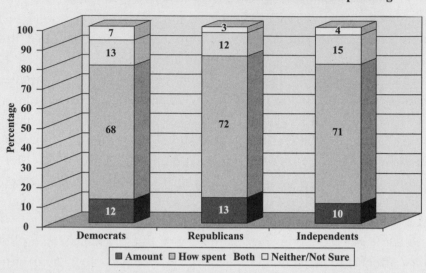

are conceived and defended in this way: Work, and the government helps you save for the day you are unemployed or retire; borrow money to educate yourself, and the government pays the interest while you're studying; buy a home, and the government lets you deduct the interest paid on your mortgage.

Aren't Americans upset with all these social programs and the big-government bureaucrats in Washington who run them, you ask? Wouldn't they rather—as Republicans repeatedly assert—send less money to the feds and instead be trusted to invest on their own? Not according to a March 2005 Fox News/Opinion Dynamics survey. In an America where Republicans, Democrats, and Independents agree on almost nothing, notice from Figure 6.3 how startingly uniform attitudes toward government taxes and spending are. Americans are not concerned with *how much* they pay to the government in taxes, but *how it spends* their tax monies—and a slightly higher share of Republicans than Democrats (72 percent to 68 percent) express dissatisfaction with how their taxes are spent rather than the amount of those taxes! The era of big government is not over, but the era of hating big government seems to be ending.

We are also seeing a revival in state government investing. Consider the difficult position Michigan governor Jennifer Granholm finds her-self in. Second perhaps only to Ohio, Michigan residents are bearing the brunt of America's transition from an industrial to a postindustrial economy. In October 2005, I followed the governor around a Detroit jobs fair cosponsored by state employers and a coalition of civic organ-izations and nonprofits led by the United Way, the goal of which was to give job seekers resume-writing advice or information about child care services, and then introduce them to prospective employers. After she toured the state fairgrounds where the event was held (just a few blocks south of the city's infamous 8 Mile Road), I asked Granhold how her administration is dealing with the rapidly changing American economy:

> We need to create jobs today and create jobs for tomorrow. We've got basically two economies in Michigan. We have a manufactur-ing sector that is struggling, and we have a high-tech sector that is growing. What we need to do is take the unemployed people today and match them with the ninety thousand vacancies [in Michigan]. What we are lacking in between are the skills to take those vacancies on, which are largely in the area of skilled trades and health care. We've got to restructure our taxes to make our-selves competitive. We have got to invest in infrastructure to jump-start the economy. We have to invest in diversifying our economy. And we have to let every child know they are college material.

This spirit of unapologetic state investment is hardly limited to postin-dustrial states like Michigan. To wit, in 2005 alone: Colorado elimi-nated its revenue-restricting taxpayer bill of rights; Washington voters rejected a ballot measure that would have repealed a 9.5-cent state gas tax enacted by the state's narrowly elected, gutsy Democratic gover-nor, Christine Gregoire; and Virginia Republicans joined Democratic governor Mark Warner in raising taxes, with no electoral damage suf-fered by Warner heir Tim Kaine. Most shocking of all, just eight days into office, Republican governor Mitch Daniels, who served as George W. Bush's first director of the Office of Management and Budget, broke his own no-tax pledge and raised taxes 29 percent on Indiana's wealthiest citizens. "Antitax groups such as [the Americans for Tax Reform], the Club for Growth, Americans for Prosperity, and Freedom Works seem to have feet-on-the-desk privileges in the White House and Republican Congress," Daniel Franklin and A. G. Newmyer III, in a *Washington Monthly* piece about the growing frustration of antitax advocate Grover Norquist, remark. "But with the red ink still flowing, even after collectively closing more than $200 billion in [state] budget shortfalls over the last three years, cracks are forming within the no-tax coalition."

Government haters had their moment a decade ago during the national debate over health care. Republicans and their HMO and insurance company benefactors like to cite then-First Lady Hillary Clinton's failure to enact comprehensive health care reform in the early 1990s as proof that the public doesn't want a nationalized health care system. This is simply untrue. In survey after survey, Americans express their desire to reform the American health care system, and no wonder: It's severely broken. The United States spends more than twice as much per capita than other industrialized nations do on health care, yet almost 45 million citizens are uninsured and America ranks poorly among the thirty member nations in the Organization for Economic Co-operation and Development in terms of life expectancy (rank: 22), infant mortality (25), and obesity (30). Roughly 4 in 5 Americans would accept higher taxes to ensure that everybody had health care coverage.

Clinton herself has subsequently admitted that her commission took too long to produce a proposal that in the end was too complicated for most Americans to understand. This was a tactical blunder. Her strategic error was not doing a better job of selling health care as an immediate and long-term investment that not only makes individual Americans healthier but makes America collectively more productive and prosperous. Because those with insurance can access preventative care and medications to stay healthy in the first place, they miss fewer days of work and contribute more to the economy and tax base. Failing to find a solution for national health care—and national doesn't necessarily mean *nationalized*—is costing the country billions of dollars in inefficiencies and lost productivity.

Just like the clever ads used by the recording industry and cable television companies to combat piracy, which emphasize the point that somebody else always pays for the costs created by those who pirate music online or wire themselves free cable, Democrats should remind the insured that their rates are higher because they are picking up the tab for walk-in emergency care patients who don't have insurance—so we may as well figure out ways to get folks insured in the first place. One of the most delicious ironies of the political troubles that arose when Majority Leader Bill Frist made some curiously timed stock sales in Hospital Corporation of America (HCA), his family's medical company, is that the stock's decline was partly because so many HCA facilities are located in the South, where the uninsured rate (18 percent) is highest in the country. Because HCA has to treat so many uninsured walk-ins, its profit margins are suffering. Frist's complicity in the do-nothing approach on covering the uninsured had finally caught up with him where it really matters: his own wallet. Of course, many of these costs eventually get passed along to the southerners with insurance who use HCA facilities.

Corporate America also understands the problems created by having so many millions uninsured, and is not as opposed to nationalizing health care as Republicans contend. Sociologist Jill Quadagno, author of *One Nation, Uninsured,* reminds us that even before the Clintons arrived on the scene to revive the idea of national health care solution, many leading executives, including celebrity CEO Lee Iacocca of Chrysler, were receptive if not openly supportive of creating some sort of a national taxpayer system. A survey of Fortune 500 executives revealed that about a third favored a public health system, and half think the government should force employers to provide health care for their workers.

If much of the public and the business community wanted a solution, why did "Hillarycare" fail? The reasons are manifold but one contributing factor, says Quadagno, is familiar: Post–civil rights racial dynamics in the South transformed what was once wholehearted support among southerners for programs like national disability insurance (so long as states maintained control and recipiency could be limited to whites) to opposition to nationalized health care that would benefit all.

While overt racial barriers such as separate white and colored entrances, wards, waiting rooms and cafeterias were removed in the wake of Medicare, racial dynamics have not disappeared entirely from policy-making processes. As jobs-based benefits have become a surrogate for national policy, racial inequality in access to benefits has become a secondary benefit of employment. Racial politics has also been transmitted through coded messages implying that minorities are undeserving beneficiaries of social programs. Such messages permeated the welfare reform debate of 1996, in which welfare recipients were implicitly portrayed as black, promiscuous, and lazy, even though the majority of [Aid to Families with Dependent Children] recipients were white. They also provided a subtle subtext in debates on Clinton's Health Security plan.

It is sickening—literally and metaphorically—that opposition to social programs can be so easily triggered by frightening citizens with the notion that the government will redistribute to those who are viewed as "undeserving." That the undeserving can be easily demonized based on race is more appalling, and helps explain why Clinton's major domestic triumph turned out to be welfare reform rather than health care reform. (Even though the sums that individuals and the federal government spend on health care dwarf what was spent on the Aid to Families with Dependent Children program reformed by the 1996 welfare reform Bill Clinton signed into law.)

Despite winning reelection by a wider margin than he was first elected, the best President Clinton could do was pass his health care agenda piecemeal and retrench into the position of advocating balanced budgets and vaguely promising to "build a bridge to the twenty-first century." As *Salon*'s Joan Walsh explains, Clinton's opportunity to create a truly investiture-based government eluded him:

Thanks in part to the Lewinsky scandal, in part to his own political caution, Clinton never mustered the political capital, or the nerve, to make bold investments that would convince the base that sacrifice led to rewards down the line—the delayed gratification that DLC types like to preach about. He rehabilitated the idea of government, but hardly managed to muster its power on anybody's behalf (besides laudable but stealthy boosts in the Earned Income Tax Credit and college tuition programs that only wonks knew about). So after eight years of fiscal discipline, there was little payoff—and then, suddenly, there was no Clinton. And here we are.

Walsh is a bit tough on Clinton, who was undoubtedly boxed in after the Democrats lost the Congress in 1994. To his credit, Clinton's bridge-building slogan strikes the right note in terms of advocating long-term public investments. That said, the Democrats can pay tribute to Clinton's legacy by turning his slogan into a general theme and apply it not only to health care but to the full panoply of educational, environmental, infrastructural, and human capital programs to create a post–Great Society "culture of investment" that will do far more for the

Table 6.1

State and Federal Spending in the South

State	Per-capita state expenditures		Federal receipts for every tax dollar	
	Amount	Rank	Amount	Rank
Alabama	$4,101	33	$1.69	6
Arkansas	$4,430	29	$1.47	14
Florida	$3,313	50	$1.00	32
Georgia	$3,749	44	$0.95	36
Louisiana	$4,157	32	$1.47	14
Mississippi	$4,684	24	$1.83	3
North Carolina	$4,080	35	$1.09	26
South Carolina	$5,071	17	$1.36	15
Tennessee	$3,597	46	$1.29	20
Texas	$3,456	49	$0.98	34
Virginia	$3,955	39	$1.58	8
United States	**$4,683**	—	**$1.00**	—

long-term health—literal and fiscal—of the country than the bogus "ownership society" wealth-accumulation schemes the Republicans are peddling.

One thing is certain: The last place Democrats ought to turn for investiture advice is the South. Republican fiscal hypocrisy on the national level is only outpaced by southerners who demonize the national government while nursing from the federal teat. If southern conservatives truly believed in federalism—in raising and spending money within their states rather than sending it to Washington for bureaucrats to redistribute—then the South would refuse the massive federal outlays it receives, and compensate by spending more on the state level. Neither is the case, as Table 6.1 shows. Most of the southern states rank near the bottom in terms of per capita state spending, with all but Mississippi and South Carolina spending less than the U.S. average. Meanwhile, all but three southern states (Florida, Georgia, and Texas) benefit from the federal redistributive bargain that sends money from high-income, blue states like California, Connecticut, Illinois, New Jersey, New York, and Rhode Island down to Dixie. In 2004, Bush won all ten states with the nation's highest personal bankruptcy rates, six of which are in the South. "We now have a new red-state political majority comprising voters who, while professing distrust of government and disdain for the values of the blue-state minority, are only too happy to rely on Washington and blue-state wealth to keep them in the style to which they have become accustomed," writes the *Washington Post*'s Steven Pearlstein. Most of the transfers come in the form of Social Security and Medicare payments, two cornerstones of the Great Society the southern-based Republican Party is trying to dismantle.

"Much of what we do via government contributes vitally to economic growth and efficiency," writes *American Prospect* magazine's cofounder Paul Starr. "Conservative views of public spending typically portray it entirely as a drain on wealth. But public expenditures on education, science and technology, health, and many programs for children are critical forms of investment, with a demonstrable history of long-term payoffs." Boilerplated into a "culture of investment" theme, Starr's sentiment is exactly the sort of unapologetic, visionary, progressivism-as-the-real-conservatism investiture model around which Democrats must rally themselves to build a non-southern majority. We are not spending your money, Democrats should remind Americans, but *investing* those monies in programs that produce long-term benefits rather than wasteful, short-term payouts. The South has generally rejected this long-term investment philosophy, which is why it has fewer major research universities and top-performing high schools that the rest of the country.

The Exercise of Inalienable Liberties

Democrats who may have forgotten why they voted proudly for Al Gore in 2000 obviously missed the speech the former vice president gave at Washington's Constitution Hall on the Martin Luther King Jr. holiday in January 2006. Just a few weeks after the *New York Times* revealed that the Bush administration has been using illegal wiretaps to spy on Americans, the former vice president drew parallels between Bush's domestic wiretapping and the Federal Bureau of Investigation's counterintelligence spying on King during the 1960s. Gore called the president's activities illegal, chastised the Congress for abdicating its oversight responsibilities, and asked for a special counsel to investigate the wiretapping program authorized by the president and subsequently defended by Attorney General Alberto Gonzales.

Dressed in a dark suit and sky-blue tie, with nine American flags as backdrop, Gore thundered away at the administration with a statesmanlike authority and equipoise that has seemingly disappeared from our public discourse:

> [A]s you know, the president has also declared that he has a heretofore unrecognized inherent power to seize and imprison any American citizen that he alone determines to be a threat to our nation, and that, notwithstanding his American citizenship, that person imprisoned has no right to talk with a lawyer—even if he wants to argue that the president or his appointees have made a mistake and imprisoned the wrong person. The president claims that he can imprison that American citizen—any American citizen he chooses—indefinitely for the rest of his life without even an arrest warrant, without notifying them about what charges

have been filed against them, without even informing their families that they have been imprisoned. No such right exists in the America that you and I know and love. It is foreign to our Constitution. It must be rejected.

Though mocked by conservative demagogues on television and Republican National Committee mouthpieces, Gore's views are shared by quite a number of Republicans and principled conservatives. In fact, only a technical snafu prevented the most unlikely of persons from introducing Gore via video feed from Atlanta: Bob Barr, the former Republican congressman from Georgia who was the first major politician to call for Bill Clinton's impeachment. Of course, it fell to a fellow southerner, deposed Senate majority leader Trent Lott of Mississippi, to defend the Bush policy. "I want my security first," said Lott. "I will deal with all the details after that." Leave it to the man who wishes the United States could have avoided the civil rights movement to reduce the Fourth Amendment to a trifling "detail" to be worried about later.

Until recently, the "exercise of inalienable liberties" would not be elevator pitch–worthy because such themes would be incapable of moving more than a few voters. However, the conservatives' repeated assaults on reproductive choice, personal privacy, the rights of homosexuals, and control over quality-of-life issues like medical marijuana or end-of-life decisions have polluted the political climate in the post–September 11, evangelized Bush era. More to the point, reasserting the importance of the protections in the Bill of Rights provides a powerful tonic for liberals when fighting the culture wars.

The Atlantic Monthly's Paul Starobin recently reflected on the inherent tension within the American political psyche between the libertarian values of self-expression on one hand, and self-abnegating faith and hyper-patriotism on the other. The irony, says Starobin, is that whereas the first element of this duality sets the United States apart from many less-developed countries, the second distinguishes American culture from most of the developed world. "Our remaining exceptionalism resides in our culture's striking combination of deep religious faith and nearly libertarian social permissiveness," says Starobin.

"These qualities don't rub elbows easily, and their twinned presence separates the United States from nearly all other countries, rich or poor . . . Having a foot in both fixed traditionalism and permissive modernism makes us still something of an outlier nation—astride both camps and at home in neither." To avoid this unusual balancing act, social conservatives would prefer that America simply chop off its left foot and hop feebly along toward a compliant, crypto-corporate Christian fundamentalism. In response, liberals need not advocate the opposite solution, for there is a dexterous balance to be achieved from sure-footed expressions of American patriotism and spirituality. The problem occurs when spirituality leads to a church-driven state and patriotism morphs into jingoism, because at that point the crusader's war footing threatens to pull the body politic into the chasm. As that chasm widens, inch by inch, we have reached the moment where Democrats must make the libertarian leap.

Democrats seeking an agile way to make this jump should behold the wise counsel of Paul Hackett. The former Marine officer and Iraq war veteran captured the nation's attention in 2005 when he ran for and nearly won a special election to the U.S. House of Representatives from Ohio in one of the most Republican-leaning seats in the country. Tall and sinewy, with close-cropped sandy brown hair and a voice like a Skilsaw, Hackett evokes a curious combination of deadpan seriousness and self-effacing humility. I caught up with him in October 2005 at a speech he gave at a union hall in Dayton, Ohio, just a few months after his loss to Jean Schmidt, a shrill Republican whose lack of military experience did not prevent her from quickly embarrassing herself in front of the entire country by calling Congressman John Murtha, a Vietnam vet, a "coward" on the House floor. Here's what Hackett told the assembled union members in Dayton:

> When I pull the lever when I walk in that ballot booth, it's not to send a spiritual leader to Washington, DC. I get that when I go to church on Sunday. I don't need Washington, DC, to come into my personal life, to try to run my personal life, tell me how to worship my God, and dictate to my wife the decisions she makes with her

doctor any more than I need Washington to come in, knock on the door, open up the gun safe, and tell me how many and what types of guns I get to keep in my gun safe.

But I'll tell you what I do need from Washington: I need Washington to watch the piggy bank. I need Washington to watch the economy and keep the economy strong, and do right by working men and women in the United States. That's what I send somebody to Washington for.

There are two precious nuggets to be mined from Hackett's pithy sermon. The first is the deft way he reduces the salience of social issues by suggesting what national politicians ought to be doing instead of fighting diversionary culture wars. The deeper genius is the way Hackett defends the other nine amendments of the Bill of Rights by securing them behind the ramparts of the social conservatives' beloved Second Amendment. This is a brilliant tactical move, and one even the most anti-gun Democrat ought to respect.

Liberals may choose not to keep guns in their homes, but how can civil libertarian absolutists embrace the parts of the Bill of Rights they like and ignore the parts they don't? Bill Clinton, Al Gore, and John Kerry all tried to take the gun issue off the table, with Kerry going so far as to fuss over his purchase of a goose-hunting license in Ohio during the late stages of his presidential bid. Forget such charades. To simultaneously disarm the National Rifle Association and apply pressure on the Republicans, Democrats should argue broadly for privacy against invasion by wiretap or into the womb by binding up these civil liberties with gun rights and defending them—pardon the pun—as all of a piece. The only deficiency in Howard Dean's much-discussed 2004 "God, guns, and gays" tagline is that the Dean should have realized that defending guns can be *used* to defend gay rights and religious freedom, because the one way to appeal to moderates is to convince them that an American who wants to buy a home with his partner is an equivalent, if different, expression of the same liberties they exercise when they license their guns or pray on Sunday. The belief that Americans are incapable of this level of political nuance is the insulting premise upon which almost every campaign of fear and objectification perpetrated by social conservatives is built. Voters are smarter than that, and Democrats can do better. Moreover, support for the Second Amendment is important to Midwest and interior West voters who will be more amenable to listening to Democrats who support gun rights. This is also true in the South, but in western states the libertarian ethic does not also require Democrats to move rightward on cultural issues like abortion and gays, as we will see in the next chapter.

Both presidential candidates in 2004 publicly opposed gay marriage but supported civil unions. The only distinction was that President Bush called for a constitutional amendment he knew would never get the two-thirds vote necessary to send to the states—an act of sheer political-electoral aggression with but one objective. "It's a vehicle for scaring people," Wisconsin congresswoman Tammy Baldwin, who is openly gay, says. "They didn't introduce it because they were serious about getting anything done but to keep it in the headlines and strike you over the head with it." Baldwin told me she had several "heart-warming" conversations with her Republican colleagues, many of whom admitted to her privately that they had friends or even family members who are gay. "They said, 'I can't believe our party is doing this,'" Baldwin recalls. "But of course their public rhetoric was quite different."

Though the House was saved from having to vote on the proposed amendment when the Senate killed the measure, 48–50, Georgia Democrat Zell Miller joined every southern Republican senator in voting for the amendment. The six Republicans who voted against it include most of the usual northeastern nonconformists: Maine's Susan Collins and Olympia Snowe; New Hampshire's John Sununu; Rhode Island's Lincoln Chafee; plus Arizona's John McCain and Colorado party switcher Ben Nighthorse Campbell, who had already announced he wasn't running for reelection in 2004. The regional disparities in support for the Federal Marriage Amendment are not surprising, given that twenty-one of the thirty-nine non-southern states have hate crime provisions that include sexual orientation, whereas only three of the eleven southern states (Florida, Louisiana, and Tennessee) do.

Quality-of-life and end-of-life issues are also debilitating the Republicans. According to a survey by the American Association of Retired

Persons, 72 percent of Americans aged 45 and over approve of physician-recommended medical marijuana use, and support levels will only increase with time because opposition is strongest among older seniors. In early 2006 the Supreme Court, with a vote to spare, upheld Oregon's assisted suicide law. Support for stem cell research has jumped more than 10 percent since 2003, and Republicans ranging from Bill Frist to Maryland governor Bob Ehrlich have distanced themselves from their party's religious base with their advocacy on this issue.

Meanwhile, capital punishment itself seems destined for death row, with support fading in response to an increasing number of convictions overturned because of DNA-based and other new forms of scientific evidence now available. Despite southern support for what President Bush likes to call the "culture of life," that culture apparently does not apply to the South's death row inmates. Since the Supreme Court's landmark 1976 *Gregg* decision, of the 1,000 executions in the United States more than 70 percent have occurred in the eleven southern states. Although Virginia is fast approaching its hundredth execution, with an eye-popping 348 executions Texas leads the way and is the only state thus far to reach triple digits. As governor, Bush spent little time reading the single-page memos prepared for him by counsel Alberto Gonzales before signing final death warrants. (The state of the southernized Christian ethic is such that Bush, who cites Jesus as his favorite philosopher, laughingly mocked the pleadings of a female felon he put to death.) Even with Texas removed from the totals, the remaining ten southern states still account for more than half of all executions during the past thirty years. Prior to a 2005 Supreme Court ruling that banned juvenile executions, only Oklahoma, Texas, and Virginia had executed minors during the past decade, and Texas accounted for thirteen of the twenty-two minors executed since 1976. Despite all the New Testament talk, the Old Testament's "eye for an eye" maxim still dominates the southern philosophy toward criminal justice.

Liberals have long upheld the principles contained in the Bill of Rights, and for these good deeds they have been targeted by Republicans for punishment. In a perfect example of the saliency trap, Democrats get vilified for defending the rights of criminals, free-speech radicals, and generally showing allegiance to the principles espoused by the American Civil Liberties Union. The slurs are familiar: *soft on crime, politically correct*. No such demonizing attends the Republicans' defense of the legal rights of white-collar criminals or the Janet Reno-loathing, black helicopter hysteria of Freemen militia types. Meanwhile, almost nobody in the country is aware of the deplorable replacement of our civil court system with a shadow system of business-friendly "binding mandatory arbitrators," which is a far more egregious violation of civil rights (not to mention the court system paid for by tax dollars) than, say, school prayer disputes, which garner infinitely more attention.

The moment has arrived for the "permissive modernism" half of the nation's cultural identity to stop being treated like Mr. Hyde to the "deep religious faith" Dr. Jekyll of America's split personality. It is not enough for Democrats to muse about the ironies of the Bush administration's stated intent of spreading freedom abroad at the very moment it restricts it at home. The Democrats must trigger the powerful instinct shared by most Americans to exercise their inalienable constitutional liberties and pursue happiness as long as it does not infringe upon the rights and freedoms of others. To obfuscate the larger issues, Republicans talk about people wanting to marry box turtles or how al Qaeda is making cell phone calls to the stock boy who bags your groceries as a way of exaggerating to the extreme Americans' basic desire to express quite reasonably their fundamental constitutional rights. At this point there shouldn't be a single Cato Institute libertarian in the country who can look herself in the mirror after voting for the modern Republican Party. That said, "an exercise of inalienable liberties" theme is the perfect antidote to the culture war Republicans will continue to wage until Democrats alert Americans that one half of their bipolar American cultural psyche is threatening to destroy the other.

THE NON-SOUTHERN PLATFORM

Great leaders and strong parties change the country by educating citizens and persuading them, not by figuring out where the voters are and moving toward them. According to Democracy Corps, the polling firm run by Stanley Greenberg and James Carville, the Democrats' largest two-party deficit is not on taxes, foreign policy, or even moral values—it's on "knowing what it stands for." Though Republicans talk fiscal responsibility while running massive deficits, thump their chest about being pro-military and strong on defense without any workable solutions for postwar Iraq, and George "restore honor and integrity to the White House" Bush had to order his White House staff to take ethics classes, the Democrats are still rated a whopping 28 points lower than Republicans in knowing who they are. And that's because Democrats spend far too much time chasing after voters and far too little time staking out bold and consistent positions and persuading voters to move toward them.

Shrewd Republican rhetoric and Democratic diffidence have combined to turn what otherwise might be a winning policy portfolio for Democrats into unnecessary and avoidable defeats at the polls. Democrats get themselves caught in saliency traps that make them appear too concerned with peripheral issues and not concerned enough about important matters. Presidential candidates like John Kerry end up offering tongue-twisting explanations like the infamous I-voted-for-it-before-I-voted-against-it quote on the Iraq war funding. These problems are compounded by the fact that Democrats often focus on low-efficacy issues for which it is either too hard to deliver results or too hard to claim credit for results once delivered. The overall effect is to make Democrats seem too unserious, too unsteady, or too unprepared to govern.

The notion that Democrats have no ideas, or no new ideas, is ridiculous. As Jonathan Chait of the *New Republic* points out, the case for new ideas is not all it's cracked up to be anyway because Democrats have a lot of solid, *old* ideas that have worked well for the country. On issue after issue, the Democrats find themselves a minority party despite advocating positions supported by a majority of Americans. This is because issue popularity does not necessarily translate into electoral victories, and good policies do not always make for good politics. Elections are not—and, indeed, perhaps shouldn't be—contests to get Americans to agree with a party and its candidates. They are contests to get people to *vote* for a party and its candidates.

To build and unify themselves, and begin to drive a wedge straight through the heart of the conservative base of the Republican Party, the Democrats need to spend a little less time micro-targeting messages to this or that group based on the latest focus group results. Chasing voters only scares them away, and so Democrats ought to spend less time in pursuit and more effort luring voters by staking out firm positions and showing the resolve not to budge. The party also must cease the costly, center-left infighting and stop trying to fit every issue on some single left-right axis that doesn't even exist. Finally, the party should promote a forward-thinking elevator pitch that emphasizes a strong defense and a smart offensive foreign policy, a culture of public investment, and the defense of every American to exercise the shared, inalienable liberties the Constitution guarantees each of us by birthright.

In conjunction with the demographic profile outlined in the previous chapter, it is clear from this chapter that the Democrats will be better able to advance a progressive agenda once they are freed from the shackles of trying to please the least-satisfiable, southern elements of its own and the opponents' party. No party should define itself entirely by its base, but neither should a party define itself by starting with the elements of its coalition *farthest* from that base. That said, it is time for Democrats to replace the party's passive, confused, and muddled national message with a muscular, unapologetic advocacy of an elevator pitch that will not only poll well in the swing states and regions of the country but, properly politicized, can win elections, too.

7

The Path to a National Democratic Majority

Our national party is a stigma in many parts of the country. Many of our party leaders come from safe southern districts. They're insulated from the reality of everyday [political] life.

—Republican strategist John Weaver

Everybody always makes the mistake of looking south.

—Democratic presidential candidate John Kerry, January 24, 2004, five days after he won the Iowa caucuses

A NATIONAL PARTY NEED not compete and succeed in every corner of the country. A governing majority is precisely that—a *majority,* not a unanimous coalition. The Republicans are presently governing on the strength (if that is the word) of the thinnest of majorities, and one that exists in part because of the disproportionate weight assigned to smaller states in the Senate and Electoral College, without which George W. Bush would never have become president. Following Bush's minoritarian victory in 2000, Republican validator-in-chief George Will gloated that elected presidents win all, not half, of the Oval Office.

That's a fair enough point, but it's equally true that controlling all of the White House does not mean a president commands the support of the entire country, or even half of it. This much is certain: Whatever fraction of the country Bush initially won over is shrinking on a monthly, if not weekly basis. Bush's tarnished crown has grown heavy upon his head, and the Republican empire is weakening.

Democrats need to win something—anything. They don't need landslides and they don't need mandates: What they need is a political foot in the door. Although there were a variety of obstacles to beating a self-proclaimed "war president" who had a three-year head start in building his reelection machine, the presidency was the only sensible goal for Democrats in 2004, but John Kerry just wasn't strong enough to win it. Although there are key governorships and state legislative chambers to pursue, in 2006 Congress is the obvious target. Again in 2008, the primary goal for Democrats will be recapturing the White House, no matter how thin or regionally confined the winning combination of states may be. The House, the Senate, the presidency, a majority of governorships—if Democrats can first win *something,* their newly established political and policy leverage will enable them to go beyond opposing the Republican agenda to presenting alternatives.

The best strategy for winning in the immediate term is to consolidate electoral control over the Northeast and Pacific Coast blue states, expand the party's midwestern margins, and cultivate the new-growth areas of the interior West. Buffeted by newly elected Democrats from the "Diamond" and brimming with the confidence from policy successes, the party can then bring its case to the more difficult electoral outposts of the country, including the South. In the interim, if nostalgic Democrats must dream about Dixie, let them envision a future wherein the party is competing seriously to win electoral votes in places like Alabama, Mississippi, or South Carolina, for that will mean the only uncertainty on Election Day is whether Democrats will coast to a forty-state or forty-five-state landslide. It will also mean that Democrats have led the country toward stronger security, broader peace, and wider prosperity—and succeeded so well that even the most wary southern skeptics have been compelled to rethink their partisan commitments. For now, however, such dreams must be delayed because any attempt to skip the important, intervening steps will only jeopardize the party's future. Sentimentality is no substitute for strategy.

In the three preceding chapters, I unfurled a blueprint for a non-southern strategy for Democrats to become the majority party of the future: in which states and regions the Democrats can build it; the voting coalition to be assembled in those states; and the policy platform and messages to attract that coalition. The only question remaining is the tactical one—*how* to do it. What follows are seven tactical recommendations for bringing the non-southern strategy to fruition.

1. RUN AGAINST THE CONSERVATIVE SOUTH

To define one's opponents is to define oneself. This maxim is true on two different levels. First, a party has to define itself and whom and what it opposes. Second, whenever and wherever possible a party must create the least favorable image in the public's mind of who those opponents are and what they represent. This is politics at its most elementary level.

Yet on both counts the Republicans do a much better job than Democrats. They mock Democrats as weak, indecisive, tax-happy, big-spending, unpatriotic, and morally permissive elites who are obsessed with marginal issues and, in general, not to be taken seriously. That's quite a mouthful, so when Republicans need a geographic shortcut they just dismiss Democrats as a pack of northeastern liberals and California wackos. The incomparably sarcastic liberal commentator Michael Kinsley testifies to the pervasiveness of this caricature:

> Democrats represent no one who is not actually waiting in line for a latte at a Starbucks within 150 yards of the east or west coastline. They are mired in trivial lifestyle issues like, oh, abortion and gay rights and Americans killing and dying in Iraq, while the Republicans serve up meat and potatoes for real Americans, like privatizing Social Security and making damned sure the government knows who is Googling whom in this great country. Just repeat

these formulas until a Democrat has been sent into frenzies of self-flagellation or reduced to tears.

If Sean Hannity and Rush Limbaugh continue to have their way, within a decade the staple media depiction of a Democrat will be a tenured, atheistic African-American cultural studies professor at Berkeley who writes about postmodern feminist thought for a few hours a day, then knocks off early to go home to have sex with his unionized, socialist, Hispanic postal clerk boyfriend as their three adopted sons are locked in the next room playing Grand Theft Auto on PlayStation2. It's doubtful that a single American fits this profile. There certainly are not 59 million of them—the number of people who voted for a supposedly out-of-the-mainstream Massachusetts senator in 2004.

It is long past time for the Democrats to respond in kind. Though it's true that the northeast is the most liberal section of the country, northeasterners are far closer to the mainstream of public opinion than southerners—and much closer than the conservative southern majority that dominates the region's and the nation's politics. In his book *Democracy Heading South,* southern political expert Augustus Cochran describes what has happened as Dixie's political traditions have overtaken Washington:

> Certainly American politics after the year 2000 will not mirror Southern politics before 1950, but today's national politics does display some of that old Southern "distinctiveness": blurred or insignificant issues, manipulative leadership, nondecisions on critical new challenges, disenchanted citizens, pervasive political corruption, and outcomes that favor elites at the expense of ordinary Americans. In some ways, then, the Solid South with its perversions of democracy stands as a warning to the nation that without nurturing the roots of democratic institutions, the substance of democracy can be lost even while the trappings of democracy are retained.

If this is the political ethic that suffuses our national politics, why won't Democrats point to the conservative South as the root of so many of the problems facing the country? Indeed, the South proxies for a variety of national pathologies. To wit:

• In the world's richest country, where two of every five children live in poverty, the South has some of the most pronounced and pervasive gaps between rich and poor—and those gaps are not just between black and white southerners, but *among* white southerners.

• The South is a place where racial animosities run deepest and xenophobia toward outsiders—foreign or domestic—is most palpable.

• The South is home to some of the most conspicuous overconsumption of commodities like beef, oil, and tobacco, which in turn lead to greater dependence on scarce domestic water resources, scarce foreign oil resources, and scarce health care services.

• At a time when personal and public debts are growing and the Republicans have raised the national borrowing limit four times, the welfare-addled South receives more in federal outlays and subsidies than it sends to Washington in taxes, and yet personal bankruptcy rates in the South are among the highest in the nation.

• Evangelicals are many and libertarians few in the South, a combination that legitimizes government interference in personal decisions from the point of conception to the end of life—with ample support for warrantless spying and corporate surveillance of Americans' personal behavior in between.

• The South is the most militarized region of the country, but only because so many military bases are stationed there—not because the South produces any more of America's soldiers and

Marines, as the region's share of men and women killed thus far in Iraq attests.

Is characterizing the conservative South in these terms unfair or inaccurate? Given the Republican domination of the region, would it really cost the Democrats that much, political or electorally, to do so? And how is it that southerners are endowed with the inherent moral authority to question the values of blue-state Americans, but never the reverse? "There is a big problem with having a southern, as opposed to a midwestern or California, base," Christopher Caldwell, senior editor of the *Weekly Standard,* warned the GOP even before Bush rose to power. "Southern interests diverge from those of the rest of the country, and the southern presence in the Republican Party has passed a 'tipping point' at which it began to alienate voters from the other regions." If conservative commentators like Caldwell and Republican strategists like John Weaver—whose quote began this chapter—concede that insular, radical southern Republicans are out of step with the rest of the country, why are Democrats so hesitant to agree? If the most conservative elements within the most conservative region of the country will not suffice as a "them" against whom Democrats can define themselves, nobody will.

It's time the Democrats stood for something. No doubt, that requires affirmative messages, proactive solutions, a solid record of effective governance, and a dose of optimism. But it also requires the guts to pick and win fights, and the willingness to define an "us" by recognizing a suitable "them" to oppose. Ken Lay and Jack Abramoff are convenient but ultimately fleeting foes. Democrats must think bigger. "You can't say, 'Please don't be mean to me. Please let me win sometimes,' " President Clinton admonished his fellow Democrats in the fall of 2005. "Give me a break here. If you don't want to fight for the future and you can't figure out how to beat these people, then find something else to do." It's not clear who, exactly, President Clinton had in mind when he referred to "these people" during a speech at the Texas Book Festival in Austin, George W. Bush's political backyard. But surely the southern conservatives who call the Republican tune in national politics fit the bill.

Consider South Carolina, which has opposed or defied almost every beneficent social and political change in American history. To appease South Carolinian slaveholders, Thomas Jefferson removed language condemning slavery from the Declaration of Independence. Four years later, backcountry loyalists in South Carolina helped the British Army recapture the state in 1780 from the patriots. By 1828, Palmetto State native and vice president John C. Calhoun was agitating for state "nullification" of federal powers, generating secessionist calls a full generation before the outbreak of the Civil War. On December 20, 1860, South Carolina became the first state to secede, four months later Confederate forces in Charleston fired the opening shots of the Civil War on the Union garrison at Fort Sumter, and South Carolina even threatened to secede *from* the Confederacy because the other southern states would not agree to reopening the slave trade. Soon after the state's chapter of the Ku Klux Klan formed, "red shirt" Democratic rifle clubs used physical intimidation and ballot manipulation to alter results of the 1876 election. In the 1890s, Governor Ben "Pitchfork" Tillman—who earned his nickname by threatening to stab President Grover Cleveland in the ribs with said implement—served two terms as governor before embarking on a twenty-three-year Senate career during which he defended segregation as vigilantly as his fellow Edgefield County native, Strom Thurmond, later did for most of his career.

Well into the twentieth century, South Carolina's black citizens observed the Fourth of July mostly alone because the vast majority of whites refused to, preferring instead to celebrate Confederate Memorial Day, May 10. State politicians repeatedly averted their eyes as textile industry executives employed children and quashed attempts by mill workers to organize for fair wages. In 1920, the South Carolina legislature rejected the proposed women's suffrage amendment and took almost a half century finally to ratify it, in 1969. In 1948, the same year the South Carolina legislature declared President Harry Truman's new civil rights commission "un-American," Thurmond's full-throated advocacy of racial segregation as the States' Rights Democratic Party presidential nominee helped him carry four Deep South states. Six years later, the Clarendon County school district—where per-pupil spending on whites was quadruple that for blacks—was pooled with three other districts in a failed defense of the "separate but equal" standard in the landmark *Brown v. Board of Education* case. And when Congress passed the 1965 Voting Rights Act, the law that finally banned the creative and vicious methods used to disfranchise blacks, South Carolina became the first state to challenge its constitutionality. By 1968 Harry Dent, the most legendary of Thurmond's political protégés and a key architect of the "southern strategy," was helping Richard Nixon translate racial antagonisms into crucial Republican votes, a victory in South Carolina, and a ticket to the White House.

If all of this seems like so much ancient history, consider that South Carolinians are still debating the merits of public displays of the Confederate battle flag. Indeed, more than a few pundits believe Republican David Beasley won the 1994 governor's race in part because of his pledge to support displaying the Confederate flag over the state capital—then promptly lost his 1998 reelection bid later after a "religious epiphany" caused him to reverse position. After two decades of adverse judicial rulings, in 2000 Bob Jones University, the state's largest private liberal arts college, founded by its anti-Catholic namesake, finally ended its policy of prohibiting interracial dating. Last year, South Carolina was sued for issuing "choose life" vanity plates while refusing the same option to pro-choice citizens, justifying its decision by claiming that the anti-abortion message constitutes protected government speech. Today, more than eight decades after women first won the right to vote, the South Carolina state legislature is the only one in America where women do not hold at least 10 percent of all seats.

Other Deep South states may stake their own claims, but South Carolina is America's most conservative state. From a strictly constitutional-historical standpoint, its legacy of firsts and lasts reads like a rap sheet: first to overturn a provincial government during the revolutionary period; last to abandon the Atlantic slave trade; first to call for nullifying the Constitution's federal authority; first to secede from the Union; last to abolish the white primary; first to litigate against the integration of public schools and challenge the Voting Rights Act. Whenever America finds itself at some social or political crossroads and in need of direction, perhaps the best thing to do is ask, "What would South Carolina do?" And then do the opposite. South

Carolina is the "Republican Massachusetts," the state from which national Republicans gladly receive electoral support but with which they would least like to be identified.

The Democrats must use caution and be specific when criticizing the conservative South. The party should not antagonize anyone unnecessarily, just as Republicans make clear that they are attacking northeastern *liberals* rather than northeasterners. The bull's-eye should be affixed squarely to the back of southern *conservatives,* for they run the country and it is their political agenda against which Democrats must stand forthrightly and unapologetically in opposition. Most Americans reject the political philosophies of the conservative South. So oppose them Democrats must, and by name if necessary.

2. REJECT THE "KEEP THEM HONEST" FALLACY

A common fallacy offered in defense of investing in the South or other red states during the presidential election is the idea that, even if the Democrats are going to lose, these investments "keep the Republicans honest." Forcing the GOP to waste resources defending its home turf, goes the logic, thereby allows Democrats to be more competitive in the swing states. This sounds nice. However, basic laws of mathematics prove it to be logically false and likely to have the inverse effect—especially if the Democrats are, as usual, the party with fewer resources. Allow me to explain.

Although the Kerry campaign and the center-left groups raised and spent millions in 2004, thanks to the deeper pockets of their corporate supporters and the sophistication with which they raise small-dollar amounts through direct mail, Republicans will continue to be the resource-advantaged party they have been for years. For simplicity's sake, let's assume Republicans have eight dollars to spend in the presidential race for every seven dollars the Democrats do—that is, rough parity with a slight Republican advantage. In an effort to "keep them honest" in the South, Democrats decide to gamble a small but not insignificant share of their resources in the region, say, one of their seven dollars. Although Republicans have a built-in regional advantage, they play it safe by matching the Democrats dollar-for-dollar and easily hold all eleven southern states. The analogy often used in this situation is that of two sailboats racing: The lead sailboat duplicates the tacking movements of the trailing boat so that no matter how fast or slow the winds carry them both, the leader cannot be caught.

What's the result? The Democrats are now in a *worse* position in the swing states, because identical sums subtracted from any ratio always yield a more disparate ratio: The Democrats are left with six dollars for every seven the Republicans spend winning in the battleground states outside the South. The more Democrats invest in keep-them-honest ploys the wider that ratio becomes. Remember, too, that the above scenario presumes that Republicans need to match the Democratic investment dollar-for-dollar, when the GOP probably could spend *half as much* and still win all the southern electors, thanks to their preexisting leads in the southern states and the winner-take-all rule. If keep-them-honest tactics really worked, in 2000 Karl "Boy Genius" Rove would not have been regretting all the late money he dumped into California instead of Florida, and likewise for the millions John Kerry invested in Virginia in 2004 that might have been better spent in Ohio.

No campaign can know for sure which states will be close enough to merit some investment. (Al Gore, for example, underestimated his chances in Ohio in 2000.) Still, given the very predictable nature of the electoral map lately, targeting is more obvious than ever. What's less obvious is that keep-them-honest tactics are inherently counterproductive for the resource-disadvantaged party, and what's true of money is also true of time. Each party in a presidential contest has two candidates and two spouses, and these four principals have the same twenty-four hours per day and seven days per week during the campaign season. In the South, however, the larger number of Republican governors and congressmen gives the GOP more surrogates to stump on behalf of the presidential ticket. As the surrogate-disadvantaged party in the region, Democrats in 2008 would be better off sending their southern congressional delegations into the Midwest and Southwest to stump for its presidential nominee.

If there is a legitimate chance to win a state's electors, then sinking resources in that state makes sense. The decision becomes how much to invest, where and when, and on what assortment of advertising, staff, or other campaign commodities. Between elections, of course, the state and national Democratic parties should make smart, long-term grass-roots and infrastructural investments to begin to turn red states to purple, and purple states to blue, as these seed monies will improve the playing field for future presidential nominees. Democratic National Committee chairman Howard Dean's promise to invest in all fifty states is a good, long-term idea. During election season, however, when the race is tight and every dollar and minute matters, spending money or time in lost-cause states for the sake of keeping the other party "honest" is self-depleting and self-defeating.

3. PUT A SOUTHERNER (OR TWO) ON THE PRESIDENTIAL TICKET

Does a non-southern strategy preclude having southerners on the Democratic presidential ticket? Absolutely not. In fact, the non-southern strategy works just fine with the right southerner—if not two—on the ballot. The Clinton-Gore ticket is the perfect case in point: The Arkansas-Tennessee tandem, remember, won a higher share of votes *outside* the South than inside the South.

The reason a non-southern strategy works so well with a southern nominee on either the top or bottom of the ticket (or both) is that key portions of non-southern states share southern sensibilities, and the threshold for flipping these states into the blue column is much lower. As my colleague David Lublin and I wrote during the early moments of the 2004 Democratic presidential primary—when Kerry appeared to be separating himself from the field—North Carolina senator John Edwards made a good choice for Kerry's vice presidential running mate:

Consider the case of the vaunted "NASCAR dad." We reject the notion that any niche demographic holds the key to the election, but, for the sake of argument, let's assume that NASCAR dads will be a key target group this year. If so, they are less likely to be the decisive voting bloc in Tennessee, Arkansas, Louisiana, or even Edwards' North Carolina. But notice that there are plenty of NASCAR dads in Missouri, Ohio, Pennsylvania, and West Virginia—in other words, in states where the votes of white moderates and independents are more likely to prove decisive . . . [E]ven if the Democrats no longer need the South, it doesn't mean that they can't use a solid southerner like Edwards on the ticket to help them elsewhere.

The Kerry campaign could have used Edwards more effectively. Afraid to unleash him on President Bush—much as the speeches at the Democratic National Convention in Boston were foolishly "scrubbed" to remove criticisms of Bush—Edwards was dispatched to bring his "two Americas" message to rural communities and smaller media markets in swing states, especially Ohio. This was the right idea, even if Edwards proved to be too little, too late to counterbalance the massive Republican investments of staff and money in pivotal places like those western Ohio counties discussed in chapter 4.

The Democrats had little success electing presidents between the Civil War and the New Deal, but when they did, the winning formula was to nominate a southern-friendly northerner. Now that the electoral map from the late nineteenth century has been flipped, red for blue and blue for red, the Democrats should not hesitate to nominate red-state politicians like Indiana's Evan Bayh, North Carolina's Edwards (again), Montana's Brian Schweitzer—or, yes, a southerner like Tennessee's Phil Bredesen or Virginia's Mark Warner—as either presidential or vice presidential candidates in 2008 and beyond. Dick Harpootlian, the colorful former chairman of the South Carolina Democratic Party, believes the South helps toughen the party's presidential candidates for the general election. "Had John Kerry stayed in South Carolina [during the 2004 primary] and gone toe-to-toe with John Edwards, he would have understood that the psychobabble crap that he developed in the campaign wasn't gonna work in Ohio, wasn't gonna work in Pennsylvania," Harpootlian told me, shaking his head as he leaned back in his chair at his law offices in Columbia. "His problem was that he was going home to the Heinz estate every weekend and Bob

Shrum and those guys were telling him, 'Attaboy, go get out there on that windsurfer.' " Harpootlian strongly disagrees with the idea of Democrats abandoning the South, but he's right about the South as a natural proving ground. That said, why *train* a candidate in the South when the party can *take* a candidate from there?

Democrats might consider another tactic to shake up the 2008 presidential election: Running as presidential–vice presidential tandems *through* the primaries, rather than the traditional practice of securing the nomination first and then picking a running mate. There are a variety of nongeographic advantages to doing this. A paired ticket offers a second candidate and spouse to tour the country and make news. It provides a second base of donors, fund-raisers, volunteers, and supporters to generate resources. Because some fences inevitably need mending when a presidential candidate disappoints Democrats whose favored candidates were not chosen, an early selection also provides more time to restore alliances. The phenomenon of running in tandem through the primaries is already taking root at the state level.

From a geographic standpoint, running in tandem through the presidential primaries has another advantage: the ticket can be regionally balanced at the *start* of the campaign. If two Democrats pair up to announce their joint candidacy early in 2007—say, Warner and Bayh— they could threaten the perceived inevitability of former First Lady Hillary Clinton's nomination. On the other hand, a smart, preemptive pairing by Clinton would make the New York senator tougher to beat: It would divert some attention to her running mate, thereby preventing Clinton from becoming overexposed too early in the campaign, and could also help soften her national image among voters still wary of her candidacy, especially those outside the Northeast.

4. ESTABLISH CREDIBILITY IN THE WEST ON GUN RIGHTS AND LAND MANAGEMENT

As discussed in the opening chapter, Democrats have trouble first clearing the "culture-credentialing" hurdle with many Americans in order to get a hearing on the rest of their agenda. Gun rights are a key part of this hurdle, and for millions of American voters the failure to support the Second Amendment's right to bear arms is a political disqualifier. It's not that hunters, anglers, and other outdoorsmen are unconcerned about terrorism, health care, or gas prices. They just have very strong feelings about hunting and fishing, as Montana Governor Brian Schweitzer of Montana explained to me while flying over his beautiful state, which is one of the nation's per-capita leaders in outdoor participation:

> When you want to get people [in Montana] worked up, talk about road closures for hunting and fishing. Talk about reducing the number of permits for elk or deer. That's what gets people worked up. There's a passion there. It's not something that's going to pop on polling, because pollsters will say, "What's the most important issues to you?," and voters will say "education, jobs, and health care" like everyone else—like they're expected to say that. But they're passionate about hunting and fishing, outdoor stuff.

The voters' intensity toward this issue is a perfect example of a high-salience and high-efficacy issue, as discussed in the previous chapter.

The outdoors community is substantial. In *Foxes in the Henhouse*, Democratic consultants Steven Jarding and Dave "Mudcat" Saunders list the hundreds of thousands if not millions of Americans in each of the fifty states who, according to a 2001 national survey conducted by the U.S. Fish & Wildlife Service, either hunt, fish, or watch wildlife. "Democrats too often do not even attempt to garner the support of the hunting, gun-owning, sportsmen group of voters," they lament. "This is another prime example of practicing the politics of subtraction instead of addition and conceding a voting block to the Republicans even though Democratic positions and votes address the real threats to this group far better than do those of Republicans." A look at the regional breakdowns of the Fish & Wildlife Service data in Figure 7.1 shows that westerners and even midwesterners participate in outdoor activities at greater rates than do southerners—although the share of white outdoorsmen in the South is surely comparable if not higher in some cases to that of whites in the Midwest and interior West states.

Figure 7.1
Outdoor Participation by Region, 2001

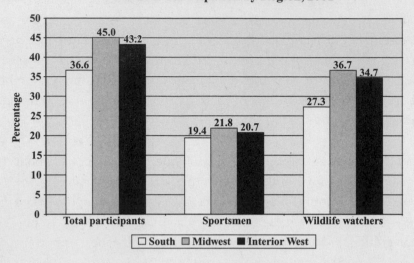

But even if white southerners hunt and fish at higher rates than white Americans from the Midwest and interior West, the real question is whether Democratic support for the Second Amendment is sufficient to clear the culture-credentialing hurdle in the South. Because southerners hold more conservative opinions on a variety of other so-called values issues, there's plenty of reason to believe it will not. To get a more precise sense of the regional differences, Figure 7.2 depicts the opinions of the subset of white respondents to the 2000 National Annenberg Election Survey on five non-firearm cultural issues: abortion, the death penalty, school prayer, gays in the military, and affirmative action. The figure shows the percentage of respondents, by region, who take the conservative position on each issue. White southerners are more conservative than midwesterners on all five issues and are significantly more conservative than westerners on four of the five (the death penalty excepted). These differences are not really that surprising, given that midwesterners are second only to southerners in their evangelism and westerners pride themselves on a tradition of libertarian values.

So, if a Democratic candidate approaches a midwestern or western voter and says, "Hey, I support the Second Amendment," that voter may reply, "Great, let's hear what you have to say about taxes, health

Figure 7.2
Support for Conservative Values by Region, 2000

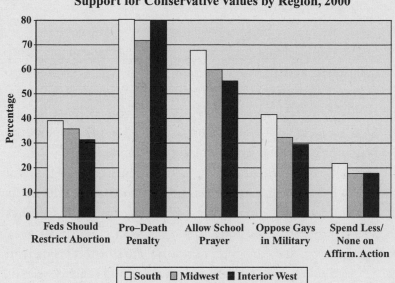

care, and education." If a Democratic candidate says the same thing to a southern voter, the response is more likely to be, "Great, but what are your views on abortion, teaching evolution in schools, or civil unions?" At that point, if the Democratic nominee does not support conservative positions on these issues, he will have to start fumbling around to explain why not. Pretty quickly, many southern voters are going to tune that candidate out, especially if those voters are non–college educated. Outside the South, where the culture-credentialing hurdle is lower, Democrats may be able to get a hearing with tens of millions of otherwise wary westerners and midwesterners just by supporting the Second Amendment.

Democrats can further capitalize out West by advocating measures necessary to protect natural resources and wildlife that make hunting and fishing locations so special in the first place. Indeed, many westerners are finally starting to realize that the Republicans' laissez-faire attitude toward land management has morphed from a "hands-off" approach into a disturbingly "hand-it-over-to-corporations" ethic. As the *New York Times* reported in the summer of 2005, Republican advocacy for deregulation and the selling off or ignoring of local property rights in the name of energy profits—call it the "Cheney-ization" of the West—is beginning to catch up with the GOP:

> Amid the clank, clatter and fire of the largest natural gas boom ever on public land in the West, a new kind of sagebrush rebellion is stirring. Ranchers, cowboys, small property owners and local government leaders—the core of the Republican base in the Rocky Mountain West—are chafing at the pace and scope of the Bush administration's push for energy development . . .
>
> The battle cry is the same as in past movements: a call for local control over a distant federal landlord. But for the first time, it is the Republicans who find themselves the target of angry speeches about lost property rights and tone-deaf federal land managers. And people who have been on opposing sides of the major land battles in the West—mainly property owners and ranchers versus environmentalists—are now allies.

In short, the terrain is changing out west as a result of the Republicans losing credibility on land and water management. Supporting the Second Amendment allows Democrats to insert themselves into this discussion. In the South, however, the Democrats have to leap higher to clear the taller and more numerous cultural hurdles just to be heard.

5. WESTERNIZE THE PRESIDENTIAL SELECTION PROCESS

A bipartisan group of top western politicians joined together in 2005 to agitate for a greater role for western states in the presidential nomination process. Led by Republican Utah governor Jon Huntsman Jr. and Democratic New Mexico governor Bill Richardson, this group is calling for an eventual "Mountain States Primary" or, in the interim, at least a bigger role for one western state in the presidential nominating process. "The objective is to increase the diversity in the early primaries by having western states participate earlier in both primaries and caucuses," says Richardson, citing the possibility of an early caucus in either Colorado and Nevada.

The Democratic National Committee should heed these calls. If putting a block of states together to create a western version of the "Super Tuesday" southern primary is too much to ask, at minimum the DNC should move a western state up in the calendar, perhaps simultaneous to the Iowa caucuses or the New Hampshire primary. Though Iowa and New Hampshire Democrats guard jealousy and take seriously their first-in-the-nation status, traditions must end when they jeopardize the party's larger agenda. Iowa and New Hampshire have always been decidedly unrepresentative of the Democratic coalition, and neither is among the states experiencing the most rapid changes and population growth. The only present advantage to assigning so much early attention to Iowa and New Hampshire is that both have been swing states in recent presidential elections. (They were two of only three states that flipped between 2000 and 2004.) Still, if both parties are spending time in Iowa and New Hampshire during the 2007 pre–primary season it's a wash: Any added attention Democrats give these states during the nomination process will be offset by extra attention from Republicans.

As for the host city for the 2008 national convention, in the past eighty years the Democrats have held their convention west of the Mississippi River only three times, all in California: twice in Los Angeles (1960, 2000) and once in San Francisco (1984). New York, Chicago, or Philadelphia hosted the DNC meeting a combined twelve times since 1928, when the convention met in Houston—the last time it wasn't held in either California, Chicago, or another site east of the Windy City. In 2008, the Democrats should flip the script, picking a city west of Chicago but east of California.

Eleven cities have expressed interest in hosting the 2008 Democratic National Convention: Anaheim, Dallas, Denver, Detroit, Minneapolis, Las Vegas, New Orleans, New York, Orlando, Phoenix, and San Antonio. Though New Orleans is the sentimental favorite in the post-Katrina era, the Big Easy will probably be incapable of hosting an event of this magnitude so shortly after the hurricane. (But wouldn't it be something if Democrats held a two-day convention there and spent the final two days of the traditionally four-day event in a Jimmy Carter–led reconstruction effort with every delegate, politician, and party official on deck?) New York should be ruled out because the Democrats have been there, and the Republicans did that post–September 11 exploitation maneuver already in 2004. Holding it in Dallas and San Antonio would send a shot across Bush's bow, but Texas is not a swing state. The 2000 convention in Los Angeles makes Anaheim redundant. Las Vegas would invite far too many media references to cultural depravity, and all it takes is one group of drunk delegates at a strip club to provide all the material that conservative talk radio hosts need to howl all the way through to Election Day.

That leaves Denver, Detroit, Minneapolis, Orlando, and Phoenix—a nice mix of cities in the Diamond, with two in the Midwest, two in the interior West, and one in the heart of the Florida's Diamond "setting." Given the amazing growth in the Denver and Phoenix suburbs, and the fact that Democrats need to do everything they can to start winning Colorado and Arizona, the Democratic National Committee can signal a new era by picking one of these two cities as the host site for 2008.

Finally, at the 2008 convention the Democrats can once and for all dispel the notion that they have no unifying message. How? By requiring every speaker, from the county party chair who has a three-minute slot in the middle of Monday afternoon to the presidential nominee's prime-time speech on Thursday night, to begin her or his speech with the same opening lines:

> *My name is _____ , and I'm a Democrat because we in the Democratic Party believe in a strong defense/smart offense approach to our national security, we believe in a culture of investment that will help America build a more prosperous future together, and we believe that every American has the right to exercise the inalienable liberties that our Constitution guarantees us all. As the _____ from the great state of _____ , to me being a Democratic also means . . .*

And at that point the speaker details whatever specific story or message affirms one or more of the three overarching themes. If the nominee and

the national party can develop a better elevator pitch and way to articulate it, that's great, but the DNC and the presidential nominee should
insist that every speaker begin his or her speech with the same few sentences. The direct policy message will be that the Democrats believe in
strong defense/smart offense, a culture of investment, and the right to
exercise our inalienable liberties. The indirect, political message will be
that the Democratic Party has finally gotten its act together.

6. SMALL-STATE SENATE TARGETING

As discussed previously, the Senate Republican majority benefits from
the election of many members from small states. Because it violates the
one-person, one-vote principle of equal representation, there have
been many calls from many quarters to abolish the U.S. Senate, and
long before the Republicans took control of the Senate in 1995. Eliminating the Senate would take a constitutional amendment, of course,
and proposing one requires either the first constitutional convention in
the United States since 1787 or the willingness of the Senate to propose
an amendment abolishing itself. That's not going to happen, so the best
strategic option for Democrats is to try to win as many as possible
small-state Senate seats because doing so is more efficient in cost-per-
voter terms.

Table 7.1 lists the forty U.S. senators from the twenty least-populous
states, the combined registered populations of which total about 15
million—not much more than the 14.2 million registered Californians
who share just two senators. The Democrats hold seventeen of the forty
small-state Senate seats; a switch of just three states would bring them
to parity. Notice there are only two southern states in the list: The Democrats have both senators from Arkansas and neither from Mississippi.
Had Mississippi's Trent Lott opted to retire in 2006, former attorney
general Mike Moore would have had a decent shot of giving Democrats
a rare pickup in the Magnolia State. Still, small state or large, winning
Senate seats in the South has become harder and harder. The Democrats
had good candidates in 2004 in the five open Senate seats, and all
Republicans did was depict them as national Democrats to beat them.

Former Democratic congressman Glen Browder of Alabama calls this phenomenon the "national rationalization of politics" in the South—though it would be equally fitting to call it the "rational nationalization" of southern politics by the Republicans.

Snagging any of the eight Republican-held seats in Idaho, Kansas, Utah, and Wyoming will be difficult, although the current Democratic governors in Kansas (Kathleen Sebelius) and Wyoming (Dave Freudenthal) would make good Senate candidates should one of the seats in their states open up in the near future. Democratic pollster Jim Gerstein makes the important point that winning governorships is very critical for Democrats—not only because governors control state politics and help in political-electoral matters like party fund-raising or their state's redistricting processes, but also because sitting or former governors make excellent Senate candidates.

The real opportunities to pick up Senate seats "on the cheap," so to speak, are in Northeast and Southwest. The incumbents there, including Maine's Olympia Snowe, New Hampshire's Judd Gregg, and New Mexico's Pete Domenici, will be tough to beat head-to-head, but once they retire their seats should be on the Democrats' target list. Others, like Rhode Island's Lincoln Chafee and Nevada's John Ensign are more vulnerable right now. Wherever they are located, when the small-state Republican incumbents either become vulnerable or their retirements open up seats, the Democrats must strike. Until then, the national and state party should continue to make the seed-money investments in candidate training and voter contacting so that Democrats will be in an at-the-ready posture when those opportunities arise. Every Senate vote cast in committee or on the floor counts the same, whether that senator represents 14 million registered voters or a few hundred thousand. If there are small-state openings, the Democrats must funnel whatever resources are necessary to win them.

7. RE-GERRYMANDERING U.S. HOUSE SEATS FOR 2012

Too many Democrats in the U.S. House are representing too-safe districts, and this fact prevents the party from maximizing its House seat

Table 7.1
Small-State Senators

State	Registered Voters*	Senators	
Wyoming	265	**Thomas**	**Enzi**
Alaska	334	**Stevens**	**Murkowski**
Vermont	354	Leahy	Jeffords
North Dakota	412	Conrad	Dorgan
Delaware	415	Biden	Carper
South Dakota	425	Johnson	**Thune**
Hawaii	497	Inouye	Akaka
Montana	519	Baucus	**Burns**
Rhode Island	522	Reed	**Chafee**
Idaho	663	**Craig**	**Crapo**
New Hampshire	716	**Gregg**	**Sununu**
Maine	824	**Snowe**	**Collins**
Nebraska	918	**Hagel**	Nelson
West Virginia	935	Byrd	Rockefeller
New Mexico	936	**Domenici**	Bingaman
Nevada	965	Reid	**Ensign**
Utah	1,141	**Hatch**	**Bennett**
Arkansas	1,328	Lincoln	Pryor
Kansas	1,338	**Brownback**	**Roberts**
Mississippi	1,510	**Lott**	**Cochran**
Totals	15,017	22R, 18D	

* Data for registered voters (in thousands) taken from U.S. Census Bureau.

Senior senators appear in left column, with junior senators in the right;

Republican members are in **boldface**; and Jeffords (I) is counted as a Democrat.

share, especially in the critical Northeast-Midwest corridor discussed in chapter 4. The "unholy alliance" forged between Republicans and minority Democratic legislators—and especially Congressional Black Caucus (CBC) and Congressional Hispanic Caucus (CHC) members—led to the election of more minority Democrats to Congress, but also more Republicans. A new alliance between white and minority Democrats must be forged, with the goal of redrawing the 2012 maps to enable

Democrats to recapture—or, if already recaptured, to retain—a majority in the U.S. House of Representatives.

To understand the magnitude of this problem, look at Figure 7.1, which depicts the Partisan Voting Index of all 435 House districts. As discussed earlier, PVI measures how well presidential candidates perform by congressional district: Positive numbers indicate districts Bush carried in 2000 and 2004, and vice versa for the Kerry-Gore districts. For visual clarity, the Democratic districts were signed positively and then all 435 districts were arrayed, left to right, from the most Democratic district (José Serrano's NY16 = 43.4 percent for Kerry-Gore) to the most Republican (Chris Cannon's UT3 = 26.2 percent for Bush). Including Serrano there were thirty-one districts with higher PVIs than Bush's 26.2 percent figure in Cannon's Utah district. The figure's tilt confirms that racial gerrymandering ostensibly intended to help African Americans and Hispanics is actually partisan gerrymandering done to benefit Republicans. Democratic voters are distributed so inefficiently than the 199 Democratic-leaning districts on the left side of the figure comprise a greater total area than the 236 Republican districts on the right side. Given that Bush's combined popular vote from 2000 and 2004 exceeds that of Gore and Kerry combined, what explains the apparent paradox of the right side containing less area than the left? The answer is simple: The bars in the figure are *percentages,* not absolute vote margins, and only if turnout were identical in every district would the Republican side necessarily be larger.

These noncompetitive congressional districts have vastly different turnouts, however. Table 7.2 reports 2004 congressional turnouts from twenty districts: a set of ten Democratic districts and a second set of Republican districts with nearly identical PVI ratings. The average turnout in the ten Republican districts was 253,837, compared to just 214,121 in the ten Democratic districts—about 40,000 fewer votes, or 16 percent lower turnout. These differences cannot be explained by the 2004 presidential contest, because the only district among the twenty in a swing state was Democrat Gwendolyn Moore's 5th District in Wisconsin that, not coincidentally, had the highest turnout of the group. Despite Moore's total, the ten Republican-represented districts *still* had higher turnout.

Figure 7.3
Partisan Voting Index

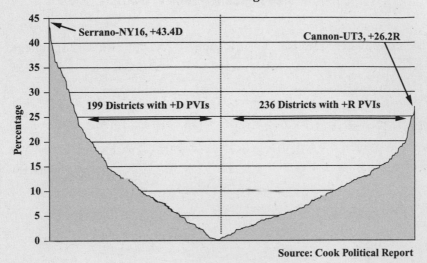

Source: Cook Political Report

All but three of the ten Democrats (Moore; New York's Carolyn Maloney; and California's Howard Berman) are members of the Congressional Black or Hispanic caucuses. Because voting varies with socioeconomic status, the majority-minority districts represented by members of the Congressional Black and Hispanic caucuses often have among the lowest turnouts in the country. Still, who can blame their constituents for not showing up? If they live in a non-swing state with a safe Democratic incumbent running literally, if not virtually unopposed, why bother? The Democrats can correct this egregious situation by producing maps in 2012 that are more competitive but which still ensure the election of minority Democrats. To accomplish this, in any state where they exert power over the redistricting process Democrats should duplicate what might be called the *Cummings-Wynn model* from the 2000 round of redistricting in Maryland.

Prior to 2002, in a state that was overwhelming Democratic in both legislative chambers and had not elected a Republican governor since 1966, Maryland's eight-member U.S. House delegation was split, four seats for each party. The inability of Democrats to defeat moderate Republicans Bob Ehrlich and Connie Morella was particularly aggravating. Ehrlich and Morella were likable, media-savvy politicians who

Table 7.2

Turnout Differences in Congressional Districts, 2004

District: Member	+DEM	Turnout		+GOP	District: Member
NY14: Maloney	26.4	274,043	272,928	26.2	UT3: Cannon
MO1: Clay	25.6	283,771	235,071	25.3	TX11: Conaway
MD7: Cummings	25.2	244,018	268,043	25.1	AL6: Bachus
CA28: Berman	24.8	162,510	233,514	24.9	TX19: Neugebauer
TX18: Jackson-Lee	23.4	152,988	205,241	24.6	TX13: Thornberry
GA5: Lewis	23.2	201,773	250,138	23.6	NE3: Osborne
CA34: Roybal-Allard	23.0	110,457	219,136	22.9	GA10: Deal
NJ13: Menendez	22.9	159,541	258,982	22.6	GA7: Linder
GA4: McKinney	22.7	246,970	293,961	21.8	UT1: Bishop
WI4: Moore	20.5	305,142	301,156	20.6	GA8: Westmoreland
Average turnout →		214,121	253,817		← Average turnout

drew enough votes from independents and moderate Democrats to win: Ehrlich, because he was a working-class guy liked by blue-collar whites in eastern Baltimore and Harford County; and Morella, because she was a pro-choice woman supported by suburban mothers in up-scale Montgomery County towns like Potomac and Bethesda. Staffers for the Democratic troika then running the state—Governor Parris Glendening, Senate president Mike Miller, and House speaker Cas Taylor—sat down in 2001 and drew a new map in which some African-American voters from black Congressman Al Wynn's Prince George's—based 4th District were moved into Morella's 8th District, and white suburban voters from Howard County were moved into black Congressman Elijah Cummings's 7th District to free up extra Democrats for the 2nd District Ehrlich was vacating to run for governor.

It worked: In 2002, Democrat Chris Van Hollen ousted Morella and Democrat Dutch Ruppersberger won the open-seat race to replace Ehrlich, turning Maryland from a 4–4 delegation to a 6–2 Democratic delegation overnight. The key to capturing both seats was the willingness of Cummings and Wynn to assume the burden of slightly less favorable districts. Sure, they had to introduce themselves to some new voters and say good-bye to familiar friends, but their name recognition, constituent operations, fund-raising capacities, and various other incumbent advantages were more than enough to survive. Cummings and Wynn easily won reelection in their newly configured districts, and returned in January 2003 for the seating of 108th Congress with two new Democratic colleagues in their state delegation.

The lesson of the Cummings-Wynn model is that black and Hispanic Democrats have the surplus voters the party needs to redistribute to create a larger set of competitive districts. This is an asset CBC and CHC members should neither horde nor bargain away. If Nancy Pelosi wants to be the first woman Speaker of the House of Representatives, she ought to sit down with the CBC and CHC and broker a deal wherein the minority members of the Democratic House caucus agree to assume a bit more electoral risk in exchange for two promises: first, that the Democratic Congressional Campaign Committee will rally to the defense of any black or Hispanic incumbent who faces a serious primary or general election threat; and second, that the CBC and CHC will enjoy some mix of greater leadership or committee assignments if their cooperation helps produce a new Democratic majority. Democrats should do the same with state legislative maps, because the identical problem of overpacked majority-minority districts exists in many states, as Tyson King-Meadows and I document in our study of black state legislators.

In previous decades, African American and Hispanic elites could hardly be blamed for doing what was necessary to break through the electoral glass ceiling. But the 2010 redistricting will be the *fifth* map-making round since the Supreme Court ruled malapportionment unconstitutional in the 1960s. Black and Hispanic legislators today are political enterprises in their own right, who have built up their own personal constituencies, name recognition, legislative accomplishments, and fund-raising connections. In additional to these advantages, they no longer need districts so overwhelmingly packed with minorities that they run unopposed or against token opposition.

Congressman Raúl Grijalva, who represents the Tucson area, is not shy about admitting how badly the districting situation is, and the complacency it creates:

> I think the Latino leadership suffers from the same myopic view that the Democratic Party and its Anglo leadership suffers from— it's myopic. It's "I have mine, let's keep it," as opposed to "How do we build this, how do we make it stronger, how do we integrate new faces, new realities, and new leadership into what we're doing?" Many times with the Latino elected leadership, they get into a comfort zone and security with their position because the Republican leadership has guaranteed a certain number of seats. So the security comes in maintaining that as opposed to working on a coalition to take back the power.

What black and Hispanic Democrats in Congress need is more power. To obtain it, they should join with equally complacent white Democrats in an effort to apply the Cummings-Wynn model wherever possible. Doing so will give minority Democrats and their constituents more influence. It will also encourage higher turnout, which will help statewide Democratic candidates for president, Senate, and governor.

EXTENDED LADDERS AND A
DEMOCRATIC SOUTH BY 2028

Dreams die hard, especially in politics, and for Democrats no dream has died harder than the idea of a party revival in the South. Perhaps the lasting power of the party's brand name in parts of the South, especially in state and local races, produces an ember of hope that seems to glow hotter and brighter than it actually is. Perhaps Democrats feel obligated to fight for the South to honor the party's traditions, or to refute the charge that southern rejection somehow implies a core inadequacy. Or maybe it's just a donkey's innate stubbornness. Whatever its origins, the persistent dream of a Democratic South is potentially ruinous to the party's hopes of reasserting itself as a national majority. The conventional wisdom that the Democrats cannot build a majority without the South is, to put it bluntly, more conventional than wise.

The Democrats' steady decline began in the mid-1960s and has continued since. By any measure—control of elected offices, party registration, partisan self-identification—the Democrats have been sliding, sometimes slowly and other times more precipitously, into minority status. The 2004 election marked sixty years since Franklin Delano Roosevelt won his unprecedented fourth term in 1944. In the fifteen presidential contests since, the Democratic nominee has won an absolute majority of the popular vote just twice—and in 1976 Jimmy Carter did so by the narrowest of margins: 50.1 percent. Winners Harry Truman in 1948, John Kennedy in 1960, and Bill Clinton in his 1996 re-election each came close, but crested at 49 percent. By comparison, in the same post-FDR era, the Republicans have claimed a majority seven times.

The fact is Democrats have been coasting for more than two generations on the fumes of their once-strong but faded post–New Deal majority. The time has come to develop a new geo-demographic winning formula. The alternative is to hope for the revival of a coalition that no longer exists and will not return any time soon—the sort of wistful thinking that only encourages southern Republicans like former Texas Congressman Tom DeLay. "The Republican Party is a permanent majority for the future of this country," predicts DeLay, who resigned from office but undoubtedly will continue working behind the scenes toward that goal. "We're going to be able to lead this country in the direction we've been dreaming of for years."

It is time for the Democrats to set into motion a non-southern strategy to forge that new governing majority. The hallmark of strategic coalition building is efficiency, and the political-electoral calculus of the moment demands that Democrats invest smartly and target wisely. Not every district, state, or region can be won, especially in a country as heterogeneous and divided as America is at the opening of the twenty-first century.

Because Democrats cannot possibly go after every voter in every demographic group in every corner of the country, they must decide how best to fill their partisan baskets. The most logical approach is to invest initially in gathering the electoral windfall from their blue-state back-yards in the Northeast and Pacific Coast. The fruits of the Midwest hang within arm's reach on the lower branches, and those of the interior West are only midway up the tree. Finally, at the far-removed tree-tops are the southern fruits that were once so plentiful but today require an extended ladder just to reach. Ascending to these heights is an ambitious, noble goal in the long term, but a risky endeavor that entails bypassing fruit much closer at hand. In strategic terms, beginning there could hardly be more perilous or less efficient.

Unfortunately, those calling for a southern revival are advocating extended-ladder politics. Why would Democrats turn to the most rural, economically stratified, racially polarized, anti-union, evangelized, and culturally conservative region of the country to begin the process of building a strong and sustainable majority for the twenty-first century? It makes absolutely no sense for a progressive party to repair itself by first targeting the nation's most conservative region. Indeed, the Republicans would be delighted if Democrats continued to obsess over the South: That way, the GOP can deplete the Democrats' resources and more easily capture the Midwest and Southwest. In his compelling new book, *Being Right Is Not Enough,* Paul Waldman nicely summarizes the dangers of Democratic pandering to the South:

> Fear of losing the South has led Democrats to look apologetic and weak, so that their attempts to win votes in the South not only fail there, they hurt them everywhere else in the country. When they cross the Mason-Dixon Line and say, "I love NASCAR and hunting, see, I'm one of you," they look ridiculous. Southerners can smell that kind of pandering a mile away, and it only makes the Democrat look unprincipled to the rest of the country. What they need to do is make their case to Southerners in a way that demonstrates to everyone their strength and their values.

Though easier said than done, the task of demonstrating that strength and those values is best made by winning elsewhere first, governing confidently and successfully, and then putting that record of accomplishment before southerners for their inspection. If, at that point, southerners still feel compelled to vote Republican because of cultural issues, well, there's just not much Democrats can do about it unless they are prepared to abandon their support for reproductive freedom, affirmative action, and civil rights and liberties more broadly.

On second thought, hasn't this proposition *already* been put to the test in the South? A native southern son, Bill Clinton, had the guts to couple fiscal responsibility with welfare reform, thereby shepherding American through its greatest period of peacetime prosperity, and when his southern heir apparent ran, what happened? The South rejected the Clinton-Gore legacy record by voting solidly for the Bush-Cheney ticket in every state but Florida. The 2000 Democratic ticket, mind you, didn't pair George McGovern and Michael Dukakis: It was Tennessee Southern Baptist Al Gore and Connecticut Orthodox Jew Joe Lieberman. It's convenient to chalk up Gore's poor showing in the South to the lingering problems of Clinton's sexual indiscretions or the fact that Florida was the only southern state the Gore campaign really targeted. But as discussed in chapter 2, the white South was already moving away from the Democrats, as it more or less has been since 1976. The Democrats governed well during the 1990s, and brought their case to the South. Southerners just weren't interested.

The states of the former Confederacy are changing. As a region, the South is no longer as exceptional as it once was. Though starting from some rather small baselines, southern states are experiencing some of the fastest rates of growth in their Hispanic populations. Americans are in-migrating to the South, and southerners are either relocating to other parts of the country or migrating within their home region to the "new South's" growth areas. As this mobility continues, the South will gradually assimilate with the rest of the country, and by consequence will lose some of its cultural and political distinctiveness. This process is already well under way in Florida, and Virginia and North Carolina have some distance to go but are not too far behind. The future Hispanic majority coming to Texas, which is solidly Republican now, will inevitably put the Lone Star State back into play. From base camps in Austin, Alexandria, and Orlando, perhaps by 2028 the next generation of Democrats will be able to surround the region, steadily convert the Outer South, and eventually press inward toward the Deep South.

When the Democrats conquer Alabama, Mississippi, and South Carolina, the process of recapturing the South will be complete and the party will have come full circle.

Forty years ago, Kevin Phillips envisioned a southern-based Republican majority, a vision that has since become reality. In *The Emerging Republican Majority,* he wrote:

> My own feeling, as a Northeasterner born and bred, is that no region of the country has a worse record—from the Federalist era to Herbert Hoover—of defending worn-out and institutionalized political credos. Today, the Northeast, its Eastern Establishment Republicans in the vanguard, is once again the final bastion of status quo liberalism. I hold no great brief for the politicians of the Liberal Establishment, but I very much oppose "writing off" the Northeast.

Today, Phillips talks of an "American theocracy" built on three cornerstones—rabid evangelism, oil dependence, and our massive national debt. In the White House is a southerner who personifies all three of these problems: George W. Bush is an evangelical Texas oilman who hasn't vetoed a single spending bill sent to him by his fellow Republicans in Congress. It is the modern Republican Party that defends worn-out and institutionalized credos, from "trickle-down economics" to "deficits don't matter," from "Star Wars missile defense" to the "culture of life." It is the southern Republicans who are the final bastion of status quo conservatism.

Democrats need not write off the South forever, but neither should they hold any great brief for the politicians of the Conservative Establishment who own the South and, by virtue of that ownership, have a temporary lease on the national government. Democrats must decide whether they want to surrender full ownership of the country to the Republicans for the next generation, maybe two. The thin majorities the Republicans presently exploit for every possible advantage will only grow stronger and become more durable if the Democrats hesitate, if they continue to think retrospectively. That would be a tragedy and a shame, for there is a future Democratic majority right in front of their eyes if they are only willing to let go of the past to see and seize it.

Afterword

The 2006 elections brought many messages, but few as clear as this one: For Democrats, the non-southern strategy is *working*.

For the first time since 1994, Democrats are now the majority party among governors, in both chambers of Congress, and in the state legislatures. While electoral analysts and pundits continue to debate why Democrats won, when the voters turned against the GOP, and which electoral subgroups triggered the partisan reversal, the "where" of the Democrats' 2006 victories is not in dispute—they won 85 percent of their seats outside the South. The results provide powerful confirmation of *Whistling Past Dixie*'s central thesis:

- Five of the Democrats' six net new governors, five of their six new U.S. senators, and twenty-four of their thirty new U.S. House members were elected outside the eleven former Confederate states.

- In U.S. House contests, Democrats defeated or replaced 31 percent of Republicans in the Northeast, 15 percent in the Midwest, 9 percent in the West, and just 7 percent in the South. Most amazing, for the first time in more than half a century—since the 83rd Congress of 1953–54—the party with a *minority* of seats in the southern House and Senate delegations to Congress is nevertheless the *majority* party in both chambers.

- More than 90 percent of the Democrats' net new state legislative seats were won outside the South, and all ten of the state legislative chamber majorities Democrats captured in 2006 were non-southern.

- Despite the best midterm election cycle in thirty-two years, exit polls showed Democrats winning every region except the South (which they lost by 8 points), carrying the Northeast by 28 points, the Midwest by 5, and the West by 11.

The 2006 results magnified the pre-existing regional disparities within the Democratic coalition: Forty-six of the fifty-one Democratic senators are now non-southern, just four shy of half the chamber; twenty-three of their twenty-eight governors are non-southern, just two shy of half the nation's fifty state chief executives; and if Speaker Nancy Pelosi is allowed to include black and Latino House members from the South— many of whom, after all, were aided by district packing engineered by Republicans to produce an overall GOP edge in the region—she has more than two hundred seats without a single southern white member.

The 2006 midterms were neither an earthquake nor a tidal wave, but an old-fashioned nor'easter. A blizzard swept through the Rust Belt, freezing out Ford- and Rockefeller-style moderate Republicans, much in the same way Republicans spent the past four decades defeating or replacing moderate Dixiecrats in the South. Toss in a few western victories for the Democrats and what we witnessed was the very formula I prescribed in the book when I wrote that the "best strategy for winning in the immediate term is to consolidate electoral control over the Northeast and Pacific Coast blue states, expand the party's Midwestern margins, and cultivate the new-growth areas of the interior West."

There have been elections in which Democrats did well in the South and well nationally, such as 1986, and others when the party did poorly in both the South and nationally, like 1994. But until 2006, there has never been an election in which Democrats made such significant gains nationally—capturing new majorities at every level except the presidency, which was not on the ballot—despite little contribution from southern electorates.

To repeat: The non-southern strategy is working.

Turning to the upcoming presidential election, how relevant will the non-southern strategy be in 2008?

In the past four presidential contests, Bill Clinton, Al Gore, and John Kerry won 331, 328, 267 and 252 non-southern electors, respectively. That's an average of 295 electors—compelling evidence that Democrats can win without southern electors. In winning both election and re-election, Clinton captured more than 270 non-southern electors, and Gore (New Hampshire) and Kerry (Ohio) came within a single state of reaching that winning threshold. Ironically, the Kerry case is most revealing: Despite having the lowest total of the four, the fact that a flawed candidate running against an incumbent president in the first presidential election after the September 11 attacks still came within just one state of winning testifies to how solid and sizeable that block of non-southern electoral votes truly is.

Starting with that core of 252 electors, how can the 2008 Democratic nominee get over the top to reach 270? The five most obvious paths, in rough order of possibility, are:

1. **Single-shot Ohio.** Along with Colorado and New Hampshire, Ohio has been home to a dramatic turnaround for Democrats. The only state to produce for Democrats a new governor and U.S. senator in 2006, with its 20 electors Ohio should again live up to its "as it goes, so goes the nation" reputation in 2008.

2. **Single-shot Florida.** The least southern of the southern states, no less one with a burgeoning Latino population, Florida and its 27 electors remain a key target for Democrats, particularly in the post-Bush (George W. and Jeb) era.

3. **The Southwest Passage.** This is the game-changing region. Winning all four states produces 29 new electors, and even without the 10 electors from Arizona (where Kerry lost ground relative to Gore), the 19 from Colorado, Nevada, and New Mexico are sufficient to reach 270.

4. **The 36th Parallel, Variant 1.** The 36th latitude is the border that splits Virginia from North Carolina, Kentucky from Tennessee, and Missouri from Arkansas, and there are two 36th Parallel routes to winning the White House. One option is to turn Kentucky and Missouri, with their combined 19 electors,

from red to blue. These two border states, both of which Gore and Kerry lost, were key to Clinton's twin victories.

5. **The 36th Parallel, Variant 2.** A final route involves flipping Virginia—the southern state that, after Florida, is the Democrats' next big southern opportunity—and West Virginia, which used to be a bedrock Democratic state and needs to be again. That would provide 18 electors, just enough to get to 270.

When added to the 252 base electors Kerry won, any of these five routes will give Democrats back the White House. Any two will raise the electoral total to about 300; three will bump it closer to 320; some combination of four would push it toward 350; and all five would return the Democratic electoral total to Clintonian levels.

For Democrats, these are the paths back to the White House—the only institution in the American system where they have not already built a non-southern-based majority.

THOMAS F. SCHALLER
Washington, D.C.
June 2007

Acknowledgments

Many thanks go first to Alice Mayhew of Simon & Schuster for believing in me and this project, and for her legendary editorial guidance. I am also grateful to Aileen Boyle, Mario Florio, Lisa Healy, Serena Jones, Roger Labrie, Victoria Meyer, Leah Wasielewski, and the rest of the Simon & Schuster team for their editorial and marketing support.

I am blessed to have dozens of great friends and colleagues who shared their ideas, data, suggestions, or chapter edits to help improve some portion of this book, including Alan Abramowitz, Sean Aday, Gerard Alexander, Kenny Baer, Steve Benen, Chris Bowers, Maria Cardona, Matt Continetti, Charlie Cook, Jim Cox, Todd Estes, Glenn Feldman, Tom Frank, Jim Gerstein, Jon Goldstein, Jon Gordon, Josh Green, Shane Ham, John Harwood, Lou Jacobson, Leonard Kastle, Tyson King-Meadows, Ezra Klein, Phil Klinkner, Chris Lindland, Ryan Lizza, David Lublin, Eric Lyman, Pete Melcavage, Markos Moulitsas, David Nir, Tim Noah, Rick Perlstein, Ken Rudin, Cliff Schecter, Byron Shafer, David Sirota, Jeff Stanger, Ruy Teixeira, Chuck Todd, Susan Turnbull, Josh Tzuker, Paul Waldman, Amy Walter, Patricia Weitsman, and Ivan Zapien. I am also fortunate to have written for several magazine and newspaper editors who helped shape my ideas over the years: Sid Blumenthal, Patrick Gavin, Michael Hill, Tara McKelvey, Jeff Price, Mike Tomasky, Larry Williams, and, most especially, former *Washington Post* Sunday "Outlook" section editor Steve Luxenberg, who published an early version of the book's argument in the *Post* in November 2003.

I learned a lot from traveling the country and talking to a variety of Democrats—a trek that took me from the indescribable Sip-n-Dip bar in Great Falls, Montana, to Colorado congressman John Salazar's seed potato farm near the New Mexico border, to a ride through Cleveland's

Flats in the passenger seat of Congressman Sherrod Brown's beloved, if cluttered car. Thanks are due to dozens of public officials, party operatives, and political observers who agreed to be interviewed for this book, not to mention the staffers and press secretaries who helped me gain access to them. Though not all interviewees were quoted in the text, their comments and insights were invaluable. Specific thanks are due to folks who live in or have political roots in six states—the five discussed in detail in chapter 4, plus South Carolina—where I spent the bulk of my travel time: State Representative Meg Burton Cahill, Kris Garcia, Congressman Raul Grijalva, State Representative Phil Lopes, Ana Ma, David Waid, and Doug Wilson in Arizona; Jim Carpenter, Bob Drake, State Senator Joan Fitz-Gerald, Rob Johnson, Tim Gill, Paul Harstad, Mike Huttner, Jared Polis, State Representative Andrew Romanoff, Congressman John Salazar, Wally Stealey, Mike Stratton, and Ted Trimpa in Colorado; Mike Dennison, Sarah Elliott, Chuck Johnson, Daniel Kemmis, Bill "Lumpy" Lombardi, Brad Martin, State Auditor John Morrison, Governor Brian Schweitzer, Matt Singer, Eric Stern, State Senator Jon Tester, Ed Tinsley, Tim Warner, and Anna Whiting-Sorrell in Montana; Congressman Sherrod Brown, David Cohen, Mike Culp, John C. Green, Paul Hackett, Joe Hallett, Congresswoman Marcy Kaptur, Dan Lucas, Brian Rothenberg, Congressman Ted Strickland, and Congresswoman Stephanie Tubbs-Jones in Ohio; State Representative Paul Agnew, Jack Bass, Walter Edgar, Donnie Fowler, John Frank, Dick Harpootlian, Lachlin McIntosh, and Rod Shealy in South Carolina; and George Aldrich, Congresswoman Tammy Baldwin, Kirk Brown, Doug Burnett, Governor Jim Doyle, Shirley Ellis, Craig Gilbert, Ken Goldstein, Rich Judge, Steve Kean, Paul Maslin, Chuck Pruitt, Teresa Vilmain, and Brady Williamson in Wisconsin. Beyond these six states thanks also go to Amy Chapman, David Eichenbaum, Karen Finney, Celinda Lake, Terry McAuliffe, New Mexico governor Bill Richardson, Simon Rosenberg, Amy Simon, Rob Stein, and Rick Weiner for agreeing to be interviewed for the book.

The faculty and staff at the University of Maryland, Baltimore County, provided the time and resources I needed during 2005 and early 2006 to research and write. I'm indebted to my UMBC political science department colleagues and then-chair Cindy Hody, Provost

Art Johnson, and President Freeman Hrabowski. A major hat-tip goes as well to the entire Institutional Advancement team headed by Vice Provost Sheldon Caplis, including Lisa Akchin, Eleanor Lewis, Mike Lurie, Liz Moseley, and the incomparable Chip Rose. As an educator, I would be remiss if I did not pause to recognize a few of the great teachers who taught me over the years: the late Marge Dinova of Bethlehem Central High School, Ron Davis at SUNY-Plattsburgh, John Kares Smith at SUNY-Oswego, Bill Claggett at Florida State University, and Mike Munger at the University of North Carolina (now at Duke University).

In addition to the lifelong support of my parents, family and friends, three individuals—each of whom is indispensable to me both personally and professionally—merit special recognition:

- I have taught countless smart, diligent, and self-assured students, many of whom were political junkies. But none compare to Sean Latanishen in terms of both his scholastic ability and near-encyclopedic knowledge of American politics. Without his dogged research assistance I would have been sunk. I only wish I had better contacts in the conservative political community in Washington to help Sean find the kind of job that best suits his many talents.

- Walter Ludwig, the big brother I never had, encouraged me to write this book. He helped shape my thinking and provided an anchor when I needed one. Formerly of the publishing industry but now one of America's rising new political consultants, he not only introduced me to my literary agent but was crucial during the book proposal stage.

- Will Lippincott proved to be everything anyone could want in a literary agent. He shepherded me through all the business elements of the process, believed in this project the whole way, and kept me focused. He alternatively coaxed, cajoled, cheerleaded, and criticized me when I needed it. I am lucky to have him as an agent and proud to call him my friend.

Finally, I owe a special debt of gratitude to my loving and lovely wife Traci Siegel, who has endured more than a year of my absence, literally if not spiritually. She managed the renovations and move into our new home during the summer and autumn of 2005 while I crisscrossed the country to conduct interviews, and she helped coordinate my finances and logistics during my travels. Her advice, recommendations, editing, and ability to open political doors made the book possible. It will take me the better part of a decade to pay her back for all her support, encouragement and, most especially, her love and patience during these past two years.

Thanks, sweetie: I love you very much, and promise you and Max a nice, long walk together.

Thomas F. Schaller
May 2006

Notes

1 Partisan Graveyard

1 *"[A]nyone who believes Democrats"*: "Democrats Covet the West, but Can't Keep Losing the South," by Ronald Brownstein, *Los Angeles Times,* May 16, 2005.

1 *"For Democrats, the South"*: "Forget the South, Democrats," by Timothy Noah, Slate.com, January 27, 2004.

1 *Fewer than half of all:* "A Time for Democratic Purpose and Renewal," polling and strategic memo issued by the Democracy Corps, Washington, DC, March 2, 2005.

2 *"Democrats cannot afford to"*: *Foxes in the Henhouse: How the Republicans Stole the South and the Heartland,* by Steve Jarding and Dave "Mudcat" Saunders (2006: Touchstone), p. 114.

4 *What Thomas Frank laments: What's the Matter with Kansas?,* by Thomas Frank (2004: Metropolitan Books).

5 *"The first is a credentialing"*: Quoted in "Southern Man," by Clay Risen, *The New Republic,* January 31, 2005.

7 *No region boasts:* See, "Southern Exposure," by Richard Morin, *Washington Post,* July 14, 1996; "The American Religious Landscape and Politics," a national survey conducted by John C. Green and published by the Pew Forum on Religion and Public Life, April 2004; and chapter 2 in *Being Right Is Not Enough: What Progressives Must Learn from Conservative Success,* by Paul Waldman (2006: Wiley and Sons).

9 *"The future Democratic coalition"*: Interview with author, Madison, Wisconsin, October 31, 2005.

11 *The 2005 estimates further:* "Cumulative Estimates of Population Change for the United States and States, and for Puerto Rico and State Rankings: April 1, 2000 to July 1, 2005," U.S. Census Bureau report, revised December 21, 2005.

11 *Half of the southern states:* Unless otherwise indicated, throughout this book the South is classified as the eleven states of the former Confederacy. Alabama, Arkansas, Mississippi, South Carolina, and Tennessee all have smaller House delegations now than they did in 1906, with Louisiana's delegation the same and the other five states' larger.

13 *If Florida—the most non-southern:* Incidentally, I scaled the Y-axis in both figures between 10 percent and 40 percent, which makes these changes look much bigger than they would if it were fully scaled between 0 percent and 100 percent.

13 *Between 2000 and 2030, Frey projects:* "The Electoral College Moves to the Sunbelt," by William H. Frey, Brookings Institution paper, published May 5, 2005.

13 *Some commentators cite Frey's:* Quoted in "Democrats Covet the West, but Can't Keep Losing the South," by Ronald Brownstein, *Los Angeles Times,* May 16, 2005.

13 *"The turbulent demographic change"*: Quoted in "Fastest Growth Found in 'Red' States," by Haya El Nasser and Paul Overberg, *USA Today,* December 22, 2004.

14 *"This power imbalance"*: *The Great Divide: Retro vs. Metro America,* by John Sperling, with Suzanne Helburn, Samuel George, John Morris, and Carl Hunt (2004: PoliPoint Press), p. 47.

14 · *Following the 2004 elections:* The thirty-one states Bush carried in his 2004 reelection victory over John Kerry did, however, boast a slight majority of the national population. For simplicity's sake, Vermont's Jim Jeffords is counted as a Democrat.

15 *"[I]f there is a new political":* "Where the Votes Are: The Electoral Geography of the Coming Democratic Majority," by Todd Estes, *The Forum,* 2006, vol. 3, issue 4, article 4.

16 *The party elected only two:* Wilson, though born in the South, was president of Princeton University and then governor of New Jersey before winning the White House.

2 The Southern Transformation

21 *Democrats everywhere are aware:* "Entrenching Democratic Minority: The Democrats Are Destined to Be the Minority Party in a Rational/National Two-Party System as Long as They Forfeit the Solid South," manuscript by Glen Browder, www.future ofamericandemocracy.org.end_061305.htm.

21 *[T]he GOP's Southern base:* "Bush Has Limited His Options on Race," by Robert Novak, *Chicago Sun-Times,* December 23, 2002.

23 *Under the famed tin-roof:* The tradition of famous speeches in Neshoba dates back more than a century. Although Reagan's 1980 visit tripled the usual fair attendance, the informal honor for most famous moment at the Neshoba County Fair apparently belongs to the late Governor Ross Barnett, who used to whip up attendees by saying: "Ladies and gentlemen, I submit to you today that Teddy Kennedy, that GREEAAT senator from Massachusetts, that GREEAAT driver, that GREEAAT lover, you know who I'm talking about. I tell you today that the ONLY time Teddy ever turned right in his life was off the bridge at Chappaquiddick!" ("Thunder Under the Pavilion," by Sid Salter, *The (Jackson) Clarion-Ledger,* July 28, 2002.)

23 *"Reagan was the first Republican":* The Rise of Southern Republicans, by Earl Black and Merle Black (2002: Belknap Press, pp. 205–6.

25 *Despite Nixon's adoption:* The Deep South states are generally defined as Alabama, Georgia, Louisiana, Mississippi, and South Carolina, and that is the definition I use throughout the book unless otherwise noted.

28 *Figure 2.1 depicts the partisan:* By "combined" I mean that I did not simply average the party's vote share across the nine elections, which would weight each year equally; rather, I summed all votes cast for each party's candidate in every state across the nine elections and divided that total by all votes cast statewide, including votes cast for candidates from other than the major parties. Thus the final percentages are properly weighted and, of course, do not sum to 100 percent because of the inclusion of third-party, independent, and write-in votes.

29 *"The creation of a Solid Republican":* The Vital South: How Presidents Are Elected, by Earl and Merle Black (1992: Harvard University Press), p. 326.

30 *"That thing with Zell":* Interview with author, Charleston, South Carolina, December 7, 2005.

30 *Allen promised that the:* "109th Congress Convenes with Larger GOP Majorities," by Charles Babington, *Washington Post,* January 5, 2005.

31 *Rare is the Democratic candidate:* "The Republicans' Great Gerrymander," by Mark Gersh, *Blueprint,* June 30, 2003.

33 *Overall, the Democrats control:* Data as of January 2005, courtesy of National Conference of State Legislatures website, www.ncsl.org.

33 *During the 2003 and 2004:* Louisiana and Mississippi conduct odd-year elections in the year prior to president elections, while Virginia holds odd-year elections in the year immediately following presidential elections. Nebraska has a unicameral legislature with nonpartisan elections, so the total number of states is forty-nine.

33 *Figure 2.2 chronicles the dramatic:* David Lublin graciously provided the data through

2002 he used in writing chapter 2 of his book, *The Republican South* (2004: Princeton University Press). For Figure 2.2, I merely updated Lublin's data to include 2003 and 2004 results.

34 *"At the same time": The Republican South,* p. 64.

38 *"In the [1963] Mississippi": Before the Storm: Barry Goldwater and the Unmaking of the American Consensus,* by Rick Perlstein (2001: Hill and Wang), p. 237.

38 *Perlstein describes the mind-set:* Ibid., p. 235.

39 *Shut out in every western state:* Goldwater lost Florida and Virginia by single digits despite getting swamped by 22.6 percent nationally.

39 *"In Republican circles that fancied": Before the Storm,* p. 253.

40 *More telling is the fact:* This fact may astonish, but every other president directly elected to his first term did so. Presidents who succeeded via the vice presidency and then won, and several incumbents during their reelection, have also failed to carry either chamber. But Nixon was the first in his initial election unable to do so. George H. W. Bush is the second and only other president thus far in this category.

41 *Thurmond adviser Harry Dent wrote: Nixon's Piano: Presidents and Racial Politics from Washington to Clinton,* by Kenneth O'Reilly (1995: Free Press), p. 298.

41 *"Nixon further strengthened his": Chain Reaction: The Impact of Race, Rights, and Taxes on American Politics,* by Thomas Byrne Edsall and Mary D. Edsall (1992: Norton), p. 83.

42 *"A sober review of Reagan's":* "Reagan's Liberal Legacy," by Joshua Green, *Washington Monthly,* January/February 2003.

44 *"You can say Bush was politically":* "Father Superior," by Jonathan Rauch, *The New Republic,* May 22, 2000.

44 *Coupled with his appointment:* It is interesting, and perhaps a sign of overcompensation for Bush's lack of regional and ideological legitimacy, that the 1988 and 1992 conventions were held in southern cities.

45 *Political observer Michael Lind: Made in Texas: George W. Bush and the Southern Takeover of American Politics,* by Michael Lind (2004: Basic Books), p. 80.

46 *Bush's neoconservative advisers stovepiped:* "The Stovepipe," by Seymour M. Hersh, *The New Yorker,* October 27, 2003.

46 *Bush has held the fewest:* "Fortress Bush," by Ken Auletta, *The New Yorker,* January 19, 2004.

46 *Most egregious, the Bush campaign:* "Pay to Play," by Steve Benen, *The Gadflyer,* September 9, 2004.

48 *Congressional reporter Michael Crowley:* "The Not-So-Fantastic Four," by Michael Crowley, Slate, March 24, 2005.

49 *Back home, the conservative:* "Specter's Shot," editorial, *Pittsburgh Tribune-Review,* November 7, 2004.

50 *The disappearing cadre of Republican:* See "Chafee Ends Speculation: He'll Remain a Republican," by John E. Mulligan, *Providence Journal,* November 9, 2004; open, online letter written to Club for Growth members by Andrew Roth, December 11, 2005, www.clubforgrowth.org/blog/archives/027501.php; "Sen. Schumer Sets Sights High for 2006," by Devlin Barrett, Associated Press, December 28, 2005.

50 *For decades, this was the very device:* The 1957 Act passed but wasn't particularly effective legislation, as evidenced by the passage in 1960 and 1964 of follow-up laws. One wonders if Thurmond wishes he had saved his energies for later, when it mattered more.

51 *"The South has twice sought":* "Our Imperiled Union," by Leslie Dunbar, in *Where We Stand: Voices of Southern Dissent,* Anthony Dunbar, ed. (2004: NewSouth Books), pp. 88–9.

52 *The conservative rage toward:* See: "Robertson: Judges Worse Than al Qaeda," by Derek Rose, *New York Daily News,* May 2, 2005; "Failed Politico Gains Weird Clout

over GOP," by Stephanie Grace, *(New Orleans) Times-Picayune*, April 26, 2005; "And the Verdict on Justice Kennedy Is: Guilty," by Dana Milbank, *Washington Post*, April 9, 2005.

53 *Forget for a moment that:* See *The Rehnquist Court: Judicial Activism on the Right*, Herman Schwartz, ed. (2002: Hill and Wang); and *The Most Activist Supreme Court in History: The Road to Modern Judicial Conservatism*, by Thomas Keck (2004: University of Chicago).

54 *Counting the time he spent:* See "Vacationing Bush Poised to Set a Record," by Jim VandeHei and Peter Baker, *Washington Post*, August 3, 2005; and "Down on the Ranch, President Wages War on the Underbrush," by Lisa Rein, *Washington Post*, December 31, 2005.

58 *On March 1, 2005, the Supreme Court's:* "5–4 Supreme Court Abolishes Juvenile Executions," by Charles Lane, *Washington Post*, March 2, 2005.

58 *Asked a few weeks later:* Transcript of April 13, 2005, interview with Tom DeLay, published in *The Washington Times*, April 14, 2005.

58 *DeLay's remarks moved:* "Without DeLay," by Hendrik Hertzberg, *The New Yorker*, April 25, 2005.

59 *According to* National Journal's *annual: National Journal*, February 12, 2005. Note: Billy Tauzin, LA-3; Speaker Dennis Hastert, IL-14; and Doug Bereuter, NE-1, did not cast sufficient number of roll call votes to be rated.

59 *Some Republicans who worried:* "Few Tears Fall for 'The Hammer,' " by Bruce Davidson, *San Antonio Express-News*, October 2, 2005.

60 *Shortly after Schiavo died:* Poll taken April 1–2, 2005, and reported by both media outlets and the Gallup Organization.

60 *"Here's the troubling thing":* "Here Comes the Scalias," by Farhad Manjoo, Salon.com, April 11, 2005.

61 *Former Clinton adviser Sidney Blumenthal:* "Distortion of Things Past," by Sidney Blumenthal, *Salon*, August 31, 2004.

62 *"Republicans have a race problem":* "Ed the Quipper," by Ann Gerhart, *Washington Post*, April 5, 2004.

62 *"After 20 years in Washington":* "Tom DeLay's Hard Drive," by Sam Tanenhaus, *Vanity Fair*, July 2004.

65 *"Removing the segregationist stigma":* Democracy Heading South: National Politics in the Shadow of Dixie, by Augustus B. Cochran III (2001: University of Kansas Press), p. 87.

65 *For example, you won't hear:* "Study Ties Political Leanings to Hidden Biases," by Shankar Vedantam, *Washington Post*, January 30, 2006.

65 *"[T]he South has proven":* "Ignoring Inequality," by Gene Nichol, in *Where We Stand: Voice's of Southern Dissent*, Anthony Dunbar, ed. (2004: NewSouth Books), p. 62.

66 *"The national image":* Quoted in "Conservative Southern Dems Disappearing," by Jeffrey McMurray, Associated Press, April 25, 2005.

3 Blacklash and the Heavenly Chorus

68 *Some Republicans gave up:* July 14, 2005, speech in Milwaukee, Wisconsin.

68 *This Republican party of Lincoln:* "G.O.P. Right Is Splintered on Schiavo Intervention," by Adam Nagourney, *New York Times*, March 23, 2005.

69 *"I am surprised because":* Interview with author, Richmond, Virginia, November 8, 2005.

70 *A top Reagan White House: The Two-Party South*, by Alexander Lamis (1990: Oxford University Press), p. 26.

71 *The nearly 18 million African Americans:* According to Census Bureau 2004 estimates, African Americans constitute 19.8 percent of the eleven southern states (17.7 million

of a total population 89.5 million), but only 9.7 percent of the other thirty-nine states and the District of Columbia (19.8 million of 204.1 million). In addition to the District of Columbia, the ten non-southern states with African-American populations above 10 percent are, in decreasing order: Maryland (29.4 percent), Delaware (20.4 percent), New York (17.5 percent), Illinois (15.1 percent), New Jersey (14.5 percent), Michigan (14.3 percent), Ohio (11.9 percent), Missouri (11.5 percent), Pennsylvania (10.5 percent), and Connecticut (10.1 percent).

71 *The majority of local, state, and national:* For purposes of consistency, I use the term "African American/s" as a noun or adjective to refer to masses (e.g., citizens or voters) but "black/s" to refer to elites (leaders, politicians, and their organizations). Indeed, partly because of the dates of their founding, most contemporary organizations of black political officials (e.g., the Congressional Black Caucus or the National Black Caucus of State Legislators) still self-describe their members as "black."

71 *The South has sent more black:* A total of forty-four CBC members are serving in the 109th Congress, including two non-voting House delegates (Eleanor Holmes Norton, District of Columbia; Donna Christian-Christensen) and the lone senator, Barack Obama of Illinois.

72 *Yet only a third of black members:* Mississippi selected the first two black U.S. senators, Hiram R. Revels and Blanche K. Bruce, during the period of Reconstruction without white support and before the popular election of U.S. senators established in 1913 by the Seventeenth Amendment. There have only been three black U.S. senators since, and so far only Edward Brooke (R, MA) has been reelected. Carol Moseley Braun (D, IL) was elected in 1992 but lost reelection in 1998; Barack Obama (D, IL) was elected in 2004.

72 *Look at Mississippi in 2004:* U.S. Census Bureau, "Voting and Registration in the Election of November 2004," Table 2, www.census.gov/population/www/socdemo/voting/cps2004.html.

74 *Southern black politicians do not:* "Dixie Democrats Voice Frustration," by Tom Curry, MSNBC online, October 6, 2003.

75 *"John and Robert Kennedy remained":* Nixon's Piano: Presidents and Racial Politics from Washington to Clinton, by Kenneth O'Reilly (1995: Free Press), p. 236.

75 *As the national Republican leadership: Before the Storm: Barry Goldwater and the Un*making of the American Consensus, by Rick Perlstein (2001: Hill and Wang), see especially chapter 15.

76 *"Goldwater's success demonstrated": Chain Reaction: The Impact of Race, Rights,* and Taxes on American Politics, by Thomas Byrne Edsall and Mary Edsall (1991: W. W. Norton), p. 41.

76 *As Jeremy D. Mayer writes: Running on Race: Racial Politics in Presidential Campaigns, 1960–2000,* by Jeremy D. Mayer (2002: Random House), p. 94.

77 *The campaign's constant complaining: Nixon's Piano,* p. 353.

78 *"What Clinton got out":* Ibid., pp. 413–5.

79 *One-seventh of black members:* Of the 110 black House members elected since 1900, 15 were first elected as part of the 103rd Congress. I intentionally use the word *cycle* here to account for the fact that Virginia and New Jersey have odd-year elections. For more information on black state legislators, consult the book I coauthored with Tyson King-Meadows, *Devolution and Black State Legislators: Challenges and Choices in the 21st Century,* (2006: SUNY Press).

80 *In a case study of congressional: Race, Campaign Politics, & the Realignment in the South,* by James M. Glaser (1996: Yale University Press), p. 136, emphasis in original.

80 *As The New Yorker's Jeffrey Toobin:* "The Great Election Grab," by Jeffrey Toobin, *The New Yorker,* December 8, 2003.

80 *There is a long tradition:* The phrase is Richard Fenno's in *Home Style: House Members in Their Districts* (1978: Little Brown).

81 *Attitudes on abortion and national defense:* "Old Times There Are Not Forgotten: Race and Partisan Realignment in the South," by Nicholas A. Valentino and David O. Sears, *American Journal of Political Science,* 2005, vol. 49, pp. 672–88, table 2.

82 *In a similar study:* "Racial Resentment and the Changing Partisanship of Southern Whites," by Jonathan Knuckey, *Party Politics,* 2005, vol. 11, p. 23.

83 *In a* Claremont Review of Books *essay:* "The Myth of the Racist Republicans," by Gerard Alexander, *Claremont Review of Books,* spring 2004.

83 *To be sure, suburbanization:* The sources here are many, but three I recommend are: *The Rise of Southern Republicans,* by Earl Black and Merle Black; *The End of Southern Exceptionalism: Class, Race, and Partisan Change in the Postwar South,* by Richard Johnston and Byron Shafer; and *The Republican South,* by David Lublin.

85 *Seven months later Barbour:* "Survey Data Help Explain GOP Victories in Kentucky, Mississippi," Associated Press, November 10, 2003.

86 *If Tuck's victory can be:* "Will Gary Anderson Make State History?" by Bill Minor, *The (Jackson) Clarion-Ledger,* August 2, 2003. Election results courtesy of Mississippi State Board of Elections website.

87 *"The Confederate flag's meaning":* The Confederate Battle Flag: America's Most Embattled Emblem, *by John M. Coski (2005: Belknap), p. 294.*

87 *Helms never won by:* "Jesse Helms, White Racist," by David S. Broder, *Washington Post,* August 29, 2001. Helms shares the state's service record of thirty years with Furnifold Simmons (1901–1931).

87 *The legendary days of:* See chapter 14 in *Hard Right: The Rise of Jesse Helms,* by Ernest B. Furgurson (1986: W. W. Norton).

88 *With foreboding music playing:* Video of the ad, along with commentary by Castellanos, is available at PBS's "30 Second Candidate" archives at www.pbs.org/30 secondcandidate.

88 *"[Helms] has a view of a fundamentalist":* Quoted in "What You Need to Know About Jesse Helms," by Eric Bates, *Mother Jones,* May/June 1995.

89 *Helms also systematically frustrated:* "Appellate Judicial Appointments During the Clinton Presidency: An Inside Perspective," by Sarah L. Wilson, *Journal of Appellate Practice and Process,* Spring 2003, vol. 5, no. 1, pp. 29–47.

89 *Helms's congressional career was:* "The Old Carolinians," by David Plotz, *Slate,* June 22, 1997.

90 *Southern women in the pre–New Deal South:* "Gender and Sectionalism in New Deal Politics: Southern White Women's Campaign for Labor Reform," by Landon R. Y. Storrs, in *Searching for Their Places: Women in the South Across Four Centuries,* Thomas H. Appleton Jr. and Angela Boswell, eds. (2003: University of Missouri Press), pp. 218–37.

91 *But as University of Alabama historian:* "Ugly Roots: Race, Emotion, and the Rise of the Modern Republican Party in Alabama and the South," by Glenn Feldman, in *Before Brown: Civil Rights and White Backlash in the Modern South,* Glenn Feldman, ed. (2004: University of Alabama Press), p. 303.

91 *Indeed, not only could Republicans:* The Emerging Republican Majority, *by Kevin P. Phillips (1969, Arlington House), pp. 468, 464.*

92 *"Now that the GOP has been":* "How the GOP Became God's Own Party," by Kevin Phillips, *Washington Post,* April 2, 2006.

92 *On almost every possible measure:* Though there are many sources, the Barna Group—a Christian polling firm—conducts national polls on a variety of religion-oriented topics. They include Kentucky, Oklahoma, and West Virginia along with the eleven former Confederate states in their regional definition of the South.

92 *According to 2004 presidential exit polls:* Figures for non-South church attendance were derived by subtracting the 51 percent of 4,456 southern respondents (2,273) from the 33 percent of respondents nationwide (5,737 of 13,360), and dividing the difference (3,465) by the total number of non-southern respondents in the survey (9,204).

92 *Among religious donors, southerners:* See table 8.5 in "Politics in a New Key: Religiosity and Participation among Political Activists," by James L. Guth and John C. Green, in *Religion and the Culture Wars: Dispatches from the Front,* John C. Green et al., eds. (1996: Littlefield Publishers, Inc.), pp. 117–45.

92 *Not surprising, the sixteen largest:* "Godless Hollywood? Bible Belt? New Research Exploring Faith in America's Largest Markets Produces Surprises," polling report issued by the Barna Group, August 23, 2005.

93 *In* The Transformation of American Religion: *The Transformation of American Religion: How We Actually Live our Faith,* by Alan Wolfe (2003: Free Press), p. 36.

93 *The growth of evangelism:* "More Money, More Ministry: The Financing of American Evangelicalism Since 1945," by Michael S. Hamilton, in *More Money, More Ministry: Money and Evangelicals in Recent North American History,* Larry Eskridge and Mark A. Noll, eds. (2000: William B. Eerdmans Publishing Company), pp. 104–38.

93 *For example, a creative ad:* "Protestant Groups Put Their Faith in Advertising," by Julia Duin, *Washington Times,* October 20, 2005.

94 *The South is home to more:* According to data from 2000 National Annenberg Election Survey.

94 *Yet evangelism actually arrived:* There are many treatments of southern evangelism during the colonial and postcolonial period, but I found Christine Leigh Heyrman's *Southern Cross: The Beginnings of the Bible Belt* (1998: University of North Carolina Press) to be especially useful.

94 *"[S]outhern Evangelicals intoned": Religion in the Old South,* by Donald G. Mathews (1977: University of Chicago Press), pp. 156–7, emphases in original.

94 *Meanwhile, southern clergymen bullied:* See *Evangelicals and Politics in Antebellum America,* by Richard J. Carwardine (1993: Yale University Press); *The Bonds of Wickedness: American Evangelicals Against Slavery, 1770–1808,* by James D. Essig (1982: Temple University Press); and chapter 7 of *Southern Evangelicals and the Social Order, 1800–1860,* by Anne C. Loveland (1980: Louisiana State University Press).

95 *"The defeat of the Confederacy": Baptized in Blood: The Religion of the Lost Cause, 1865–1920,* by Charles Reagan Wilson (1980: University of Georgia Press), p. 38, emphasis added.

96 *"A private introspectiveness":* "Northern and Southern Varieties of American Evangelicalism," by Samuel S. Hill, in *Evangelicalism in the Nineteenth Century: Comparative Studies of Popular Protestantism in North America, the British Isles, and Beyond, 1700–1990,* Mark A. Noll, David W. Bebbington, and George A. Rawlyk, eds. (1994: Oxford University Press), pp. 278–9.

97 *Yet, according to Pulitzer Prize winner: Summer for the Gods: The Scopes Trial and America's Continuing Debate over Science and Religion,* by Edward J. Larson (1997: Harvard University Press).

97 *Riley called evolutionists atheists:* Ibid., p. 44.

98 *The Scopes trial sent: The Evangelicals: A Historic, Thematic, and Biographical Guide,* by Robert H. Krapohl and Charles H. Lippy (1999: Greenwood Press), p. 48.

98 *These actions, as Mark Shibley explains: Resurgent Evangelism in the United States: Mapping Cultural Change Since 1970,* by Mark A. Shibley (1996: University of South Carolina Press), p. 17.

99 *"In contrast to the mainline pattern": The Transformation of American Religion,* p. 83.

99 *As evidenced by their denomination:* See table 11. 1 in "Measuring Fundamentalism: An Analysis of Different Operational Strategies," by Lyman Kellstedt and Corwin Smidt, in *Religion and the Culture Wars: Dispatches from the Front,* John C. Green et al., eds. (1996: Rowman & Littlefield), pp. 193–218.

99 *Even Catholics, as few as:* "Reclaiming the White Catholic Vote," polling memo issued by Democracy Corps, March 29, 2005.

99 *Religious-based conservatism among southerners runs:* Results of General Social Survey, adapted from tables 7.4 and 7.5 in Shibley, Resurgent Evangelism (1996).

100　*In September 2005, SurveyUSA's poll:* Data courtesy of SurveyUSA's survey of adults age 18 or over, conducted between August 12 and 14, 2005. I used the same 2004 Census population shares to weight the eleven southern and thirty-nine non-southern estimates.

101　*"Without the unifying and galvanizing":* Not by Politics Alone: The Enduring Influence of the Christian Right, by Sara Diamond (1998: The Guilford Press), p. 132.

101　*In fact, when the Christian Coalition:* Onward Christian Soldiers: The Religious Right in American Politics, by Clyde Wilcox (2000: Westview Press), p. 112.

102　*Since then, the rapid political:* Some argue about whether the terms "Christian Right" and "Religious Right" are interchangeable. I suppose my position, insofar as I have one and it matters, is that the Religious Right is technically broader than the Christian Right as it includes, among others, conservative/orthodox Jews. To avoid any confusion, and given the small fraction of the southern population that is Jewish, I use "Christian Right" throughout.

102　*"[C]onservative Christians are to the Republican Party":* "The Southern Captivity of the GOP," by Christopher Caldwell, *The Atlantic Monthly,* June 1998.

102　*Though survey data do not exist:* See "Southern Baptist Clergy, the Christian Right, and Political Activism," by James L. Guth, in *Politics and Religion in the White South,* Glenn Feldman, ed. (2005: University of Kentucky Press), pp. 187–213, especially table 7.1. Quote taken from p. 194.

103　*Guth has also documented:* "The Bully Pulpit: Southern Baptist Clergy and Political Activism, 1980–1992," by James L. Guth, in *Religion and the Culture Wars: Dispatches from the Front,* John C. Green et al., eds. (1996: Rowman & Littlefield Publishers).

103　*Wherever founded or headquartered:* See table 8.5 in "Politics in a New Key: Religiosity and Participation Among Political Activists," by James L. Guth and John C. Green, chapter 8 in *Religion and the Culture Wars: Dispatches from the Front,* John C. Green et al., eds. (1996: Rowman & Littlefield Publishers, Inc.).

104　*Based on 2004 exit polls:* Data taken from Edison/Mitofsky National Election Pool. There are no results for Florida, Virginia, and Texas because the exit poll questionnaire in those states did not ascertain EBA self-identification. This fact may also explain why the overall regional total for the South reported in the exit poll data is so low, given the much higher figures in the eight southern states for which data do exist.

106　*Comparative results from the:* See "Key Findings" section of the American Religious Identification Survey, conducted by principal investigators Barry A. Kosmin and Egon Mayer, City University of New York, December 19, 2001, www.ga.cuny.edu/faculty/research_studies/aris.pdf.

106　*Generational differences are driving:* "OMG! How Generation Y Is Redefining Faith in the iPod Era," report by Greenberg Quinlan Rosner, April 2005.

106　*In 1870, church income:* See table 1 in "American Evangelism and the National Economy, 1870–1997," by Robin Klay and John Lunn, with Michael S. Hamilton, in *More Money, More Ministry: Money and Evangelicals in Recent North American History,* Larry Eskridge and Mark A. Noll, eds. (2000: William B. Eerdmans Publishing Company).

107　*So did a few courageous:* "G.O.P. Right Is Splintered on Schiavo Intervention," by Adam Nagourney, *New York Times,* March 23, 2005.

107　*Former Republican senator John Danforth:* "In the Name of Politics," by John C. Danforth, *New York Times,* March 30, 2005.

108　*A few months later, Danforth:* "Danforth Criticizes Christian Sway in GOP," by Daniel Connolly, Associated Press, October 27, 2005.

108　*"Republicans think this new":* "Deepening the Religious Divide," by Robert B. Reich, *American Prospect,* May 2005, p. 26.

108　*True to Reich's assessment:* "Republicans Splinter on Bush Agenda," by John Harwood, *Wall Street Journal,* April 7, 2005, p. A4.

108 *"Even many evangelicals":* "Reining in the G.O.P.'s Parade," by David Brooks, *New York Times,* April 9, 2005.

109 *A decade ago in his book: Dead Right,* by David Frum (1994: Basic Books), pp. 172–3.

110 *Michael Lind, author and resident scholar: Made in Texas: George W. Bush and the Southern Takeover of American Politics* (2003: Basic Books), pp. 113–14.

111 *Even Richard Cizik, who lobbies:* Quoted in "The Dobson Way," by Dan Gilgoff, *U.S. News & World Report,* January 17, 2005.

111 *Christian fundamentalism also bears: Our Endangered Values: America's Moral Crisis,* by Jimmy Carter (2005: Simon & Schuster), chapter 3.

112 *"If the Republicans are daily": The Right Nation: Conservative Power in America,* by John Micklethwait and Adrian Wooldridge (2004: Penguin Press), pp. 263–4.

113 *As Jim Wallis argues in: God's Politics: Why the Right Gets It Wrong and the Left Doesn't Get It,* by Jim Wallis (2005: HarperCollins), p. 18.

4 Go West, Young Democrats

116 *"Arizona, Colorado, Nevada, New Mexico are clearly":* Interview with author, Washington, DC, January 19, 2006.

116 *If we don't expand our base:* "Democrats May Look West for Votes," by Doug Abrahms, *USA Today,* November 26, 2004.

118 *But in a seminal 1963 article:* "Crossroads for the GOP," by William Rusher, *The National Review,* February 12, 1963, pp. 109–12.

119 *The share of "landslide" counties:* "Red and Blue Déjà Vu: Measuring Political Polarization in the 2004 Election," by Philip Klinkner and Ann Hapanowicz, *The Forum,* 2005, vol. 3, issue 2, article 2.

121 *"Throughout American history, national parties":* "Mapquest.Dem," by Michael Lind, *American Prospect,* January 4, 2005.

124 The Cook Political Report: The PVIs are a composite measure of party performance by district for the past two presidential elections.

125 *The remaining fifty-four districts:* Based on data from table 6–3 in *The Politics of Congressional Elections, 6th Edition,* by Gary Jacobson (2003: Longman), and updated with the help of Amy Walter and Charlie Cook of the *Cook Political Report.* The number of split districts was far higher in close elections like 1968 (139) and 1976 (124) than it was in either 2000 (86) or 2004 (54).

125 *Of those twenty-nine House Democrats:* All but three of these sixteen districts are represented by whites, the exceptions being Sanford Bishop, Jr. of GA-2 (PVI = 1.1); Ruben Hinojosa of TX-15 (1.4); and Solomon Ortiz of TX-27 (1.1). The other thirteen districts are: AL5 (Cramer, 6.4); AR2 (Snyder, 0.1); FL2 (Boyd, 2.2); GA3 (Marshall, 2.7); LA3 (Melancon, 4.8); MS4 (Taylor, 16.3); NC2 (Etheridge, 2.7); NC7 (McIntyre, 2.8); SC5 (Spratt, 5.6); TN4 (Davis, 3.2); TN6 (Gordon, 3.8); TX17 (Edwards, 17.7); and VA9 (Boucher, 7.0).

126 *The result, observes Capitol Hill:* "Conservative Southern Dems Disappearing," by Jeffrey McMurray, Associated Press, April 25, 2005.

128 *Meanwhile, Fitzpatrick and Weldon:* "Magic Bullet," by Jason Zengerle, *New Republic,* February 6, 2006.

128 *"While the Congressional realignment":* "Competitive House Races: Some States Shoulder the Burden," by Louis Jacobson, *Roll Call,* October 26, 2005.

129 *Republicans Jodi Rell of Connecticut:* At one point in late 2005, according to SurveyUSA, Rell was the nation's most popular governor. But even in SurveyUSA's January 2006 roundup of the fifty most recent statewide polls, Rell ranked third and Douglas seventh.

129 *"Republicans who win statewide":* "The Northeast: All But One, Blue," by Kevin J. McMahon, chapter 5 in *Winning the White House 2004: Region by Region, Vote by Vote* (2005: Palgrave Macmillan), p. 98.

131 New York Times Magazine*'s Matt Bai:* "The Multilevel Marketing of the President," by Matt Bai, *New York Times Magazine,* April 25, 2004; "Who Lost Ohio?" by Matt Bai, *New York Times Magazine,* November 21, 2004.

133 *Nebraska, Oklahoma, and both Dakotas:* Nebraska, of course, is unique in that it is the only state with both a unicameral legislature and nonpartisan elections to its lone state legislative chamber.

134 *The relative rate of population:* The twelve northeastern states dropped only 17 percent, from 144 electors in 1904 to 119 by 2004; the drop in midwestern electors from 160 to 123 is 23 percent.

136 *Overall, the region's 2004 exit polls:* "The Midwest: The Arching Divide," by David M. Rankin, in chapter 7 in *Winning the White House 2004: Region by Region, Vote by Vote* (2005: Palgrave Macmillan).

136 *Michael Lind summarizes the region's:* "Mapquest.Dem," by Michael Lind, *American Prospect,* January 4, 2005.

137 *As Charlie Cook has observed:* Sources: "Republicans Were Already Reeling," by Charlie Cook, *National Journal,* October 1, 2005; "First Comprehensive 2006 House Forecast, Part I," by Chris Bowers, www.mydd.com/story/2006/2/10/119/32630; "Three More Lawmakers Linked to Abramoff," by Toni Locy and Pete Yost, Associated Press, February 11, 2006; "Rothenberg's 10 Most Endangered House Incumbents," by Stuart Rothenberg, *Roll Call,* February 16, 2006.

137 *"best chance at a pickup":* "First Comprensive 2006 House Forecast, Part I," by Chris Bowers, MyDD.com, February 10, 2006, www.chris_bowers.mydd.com/story/2006/2/10/119/32630.

138 *Emanuel has promised to:* "The Man Who Democrats Hope Can Take That Hill," by Linda Feldmann and David T. Cook, *The Christian Science Monitor,* March 11, 2005.

139 *Since 2000, Nevada's 19.7 percent:* "Table 1: Annual Estimates of the Population for the United States and States, and for Puerto Rico: April 1, 2000 to July 1, 2005," report by the Population Division of U.S. Census Bureau, released December 22, 2005.

140 *"The new path to the White House":* "Blue States, Latino Voters," by Joe Velásquez and Steve Cobble, *The Nation,* January 5, 2004.

142 *State legislative control also reflects:* Totals reported in table 4.4 courtesy of Statenet. org as of August 2005, www.legislate.com/capitol_journal/08-15-2005.

143 *"With the Northeast, South":* "Purple Mountains Strategy: Should Democrats Look to the West?" by John Yewell, *Salt Lake Tribune,* March 12, 2005.

144 *"We want to win the West":* Quoted in "Clinton in the West, Bush in the South," by John Wildermuth, *San Francisco Chronicle,* October 22, 1992.

145 *"In retrospect, that was the mistake":* "Ohio Democrats Positioning Themselves for a Possible Comeback in 2006," by Malia Rulon, Associated Press, April 22, 2004.

145 *In fact, one pollster:* For business reasons, this pollster asked not to be named. Phone interview with author, October 11, 2005.

146 *"The state Democratic Party basically collapsed":* Interview with author, Akron, Ohio, October 24, 2005.

146 *By mid-2006 Bush's net:* Sources: SurveyUSA publication of fifty state surveys of Bush approval ratings, released January 17, 2006 (www.surveyusa.com/50State2006/50StateBush060117NetApproval.htm); SurveyUSA publication of fifty state surveys on governors' approval ratings, released January 19, 2006 (www.surveyusa.com/50State2006/50StateGovernor060119NetApproval.htm); "NRA May Back Dem Against DeWine in '06," by Peter Savodnik, *The Hill,* August 10, 2005; and "Most Republicans in Poll Say State Not on the Right Track, *Columbus Dispatch,* February 4, 2006.

147 *"For a Democrat to win in Ohio":* Interview with author, Dayton, Ohio, October 25, 2005.

147 *State Democratic Party communications director:* Interview with author, Columbus, Ohio, October 26, 2005.

148   *"Everything in Ohio has fallen short":* Interview with author, Cleveland, Ohio, October 23, 2005.

148   *Between 1910 and 1960:* "Reforms Punish Poor, Veteran Socialist Says," by Jason DeParle, *New York Times,* April 7, 1999.

149   *Steve Kean, the former chair:* Interview with author, Madison, Wisconsin, October 31, 2005.

150   *Burnett, Polk, and St. Croix are:* "County to Grow, but Not as Fast as Others," *Milwaukee Journal Sentine,* March 14, 2004.

150   *"Many work in Minnesota":* Interview with author, Milwaukee, Wisconsin, November 1, 2005.

151   *At one point, Doyle reflected:* Speech at Sentry Insurance, Stevens Point, Wisconsin, November 2, 2005.

152   *Both issues are part of the broader:* "Assembly Fails to Override Governor's Concealed Carry Veto," by Todd Richmond, Associated Press, February 1, 2006; "Wisconsin Governor Vetoes 'Conscience Clause' Bill," by Todd Richmond, Associated Press, October 14, 2005.

152   *Montana was a rare bright spot:* The most notable of the public relations fiascos of Martz's administration was a bizarre episode in which her top policy aide, Shane Hedges, after getting into a car accident that killed the house majority leader, went to the governor's mansion, where Martz washed Hedges's clothes.

152   *"We ran a good race":* Quoted in "The Progressive Frontier," by Matt Singer, *In These Times,* July 12, 2005.

153   *"Brian likes to do things":* Phone interview with author, March 10, 2006.

153   *State senator Jon Tester:* Interview with author, Great Falls, Montana, July 16, 2005.

154   *The state has a long progressive tradition:* Interview with author, Great Falls, Montana, July 15, 2005.

154   *Mike Dennison, capital bureau chief:* Interview with author, Great Falls, Montana, July 15, 2005.

155   *Baucus was on hand:* Transcript of speech to Montana Democratic Party, Holiday Inn, Great Falls, Montana, July 15, 2005.

155   *"We had a lot of resources":* Interview with author by phone, June 20, 2005.

156   *Although Coloradans cast 30,000 fewer:* Those counties are Pitkin (200 votes more for Kerry) and San Miguel (18 votes).

156   *"Having a guy like Ken Salazar":* Interview with author, Denver, Colorado, July 18, 2005.

156   *Colorado political experts Thomas: Colorado Politics and Government,* by Thomas E. Cronin and Robert D. Loevy (1993: University of Nebraska Press), p. 154.

157   *Those suburbs are growing:* Figures as of December 2005 courtesy of the Colorado Secretary of State's office.

157   *"As the Denver/Boulder area stretches":* "The West: The Electoral Gateway," by David M. Rankin, chapter 8 in *Winning the White House 2004, Region by Region, Vote by Vote* (2005: Palgrave Macmillan), p. 207.

158   *Bob Drake, a veteran Democratic:* Interview with author, Boulder, Colorado, July 21, 2005.

159   *The net effect is that Arizona:* "The Electoral College Moves to the Sunbelt," by William H. Frey, Brookings Institution paper, published May 5, 2005.

160   *"Arizona has long had a candidate-centered": Arizona Politics and Government: The Quest for Autonomy, Democracy, and Development,* by David R. Berman (1998: University of Nebraska Press), p. 58.

160   *In fact, between 1996:* Data courtesy of the Arizona Secretary of State's office, as of January 2006.

160   *The problem for Arizona Democrats:* Interview with author by phone, January 24, 2006.

162 *But one of the two where he improved:* The other was Yavapai, which, thanks to newly mobilized Native Americans who helped flipped the vote from 35.3 percent for Gore to a stunning 61.2 percent for Kerry.

162 *"Janet is going to win again":* Interview with author by phone, February 6, 2006.

163 *Political handicapper Chuck Todd:* Email exchange with author, March 28, 2006.

165 *President Bush's strong Cuban support:* Florida Cuban American Survey conducted by the William C. Velásquez Institute, June 29–July 7, 2004, www.wola.org/cuba/survey_results_7_9_04.pdf#search='cuban%20population%20share%20florida'.

165 *"Both parties know if you win":* Quoted in, "Courting the Hispanic vote," Canadian Broadcast Corporation News Online, October 20, 2004.

165 *"I think for the Republican Party":* "GOP Offensive Still Has a Few Minefields to Clear," by Gary Fineout, *Miami Herald,* July 24, 2005.

165 *"It was not a good campaign for us":* Interview with author, Washington, DC, January 19, 2006.

166 *Look no further than:* "Sen. Schumer Sets Sights High for 2006," by Devlin Barrett, Associated Press, December 28, 2005.

168 *Again, the best source for:* Interview with author by phone, February 22, 2006.

168 *Blanco is about as popular:* Figures courtesy of SurveyUSA's tracking polls of the approval ratings of the fifty state governors, as of February 2006, www.surveyusa.com/50State2006/50StateGovernor060214Net.htm.

5 Diamond Demography

170 *For far too many women:* Quoted in "Bush, Kerry Court Women and Swing Voters," by John Whitesides, *Boston Globe,* October 22, 2004.

170 *The growth of the Latino vote:* Quoted in "Sun Belt Holds Reins of Nation's Politics," by Jonathan Tilove, Newhouse News Service, May 29, 2005.

170 *Observers such as David Brooks:* "People Like Us," by David Brooks, *Atlantic Monthly,* September 2003; "Bipolar Disorder," by Jonathan Rauch, *Atlantic Monthly,* January/February 2005.

173 *Early critics of the Clinton administration: The Clinton Presidency: First Appraisals,* Colin Campbell and Bert A. Rockman, eds. (1996: Chatham House).

173 *The point is not to criticize:* "Do the Democrats Have a Prayer?" by Amy Sullivan, *Washington Monthly,* June 2003.

174 *Whether by mobilization or persuasion: The End of Southern Exceptionalism,* by Richard Johnston and Byron Shafer (2006: Harvard University Press).

175 *"If you look in the 1990s":* Quoted in "Texas Becomes a Majority-Minority State," by Alicia A. Caldwell, Associated Press, August 11, 2005.

175 *The South contains the highest:* For a good treatment of this phenomenon, see *The Promised Land: The Great Black Migration and How It Changed America,* by Nicholas Lemann (1992: Vintage).

176 *Sure enough, four are southern:* "Demographic Trends in the 20th Century," a Census 2000 Special Report by Frank Hobbs and Nicole Stoops, U.S. Census Bureau, November 2002, p. 1. West Virginia is the fifth state.

177 *Figure 5.2 depicts the white vote:* Data for Figure 5.2 sourced from Table 5.2 in "The South: Race, Religion and Republican Domination," by Donald W. Beachler, chapter 6 in *Winning the White House 2004, Region by Region, Vote by Vote* (2005: Palgrave Macmillan). Baechler includes Kentucky and Oklahoma along with the eleven Confederate states, uses the same dozen states each for Northeast and Midwest used in the previous chapter, with the remaining thirteen states as West.

178 *On a related note, although:* "Latino Legislators, 2003," table produced by the National Conference of State Legislatures, www.ncsl.org/programs/legman/about/Latino.htm.

179 *"In 2004, Hispanics outnumbered":* "Latino Power?" by Roberto Suro, *Washington Post,* June 26, 2005.

179   *Florida governor Jeb Bush:* "The Cuban Strategy," by William Finnegan, *The New Yorker,* March 15, 2004.

179   *Rosenberg laments the fact:* "Hispanics Becoming Key Presidential Swing Voters," by Chuck Raasch, *USA Today,* July 28, 2005.

180   *Nor is this problem limited:* Interview with author, Tucson, Arizona, December 23, 2005. Lopes, incidentally, is of Portuguese descent.

180   *Gregory Rodriguez, a senior fellow:* "Why We're the New Irish," by Gregory Rodriguez, *Newsweek,* May 23, 2005.

181   *"They have been more assertive":* Interview with author by phone, December 2, 2005.

182   *In fact, after returning:* Not surprising, the courts were out in front of the majoritarian branches on the matter of Native American suffrage, as state legislators and governors repeatedly attempted to thwart many efforts to extend full voting rights to Native Americans. For a good summary, see *The Right to Vote: The Contested History of Democracy in the United States,* by Alexander Keyssar (2000: Basic Books), pp. 251–5.

182   *"In the legislative process":* Interview with author, Helena, Montana, July 26, 2005.

182   *"I think in certain, key states":* Email exchange with author, March 9, 2006.

184   *Asian Americans were 4.2 percent:* "The Asian Population: 2000," a Census 2000 Report, issued February 2002 by the U.S. Census Bureau, www.census.gov/prod/2002 pubs/c2kbr01-16.pdf.

184   *The answer to both questions:* Actually, one could ask a third, preliminary question: Is there a *participation* gap in registration rates and voting rates that varies by region? The answer is also yes, but the problem for Democrats is not that women are failing to register and turn out at comparable rates to men—in fact, the participation gap by gender is actually *wider* in the South. Nationally, in 2004 women out-registered men by 3.6 percent and outvoted them by 3.8 percent. With the exception of Louisiana, every southern state had a bigger registration gap than the non-southern average of 3.2 percent, and only Louisiana (0.1 percent) and Virginia (2.9 percent) had smaller turnout gaps than the non-southern average of 3.4 percent. In other words, southern women out-participate their male cohorts to a greater degree than do women in the rest of the nation. This phenomenon is largely a function of the glaring participation gap between female and male African Americans (about 8 percent in both registration and turnout rates). See U.S. Census Bureau: "Table 4a. Reported Voting and Registration of the Total Voting-Age Population, by Sex, Race and Hispanic Origin, for States: November 2004," and "Table 7-4, Reported Voting and Registration, by Race, Hispanic Origin, Sex, Employment Status, and Class of Worker: November 2004, Black Alone." Non-southern averages were tabulated by the author.

185   *In fact, the gender gap:* A computational note on calculating the gender gap: Some simply report the gender gap as the difference within one sex or the other (usually women) in their voting for a candidate, which is fine so long as the gaps are the same magnitude for each gender. Because the expectation (and reality) is that Democrats generally do better among women and thus a positive figure implies a women voting more Democratic than men, I calculate the gender gap by subtracting the Democratic margin among men from the Democratic margin among women, and divide it by 2. Measuring it this way produces a performance gap between women and men without regard to whether the candidate won or loss either or both sexes—it merely calculates the differential in performance between the sexes. (E.g., if men vote 95 to 5 for Bush and women vote 85 to 15 for Bush, the gap is still 10, because -70 minus -90 = 20, half of which is still 10.) Dividing by two weights male and female votes equally, which is inaccurate to the degree that the ratio of male:female votes diverges from 1:1. But I calculated it this way to keep the math simple and results easy to understand. Using actual national results from 2004, Kerry won women 51–48 and Bush won men 55–44; thus, 3 minus -11 is 14, divided by 2 is 7.

186 *That's four southern states:* All figures taken from Edison/Mitofsky 2004 National Election Pool data.

186 *"The Republicans have been very":* Online question-and-answer with Celinda Lake and Kellyanne Conway, *Washingtonpost.com,* October 27, 2005.

186 *By early 2005, polls:* "Women Returning to Democratic Party, Poll Finds," by Brian Faler, *Washington Post,* Tuesday, May 10, 2005.

187 *Not surprising, the South:* See a discussion of the study of congressional elections conducted by Barbara Palmer and Dennis Simon in "Narrowing the House's Gender Gap," by David S. Broder, *Washington Post,* April 9, 2006; the southern states rank among the lowest in the share of female legislators, according to data tabulated and reported by the Center for American Women and Politics at Rutgers University, www.cawp.rutgers.edu/Facts/Officeholders/stleg.pdf.

188 *Internet-savvy young voters:* "Rise in Online Fundraising Changed Face of Campaign Donors," by Thomas B. Edsall, *Washington Post,* March 6, 2006.

188 *"Moreover, youth support for equal":* "Young Americans Most Tolerant Age Group," press release issued by the Center for Information & Research on Civic Learning & Engagement, February 24, 2005, www.civicyouth.org/research/areas/race_gender.htm.

189 *These differences are to some degree:* The African-American population share has stabilized at about 15 percent. "Electoral Engagement Among Minority Youth," report by Mark Hugo Lopez and Emily Kirby, issued by the Center for Information & Research on Civic Learning & Engagement, July 2005, www.civicyouth.org/PopUps/FactSheets/FS_04_Minority_vote.pdf.

189 *"Today's young voters could be":* "A New Progressive Majority," by Ben Hubbard, *The American Prospect* online, November 12, 2004.

189 *Curiously, despite losing Mississippi:* Whether or not the polling methodology has anything to do with Mississippi's unusual results, there was some concern about the validity of the 2004 state exit poll results. I can only report them as they were released.

189 *Why are Democrats slipping:* "Drug Plan's Start May Imperil G.O.P.'s Grip on Older Voters," by Robin Toner, *New York Times,* February 19, 2006.

191 *In* The Greater Generation: *The Greater Generation: In Defense of the Baby Boom Legacy,* by Leonard Steinhorn (2006: Thomas Dunne), p. 15.

191 *The 65+ population in the United States:* "65+ in the United States," Census Population Report by Frank B. Hobbs with Bonnie L. Damon, issued April 1996.

192 *Berthed in California's famed: Suburban Warriors: The Origins of the New American Right,* by Lisa McGirr (2001: Princeton University Press).

193 *Stratton describes what he sees:* Interview with author by phone, June 20, 2005.

196 *The demographics of these areas: The Emerging Democratic Majority,* by John B. Judis and Ruy Teixeira (2002: Scribner), p. 73.

197 *"Lack of governmental investment": Foxes in the Henhouse: How the Republicans Stole the South and the Heartland,* by Steve Jarding and Dave "Mudcat" Saunders (2006: Touchstone), chapter 3.

198 *"Rural Nevada beat John Kerry":* "Democrats May Look West for Votes," by Doug Abrahms, *USA Today,* November 26, 2004.

198 *"We put a lot of money behind":* Interview with author, January 19, 2006.

198 *To find out what working-class voters:* "The Cultural Divide: The Challenge of Winning Back Rural and Red State Voters," focus group memo by Karl Agne and Stan Greenberg for Democracy Corps, August 9, 2005, emphasis added.

200 *"President Bush carried 97":* "Bush Rode Suburban Tide," by Ronald Brownstein and Richard Rainey, *Los Angeles Times,* December 5, 2004.

200 *Mark Gersh, data wizard:* "Battlefield Erosion," by Mark Gersh, *Blueprint,* December 13, 2004.

200 *"If you looked at those three":* Interview with author by phone, March 10, 2006.
201 *"Public opinion data indicate":* "The Next Frontier: A New Study of American Exur-
     bia," by Ruy Teixeria, prepared for the New Politics Institute (www.ndnpac.org),
     March 2006.
202 *"Income is now more concentrated":* Quoted in "Rich-Poor Gap Gaining Attention," by
     Peter Grier, *The Christian Science Monitor,* June 14, 2005.
202 *Liberal* Washington Post *columnist E. J. Dionne:* "Lessons for Democrats," by
     E. J. Dionne Jr., *Washington Post,* December 31, 2004.
203 *Dionne may find some comfort:* Interview with author, Denver, Colorado, July 21,
     2005.
204 *Not coincidentally, these are among:* "Twenty Years Later, Buying a House Is Less of a
     Bite," by David Leonhardt and Motoko Rich, *New York Times,* December 29, 2005.
205 *Rick Weiner, a veteran Democratic:* Interview with the author, Lansing, Michigan,
     October 28, 2005.
205 *A March 2006 poll confirms:* "NPR Survey: Republicans Lose Ground on Foreign
     Policy, National Security; Opportunity for Democrats," poll conducted by and
     released on March 17, 2006, by Greenberg Quinlan Rosner and Public Opinion Strate-
     gies.
206 *Table 5.4 reports the share:* Data for table 5.4 taken from "Estimates of Union Density
     by State," Barry T. Hirsch, David A. MacPherson, and Wayne G. Vroman, *Monthly
     Labor Review,* July 2001, pp. 51–5. Kentucky was not a right-to-work state in Novem-
     ber 2004, but has since become one.
207 *As Columbia University statistician:* "Rich State, Poor State, Red State, Blue State:
     What's the Matter with Connecticut?" manuscript by Andrew Gelman, Boris Shor,
     Joseph Bafumi, and David Park, November 30, 2005, www.stat.columbia.edu/~gel
     man/research/unpublished/redblue12.pdp.
208 *Members of the military:* "Table 1. Employment Status of the Population 16 Years Old
     and Over in Households for the United States, States, Counties, and for Puerto Rico:
     2000," report by the U.S. Census Bureau, www.census.gov/population/cen2000/
     phc-t28/tab01.xls; "Veterans: 2000," a Census 2000 Brief issued by the U.S. Census
     Bureau, May 2003, www.census.gov/prod/2003pubs/c2kbr-22.pdf. The veteran pop-
     ulation, incidentally, is not particularly concentrated in any region; some southern
     states have above-average shares of veterans (e.g., Florida and Virginia) while others
     are below the 12.7 percent national threshold (e.g., Mississippi and Texas).
209 *At some point between 1990:* "More Homes in U.S. Go Solo," by Cheryl Wetzstein,
     Washington Times, August 17, 2005.
209 *Some election watchers foresee:* "An Alternative Account of the 2004 Presidential Elec-
     tion," by Barry C. Burden, *The Forum,* volume 2, issue 4, article 2.
209 *"If Latino voters continue":* "Parent Trap," by Joel Kotkin and William Frey, *The New
     Republic* online, December 2, 2004.
210 *"In Seattle, there are nearly":* "The Liberal Baby Bust," by Phillip Longman, *USA
     Today,* March 13, 2006.
210 *In 2003, 49.7 percent:* About a quarter of women have never been married, and an-
     other 10 percent each are either divorced or widowed. "Table A1. Marital Status of
     People 15 Years and Over, by Age, Sex, Personal Earnings, Race, and Hispanic Origin,
     2003," U.S. Census Bureau, 2003 Current Population Survey, released September 15,
     2004, www.census.gov/population/socdemo/hh-fam/cps2003/tabA1-all.xls.
210 *Kerry won unmarried women:* Edison/Mitofsky National Election Pool data.
212 *Figure 5.7 scatterplots each:* Data taken from "Rainbow Nation: Mixed-Race Mar-
     riages Among States," by William Frey, www.frey-demographer.org/reports/Rain
     bownation.pdf. Hawaii was left out of the figure because its interracial marriage share
     (29 percent) skewed the diagram too much to see differences among the other forty-
     nine states.

213 *"African Americans are much rarer":* Ibid.
213 *"Twenty-two percent of Americans":* "Guess Who's Coming to Dinner: 22% of Americans Have a Relative in a Mixed-Race Marriage," Pew Research Center report issued March 14, 2006.
214 *Figure 5.8 depicts results:* Data taken from "OMG! How Generation Y Is Redefining Faith in the iPod Era," polling analysis conducted by Greenberg Quinlan Rosner Research, April 2005.
214 *Even in Utah, the closest:* "Mormons to Lose Dominance of US State of Utah Within 30 Years," Agence France Presse, July 28, 2005.
217 *Put another way, although Hispanics: Abuelita* in Spanish translates roughly to "little grandma."

6 A Non-Southern Platform

218 *We have been in a reactive:* Quoted in "Some Democrats Are Sensing Missed Opportunities," by Adam Nagourney and Sheryl Gay Stolberg, *New York Times,* February 8, 2006.
218 *On issue after issue:* "Bush Hits Democratic 'Agenda of the Roadblock' " by Joseph Curl, *Washington Times,* June 15, 2005.
218 *As Jacob Hacker: Off Center: The Republican Revolution & the Erosion of American Democracy,* by Jacob S. Hacker and Paul Pierson (2005: Yale University Press), p. 183.
219 *In 2000, Gore actually:* "Candidates' Budget Numbers Rely on Optimistic Outlook," by Richard W. Stevenson, *New York Times,* September 17, 2000, section 4, p. 1.
223 *If issues are about more:* It is common to use the terms "policy" and "issue" interchangeably, and I'm often guilty of doing so myself. However, I try to use the word *issue* when speaking generically of matters of public contestation because not every such contestation is a matter of policy. For example, appointing judges is not a *policy*—even if semantically one might say it is the "policy" of the Republicans to appoint "strict constructionists" to the bench. Rather, the matter of judicial appointments is a public or partisan *issue,* whereas the dividend tax is a policy matter.
224 *In a recent Democracy Corps survey:* "Toward a Democratic Purpose," Democracy Corps polling memo, issued February 1, 2005.
224 *Within a month of Bush taking:* "Having Faith in the System," by George F. Will, *Chicago Sun-Times,* February 4, 2001.
226 *"The biggest reason Democrats":* "Outer Limits," by Noam Scheiber, *The New Republic,* March 14, 2005, emphasis in original.
227 *That's just fine with Republicans:* Alan Abramowitz and Walter Stone found that the states with gay marriage ballot measures had no greater increase in turnout between 2000 and 2004 than those without. "The Bush Effect: Polarization, Turnout, and Activism in the 2004 Presidential Election," by Alan I. Abramowitz and Walter J. Stone, *Presidential Studies Quarterly,* forthcoming 2006.
227 *As he puzzled over: What's the Matter with Kansas? How Conservatives Won the Heart of America,* by Thomas Frank (2004: Metropolitan Books), p. 7, emphases in original.
228 *In politics, as in life:* In 1993, at 17 percent, the "budget deficit" ranked third behind only "unemployment" and "economy (general)" as the third-most important issue; in 2006, it rated near the bottom, with just 2 percent citing it as the most important issue. "Do Deficits Matter Anymore? Apparently Not to the Public," by Carroll Doherty, Pew Research Center, March 14, 2006.
231 *Ohio congressman Sherrod Brown:* Interview with author, Cleveland, Ohio, October 23, 2005.
232 *Though union workers are declining:* National Election Survey results, tabulated and reported in "GOP Makes Gains Among the Working Class, While Democrats Hold on to the Union Vote," report published by the Pew Research Center for the People and the Press, August 2, 2005.

232   *The difference is that thirty: The Pro-Growth Progressive: An Economic Strategy for Shared Prosperity,* by Gene Sperling (2005: Simon & Schuster), p. 44.

233   *Indeed: By the time George:* "N.C. GOP Not Buying Trade Deal," by Rob Christensen, *(Raleigh) News & Observer,* July 25, 2005.

233   *The GOP's biggest gains:* "GOP Makes Gains Among the Working Class, While Democrats Hold on to the Union Vote," report published by the Pew Research Center, August 2, 2005.

233   *As political analyst David Sirota:* "Debunking 'Centrism,' " by David Sirota, *The Nation,* January 3, 2005.

233   *Despite the fact that only:* National exit polls show that in 2004 Kerry won among Ohio union households by only a 59–40 margin, compared to 58–42 nationally, and among union members by a 61–38 margin, compared to 60–39 nationally. The 17 percent figure for Ohio is also taken from state exit polls in 2004.

234   *The clips were carefully:* In the House, 82 Democrats voted for the resolution and 126 voted against it; in the Senate, the totals were 29 for, 21 against. Only seven Republicans—six House members plus Rhode Island senator Lincoln Chafee—voted nay.

234   *Still, the fact that almost:* Though I credit Josh Marshall, of talkingpointsmemo.com, for first pointing out on his website the Mafioso-style politics Republicans play, Senate minority leader Harry Reid wrote an op-ed in January 2006 comparing Tom DeLay's political style to the mafia ("If We Can Beat Mob, We Can Fight DeLay-style Politics," by Harry Reid, *Houston Chronicle,* January 12, 2006).

235   *"[The Republican] Party's split":* "GOP Rift Splits Seculars, Sacreds," by Charlie Cook, *National Journal,* May 7, 2005. Cook prefers the labels "sacred" versus "secular" to describe this cleavage, but the distinction is essentially the same.

235   *Because a majority of:* The cloture vote in the Senate on the Federal Marriage Amendment got only forty-eight of the sixty votes necessary, a far cry from the sixty-seven needed to propose a constitutional amendment. The House also failed to pass it.

236   *"Conservatives have thrived because":* "A House Divided, and Strong," by David Brooks, *New York Times,* April 5, 2005.

239   *Thanks to the Republicans':* Washington Post-ABC News poll conducted October 30–November 2, 2005, as discussed in "Voter Anger Might Mean an Electoral Shift in '06," by Dan Balz, Shailagh Murray, and Peter Slevin, *Washington Post,* November 6, 2005; "Poll Finds Bush Job Rating at New Low," by Richard Morin and Claudia Deane, *Washington Post,* April 11, 2006.

240   *Thanks to the Cheney-Rumsfeld:* The term "Cheney-Rumsfeld cabal" belongs to Larry Wilkerson, former deputy secretary of state to Colin Powell, who offered a blistering public criticism of the president and the neoconservatives in a speech delivered at the New America Foundation on October 19, 2005, in Washington, DC.

241   *Kerry put Bush on the ropes:* Commission on Presidential Debates, www.debates.org.

241   *Former presidential counterterrorism:* "Things Left Undone," by Richard A. Clarke, *The Atlantic Monthly,* November 2005, pp. 37–8.

242   *Alas, the problem is worse:* "A Formula for Disaster," by Thomas H. Kean and Lee H. Hamilton, *New York Times,* December 5, 2005.

243   *A July 2005 poll by Hart:* Survey of 858 voters, conducted by Hart Research, July 5 and 6, 2005, margin of error +/-3 percent.

244   *Bush's fight-them-over-there:* Data for figures 6.1 and 6.2 derived from results of CNN/USA Today/Gallup polls taken since beginning of war, courtesy of Polling Report archives, www.pollingreport.com.

245   *Finally, of course:* "Why Iraq Has No Army," by James Fallows, *The Atlantic Monthly,* December 2005.

246   *In a profile of Delaware:* "The Unbranding," by Jeffrey Goldberg, *The New Yorker,* March 21, 2005.

246   New Republic *editor Peter Beinart:* "A Fighting Faith," by Peter Beinart, *The New Republic,* December 13, 2004.

247 *A Garin-Hart-Yang Research:* The question was worded as follows: "Suppose for a moment that you were deciding your vote for Congress solely on the question of who you trusted more to protect America's national security and have the right policies for combating terrorism. If this were the only issue you were considering, would you be more likely to vote for a Democrat or a Republican?" Results, by percentage: Democrat, 41; Republican, 39, Depends on individual, 15; No difference, 2; Not sure, 3. Poll of 808 adults, March 24–28, 2006.

247 *During a nationally televised:* "S.C.'s Unconventional Senator," by Kevin Hechtkopf, CBSNews.com, July 11, 2005.

248 *Pork-barrel spending has nearly:* "Spending Overdose," by Veronique de Rugy and Nick Gillespie, *Washington Times,* October 6, 2005. See also table on p. 135, and appendixes I and II in *Impostor: How George W. Bush Bankrupted America and Betrayed the Reagan Legacy,* by Bruce Bartlett (2006: Doubleday).

248 *Despite all the Republican bluster:* Here's a fun party trick: Ask a self-proclaimed economic conservative if he thinks that three-cent saving is worth swapping for Mexico's quality of public services and infrastructure, and if he says yes, hand him a sombrero and Mapquest driving directions to Juarez.

248 Weekly Standard *editor Fred Barnes:* "A 'Big Government Conservatism,' " by Fred Barnes, *Wall Street Journal,* August 15, 2003; "The Accidental Radical," by Jonathan Rauch, *National Journal,* July 25, 2003; and "Interest-Group Conservatism," by Jacob Weisberg, *Slate,* May 4, 2005.

249 *They scowled at welfare:* "Holy Soybean!" by Rich Lowry, *National Review* online, February 8, 2005.

249 *The biggest abomination has:* "State Orders Help for Elderly as Medicare Glitches Spread," by Ricardo Alonso-Zaldivar and Peter Nicholas, *Los Angeles Times,* January 13, 2006.

249 *"He's the biggest-spending":* "Grand Old Spenders," by George F. Will, *Washington Post,* November 17, 2005, p. A31. Moore quoted in "The Accidental Radical," by Jonathan Rauch, *National Journal,* July 25, 2003.

250 *Bush administration Treasury under secretary:* Quoted in "A Fiscal Train Wreck," by Paul Krugman, *New York Times,* March 11, 2003, p. A25.

251 *To convince people to:* As the largest government program in the history of the planet, Social Security, despite its kinks and potentially severe intergenerational redistributive inequities, is hard to argue with in terms of its success. Senior poverty has declined precipitously since the mid-1960s, when about a third of American seniors lived in poverty; today, fewer than 1 in 10 do. And it succeeded without programmatic attendance, retirement training, or other standards or expectations for receiving the transfers other than age and economic qualification. It works as a simple transfusion of cash, and in that regard stands as a direct refutation to conservatives who scoff at the notion that throwing money at the problem of poverty is at best useless and at worst counterproductive. And good luck trying to find a hand-wringing conservative who publicly laments the way in which Social Security "welfare" destroys the very dignity and self-worth of the lazy, shortsighted, teat-suckling welfare queens on the dole who failed to plan far enough ahead for their own retirements. They'll be out of office faster than Bush can work the word *terror* into a sentence.

253 *After she toured the state:* Interview with the author, Detroit, Michigan, October 28, 2005.

254 *"Anti-tax groups such as":* "Is Grover Over?" by Daniel Franklin and A. G. Newmyer III, *Washington Monthly,* March 2005.

254 *The United States spends:* "Health Status," table produced by the Organisation for Economic Co-operation and Development for 2003 statistics, www.ocde.p4.siteinternet.com/publications/doifiles/012005061T003.xls.

254 *Roughly 4 in 5:* Washington Post-ABC News Poll, October 9–13, 2003. Question: Which of these do you think is more important (rotated): Providing health care cov-

erage for all Americans, even if it means raising taxes (79 percent), or holding down taxes, even if it means some Americans do not have health care coverage (17 percent)?

255 *Because HCA has to treat:* See, "Frist's Real HCA Scandal," by Daniel Gross, *Slate,* September 27, 2005, and table 7 from "Income, Poverty, and Health Insurance Coverage in the United States: 2004," a Census Bureau report by Carmen DeNavas-Walt, Bernadette D. Proctor, and Cheryl Hill Lee, issued August 2005. N.B.: The Census Bureau's definition of the "South" includes more states than the eleven former Confederate states used throughout this book.

255 *Corporate America also understands: One Nation, Uninsured: Why the U.S. Has No National Health Insurance,* by Jill Quadagno (2005: Oxford University Press), p. 183.

255 *Post–civil rights racial:* Ibid., p. 204.

256 *As Salon's Joan Walsh:* "Donkey in Distress," by Joan Walsh, *Salon,* November 18, 2002.

258 *Neither is the case:* Sources for Table 6.1: U.S. Census Bureau, Governments Division, 2003 Annual Survey of Government Finances, February 2005, www.census.gov/govs/state/03rank.html; "Federal Tax Burdens and Expenditures by States," special report no. 132, by Sumeet Sagoo, Tax Foundation, Washington, DC, December 2004.

258 *"We now have a new":* Statistics on bankruptcy reported by American Bankruptcy Institute, www.abiworld.org/statcharts/HouseRank.htm, "Red States Make a Mockery of Self-Reliance," by Steven Pearlstein, *Washington Post,* January 19, 2005.

258 *Most of the transfers:* "Blue States: Ready for a Less Progressive Tax Code?" commentary by William Ahern of the Tax Foundation, December 15, 2004, www.taxfoundation.org/news/show/75.html.

258 *"Much of what we do":* "The Price of a Free Society," by Paul Starr, *American Prospect,* May 2005.

259 *The South has generally:* On this point, see educational data from *The Great Divide: Retro v. Metro America,* by John Sperling, et al. (2004: PoliPoint Press).

260 *Of course, it fell to:* "Wiretap Furor Widens Republican Divide," by Neil King Jr., *Wall Street Journal,* December 22, 2005.

260 *"Our remaining exceptionalism":* "Misfit America," by Paul Starobin, *The Atlantic Monthly,* January/February 2006.

261 *Here's what Hackett:* Speech at labor union hall in Dayton, Ohio, October 25, 2005.

263 *"It's a vehicle for scaring":* Interview with author, Washington, DC, December 18, 2005.

263 *The regional disparities:* Hate Crimes Laws table compiled for the Anti Defamation League, www.adl.org/99hatecrime/provisions.asp.

263 *According to a survey:* "Medical Uses of Marijuana: Opinions of Americans 45+," survey published by the American Association of Retired Persons, December 2004, www.aarpmagazine.org/health/Articles/a2005-01-18-mag-marijuana.html.

264 *Earlier this year: Gonzales v. Oregon,* 04–623. The vote was 6–3, with associate justice Anthony Kennedy writing the opinion signed by justices John Paul Stevens, Sandra Day O'Connor, David Souter, Ruth Bader Ginsburg, and Stephen Breyer. Newly confirmed chief justice John Roberts, along with associate justices Antonin Scalia and Clarence Thomas, dissented.

264 *Support for stem cell:* According to the 2005 Virginia Commonwealth University Life Sciences Survey, support for stem cell research jumped from 47 percent in 2003 to 58 percent by late 2005, www.vcu.edu/uns/Releases/2005/oct/102405a.html.

264 *As governor, Bush spent:* "The Texas Clemency Memos," by Alan Berlow, *The Atlantic Monthly,* July/August 2003.

264 *Even with Texas removed:* Data courtesy of the Death Penalty Information Center, www.deathpenaltyinfo.org. The subtotal of the 978 executions nationwide as of September 2005 for the eleven southern states is 703. Figures for the other nine southern states are: Alabama (33), Arkansas (26), Florida (60), Georgia (39), Louisiana (29), Mississippi (6), North Carolina (36), South Carolina (33), and Tennessee (1). The 2005 de-

cision that outlawed juvenile executions is *Roper v. Simmons* (U), but see also, "5–4 Supreme Court Abolishes Juvenile Executions," by Charles Lane, *Washington Post*, March 2, 2005.

264 *Prior to a 2005 Supreme Court: Roper v. Simmons,* 543 U.S. 551 (2005).

266 *As Jonathan Chait:* "The Case Against New Ideas," by Jonathan Chait, *New Republic,* July 11, 2005.

7 The Path to a National Democratic Majority

268 *Our national party is a stigma:* Quoted in "The Other Republican," by Joshua Micah Marshall, *The American Prospect,* December 18, 2000.

270 *The incomparably sarcastic:* "Kick Me, I'm a Democrat," by Michael Kinsley, *Slate,* January 29, 2006, www.slate.com/id/2134929.

271 *In his book: Democracy Heading South: National Politics in the Shadow of Dixie,* by Augustus B. Cochran III (2001: University of Kansas Press), p. 205.

272 *The South is home to:* Smoking rates are highest and tobacco taxes and anti–smoking campaign monies, not surprising, are lowest—in the South, but see www.tobacco freekids.org/research/factsheets/pdf/0176.pdf; according to USDA figures, the South is second only to the Midwest in beef consumption, and as a source of protein beef requires far more water than growing crops do; www.ers.usda.gov/publica tions/ldp/Oct05/ldpm13502/ldpm13502.pdf; every single southern state has a per capita gasoline consumption rate higher than the national average of 464 gallons per year (www.energy.ca.gov/gasoline/statistics/gasoline_per_capita.html), which is unsurprising given that trucks and buses as a share of all vehicles is 45.2 percent in the South, compared to 40.8 percent for the rest of the United States, according to the latest figures from the National Automobile Dealers Association www.nada.org/Content/NavigationMenu/Newsroom/NADAData/20062/NADA_Data_2006.pdf.

272 *At a time when personal:* The Tax Foundation numbers were reported in chapter 7. As for bankruptcy rates, the ten states with the highest bankruptcy rates all voted for Bush in 2004, and five of them are southern states: Tennessee (ranked number 2, with 38.7 households per bankruptcy filing); Georgia (number 3, 42.4); Alabama (number 6, 47.2); Arkansas (number 7, 48.4); and Mississippi (number 9, 54.8). Source: American Bankruptcy Institute, www.abiworld.org/statcharts/HouseRank.htm.

272 *Evangelicals are many:* SurveyUSA's summary of the fifty states revealed that 40 percent of Americans believe that Bush "clearly broke the law" with his wiretapping policies; Florida, at 41 percent, is the only southern state above the national average. Results released February 27, 2006; www.surveyusa.com/50State2006/50StateWire Tap060227Broke.htm.

272 *The South is the most:* As for March 28, 2006, the eleven southern states were home to 747 of the 2,325 fatalities, or 32 percent. The region's national population share is about 30 percent.

273 *"There is a big problem":* "The Southern Captivity of the GOP," by Christopher Caldwell, *Atlantic Monthly,* June 1998.

273 *"You can't say":* "Clinton to Dems: Don't Fear Tough Issues," by Liz Austin, Associated Press, October 29, 2005.

275 *Last year, South Carolina:* "Court Declines License Plate Case," Associated Press, January 25, 2005.

277 *What's less obvious is:* It often does not help the resource-advantaged party, either, precisely because the party that has an existing voting advantage in a state or region probably doesn't have to spend the same amount to hold those states. If Kerry had foolishly poured even $10 million into, say, Mississippi, would the Bush campaign have had to match that dollar for dollar? Would the campaign have had to spend even a nickel?

278 *As my colleague David Lublin:* "Southern Comfort," by David Lublin and Thomas F. Schaller, *American Prospect* online, February 4, 2004.

279 *Afraid to unleash him:* "Scrub In," by Ryan Lizza, *The New Republic,* August 9, 2004.

279 *"Had John Kerry stayed":* Interview with author, Charleston, South Carolina, December 7, 2005.

280 *The phenomenon of running:* "For Democrats, Teaming Up Now Is Just the Ticket," by Thomas F. Schaller, *Washington Post,* June 8, 2003; "O'Malley Hopes Early Bird Gets Political Worm," by Chuck Todd and Thomas F. Schaller, *Baltimore Sun,* December 11, 2005.

281 *They just have very:* Interview with author, flying over Montana, July 26, 2005.

281 *A look at the regional:* See chapter 9 in *Foxes in the Henhouse: How the Republicans Stole the South and the Heartland,* by Steve Jarding and Dave "Mudcat" Saunders (2006: Touchstone). Data for Figure 7.1 taken from Table 50 of "2001 National Survey of Fishing, Hunting and Wildlife-Associated Recreation," a report issued October 2002 by the U.S. Fish & Wildlife Service. Given that the overwhelming majority of hunters, anglers, and wildlife watchers nationwide are white, it is more than safe to make the supposition about participation rates among white southerners being comparable if not higher than those of whites in the Midwest and interior West.

282 *To get a more precise:* The states for each region are grouped the same as they are in chapter 4.

283 *As the* New York Times *reported:* "Drilling in West Pits Republican Policy Against Republican Base," by Timothy Egan, *New York Times,* June 22, 2005.

284 *A bipartisan group:* "A Primary in the West?" by Lisa Riley Roche, *Deseret Morning News,* June 15, 2005.

284 *"The objective is to increase":* Interview with author by phone, February 22, 2006.

288 *Former Democratic congressman:* For a good treatment of how Republicans destroy Democrats in the South by turning them into "national Democrats," see "In the South, Partisan Voting Gets Stronger," by Louis Jacobson, *Roll Call,* June 9, 2005.

288 *Democratic pollster Jim Gerstein:* Phone conversation with author, April 5, 2006.

290 *The answer is simple:* Theoretically, it is also possible because populations of districts change during the course of a decade following reapportionment, as well as the complicating matter of at-large districts in the seven states that have only one House seat. But these differences are small; the main contributing factor is lower average turnout in Democratic districts.

293 *Democrats should do the same:* See, especially, chapter 3 in *Devolution and Black State Legislators: Challenges and Choices in the 21st Century,* by Tyson King-Meadows and Thomas F. Schaller (2006: SUNY Press).

294 *Congressman Raúl Grijalva:* Interview with author by phone, February 9, 2006.

295 *"The Republican Party is a permanent":* Quoted in "A GOP Plan to 'Fix' the Democrats," by E. J. Dionne Jr., *Washington Post,* May 10, 2005, p. A21.

296 *In his compelling new book: Being Right Is Not Enough: What Progressives Must Learn from Conservative Success,* by Paul Waldman (2006: Wiley & Sons), p. 36.

298 *Forty years ago: The Emerging Republican Majority,* by Kevin P. Phillips (1969: Arlington House), p. 23.

Index

Page numbers beginning with 303 are endnotes; page numbers in *italics* refer to figures and tables.